MORE GENERALS IN GRAY

MORE GENERALS IN GRAY

Bruce S. Allardice

LOUISIANA STATE UNIVERSITY PRESS
Baton Rouge

Louisiana Paperback Edition, 2006
15 14 13 12 11 10 09 08 07 06
5 4 3 2 1

Designer: Glynnis Phoebe
Typefaces: display, Caslon Openface / text Goudy
Typesetter: Moran Printing, Inc.

Library of Congress Cataloging-in-Publication Data

Allardice, Bruce S.
    More generals in gray / Bruce S. Allardice
        p. cm.
    Includes bibliographical references and index.
    ISBN 0-8071-1967-9 (cloth)
    1. Generals—Confederate States of America—Biography
    2. Confederate States of America. Army—Biography.   3. United
States—History—Civil War, 1861–1865—Biography.   I. Title.
E467.A4   1995SS
973.7'41'0922—dc20   94-43870
[B]   CIP

ISBN 0-8071-3148-2 (pbk.)

To Ezra Warner

CONTENTS

PREFACE

Civil War literature is filled with the names and deeds of the generals who commanded the armies, corps, divisions, and brigades of the Confederate army. Entire books have been written on the lives of many individual generals. Other books, biographical encyclopedias, briefly cover the lives of every general. This focus on the leadership of the southern armies is justifiable; the men who provided the leadership in camp and on the battlefield gave the Confederacy an existence (however brief) and a sense of nationhood.

However, a class of officers who performed the duties of a general of the southern armies, in either Confederate or state service, have been virtually lost to history because of a lack of evidence of their formal appointment to general's rank. Among this class of officers are numbered the Confederacy's most famous naval hero (Raphael Semmes), its first war martyr (the fatally eloquent Francis Bartow), the commander of its forces in the last battle of the war (ex–Texas Ranger "Rip" Ford), and the men who led the armies of the individual Confederate states in the beginning of the war. Contemporaries considered these men Confederate generals, and the evidence suggests that President Davis appointed at least two (and probably more) of these officers to general's rank.

This book contains concise biographical articles on these officers, correcting errors in and adding to accounts in standard reference works and, for the many men whose lives have never been sketched, recreating their careers. About half of each article is devoted to the officer's war career and half to his pre- and postwar life. The book intends to present a standard body of information for each officer, including exact dates and places of birth and death, the place of burial, the names and occupations of his parents, a likeness of the officer, and an outline of his military record, including an evaluation of his claim to the rank of Confederate general. Every effort has been made to verify the facts presented, including, in many instances, tracking down the descendants of the officers and benefiting from their input.

For the reader who wishes to research an officer beyond the narrow confines of this work, a small bibliography has been provided for each officer's article, with suggestions for further reading. A general bibliography at the end of the volume provides a useful list of sources. In addition, readers are encouraged to write the author with requests for further information.

Writing a book places an author in the debt of many institutions and hundreds of people who have generously contributed their time and expertise. The credit for this book belongs to them; the imperfections that remain are the responsibility of the author. I would especially like to thank Bob Krick, historian and author, whose works provide inspiration for all those who aspire to write Civil War biography; Professor Herschel Gower, whose sage advice smoothed over many a rough spot; and the staff at Louisiana State University Press, especially John Easterly and Nicola Mason. The following people are also owed special thanks (to all those I may have inadvertently omitted, my apologies and deepest gratitude):

Lily Ambrose, Wadmalaw Island, South Carolina (relative of William P. Shingler); Dale Anderson, Philadelphia, Pennsylvania (descendant of Charles DeWitt Anderson); J. Thomas Bagby, Houston, Texas (descendant of Arthur Bagby); Clinton Bagley, Greenville, Mississippi; Anne Bailey, Professor, Georgia Southern College; Russell P. Baker, Deputy Director, Arkansas History Commission; John D. Barbry, Manuscripts Research Supervisor, The Historic New Orleans Collection, New Orleans, Louisiana; Douglas E. Barnett, Managing Editor, *Handbook of Texas*; John Berg, New York City (descendant of Charles Dahlgren); Arthur Bergeron, Baton Rouge, Louisiana; Lionel Bienvenue, Military Historian, Louisiana Army and Air National Guard; Carolyn Earle Billingsley, Alexander, Arkansas; Lynn N. Bock, New Madrid, Missouri; Laurel Boeckman, The State Historical Society of Missouri; Keith Bohannon, Athens, Georgia; Lena Canady Bonner, Freestone County (Texas) Genealogical Society; Dewayne Borror, Franklin, West Virginia; Raymond Bouska, Greenwood Cemetery Association, Dallas, Texas; Ellen Brown, Archivist, Baylor University; George Brown, Cave Hill Cemetery, Louisville, Kentucky; Tim Burgess, White House, Tennessee; Katherine G. Bushman, Augusta County (Virginia) Historical Society; Barbara Cade, Fredericksburg, Texas (descendant of Sidney Jackman); Ellamarie Calhoun, San Antonio, Texas (relative of Reuben Carswell); Cherry Caliway, Shreveport, Louisiana (descendant of Robert P. Maclay); Loman D. Cansler, Kansas City Public Library; Ellison Capers IV, Columbia, South Carolina (relative of Francis W. Capers); Elizabeth Carroll, Knoxville, Tennessee (descendant of James Hagan); E. W. Carswell, Chipley, Florida (relative of Reuben Carswell); Connie Jean Casilear, Winchester, Virginia; C. Pat Cates, Woodstock, Georgia; Clark Center, Reference Archivist, University of Alabama; Joe and Ann Cerny, Wichita Falls, Texas (descendants of William Parsons); Charles Chambers, Houston, Texas; Nicholas B. Clinch, Palo Alto, California (descendant of Charles Crews); Bob Cochran, Registrar, University of Tennessee; David J. Coles, Florida Dept. of State, Division of Library and Information Services; Alice C. Cormany, Public Services Division, Georgia Secretary of State; Tommy Covington, Librarian, Ripley (Mississippi) Public Library; Professor Lynda Crist, Rice University;

Paxton Davis, Roanoke, Virginia (relative of Alfred Beckley); Robert O. DePriest, Archivist, Tennessee State Library and Archives; John R. Dulin, Henderson, Texas; Faye Duncan, Waynesboro (Virginia) Public Library; John C. Edwards, Archivist, University of Georgia; Warner D. Farr, M.D., Clarksville, Tennessee; John L. Ferguson, State Historian, Arkansas History Commission; V. Poindexter Fiser, Elaine, Arkansas (relative of John C. Fiser); Barry Fleig, Chicago (Illinois) Genealogical Society; Mrs. Jack Fleming, Pensacola, Florida, and Mrs. Deborah Fleming, Chevy Chase, Maryland (relatives of Gilbert J. Wright); Donna Flowers, State Coordinator, North Carolina Cemetery Survey, Raleigh, North Carolina; Peggy Fox, Confederate Research Center, Hillsboro, Texas; G. W. French, Jr., Dallas, Texas; Mike Gillespie, Independence, Missouri; David L. Gilliam, Hollywood (Richmond, Virginia) Cemetery; Mrs. George B. Gordon, Lexington, Missouri (relative of Benjamin Frank Gordon); Leslie F. Gray, Glenview, Illinois (relative of Benjamin F. Gordon); Casey Edward Greene, Assistant Archivist, Rosenberg Library, Galveston, Texas; Martha F. Greer, The Friends of Magnolia Cemetery, Mobile, Alabama; Bob Gremillion, Fordoche, Louisiana; Martha K. Griffin, Elmwood Cemetery, Memphis, Tennessee; Hiram F. Griffith, Windham, Maine; Olinde Haag, New Roads, Louisiana; Ron Hale, Forest Hills Cemetery, Chattanooga, Tennessee; Mrs. R. James Hancock, Cobb County (Georgia) Genealogical Society; Pauline Harman, Pendleton County Historical Society, Franklin, West Virginia; Mrs. William Heard, Ponte Vedra Beach, Florida (descendant of George C. Gibbs); Catheryn Wiley Heatly, Dallas, Texas (descendant of Moses Hannon); Margaret Henson, Huntsville-Madison County Public Library, Huntsville, Alabama; Dr. Lawrence L. Hewitt, Hammond, Louisiana; Lisa Hill, Anderson, Texas (descendant of James W. Barnes); Sharon Hinson, Secretary, Natchez (Mississippi) Cemetery; Brent H. Holcomb, Columbia, South Carolina; Jim Huffman, Picayune, Mississippi; Roger Hunt, Rockville, Maryland; Ogretta Huttash, Jacksonville, Texas; Ned Irwin, Chattanooga-Hamilton County Bicentennial Library, Chattanooga, Tennessee; Diane B. Jacob, Archivist, Virginia Military Institute; Maida Jaggers, Rusk County (Texas) Historical Commission; Eileen A. Jelmini, Archivist, Georgia Historical Society; Ann Martin Jennings, Lanett, Alabama (descendant of John D. Martin); Libba Johnson, Columbus, Mississippi (relative of Jeptha V. Harris); Major Jack Johnson, Historian, Minnesota Army and Air National Guard; Sandra Johnson, Curator, Pensacola (Florida) Historical Society; J. Tom Jones, Dallas, Texas (relative of Horace Randal); Joyce F. Jones, Vice President, Cherokee County (Texas) Genealogical Society; Norwood A. Kerr, Alabama Dept. of Archives and History; Peter G. DeSaussure Kershaw, Port Charlotte, Florida (descendant of Wilmot DeSaussure); Virginia Knapp, Rusk County (Texas) Historical Commission; Patricia M. LaPointe, Memphis-Shelby County Public Library; Jerry V. Lawrence, Pine Bluff, Arkansas; William E. Lind, Military Service Branch, National Archives; Mrs. Edward Long, Kansas City, Missouri (relative of B. Frank Gordon); Sally M. Marks, National Archives; Bruce Marshall, Austin, Texas (descendant of John Marshall); John D. Martin III, Memphis, Tennessee (descendant of John D. Martin); Mrs. John D. Martin, Memphis, Tennessee (relative of John D. Martin); Mrs. W. E. Martinsons, St. Augustine (Florida) Historical Society; Mrs. M. H. McBryde, Bermuda Run, North Carolina (descendant of James Hagan); Sue Lynn McGuire, Manuscripts Librarian, Western Kentucky University; Ruth Ellenwood McGuyre, Wichita, Kansas (relative of James Yell); Richard McMurry, Decatur, Georgia; Donald W. Meyer, Bellefontaine Cemetery Association (St. Louis, Missouri); Virginia Meynard, Columbia, South Carolina (relative of Richard Harrison); Whitney Miller, Archivist, McKissick Museum, Columbia, South Carolina; Bobby Mitchell, Holly Springs, Mississippi; Margaret G. Mottley, National Grigsby Family Society; Debra S. Moxey, *Dorchester County* (Maryland) *Genealogical Magazine*; Jim Mundie, Houston, Texas; Mary L. Murray, Secretary, Green Mount Cemetery, Baltimore, Maryland; Pauline Spivey Muth, Dallas, Texas (descendant of Robert Cumby); Ellen Nemhauser, Emory University; R. C. O'Ferrall, Chattanooga, Tennessee (descendant of John W. O'Ferrall); William Wade O'Neill, Oklahoma City, Oklahoma (descendant of William B. Wade); Carlus Page, Scottsboro, Alabama; Kathryn Page, Archivist, Louisiana State Museum; Jeanne C. Pardee, University of Virginia Library; William Parsons, Lake Forest, Illinois (descendant of William Parsons); Betty Hargis Peardon, Marietta, Georgia (descendant of William Phillips); D. M. Pilcher, Archivist, Mississippi Department of Archives and History; Thomas K. Potter, Nashville, Tennessee; John Potts, Administrator, Dorchester County (Maryland) Historical Society; Herman A. Price, Waynesboro, Virginia; Alana Procchi, St. Louis Cemeteries, New Orleans, Louisiana; Mrs. M. M. Ralsten, Beckley, Virginia (descendant of Alfred Beckley); Marie Reasonover, Chairman, Kaufman County (Texas) Historical Commission; Dr. Ronald Ripley, Union, West Virginia; Phillip W. Rodes, Jones Memorial Library, Lynchburg, Virginia; Connie Richardson, St. Augustine (Florida) Historical Society; William Richter, Assistant Archivist, University of Texas Library; Brenda Rigsby, Secretary, Maple Hill Cemetery, Huntsville, Alabama; Anne H. Rogers, Washington Memorial Library, Macon, Georgia; Margaret Green Rogers, Executive Director, Northeast Mississippi Museum, Corinth, Mississippi; Dr. Dan Ross, Clarksville, Tennessee (relative of Reuben Ross); Lynn P. Roundtree, Chapel Hill, North Carolina; Katherine Mahood Rugg, Greensboro, Alabama (descendant of James Carson); James W. Russell, Huntsville, Alabama (relative of Alfred Russell); Walter A. Russell, Panama City, Florida (relative of Alfred Russell); Justin Sanders, Manhattan, Kansas; Nancy Sandleback, Manuscript Specialist, University of Missouri; Oliver B. Smalls, Archivist, College of Charleston; Mr. and Mrs. L. A. Smith, Holly Springs, Mississippi (descendants of Absalom West); L. A. Smith, Jackson, Mississippi (descendant of Absalom West); Karen Southwell, Florida Department of State; Elizabeth W. Strother, East Alabama Genealogical Society; Professor Jerry Thompson, Laredo, Texas; Dr. Francis B. Trudeau, Saranac Lake, New York (descendant of James Trudeau); June E. Tuck, Hopkins County (Texas) Historical Society, Inc.; Maggie Venezia, Spring Grove Cemetery, Cincinnati; James H. Walker, McCalla, Alabama; Susan P. Walker, United States Military Academy Archives; Louise Watkins, Rockford, Tennessee (relative of Thomas McCray); Judy Watts, St. Augustine (Florida) Cemetery Association; John Terrill Wayland, Jr., Waco, Texas (relative of Alexander W. Terrell); Keith Wills, Texas Baptist Historical Collection; Terry Winschel, Vicksburg National Military Park; Curt B. Witcher, Allen County (Indiana) Public Library; Belinda Wooley, Archivist, Mississippi Department of Archives and History; Jane Yates, Archivist, The Citadel; Barbara J. Zeigler, Randolph-Macon College.

Abbreviations

CMI I Clement A. Evans, ed., *Confederate Military History: A Library of Confederate States History* (1899; 17 volume extended edition; rpr. Wilmington, N.C., 1987).

Cullum George W. Cullum, *Biographical Register of the Officers and Graduates of the U.S. Military Academy* (8 vols.; Boston and New York, 1891–1940).

CV *Confederate Veteran*. Unless otherwise noted, *CV* refers to Charles E. Jones, "General Officers of the Regular C.S. Army," *Confederate Veteran*, XVI (1908), 45–48.

Heitman Francis B. Heitman, *Historical Register of the United States Army, from Its Organization, September 29, 1789, to September 29, 1889* (2 vols.; Washington, D.C., 1890).

Lonn Ella Lonn, *Foreigners in the Confederacy* (Chapel Hill, N.C., 1940).

OR United States War Department, *War of the Rebellion: . . . Official Records of the Union and Confederate Armies* (128 parts in 70 vols.; Washington, D.C., 1880–1891).

SHSP *Southern Historical Society Papers*. Unless otherwise noted, *SHSP* refers to Charles C. Jones, "A Roster of General Officers, Heads of Departments, Senators, Representatives Military Organizations, &c., &c., in Confederate Service During the War Between the States," *Southern Historical Society Papers*, vols. I and II (printed as vols. IA and IIA: 1876–77).

Wood Robert C. Wood, *Confederate Handbook* (New Orleans, 1900).

Wright Marcus J. Wright, comp., *General Officers of the Confederate Army* (New York, 1911).

MORE GENERALS IN GRAY

Introduction

In most respects the Confederate army *was* the Confederacy. The very existence of the new nation depended far more on its fighting forces than on its new and half-formed civil government. In the 130 years since the end of our Civil War, scholars, recognizing this fact, have devoted vastly more time and effort to studying the Confederacy's military than to studying any other single aspect of the "Lost Cause."

This book explores one component of the Confederate military leadership—its generals. More specifically, it examines a class of generals that has so far largely escaped historical scrutiny. Studies of Confederate generals have been numerous: a six-volume biographical dictionary of Confederate generals was published as recently as 1991. The studies have focused on those officers who became generals through the regular procedure—appointment to that rank by Confederate President Jefferson Davis. Yet any reader of postwar literature is struck by the mention of large numbers of generals who have not been covered in these studies. Some of these men were generals in the service of an individual state but not in the service of the Confederate government. Others were appointed by Confederate military authorities rather than the president. Still others claim to have been appointed by the president, but evidence of the appointment was lost in the chaos of the last days of the war.

The intention of this book is to sketch the lives of this long-neglected group of officers.

Any analysis of Confederate generals must first attempt to define what a "Confederate general" was under Confederate law.

Two Confederate armies existed, at least in law; the "Army of the Confederate States," and the "Provisional Army of the Confederate States" (PACS). The first, envisioned as the peacetime regular army, never got much beyond the appointing of a miniscule officer corps and the raising of a few companies of cavalry and artillery.[1] The latter, based on the law of February 28, 1861, and subsequent laws, was the volunteer organization that fought the war.

1. See Ezra Warner, *Generals in Gray: Lives of the Confederate Commanders* (Baton Rouge, 1959). This book is the seminal work on the subject of Confederate generals, with biographies of all 425 reg-

Key [handwritten margin note]

The laws passed by the Confederate Congress regarding the creation of general officers required appointment by the president and, with one exception, subsequent nomination by the president to the Senate. The Senate, in turn, would refer the nomination to its Committee on Military Affairs. That committee would recommend (or not recommend) the nominee to the full Senate, at which point the Senate would vote to "advise and consent" to, or reject, the nomination. If the Senate was not in session, the president made the appointment first and the nomination was sent to the Senate later. The surviving records show 425 appointments [*No* handwritten] to one of the four grades of general.[2]

The act of February 28, 1861, Section 4, gave the president power "to appoint, by and with the advice and consent of Congress, such general officer or officers for said forces (the PACS) as may be necessary for the service." The act of March 6, 1861, as amended by the acts of March 14 and 16, 1861, authorized the president to appoint five generals in the regular Confederate army. The act of May 21, 1861, authorized the president to confer "temporary rank and command, for service with volunteers (PACS) troops, on officers of the Confederate (regular) army."

Subsequent acts provided for the grade of lieutenant general (acts of September 18, 1862, and February 17, 1864); authorized particular promotions to general (acts of October 11, 1862; October 13, 1862; February 17, 1864; and February 11, 1865); and to promote lower ranks (acts of March 1, 1861, and April 21, 1862).[3]

Under the law of May 31, 1864, the president was allowed to make (with the consent of the Senate) "temporary" appointments to all four grades of general rank in the PACS, the appointments to lapse when, in the judgment of the president, the "temporary exigency" had passed. This temporary appointment power, designed

updated by Eicher [handwritten margin note]

ularly appointed generals. See also Richard P. Weinert, *The Confederate Regular Army* (Shippensburg, Pa., 1991); and United States War Department, *War of the Rebellion: . . . Official Records of the Union and Confederate Armies* (128 parts in 70 vol., Washington, D.C., 1880–1901), hereinafter cited as OR or *Official Records.* All OR citations in this book are to Series I, unless otherwise indicated, and are cited with volume, part, and page numbers following. For example, OR Vol., XX, Pt. 1, p. 1026 is a reference to the *Official Records,* Series I, Volume XX, Part 1, page 1026; OR, V, 106 is a reference to Series I, Volume V, page 106.

2. See *Journal of the Congress of the Confederate States of America, 1861–1865* (7 vols., Washington, D.C., 1904–1905); Marcus J. Wright, comp., *General Officers of the Confederate Army* (New York, 1911). The Confederate army was organized with four grades of general officer—brigadier general, major general, lieutenant general, and general—in line with modern army practice. The Union army continued the outdated prewar United States army organization, and had only two grades of general officer—brigadier general and major general.

3. Warner, *Generals in Gray;* Wright, *General Officers;* Emory Upton, *Military Policy of the United States* (Washington, D.C., 1907), 448. Although Confederate army regulations (following the regulations of the United States Army) allowed the award of "brevet" (honorary) rank, it appears that no award of any brevet rank was ever made. The Union army contained literally thousands of colonels who, because of a brevet rank of general, swelled the rolls of the "Generals in Blue." For a listing and biography of Union brevet generals, as well as a discussion of brevet rank, see Roger Hunt and Jack Brown, *Brevet Brigadier Generals in Blue* (Gaithersburg, Md., 1990).

to allow President Davis greater flexibility in filling officer vacancies, was resorted to in fifty-three cases, most notably in the promotion of Lieutenant General John B. Hood to full general (over the heads of senior lieutenant generals) to command the Army of Tennessee.[4]

All presidential appointments to general, by law, were supposed to go through the nomination and confirmation process. Not all appointees, however, made it through the process. Some, appointed and nominated by the president, the Senate either rejected (e.g., Colonel John W. Frazier, whose hasty surrender of Cumberland Gap enraged the South) or never acted upon because of time or the death of the officer (e.g., Colonel Theodore Brevard, whose appointment was made on March 28, 1865, after the Senate had adjourned for the last time). Other officers were regularly appointed but not nominated (e.g., Colonel Lucius Northrup, President Davis' commissary general; Davis knew the Senate would reject the unpopular Northrup if given the chance), and still others had their nominations withdrawn by the president (e.g., Colonel Robert V. Richardson, criticized for not disciplining his men).

The nomination process, being handled by politicians, and with the nominees themselves often being politicians, could become quite political. Devotees of the antics of our present-day Congress will not be surprised to learn that the Confederate Congress acted just as capriciously. President Davis' nominees were sometimes rejected or kept in limbo because the nominee was unpopular, as in the year-long delay of the nomination to major general of Brigadier General Joseph Wheeler, who was confirmed only when Davis asked his bitter enemy General Joseph Johnston to lobby senators on Wheeler's behalf. Sometimes nominees were rejected because the president was unpopular: the 1864 nomination of Colonel William Browne, President Davis' aide and close political associate, made at a time when the president's prestige was at a low, was resoundingly rejected 18 to 2. And sometimes nominees were rejected because some senator demanded a payoff for his support, as in the nomination of Colonel Joseph Davis, the president's nephew, who was at first rejected 11 to 6 by the Senate, only to have the same Senate two days later vote 13 to 6 to reconsider and confirm. The reconsideration was obtained by promising patronage (a postmaster position) to opposition senator Ben Hill of Georgia.

Army colonels were usually promoted on the recommendation of their superior officer. However, ambitious officers were never shy in pressing their claims for promotion directly upon President Davis and enlisting their congressman to press their claims, even though such conduct (going over the head of their com-

---

4. To avoid confusion, the main Confederate army in the West will be called by its historic name, the Army of Tennessee, throughout. Technically, the Army of Tennessee was formed on November 20, 1862, by the merger of General Braxton Bragg's Army of Mississippi and the much smaller Army of Kentucky of Lieutenant General E. Kirby Smith. Prior to November 20, 1862, the Army of Tennessee was known as the Central Army of Kentucky and the Army of Mississippi. Similarly, the main Confederate army in Virginia will be called the Army of Northern Virginia (ANV).

manding officer) was considered a breach of military discipline. In 1862, when Jeff Thompson of Missouri desired promotion to general, he traveled to Richmond to call upon President Davis personally. In Thompson's words, he went because, with all the other Missouri officers in Richmond pressing their claims (and, like Thompson, away from their troops), he was in "fear of being overlooked in the hurry and confusion of business." [5] Colonel Thomas McCray of the 31st Arkansas wrote directly to President Davis, and enlisted Arkansas Senator Robert Johnson to lobby on his behalf, to protest an "injustice" done McCray: the promotion of someone else to lead the brigade McCray had commanded as senior colonel during the Kentucky campaign of 1862. McCray's letter acknowledged that his writing the president directly was "a breach of military rules," and in the same paragraph asked that he, the breachee, be promoted! [6]

Through a nonpresidential route, other officers were "assigned to duty" or "appointed" "acting Brigadier General" by area military commanders, such as General Edmund Kirby Smith, commander of the Trans-Mississippi Department, and through these appointments enjoyed general's rank, title, and authority. Still other officers were appointed general by the various state governors to command state militia forces. To complicate matters, some of these state militia generals exercised a general's command over Confederate volunteer forces.

We thus have six main categories of (more or less legitimate) claimants to the title "Confederate general":

1. Officers appointed and nominated by President Davis and confirmed by the Senate;

2. Officers appointed and nominated by the president but never confirmed by the Senate;

3. Officers appointed by the president but never nominated or confirmed; [7]

4. Officers appointed by a Confederate army authority but not by the president;

5. Officers who derived their general's rank from appointment by state authorities; [8]

5. M. Jeff Thompson, *The Civil War Reminiscences of General M. Jeff Thompson*, ed. Donal J. Stanton, Goodwin F. Berquist, and Paul C. Bowers (Dayton, 1988), 135–36.

6. In McCray's case, his protest deserves some sympathy—and shows that snafus did not originate with World War II. Army commander General Edmund Kirby Smith evidently recommended Colonel McCray for promotion, but the War Department thought that another Arkansas colonel in the same army (Dandridge McRae of the 21st Arkansas) was recommended and promoted McRae instead! See Colonel Thomas H. McCray to Jefferson Davis, November 21, 1862, and Colonel Thomas H. McCray to Senator R. M. Johnson, January 31, 1863, in Compiled Service Records of Confederate Army Volunteers, 31st Arkansas Infantry, Col. Thomas H. McCray, National Archives.

7. The 425 officers accepted as Confederate generals by all historians fall into one of these first three categories.

8. This book covers 71 generals of state armies and militias in instances in which that state army or militia was called into service. Not covered are 33 state army and militia generals subsequently appointed by the president to be Confederate generals. It is one of history's ironies that, in a confederacy of states where state sovereignty and state loyalty were strong enough beliefs to fight a war over, history

why?

6. Other officers, *i.e.*, colonels, who exercised brigade or even divisional command during the war, and were called "general" by contemporaries, but whose appointment to general does not show in the surviving records.[9]

By strict definition, only those officers nominated by the president (categories 1 and 2 above) should be considered Confederate generals. By a looser definition any officer who exercised authority over Confederate troops as "general" (categories 1 to 4 and part of category 5) should be considered a Confederate general. The latter definition would exclude officers who exercised general's commands with the rank of colonel (*e.g.*, Colonel John C. Fiser, who led a brigade in the Army of Tennessee in 1865) and officers whose general's rank was derived solely from state, not national, authority; but it could include state militia generals who commanded, as generals, Confederate (PACS) troops. The widest possible definition would consider all troops fighting for the Confederacy—including state militia and reservists—as Confederate troops and would include their generals as Confederate generals. This definition, which would embrace the state-appointed generals in category 5, would focus on the rank of the officer rather than the authority from which that rank was derived.

Categories 1 and 2 must, by any definition, be considered Confederate generals, category 1 under all laws and category 2 under the law of May 21, 1861.

Category 3, appointment without nomination, presents a more debatable question. Since the laws coupled appointment with nomination, in this rare case in which appointment was not followed by nomination the officer's legal status was cloudy. (There were only four instances of such an occurrence.)

It could be said that mere presidential appointment, without subsequent nomination, was of no legal force, even if the failure to nominate was through no fault of the appointee. Daniel H. Hill, for one, uniformly signed himself as major general in his 1865 official reports,[10] which is evidence that both he and the War Department believed that Hill's July 11, 1863, appointment to lieutenant general had lapsed because of the subsequent failure of President Davis to nominate him to that grade. Hill had commanded a corps at the Battle of Chickamauga with the rank of lieutenant general and has been classified by all historians a lieutenant general because of that appointment.

Category 4, appointment by military authority, embraces acting brigadier generals appointed by General P. G. T. Beauregard, Major General Earl Van Dorn, and

---

would judge only federally appointed officers to be Confederate generals. Today, when "states' rights" is a mere catchword, the victory of the centralists in the Civil War is often taken to validate the view of the Civil War period in centralist terms. Not so to contemporaries. To them, a Georgia militia general had as good a claim to the title "general" as a Jeff Davis appointee (though, of course, a militia general would not be held in as high a regard as a military man as would a regularly appointed general).

9. There were 43 with claims of some substance. Over 100 other officers were, less reliably, called "general" by contemporaries. See Appendix.

10. See for example, OR, Vol., XLVII, Pt. 2, p. 1130.

others, as well as the Trans-Mississippi Department appointments made by General E. Kirby Smith.

As noted before, military authorities had no legal right, as such, to appoint subordinate generals. Those appointed, while exercising a general's rank, usually were careful to sign their reports "acting brigadier general"—i.e., did not officially assume the rank they were exercising.[11]

The officers assigned to duty as general by General Kirby Smith constitute a special category of military appointment. The distinction lies in the quasi-civil nature of Kirby Smith's command authority. After the fall of Vicksburg in 1863, the Union navy commanded the Mississippi River, and the Trans-Mississippi Department (Texas, Louisiana, Arkansas, Missouri, and the Indian Territory) was essentially cut off from Richmond. President Davis recognized this breakdown and granted General Kirby Smith, the military head of the department, many civil executive powers—for example, the power to regulate trade and the powers of the secretary of war. President Davis did not delegate to Kirby Smith the presidential authority to appoint and nominate general officers, though Kirby Smith repeatedly asked for this power. Instead, the usual course was that Kirby Smith would assign an officer to duty pending approval of that appointment by President Davis, word of the assignment would be sent by courier to President Davis, and President Davis would independently nominate the officer. In practice the central government usually looked the other way when General Kirby Smith made appointments to general, ratifying by inaction; in the latter stages of the war Kirby Smith would not even send word of his appointments to Richmond. The officers thus appointed were treated by other officers as generals; had a general's rank, pay, and title; were paroled as generals; and were considered by their contemporaries as generals.

As to the legal basis of General Kirby Smith's actions, the best evidence comes from Kirby Smith himself. In an 1865 communication to Major Robert P. Maclay, whom Kirby Smith had assigned to duty as brigadier general, Kirby Smith frankly admitted that he had no legal authority for his appointments (he conceded that Maclay's appointment "was without authority of law at the time") but expressed the hope that the president would subsequently approve of his actions.[12]

While these appointments were not sanctioned by any specific provision of Confederate law, various Confederate laws vested Kirby Smith with "full" authority, "civil as well as military," and the Trans-Mississippi governors voted that Kirby Smith's powers extended to the powers of the Confederate executive that were "absolutely necessary" for the defense of the department, which would (logically) include a power to appoint generals.[13]

11. See OR, VI, 662 (report of "acting brigadier general" Thomas M. Jones, May 14, 1862).
12. OR, Vol. XLVIII, Pt. 1, p. 1335 (January 31, 1865).
13. For a detailed discussion of General Kirby Smith's civil and executive powers, see Robert L. Kerby, *Kirby Smith's Confederacy: The Trans-Mississippi South, 1863–1865* (New York, 1972), and Florence Holladay, "The Powers of the Commander of the Confederate Trans-Mississippi," *Southwestern Historical Quarterly*, XXI (1918), 279–98, 333–59.

Category 5, that of appointment by state authorities, presents the case of officers, each with a general's rank, commanding with that rank forces fighting for the Confederacy, although the rank, and the forces, were not "Confederate." Arguably, anyone who was a general in a state militia or state army anytime after the formation of the Confederate government (February 8, 1861) or after his state's secession, could be considered a "Confederate general." [14]

The efforts of the southern states to raise armies in 1861 followed two tracks—the main one, the raising of PACS volunteer units, paralleled by state efforts to raise their own forces under their own generals, was usually under a state militia or army framework. The framework varied from state to state. Some states (Texas, for example) retained their existing, prewar militia organization. Other states (Tennessee, for one) created their own new "provisional army." The states appointed their own generals to command these troops. Several of these generals (though not all) appear on all the contemporary lists of "Confederate generals." By early 1862 these state armies had either disbanded or had been absorbed into the PACS.

The governors and secession conventions that organized these state armies put their friends and fellow politicians in command. The regular army officers who were best qualified to lead these armies were typically little known by the local politicians and were often hundreds of miles away on the western frontier and unavailable for immediate duty anyway.

The states' rights–oriented political class of the South pressured President Davis to appoint these state officers as the generals of the Confederate army. To his credit, Davis resisted the easy, popular path of going along with local wishes. He reserved the army high command for top flight regular army officers such as Robert E. Lee, Albert Sidney Johnston, and P. G. T. Beauregard, men who had a proven record of military leadership. Davis saved the Confederate army from having as its corps and army commanders such military nonentities as Gideon Pillow, Reuben Davis, Millege Bonham, Jeremiah Clemens, and James Yell (men chosen by Tennessee, Mississippi, South Carolina, Alabama, and Arkansas, respectively, to lead their state armies). The army benefited—but Davis' political support, never unanimous, suffered.

In addition to the eleven seceding states, the pro-southern Missouri state government organized an independent state army, the "Missouri State Guard," which was allied with, but not controlled by, Confederate authorities. As late as April, 1862, one year into the war, the majority of Missourians fighting for the South were state guard, not Confederate, soldiers.

The number of southerners who were generals in the militias of the states in the period 1861–1865 would rival the number (425) of regularly appointed gen-

14. State militias are the organized force of all citizens in the state capable of bearing arms. The state armies raised in 1861 differed from militias in that they were composed of volunteers from the citizenry. The officers of these state armies were chosen by the state government, not elected by the militiamen themselves.

erals. The eleven seceding states, at the start of the war, had state militia forces organized into 78 divisions and 196 brigades, both totals far exceeding the number of brigades and divisions in the Confederate army. Typically, state laws provided that the militia generals be elected by the colonels of the regiments. The colonels were in turn elected by the company commanders, who were themselves elected by the privates. The laws also provided for a state adjutant and inspector general, with a rank of colonel or brigadier general, who would act as chief of staff to the governor, the *ex officio* commander-in-chief of the state's militia.[15]

Although largely overlooked by historians, the state militias fought in nearly every campaign of the war. Virginia militia were active in the Shenandoah Valley of Virginia in 1861, participating in the Bull Run and Romney campaigns. North Carolina militia fought at the Battle of New Bern, North Carolina, in 1862. The bloody Battle of Wilson's Creek, Missouri, in 1861 was mainly fought by the Missouri State Guard and the Arkansas militia. Georgia militiamen (immortalized in *Gone With The Wind*) manned the entrenchments of Atlanta during that city's 1864 siege. The last three Confederate victories of the war—the minor Battles of Honey Hill, Natural Bridge, and Palmito Ranch—were won by Confederate armies whose main component was state reservists or militiamen.

Regarding the status of state militias under Confederate law, the Confederate Constitution Article I, Section 6, Clause 16, which was copied from Article I, Section 8 of the United States Constitution, vested in the Confederate Congress the power "to provide for organising, arming and disciplining the militia and for governing such part of them as may be employed in the service of the Confederate states: reserving to the States respectively the appointment of the Officers." Pursuant to this, the Congress in its act of March 6, 1861, provided that the Confederate government had the power to call state militia into Confederate service for a period not to exceed six months, and while in service such militia would receive the pay of PACS soldiers. As to the legal status of militia called into service, the attorney general, in his opinion of August 20, 1861, made clear that, according to

15. The state militias were set up as follows (with all the divisions being commanded by major generals and the brigades by brigadier generals): Alabama—11 divisions and 22 brigades (Alabama Digest of 1841, Military Code, Chapter IV, Section 1, as amended by the act of March 4, 1848); Arkansas—2 divisions and 8 brigades (Gould's 1856 Arkansas Digest, Chapter 113, Section 3); Florida—2 divisions and 5 brigades (act of December 22, 1859); Georgia—13 divisions and 26 brigades (code of 1851, p. 771); Louisiana—5 divisions and 11 brigades (Napier Bartlett, *Military Record of Louisiana* [New Orleans, 1875], 237); Mississippi—5 divisions and 10 brigades, with two additional brigades of volunteer militia (Dunbar Rowland, *Military History of Mississippi* [Spartanburg, 1978], 34–35); North Carolina—10 divisions and 20 brigades (law of January 29, 1851); South Carolina—5 divisions and 10 brigades (Walter B. Cisco, *States Rights Gist* [Shippensburg, Pa., 1991], 31, citing the militia laws of 1851); Tennessee—4 divisions and 22 brigades (law of January 28, 1840); Texas—16 divisions and 32 brigades (law of February 14, 1860); in December of 1861, the Texas militia was reorganized into 33 brigades, with no divisions (law of December 25, 1861), which organization is set forth in Marcus J. Wright, *Texas in the War, 1861–1865*, ed. Harold Simpson (Hillsboro, 1965); Virginia—5 divisions and 28 brigades (Lee A. Wallace, *A Guide to Virginia Military Organizations, 1861–1865* [Lynchburg, Va., 1986], 234).

the Constitution and the acts of Congress, only troops raised by Congress (*i.e.*, PACS units) were Confederate troops.[16] By implication, this would mean that only generals appointed by the president and/or confirmed by Congress were Confederate generals.

When called into service the state militia generals would have many of the attributes of Confederate generals. They would be paid as PACS generals; they would be commanding units mobilized by the Confederate government under Confederate law; they would be commanding, as generals, troops fighting for the Confederacy under the orders of the Confederate military. In addition, under the Articles of War adopted by Congress on March 6, 1861, a militia officer's rank was officially recognized; he could issue orders, as general, to PACS colonels.[17] It is no wonder that many postbellum historians routinely included many state militia generals in their lists of Confederate generals.

Later in the war the Confederate government organized its own state reserve units under Confederate law. [18] These reserves (the young and the old, factory workers, government employees) were enrolled, organized, and mustered in by the Confederate Bureau of Conscription and placed under the command of PACS generals assigned to that duty by the president.

The *Southern Historical Society Papers* and other postwar sources list as "general" or "acting general" colonels who commanded a brigade.[19] A commonly held belief in the postbellum years was that rank followed command—that a colonel put in command of a brigade was thereby an "acting brigadier"[20] and, conversely, that when the brigade was dissolved the brigadier general's rank lapsed.[21] Brigade command was (in theory) to be exercised only by a brigadier general. However, in practice, there was hardly a colonel in the Confederate army who did not, at some time or another, command a brigade because of the absence or wounding of his superior officer. As early as the First Battle of Bull Run in 1861, three of the ten Confederate brigades went into battle under the command of colonels. At the Battle of Shiloh in 1862, eleven of the sixteen brigades were (at some point in the battle) led by colonels. By 1865, in the two main Confederate armies, only thirty-one of seventy-five infantry brigades were led by brigadiers; thirty were led by colonels, seven by lieutenant colonels, three by majors, and four by captains. To give all these

16. See Rembert Patrick, ed., *The Opinions of the Confederate Attorneys General, 1861–1865* (Buffalo, 1950), 26–32.

17. See the 62nd and 98th Articles of War, set forth in Patrick, ed., *The Opinions of the Confederate Attorneys General*, 33–34.

18. See the act of February 17, 1864, and other legislation.

19. Charles C. Jones, "A Roster of General Officers, Heads of Departments, Senators, Representatives, Military Organizations, &c., &c., in Confederate Service During the War Between the States," *Southern Historical Society Papers*, vols. I and II (printed as vols. IA and IIA, 1876–77).

20. See, for example, the Louisville *Courier-Journal*, June 17, 1889.

21. See the opinion of the Confederate Attorney General, April 22, 1864, in Patrick, ed., *The Opinions of the Confederate Attorneys General*, 424–29.

brigade commanders a general's or "acting" general's title would only serve to dilute the term "general" beyond all rational meaning.[22]

Proof of rank is an additional problem. While Union source records are plentiful and complete, the supply of Confederate records is woefully incomplete. Although the records show fairly completely which officers were regularly nominated and confirmed as generals, there have been various postbellum allegations of a whole series of otherwise unrecorded presidential appointments to the rank of general. The American mania for military title, satirized by Charles Dickens, antedated the Civil War and was only exacerbated by the comradeship of the Lost Cause. Surviving, sentimental veterans were loath to dispute a fellow veteran's claim to rank, however tenuous that claim's basis. Often the result was the attribution, in otherwise authoritative biographies, of unverifiable general's rank. An especial favorite is a Davis appointment after the fall of Richmond, when nominations were impossible and few official records were kept. To read the many assertions of such appointments, President Davis must have spent most of his waking hours not in flight but in appointing generals!

Other officers appear in the *Official Records* as "general" even though no record of such appointment has been found. For example, Major General Joseph Wheeler's official report on the last weeks of the war names three of his four subordinates (Colonels James Hagan, Moses Hannon, and Henry M. Ashby) as "generals," but no record of any presidential appointment to that rank appears.[23] Similarly, Robert J. Henderson is shown as brigadier general, commanding a brigade, on the April 9, 1865, organization chart of the Army of Tennessee.[24]

The problem of proof extends to the appointments of Kirby Smith and to other military appointments as well. Several Trans-Mississippi officers were paroled at a rank for which no surviving army order places them: Brigadier General Hamilton Bee, for example, was paroled as a major general.

Ordinarily the rank of the officer, reflected in his end-of-war parole paper, would be conclusive proof of his wartime rank. But two factors peculiar to the Confederate army lessen the value of such parole evidence.

Many officers never received parole from the U.S. Army. General E. Kirby Smith and many Trans-Mississippi generals fled to Mexico at the war's end rather than formally surrender. And of those who were paroled, their rank at war's end did not al-

22. Although only 31 of the 75 brigades were led by generals, it would be an error to assume that these armies (or the Confederacy as a whole) were lacking officers of proper rank in 1865. The "brigades" of 1865 were in actuality no stronger than the regiments of 1861–62. For example, in April, 1865, the 20 infantry brigades of the Army of Tennessee numbered 18,000 effectives—about 900 men per brigade. In April, 1862, the same army averaged 2,521 men per brigade. For these brigades, in corps, division, and brigade command, in 1865 there were 1 general for every 643 men and 1.4 generals for every brigade; in 1862 there were 1 general for every 2,251 men and .89 generals for every brigade. In the war's final year the southern armies were not lacking in generals. This point should be kept in mind when evaluating the numerous claims of end-of-the-war appointments to general's rank.

23. *OR*, Vol. XLVII, Pt. 1, p. 1132.

24. *OR*, Vol. XLVII, Pt. 1, p. 1065.

ways reflect a temporary or lapsed, though still valid, promotion to general. William W. Allen, a brigadier in Wheeler's cavalry, was promoted by the president to major general, with temporary rank, on March 4, 1865. The Senate, in the two weeks remaining before its final adjournment, did not act upon the nomination, and Allen was paroled as a brigadier.

Other postbellum Confederates termed "general" held neither an officer's rank in the Confederate army nor a wartime officer's rank in the state militias. The organizational structure of the Confederate veterans organization, the United Confederate Veterans (UCV), founded in 1889, created a host of "generals" in the UCV structure only, to confuse both contemporaries and later generations. Often the "general's" actual Confederate rank was private yet he would popularly be known as "general." [25] By 1909 one Confederate veteran was complaining that the practice of giving military titles to officers of the UCV perpetrated "a great wrong. . . . [I]t has created and will continue to create confusion as to who were officers of the Confederate army and perverts history." [26] Because war service and military title were two surefire claims to the affections of the voters, many putative candidates played up their rank—any rank—in an effort to win votes.

Any casual reader of antebellum newspapers or diaries is struck by the vast numbers of "majors," "colonels," and "generals" in public life. Many prominent antebellum politicians held some sort of military title derived through election to a state militia post. These titles persisted even though the politician lost his post at the next election. Thus, a man could be called "general" in the *Official Records* and not even hold an active state, let alone Confederate, rank.

Confusion is also caused by staff officers whose titles, such as "quartermaster general," "adjutant general," and "commissary general," contained the word *general*. Although such officers were often termed "general," both in official correspondence and in popular estimation, such officers did not usually hold the substantive rank of general. [27]

The 137 officers in this book qualify as "other Confederate generals" by meeting one or more of several criteria.

First come those shown in the *Official Records* as being "assigned to duty" by Kirby Smith, or some other military authority, to the rank of general. Second come those considered by contemporary authorities as generals, though no official record of any such promotion survives. The lists of Confederate generals in *The Confederate Veteran*, the *Southern Historical Society Papers*, Evans' *Confederate Military History*, Heitman's *Historical Register of the United States Army*, and Wood's *Confeder-*

25. See, for example, William E. Mickle, *Well Known Confederate Veterans and Their War Records* (New Orleans, 1907), 53.

26. John H. Lester, "Titles in the U.C.V.," *Confederate Veteran*, XVII (1909), 54.

27. President Chester A. Arthur was often called "General Arthur," because that portly politician had been appointed quartermaster general of New York during the Civil War. See the New York *Times*, July 19, 1880.

ate Handbook are utilized as sources here.[28] Since many of those on the contemporary lists were generals in state service only, it would seem inconsistent to accept
only those state generals on one or more lists while excluding other state generals
with identical service and claims who, for whatever reason, did not make one of
those lists. This third category thus consists of generals in either a) one of the state
armies organized in 1861; or b) a state's militia, if that militia unit was called into
service and participated in a campaign. Also added are five officers (Henry Kyd
Douglas, Claiborne Jackson, Jeffrey Forrest, Henry Ashby, and Santos Benavides)
mentioned as generals in prominent modern works, but only occasionally called
general by contemporaries.

The 137 men treated in this book were a varied lot, with backgrounds as diverse
as the country they served. Ten (Charles Adams, William Chase, Henry McCay,
Charles Dahlgren, Robert Maclay, Elisha Tracy, Kenton Harper, William Parsons,
John Pratt, and James Alcorn) were born in the North, the first two in abolition-
ist Massachusetts, but had since moved to the South. Adams, particularly, despite
(or because of) his northern upbringing, became a secessionist leader in his adopted
state of Arkansas. Nine (Peter McGlashan, James Boggs, Xavier DeBray, Benjamin
Buisson, James Hagan, Pierre Soulé, Henry Douglas, John Wagener, and Gaspard
Tochman) were born abroad, but loyally served their new country.

The following chart shows the generals' states of birth and the states for which
they served. The chart clearly illustrates the westward drift of the population in the
prewar years.

	State of Birth	State of Service
Maryland-D.C.	6	0
Virginia	22	13
N. Carolina	11	7

---

28. Charles E. Jones, "General Officers of the Regular C. S. Army," *Confederate Veteran*, XVI (1908),
45–48, lists 50 generals not included in Warner's *Generals in Gray*. Jones's list is partially supplemented
by three articles listing surviving Confederate generals: W. L. Cabell, "Confederate Generals Yet Living," *Confederate Veteran*, II (1893), 28; "Surviving Confederate Generals," *Confederate Veteran*, VII
(1899), 420; and Telamon Cuyler, "Surviving Confederate Generals," *Confederate Veteran*, XV (1907),
118–19.

Charles C. Jones, "A Roster of General Officers, Heads of Departments, Senators, Representatives,
Military Organizations, &c., &c., in Confederate Service During the War Between the States," *Southern Historical Society Papers*, vols. I and II (printed as vols. IA and IIA, 1876–77), includes 62 generals
Warner does not. Clement A. Evans, ed., *Confederate Military History: A Library of Confederate States
History* (1899; 17 volume extended edition; rpr. Wilmington, N.C., 1987), an invaluable work, is or-
ganized by states; at the end of each state's volume are biographies of those officers the writer considered generals from that state. Evans gives biographies of 18 generals not included in Warner. Francis B.
Heitman, *Historical Register of the United States Army, from Its Organization, September 29, 1789, to
September 29, 1889* (2 vols.; Washington, D.C., 1890), II, 176–79 contains a list entitled "General Officers of the Confederate Army, 1861–1865," a reprint of a document printed by the U.S. House of Representatives. It lists 40 generals Warner does not. Finally, Robert C. Wood, *Confederate Handbook* (New
Orleans, 1900), lists 27 generals Warner does not.

S. Carolina	14	9
Georgia	19	15
Florida	0	4
Alabama	6	9
Mississippi	1	16
Tennessee	23	11
Kentucky	11	2
Louisiana	1	9
Missouri	3	14
Arkansas	0	10
Texas	1	18
Other	19	0

An analysis of the generals' prewar occupations shows 9 physicians, 8 newspaper editors, a Methodist clergyman, an ornithologist, 2 students, a candymaker, 4 merchants, and a saddlemaker—occupations unusual for future generals. But the vast majority of the "other" generals (like their regularly appointed counterparts) fitted into one of two categories: professional soldier or lawyer-politician.

These officers, both before and after the war, held the highest political offices in the land. Among them were 4 U.S. senators, 3 governors, 8 congressmen, as well as state representatives and judges. Seven were members of the Confederate Congress. More than half (72 of 137) attended college prior to the war, at a time when only a small percentage of people did.

Civil War armies are characterized, with some justice, as armed mobs led by ignorant amateurs. Nevertheless, the majority (94) of these 137 officers had provable military experience prior to the war. Nineteen had attended West Point, and 10 more were officers in the armed forces. Six were educated at private military schools, 29 had fought as volunteers in the Mexican War or other wars, and 8 had experience in foreign armies or in Indian fighting. At least 22 more were prewar militia officers.

Of the regularly appointed Confederate generals, 64 percent (272 of 425) had demonstrable prewar military experience.[29] The percentage of the "other" generals with prewar military experience (69 percent) was similar, but the quality of that experience was different. Of the regularly appointed generals, 40 percent either attended West Point or were officers of the U.S. Army, compared with 21 percent of the "other" generals. A West Point graduate usually tendered his services directly to the Confederate government, rather than to his state. A prewar militia officer usually tendered his services to his state government first.

The Civil War divided families like no other war in American history. Charles Dahlgren's brother John was a widely respected admiral in the U.S. Navy; his

29. See Warner, *Generals in Gray*, xx. Warner's figure, though the best available, clearly understates the actual prewar military experience of the regularly appointed generals.

nephew Ulric, a Union cavalry colonel, was killed during a famous raid on Richmond in 1864. Alexander Steen's father was a Union colonel; Smith Bankhead's brother was a Union general; Thomas Harris' brother-in-law was the Union's Admiral Porter; Thomas Fauntleroy's son-in-law was the Union surgeon general.

Contrary to the legends of the "Lost Cause," some officers did not remain with the colors to the bitter end. Generals Edwin Price, Jere Clemens, and Alfred Beckley "made their peace" with the North while the war was still raging, the first to the dismay of his father, the Confederate commander in Missouri. Edward Gantt, a firebrand secessionist before the war, went to the opposite extreme, joining the Yankees and issuing public calls for the South to surrender. After the war he was a noted "scalawag." At the other end of the spectrum, Joseph Brent and A. C. Jones, longtime residents of northern states when the war started, came back to fight for their native South. Archibald Dobbins and A. A. Russell, after 1865, chose exile rather than life under Yankee rule, and died abroad.

Soldiering was, in the Confederacy, a family affair. To cite but a few examples, we have the Harrisons, father and son both generals. Samuel P. Moore and Stephen Westmore were brothers, as were John F. and William J. Hoke. Richard Harrison had two brothers who were generals; a third brother was a colonel killed in 1864. John Clark's son was a general; sons of David Clark, Alfred Beckley, and John McElroy were colonels, as were brothers of John Baylor, J. Warren Grigsby, and John O'Ferrall.

Of the regularly appointed Confederate generals, 96 (23 percent) died before the end of the war, mostly in battle. Of the 137 officers featured in this book, 22 (16 percent) died during the war, 15 in battle and 7 of other causes. The slightly lower rate of battle deaths follows from the higher percentage of state generals, many of whom never got near the front lines.

Nine officers achieved the rank of major general, 1 (Arthur Bagby) by military assignment, and 8 (James Yell, Reuben Davis, Jefferson Davis, Jeremiah Clemens, John Pratt, Kenton Harper, William Chase, and Walter Gwynn) through state appointment. The rest of the officers never had rank claimed for them other than brigadier general.

Undoubtedly the oldest man to serve as a brigadier general in the Confederacy was Benjamin Buisson, a Louisiana militia general born in 1793 who had been an artillery lieutenant in Napoleon's "Grand Armee." At the other end of the spectrum was John Ed Murray, colonel in the 5th Arkansas, who was not even old enough to vote when the war started. The average age of the 137 officers, when the war started, was 40. The regularly appointed generals averaged 36.25—the older age of the state militia officers accounting for the difference.

Biographical Sketches

Charles W. Adams

Charles W. Adams was born on August 16, 1817, in Boston, Massachusetts, the son of Benjamin and Susannah (Goodhue) Adams. In 1819 his parents moved to New Albany, Indiana. Young Adams clerked in a mercantile house in New Albany from 1830 to 1835. Moving to Helena, Arkansas, in 1835, he became a lawyer and was a law partner to U.S. Senator William Sebastian. A Whig, Adams served as judge from 1852 to 1854 and in1860 was a presidential elector on the Bell ticket. When the secession crises came, Adams, a large slaveholder and cotton grower, was elected to the secession convention, where he took a leading role in the movement to take Arkansas out of the Union.[1]

Arkansas History Commission

Adams' first war service was as major and quartermaster of Arkansas state troops, on the staff of Brigadier General Thomas Bradley. Upon the dissolution of the Army of Arkansas in late 1861, Adams left the staff for field duty. He recruited an infantry regiment from the Helena area, the 23rd Arkansas, and on April 25, 1862, was elected its colonel. The 23rd joined the Army of Tennessee in northern Mississippi after the Battle of Shiloh. That summer Adams was transferred back to Arkansas and put in command of a newly raised infantry regiment. The raw regiment bolted in its first battle at Prairie Grove, Arkansas, on December 7, 1862, though Adams' own performance and leadership in the battle were praised. In July, 1863, the regiment was broken up; Adams, an officer without a command, joined the staff of Major General Thomas Hindman, an old acquaintance from Helena days. Hindman led a division in the Army of Tennessee that fall, and Adams was appointed acting assistant inspector general and later chief of staff of the division. In December, 1863, Adams returned to Arkansas. In 1864 he served as commander of the Northern Sub-District of Arkansas (behind the Union army's lines) with the rank of "acting brigadier general." His service there was subject to criticism. Brigadier General Joseph Shelby, the brilliant cavalry leader, had a low opinion of Adams' military abilities. When Shelby operated in Adams' district, he took over all the military duties and relegated Adams to strictly civil matters. Shelby's chief of staff and amanuensis, John Newman Edwards, wrote of an abandoned siege that Adams had "no faith in investments, except cotton investments, perhaps." An old friend, however, remembers Adams as "a brave soldier."[2] Adams had at least titular command in the Northern Sub-District through at least December 27, 1864, though by early 1865 other officers were in command of it.

After the war Adams returned to Helena. In 1865 he settled in Memphis and formed a law partnership with his close friend General Albert Pike. General Adams died in Memphis of yellow fever on September 9, 1878. He is buried in Elmwood Cemetery in Memphis. Helen Keller, the blind deaf-mute who overcame her handicaps to become a celebrated author, was General Adams' granddaughter.

Adams is listed as a Confederate general in CV, Heitman, and SHSP, on the basis of his "acting" generalship rank. The presumption is that Adams was assigned to duty as brigadier general by General E. Kirby Smith, the commander of the Trans-Mississippi Department. However, unlike other Kirby Smith assignments to duty, no record of Adams' promotion exists.

At least two sources state that Adams was made brigadier general for "conspicuous courage" at the Battle of Missionary Ridge, Tennessee, in November, 1863. In fact, on February 6, 1864, Colonel Adams wrote the secretary of war asking to be promoted to brigadier general, giving as reason that, with his property in Union hands, he needed the extra pay.

NOTES

1. A member of the secession convention remembered that "C. W. Adams was an able man, and noted for the frequency of his orations. . . . He did inflict on us many long orations to prove the right of secession." Another contemporary noted his "great energy, strong individuality, and much force of character—a self-educated and self-made man." See Alfred H. Carrigan and Jesse Cypert, "Reminiscences of the Secession Convention," *Arkansas Historical Associations Publications*, I (1906), 308; John Hallum, *The Diary of an Old Lawyer* (Nashville, 1895), 277.

2. John N. Edwards, *Shelby and His Men* (Cincinnati, 1867), 318; Charles E. Nash, *Biographical Sketches of Gen. Pat Cleburne and Gen. T. C. Hindman* (Little Rock, 1898), 83.

MAIN SOURCE

Hallum, John. *Biographical and Pictorial History of Arkansas*. Albany, 1887.

JAMES LUSK ALCORN

James Lusk Alcorn, brigadier general of Mississippi state troops in 1861, was born on November 4, 1816, in Golconda, Illinois Territory, to James and Louisa (Lusk) Alcorn. His father operated trading boats on the Mississippi River. The family soon moved to Kentucky, where Alcorn was raised. He attended Cumberland College in 1836, but had to quit college when his funds ran out. After a brief stint teaching school in Jackson, Arkansas, Alcorn returned to Kentucky and embarked upon a long and distinguished political career. He served as deputy sheriff and state representative from Livingston County from 1839 to 1843, before moving to Delta, Coahoma County, Mississippi. There Alcorn practiced law, owned and operated a plantation, and was active in founding the Mississippi River levee system. A leader among Delta-area Whigs, Alcorn served in the Mississippi legislature from 1846 to 1860. In 1856 he ran unsuccessfully for U.S. Congress.

Mississippi Department of Archives and History

Elected delegate to the state secession convention in 1861, Alcorn, who personally opposed secession, nonetheless led a Whig faction that, in the interests of southern solidarity, consistently voted with the secessionists. This veteran Whig politico, a "handsome individual of slow and stately utterance,"[1] was elected brigadier general of Mississippi state troops by the convention. With the successive resignations of Jefferson Davis, Earl Van Dorn, and Charles Clark as major generals of Mississippi state troops, Alcorn, the senior brigadier, was in line for promotion to major general. However, Governor John Pettus, a Democrat and old political opponent, appointed fellow Democrat Reuben Davis to the rank instead. In the fall of 1861, General Alcorn and his troops were ordered to join Confederate forces in central Kentucky. An outbreak of the measles crippled the troops. Transferred to Fort Donelson, Tennessee, Alcorn's "valuable assistance" was praised by the Confederate commander. Relieved from Donelson on October 27, 1861, he returned to Mississippi to organize more regiments. In December of that year he led a brigade of three regiments of sixty-day state troops to Columbus, Kentucky. Under orders from Major General Leonidas Polk, the Confederate commander at Columbus, Alcorn and his brigade took over the post of Camp Beauregard, west of Columbus. The brigade was disbanded at the end of January, 1862. After that Alcorn saw no more field service. In 1862 he was taken prisoner in Arkansas. Upon his parole later that year, he returned to his Delta plantation. Alcorn seems to have spent the balance of the war alternately damning Jefferson Davis (in the legislature, to which he was again elected in 1863)[2] and selling cotton to both sides. Two of his sons died in service, and Alcorn contributed a large part of his personal fortune to the Confederate cause.

When the war ended Alcorn, a distinguished old-line Whig who had never been a strong secessionist, was a natural choice for office of Mississippians willing to cooperate with the newly imposed federal order. The legislature elected him U.S. senator in May, 1865; however, the radical Republican Congress refused to seat him. Turning Republican himself, he was elected governor in 1870 and U.S. senator in 1871. No emancipationist, Alcorn as governor resisted all federal efforts to enforce social equality for blacks and otherwise opposed the radical faction of the Mississippi Republican party. After his Senate term ended in 1877, General Alcorn returned to his lucrative law practice, in which his "natural vigor of intellect, remarkable industry, and thorough knowledge of the law" made him a leader of the state bar.[3] Alcorn's last official service was as a member of the Mississippi Constitutional Convention of 1890. General Alcorn died at Eagle's Nest, in Coahoma County, December 20, 1894, and is interred in a family cemetery on his estate.

Both *CMH* and *SHSP* list Alcorn as a Confederate general.

NOTES

1. Lillian Pereyra, *James Lusk Alcorn: Persistent Whig* (Baton Rouge, 1966), 19.

2. Alcorn called President Davis a "miserable, one-eyed, dyspeptic, arrogant tyrant. . . . Oh, let me live to see him damned and sunk in the lowest hell." See John K. Bettersworth, *Confederate Mississippi* (Baton Rouge, 1943), 58.

3. Pereyra, *James Lusk Alcorn*, 20.

MAIN SOURCES

Alcorn, James L. Papers. Southern Historical Collection, University of North Carolina, Chapel Hill.

Pereyra, Lillian. *James Lusk Alcorn: Persistent Whig.* Baton Rouge, 1966.

Robinson, Mary F. "A Sketch of James Lusk Alcorn." *Journal of Mississippi History,* XII (1950), 28–45.

CHARLES DAVID ANDERSON

Charles David Anderson was born on May 22, 1827, near Stone Mountain in De Kalb County, Georgia, the son of William Robert and Annie (Coker) Anderson. His father, a farmer, was the son of a Revolutionary War major and descended from Welsh immigrants. Before the war he lived in Fort Valley in Houston County, as a planter, cotton merchant, slaveowner, justice of the county court (1857 to 1858), and mayor of Fort Valley.

At the start of the war Anderson, "a man of unsullied reputation and extensive popularity,"[1] was elected captain of Company C, 6th Georgia, the "Beauregard Volunteers." The 6th, part of Colquitt's Georgia brigade, fought in Virginia for the better part of

Courtesy Georgia Department of Archives and History, Brown/Connally/Spalding Collection, AC

the war. Anderson was promoted to major on September 17, 1862, and elected lieutenant colonel on May 15, 1863. At the Battle of Antietam Anderson was wounded and captured. After exchange, he fought at Fredericksburg and Chancellorsville, losing a finger on his left hand in the latter battle. After partially recovering from his wounds, he rejoined his regiment, now part of the Charleston, South Carolina, garrison. Resigning his Confederate army commission on January 20, 1864, because of wounds, Anderson was appointed by Governor Brown as his aide-de-camp. In the summer of 1864 he was elected colonel of the 5th Regiment of the Georgia Militia. Anderson served in the Atlanta campaign and opposed Sherman's March to the Sea. The Georgia militia division joined the Army of Tennessee after the Battle of Kennesaw Mountain. At the Battle of Atlanta the militiamen advanced in conjunction with the attack of Cheatham's Corps, but did not become seriously engaged. For the remainder of the siege of Atlanta "Joe Brown's pets" (as the militiamen were derisively termed) manned the trenches about Atlanta. During the siege Anderson was unanimously elected brigadier general of the newly formed 3rd Brigade of the Georgia Militia. After the fall of the city the militia division was detached from the main army and confronted (from a distance) Sherman's advancing forces. On November 22, 1864, the militia division attacked an isolated Union infantry brigade near Griswoldville, Georgia. The veteran Union troops shot the militiamen to pieces as they charged. Leading his brigade, Anderson had his clothes riddled with bullets and his horse was shot out from under him; his coolness and precision in that unfortunate battle were marked. The brigade formed part of the Savannah garrison during that city's siege in December. After Sherman took Savannah, the brigade was sent to Augusta, Georgia, and finally ended the war guarding Macon. Anderson was elected, without his knowledge, to the state senate in late 1863 and served through 1865.

After the war General Anderson first ran a cotton warehouse and farm supply business in Macon. Both failed, and he returned to Fort Valley, where he served more or less continuously as county tax collector. General Anderson died in Fort Valley on February 22, 1901, and is buried there, in Oaklawn Cemetery.

Heitman, *SHSP*, and Wood all list Anderson as a general.[2]

NOTES

1. Wendell O. Croom, *The War History of Company "C," Sixth Georgia Regiment* (Fort Valley, Ga., 1879), 5.

2. Heitman, listing Charles D. Anderson as a Confederate general, mistakenly confuses his prewar career with that of another Charles D. Anderson, who was colonel of the 21st Alabama Infantry.

MAIN SOURCES

Atlanta *Constitution*, February 24, 1901.

Central Georgia Genealogical Society, Inc. *First Hundred and Ten Years of Houston County, Georgia*. Chelsea, Mich., 1983.

Croom, Wendell O. *The War History of Company "C," Sixth Georgia Regiment*. Fort Valley, Ga., 1879.

Daughters of the American Revolution, Gov. Treutlen Chapter. *History of Peach County, Georgia*. Atlanta, 1972.

CHARLES DEWITT ANDERSON

Charles DeWitt Anderson, colonel of the 21st Alabama Infantry, was born July, 1827, in South Carolina. In 1839 the Anderson Family immigrated to Texas. His parents died on board ship, and when the ship docked in Galveston the orphaned Anderson and his brother were taken in by the minister of the local Episcopal church, who raised the two boys. In 1846 Anderson was the first cadet appointed to West Point from the new state of Texas (Texas founder Sam Houston personally recommended Anderson for the appointment). As a result of deficiencies in math and French, Anderson left West Point after his freshman year; he was discharged in 1848. Eight years later he was commissioned lieutenant of artillery in the U.S. Army directly from civilian life. He served with the 4th Artillery in Florida and the Utah Territory until 1861.

Anderson was with his regiment in the northwest when the Civil War broke out. Securing a leave of absence, he immediately left for the South, traveling overland hundreds of miles in the dead of winter. Reaching the South after an eventful journey, he resigned from the U.S. Army (effective April 1, 1861) and enlisted in the Confederate army. A commission as captain in the regular Confederate army awaited him. Posted to Fort Morgan near Mobile, Alabama, he took command of a detachment of Confederate regulars who handled the ordnance duties at the fort. On December 9, 1861, Anderson was promoted to major of the 20th Alabama Infantry, then stationed at Knoxville, Tennessee. Anderson was detached from the 20th on February 15, 1862, and returned to Mobile to join the staff of Brigadier General Adley H. Gladden. At the Battle of Shiloh (April 6 and 7, 1862) he was Gladden's acting assistant adjutant general. Gladden was killed at Shiloh, and his staff dissolved. On May 8, 1862, Anderson was elected colonel of the 21st Alabama. The 21st, a regiment largely raised in Mobile, was sent back to that city to serve in Mobile's defenses. A "fine officer," Anderson commanded the 21st throughout 1863 and 1864.[1] During the Union army's August, 1864, operations against Mobile, Anderson commanded Fort Gaines, a small fort on Dauphin Island opposite Fort Morgan, the main defense work guarding the entrance to Mobile Bay. On August 5, 1864, Admiral David Farragut's Union fleet ran past Forts Morgan and Gaines. A Union army force landed on Dauphin Island, and in conjunction with Farragut's fleet began to bombard Anderson's fort. Although the bombardment caused only nominal damage to the fort, the officers of the garrison (six companies of the 21st, plus artillerymen and reservists) demanded that Anderson surrender. Union shells were penetrating the walls of Fort Gaines as if they were made of cheese. The small fort was encumbered with a superfluous number of conscripts and reservists, many mere boys, who could find no shelter from the shelling. Their panic spread to the rest of the garrison. At first Anderson was inclined to resist, but seeing that the officers and men were demoralized by Farragut's passage of the forts and ready to mutiny, Anderson gave in. On August 8, 1864, Anderson surrendered Fort Gaines, its 864-man garrison, and 26 cannon. Brigadier General Richard Page, Anderson's superior, criticized the surrender as a craven "deed of dishonor and disgrace."[2] Anderson was also criticized for allowing his second-in-command to abandon Fort Powell, a small earthwork guarding Mobile Bay, after an even briefer bombardment.[3] Admiral Farragut, on the other hand, thought that Anderson displayed great courage for holding out as long as he did. One of the admiral's dying requests was that Anderson's sword, surrendered at Fort Gaines, be returned to him in recognition of his gallantry. Anderson spent the remainder of the war in a Union prison in New Orleans.

After the war Colonel Anderson returned to Texas and got a job in railroad construction. He served two terms as city engineer of Austin, Texas, then returned to Galveston, where he built the Galveston lighthouse. His last six years were spent as a lighthouse keeper on Galveston Island. Anderson died (of the "grippe") on November 21, 1901, and is buried in Galveston's Old Cahill Cemetery.

Heitman lists Colonel Anderson as a Confederate general, confusing him with Brigadier General Charles D. Anderson of the Georgia militia.

NOTES

1. John K. Folmar, ed., *From That Terrible Field: Civil War Letters of James M. Williams, Twenty-First Alabama Infantry Volunteers* (University, Ala., 1981), 176.

2. Arthur W. Bergeron, *Confederate Mobile* (Jackson, Miss., 1991), 145–47.

3. With Union naval artillery, heavier than anything the fort mounted, battering down the walls, and with Farragut's fleet already inside the bay, Anderson felt that further resistance was pointless. General Page, who criticized Anderson for giving up too easily, surrendered Fort Morgan two weeks later after only a one-day bombardment. Admiral Farragut's report of the campaign stated that Anderson put up a better fight than Page. See United States Navy Dept., *The War of the Rebellion: . . . Official Records of the Union and Confederate Navies* (30 vols; Washington, D.C., 1894–1922), XXI, 414–15, 536, 541–42.

MAIN SOURCES

Edgar, Thomas H. "Col. Charles D. Anderson." *Confederate Veteran*, X (1902), 31.

Engineer Department Records of the United States Military Academy, 1812–1867. Microfilm M91. National Archives.

HENRY MARSHALL ASHBY

Henry Marshall Ashby was born in Fauquier County, Virginia, in 1836, the son of Marshall and Lucinda (Cocke) Ashby and the first cousin of future Confederate Brigadier General Turner Ashby. Ashby attended William and Mary College from 1853 to 1854, but did not graduate. His prewar career is obscure, but by 1860 he was making a living as a "trader" in Chattanooga, Tennessee.[1]

The outbreak of the war found him a guest at his uncle's home in Knoxville, Tennessee. Enlisting on July 6, 1861, Ashby organized a company of cavalry in Knoxville and was immediately elected its captain. This unit was later Company C of the 4th Tennessee

Confederate Veteran, XIV (1906)

Cavalry Battalion, which was merged with another battalion to form the 2nd Tennessee Cavalry. On May 24, 1862, Ashby was elected colonel of the newly formed 2nd, which helped guard east Tennessee during 1862 and 1863, and generally served in the cavalry brigade of Brigadier General John Pegram. Ashby participated in three raids into Union-held Kentucky during this period. In one raid Colonel Ashby was shot in the foot and lost the bones in his right heel. Pegram's brigade joined the Army of Tennessee for the Battle of Stone's River (December 31, 1862, to January 2, 1863), where Ashby's regiment helped destroy a wagon train in the rear of the Union army. Pegram's brigade rejoined the Army of Tennessee in time for the Battle of Chickamauga (September 19 to 20, 1863). After this battle Ashby's regiment remained with the Army of Tennessee. During the 1864 Atlanta campaign he was assigned to command a brigade of four Tennessee cavalry regiments in Brigadier General William Y. C. Humes's division. With this brigade Ashby helped oppose the Union army's advance on Atlanta and delay its subsequent March to the Sea. A "born soldier" "who always put himself in front" during a charge,[2] Ashby became an especial favorite of Major General Joseph Wheeler, commander of the Army of Tennessee's cavalry corps. During the 1865 Carolinas campaign Ashby again harassed the advance of Major General William T. Sherman's Union army. When General Humes was wounded in March of 1865, Ashby, as senior colonel, was put in charge of Humes's division, which he led at the Battle of Bentonville and through to the final surrender.

After the war Ashby briefly visited New York City, then returned to Knoxville. He was killed there on July 10, 1868, shot to death on Main Street by E. C. Camp, a local lawyer, during a quarrel. Colonel Ashby is buried in Old Gray Cemetery, in Knoxville.

Ashby was termed a general in the April, 1865, official report of his corps commander, Major General Joseph Wheeler, which has been followed by subsequent writers.[3] General Wheeler had unofficially received word from friends in the War Department that generals' commissions for three colonels in his corps,[4] including Ashby, had been issued, but that the commissions had never been delivered because of uncertainty, in the last day of the war, over where to send them. Ashby ended the war a colonel, signing a May 3, 1865, parole as "Colonel, commanding Division."

NOTES

1. Census of 1860, Tennessee, Hamilton County, Microfilm, pp. 148–49. The census does not show what Ashby was trading in—horses, cotton, or slaves.

2. See James P. Coffin, "Col. Henry M. Ashby," CV, XIV (1906), 121; Bennett H. Young, Confederate Wizards of the Saddle . . . (1914; rpr. Boston, 1958), 585.

3. See, for example, John P. Dyer, "Fightin' Joe" Wheeler (Baton Rouge, 1941), 224. Wheeler's report is in OR, Vol. XLVII, Pt. 1, p. 1132.

4. Colonels James Hagan, Moses Hannon, and Henry Ashby (General Wheeler to James Hagan, May 13, 1865, in the possession of Mrs. Elizabeth H. Carroll, Knoxville, great-granddaughter of Colonel Hagan). A slight variant of this story is set forth in Coffin, "Col. Henry M. Ashby," 121.

MAIN SOURCES

Coffin, James P. "Col. Henry M. Ashby." Confederate Veteran, XIV (1906), 121.
Reese, Lee F., comp. The Ashby Book. 2 vols. San Diego, 1976–78.

Arthur Pendleton Bagby

Arthur Pendleton Bagby was born on May 17, 1833, in Claybourne, Alabama, the son of Alabama senator and governor Arthur Pendleton Bagby and his second wife, Anne Connell. The Bagbys were an old (if not especially distinguished) Virginia family whose ancestor had sailed from Scotland to Jamestown in 1628. Appointed to West Point in 1847, the young Bagby graduated in 1852, thirty-sixth in his class of forty-three. He served as second lieutenant of infantry for a year in New York and Texas. Resigning from the service on September 30, 1853, Bagby returned to Alabama to study law. From 1855 to 1858 he practiced law in Mobile, where his father resided. Bagby then removed to Gonzales, Texas, practicing law there until 1861.

Evans, ed., *Confederate Military History*, XV

On October 12, 1861, Bagby was appointed major of the 7th Regiment of the Texas Mounted Volunteers. He was promoted to lieutenant colonel on April 4, 1862, and to full colonel on November 15, 1862. Bagby led a battalion of the 7th in the New Mexico campaign from 1861 to 1862. His unit was left behind to secure the rear of the main army as it advanced to Santa Fe; during the Battles of Valverde and Glorieta Bagby's troops garrisoned towns in southern New Mexico. In April, 1862, a subordinate accused Bagby of drunkenness on duty. Richmond, not wanting to lose the services of a valuable officer, refused to accept Bagby's resignation. A court-martial was arranged to clear Bagby and, in the teeth of the evidence, did so.[1] He saw further action in the retaking of Galveston in 1863, commanding a detachment of his troopers who volunteered for marine duty manning an improvised gunboat. In 1863 the 7th, part of Brigadier General Henry Sibley's (later Thomas Green's) brigade of Texas cavalry, was ordered to Louisiana. At the Battle of Berwick Bay (April 13, 1863) the 7th, dismounted for the battle, held the Confederate left. Bagby was shot in the arm, but remained with his regiment until the Union attack was driven back. In the fall of 1863, upon the promotion of Green to divisional command, Bagby took over the Sibley-Green brigade, leading it at the Battles of Fordoche and Bayou Bourbeau. In the Red River campaign of 1864 Bagby led his brigade in the rear guard actions opposing Bank's advance. At the Battle of Mansfield (April 8, 1864) the brigade, dismounted for the battle, helped to turn the Union right flank. At the Battle of Pleasant Hill (April 9) the brigade, again dismounted, captured a Union advance position, but hostile fire stalled any further advance. After Pleasant Hill the Union army commenced a long retreat to Simmesport. Throughout the month of April Bagby's cavalry brigade harassed that retreat. General Kirby Smith, who had earlier recommended Bagby for promotion, assigned the "brilliant" Bagby[2] to duty as brigadier general on April 13, 1864, to date from March 17. By September, 1864, General Bagby was transferred from his old brigade and given a new brigade (4th Brigade, 2nd Cavalry Division) of three Texas cavalry regiments. In early 1865 Bagby was given permanent command of a cavalry division. On May 16, 1865, Kirby Smith promoted Bagby to major general (to rank from May 10), but by then the Confederacy had collapsed.

After the war Bagby settled in Victoria, Texas, and resumed his legal career. From 1870 to 1871 he was the assistant editor of the Victoria *Advocate*. In the early 1870s he moved to Halletsville, Texas, and established a thriving law practice. A "learned and a fine orator," Bagby was an active and prominent member of the state bar.[3] General Bagby died at his home in Halletsville on February 21, 1921, and is buried in Halletsville City Cemetery.

CMH, SHSP, CV, Wood, Heitman, and Cullum all list Bagby as a Confederate general.

NOTES

1. For more on this unhappy episode, see Martin H. Hall, "The Court-Martial of Arthur Pendleton Bagby, C.S.A.," *East Texas Historical Journal*, XIV (1981), 60–65.

2. Dallas *Morning News*, February 23, 1921.

3. "Gen. A. P. Bagby," *CV*, XXIX (1921), 146.

MAIN SOURCES

"Gen. A. P. Bagby." *Confederate Veteran*, XXIX (1921), 146.

"Gen. Arthur Pendleton Bagby." *Confederate Veteran*, XXXII (1924), 172.

Hall, Martin H. "The Court-Martial of Arthur Pendleton Bagby, C.S.A." *East Texas Historical Journal*, XIV (1981), 60–65.

United States Military Academy. *Annual Reunion of the Association of Graduates*. N.p., 1924.

SMITH PYNE BANKHEAD

Smith Pyne Bankhead was born on August 28, 1823, at Fort Moultrie, near Charleston, South Carolina, the son of Brigadier General James Bankhead, U.S. Army, and his wife Anne Pyne.[1] From a distinguished Virginia family, young Bankhead grew up in that state and attended both Georgetown University and the University of Virginia. During the Mexican War Bankhead was captain of the Virginia Volunteers. After the war he migrated to California. In 1851 he settled in Memphis, Tennessee, which was to be his lifelong home. Bankhead founded and edited the Memphis *Whig*, a party organ. After selling that paper, Bankhead served as city attorney and later entered private law practice.

When the war started Bankhead was immediately appointed an officer in the Tennessee artillery corps. Future general W. Y. C. Humes and he organized a battery of light artillery in Memphis. "A reliable man and a well-instructed officer,"[2] Bankhead served as captain of artillery at Columbus, Kentucky, New Madrid, and Fort Pillow. Promoted major of artillery on April 1, 1862, at the Battle of Shiloh he was chief of artillery for Polk's corps and rendered distinguished service. Subsequent to that battle Bankhead's military service was in the Trans-Mississippi Department, where he often served under his first cousin, Major General John Bankhead Magruder. Promoted to colonel on November 13, 1862,[3] he was Magruder's chief of artillery from October, 1862. In the spring of 1863 Bankhead commanded the post of San Antonio, Texas. Bankhead was assigned to command the Northern Sub-District of Texas, as "acting Brigadier General," on May 30, 1863. Bankhead's tenure in command was not a success. His district was overrun with deserters and cotton speculators while his forces were still being organized. Ordered into the Indian Territory with parts of three regiments of Texas cavalry, Bankhead and his brigade skirmished with Union patrols but failed (despite orders) to link up with the main Confederate forces there. Bankhead's district command, in his absence, was assigned to another (August 29, 1863). Bankhead was also soon replaced in brigade command and returned to Texas. After this assignment he reverted to his substantive rank of colonel, but did not see field service again. On December 28, 1863, Bankhead again became chief of artillery, District of Texas.

After the war Bankhead returned to Memphis and resumed his legal practice. On March 30, 1867, he was the victim of a brutal assault in the streets of Memphis, from which he died the next day. It was speculated the "deservedly popular" Bankhead was assassinated in error, the killer mistaking him for someone else.[4] General Bankhead is buried in Elmwood Cemetery in Memphis.

Bankhead is called "acting Brigadier General" in OR and "general" in Lindsley's *The Military Annals of Tennessee*.[5] A Bankhead letter dated September 24, 1863, mentions that he was appointed brigadier by order of General Edmund Kirby Smith.[6] Kirby Smith actually approved of Magruder's assignment to duty pending action by the War Department.

NOTES

1. Bankhead's first cousin was Confederate Major General John Bankhead Magruder. His brother Henry Cary Bankhead remained loyal, and was a brevet brigadier general of volunteers in the Union army.

2. See *OR*, VIII, 760.

3. In an interesting twist more reminiscent of twentieth-century bureaucracy, Bankhead's November, 1862, appointment as colonel was never confirmed by the Confederate Senate. Evidently the promotion papers were mislaid in the Confederate war office and the Senate never saw them. Bankhead was subsequently reappointed colonel on January 14, 1865, to rank from June 15, 1864.

4. See John Hallum, *Diary of an Old Lawyer* (Nashville, 1895), 75.

5. See John B. Lindsley, *The Military Annals of Tennessee* (Nashville, 1886), 792.

6. *OR*, Vol. XXII, Pt. 2, p. 1026.

MAIN SOURCES

Elmwood Cemetery Association of Memphis. *Charter, Rules, Regulations, and By-laws of the Elmwood Cemetery Association of Memphis*. Memphis, 1874.

Hallum, John. *The Diary of an Old Lawyer*. Nashville, 1895.

Memphis *Avalanche*, April 1, 3, 1867.

JAMES WILLIAM BARNES

James William Barnes, a brigadier general of Texas state troops, was born on October 5, 1815, in Hancock County, Georgia, the son of Thomas and Sarah Barnes, planters in that county. He was educated in the local schools and at Sparta Academy. Barnes taught school for two years and then volunteered for the Seminole War, rising to the rank of sergeant. In 1839 Barnes removed to Kemper County, Mississippi. Going to Texas the next year, Barnes first lived in Polk County. In 1842 he settled in Anderson in Grimes County, establishing his farm two and a half miles east of town. When not farming, Barnes's main activity was with the Baptist Church. "One of the strongest and most

Courtesy Lisa Hill

active of the earlier great Baptist laymen," [1] he was elected treasurer of the Baptist state convention at its organization in 1848. He was also treasurer of the Union (Baptist) Association and a regular contributor to the Texas *Baptist Herald*. He was a trustee of Baylor University from 1852 to 1872, and as an active agriculturalist, he wrote learned papers for agricultural magazines.

On the outbreak of the war Barnes was commissioned colonel of the 4th Regiment of the Texas State Troops, a temporary organization. In 1863 he was elected captain of a company of Texas state troops based in Grimes County. In September of 1863 Barnes, with a detachment of militia, took over Camp Grace Military Prison. The Union prisoners, not generally respectful of their southern guards, found Barnes a model jailer, "in every thought and word and deed a perfect Christian gentleman . . . as good a man as a rebel could be."[2] In December the prisoners were transferred to another prison. At this time Governor Pendleton Murrah appointed Colonel Barnes brigadier general of Brigade No. 5, Texas State Troops.[3] Barnes's efforts in that post met with general approval; Major General John B. Magruder, the Confederate commander in Texas, praised Barnes as "a true patriot and man of good sense" after Barnes mediated a dispute between Magruder and Governor Murrah over who would control the reserve army in Texas.[4] Barnes also commanded as colonel a regiment in the "Reserve Corps of Texas" to the end of the war. Barnes saw no field duty; his duties involved hunting draft dodgers and deserters.

After the war General Barnes was heavily involved in railroad promotion in his adopted state and became vice president of the International Railroad Company. A Republican politically, Barnes never ran for elective office, yet with his statewide reputation for common sense and honesty he wielded considerable influence. General Barnes died on October 22, 1892, in Anderson. He is buried on the Barnes estate, Prairie View, southeast of Anderson.

Both *SHSP* and *CV* list him as a general.

NOTES

1. James M. Carroll, *A History of Texas Baptists* (Dallas, 1923), 274.

2. Leon Mitchell, Jr., "Camp Groce, Confederate Military Prison," *Southwestern Historical Quarterly*, LXVII (1963–64), 17, quoting Charles Nott, *Sketches in Prison Camps* (New York, 1965), 115–16.

3. Under the law of December 16, 1863, the Texas legislature created six military brigade districts, with the governor appointing a brigadier general for each brigade. The law provided that each brigadier general could supersede Texas militia generals in command of militia troops.

4. General Magruder was of the opinion that the citizens of Texas were not joining, and would not join, the Texas state forces. Governor Murrah, on the other hand, promised to recruit 4,000–5,000 men for state service. According to the governor, by April, 1864, three brigades, totaling 2,500 men, were already embodied. See *OR*, Vol. XXXIV, Pt. 3, pp. 726, 739, 749.

MAIN SOURCES

Dallas *Texas Baptist and Herald*, November 3, 1892.
"Gen. James William Barnes." *Texas Historical and Biographical Magazine*, II (1892), 172–79.

WILLIAM TAYLOR SULLIVAN BARRY

William Taylor Sullivan Barry was born in Columbus, Mississippi, on December 10, 1821, the son of Richard and Mary (Fearn) Barry. Major Richard Barry, his father, was a wealthy plantation owner and slaveholder. The younger Barry graduated from Yale University in 1841. Returning to Columbus, he practiced law and engaged in planting in Sunflower and Oktibbeha counties. Barry "had neither the taste nor patience for the dry and ponderous details of (the law)" and, as an original secessionist, soon plunged into politics.[1] Barry, a Democrat, was elected to the state legislature in 1850 and 1852 and to the U.S. Congress in 1853. Elected again to the state legislature in 1854, Barry served as speaker of the state house in 1855. One contemporary

La Bree, ed., *The Confederate Soldier in the Civil War*

remembered that "he was all orator. . . . No one was more effective in a canvass, but he abhorred the labors and responsibilities of office."[2] Barry was a member of the Mississippi delegation that bolted the Charleston Democratic Convention in 1860 over slavery. He later presided over the Mississippi Secession Convention.

Elected to the Confederate Congress in 1861, Barry advocated extremist measures such as reopening the African slave trade. Barry resigned from Congress in 1862 to enter the army. Commissioned colonel on January 27, 1862, to recruit and organize the 35th Mississippi Infantry, he led his regiment in the Corinth and Vicksburg campaigns. At the Battle of Corinth the 35th took part in the tragic assault on Battery Robinette. In the siege of Vicksburg the 35th manned the right center of the Confederate lines, just South of the 3rd Louisiana Redan. Captured and paroled at Vicksburg, Barry broke parole and led his regiment through the Atlanta campaign of 1864. As senior colonel he often led Sears's brigade during this campaign. Barry was seriously wounded in the shoulder at Altoona in October, 1864. His brigade was transferred to Mobile in 1865 and was captured in the Union attack on Fort Blakely on April 9, 1865. Confined in a New Orleans prison, he was finally exchanged on May 1, 1865.

After the war Colonel Barry practiced law in Columbus. Despondent over the war and the effects of his old shoulder wound, Barry withdrew into seclusion. He did publicly urge ex-slaves to vote for the Democratic party. He died on January 29, 1868, and is buried in Friendship Cemetery, Columbus.

Barry is called general in CV and SHSP. Although often in brigade command, it does not appear that he was ever promoted to brigadier. He is termed colonel in the OR as late as April 5, 1865, and he signed his May 9, 1865, parole as colonel, 35th Mississippi.

NOTES

1. Reuben Davis, *Recollections of Mississippi and Mississippians* (Boston, 1889), 98.
2. *Ibid.*

MAIN SOURCES

Rowland, Dunbar, ed. *History of Mississippi: The Heart of the South.* 4 vols. Chicago, 1925.
Wyatt, Lee T. III. "William S. Barry, Advocate of Secession, 1821–1868." *Journal of Mississippi History,* XXXIX (1977), 339–55.

FRANCIS STEBBINS BARTOW

Francis Stebbins Bartow was born on September 6, 1816, in Savannah, Georgia, the son of Dr. Theodosius and Frances Lloyd (Stebbins) Bartow. The son graduated first in his class at Franklin College (later the University of Georgia) in 1835 and attended Yale Law School, but did not graduate. Returning to Savannah, he studied law under Senator John Berrien and later married Berrien's daughter. Bartow soon became a prosperous Savannah lawyer, planter, and slaveowner. A Whig like his father-in-law, Bartow served in the state house in 1841, 1847, and from 1851 to 1852, and in the state senate in 1843. He made an unsuccessful run for the U.S. Congress, as a "Know-Nothing" in 1857. Once a Unionist, by 1860 Bartow had evolved into an active secessionist, delivering eloquent disunion speeches throughout the South.

Miller, ed., *Photographic History,* X

As captain of a Savannah militia company, the "Oglethorpe Infantry," Bartow helped seize Fort Pulaski from federal authorities on January 3, 1861. The previous day Bartow had been elected, as an immediate secessionist, to the Georgia Secession Convention. "Of high social standing and great personal magnetism,"[1] he was elected by the convention to the Confederate Provisional Congress. In Congress he served as chairman of its Military Affairs Committee. Preferring field duty, he left Congress that spring and on May 21, 1861, he was commissioned captain of Company B of the 8th Georgia. On June 1 he was commissioned colonel of the 8th. The regiment was ordered to the Shenandoah Valley in Virginia, where Bartow was placed in command of the 2nd Brigade of the Army of the Shenandoah. Early in the First Battle of Bull Run on July 21, 1861, Bartow's brigade became engaged with the Union flanking column. Exhibiting great personal gallantry, the "impetuous Bartow" was mortally wounded near the Henry House, shot through the heart while grasping the regimental flag and calling on his disorganized troops to rally.[2] His last words were: "They have killed me, boys, but never give up the field." He is buried in Bonaventure Cemetery in Savannah. In December, 1861, Cass County, Georgia, was renamed Bartow County in his honor.

Wood, Heitman, CV, CMH, and SHSP all list Bartow as a general. Less than a week after his death, the Richmond Dispatch made reference to the death of "Col. (acting Brig. Gen.) Francis S. Bartow," the "acting general" title referring to his leading a brigade.[3] From this sprung the widespread contemporary belief that Bartow was a general. Although he undoubtedly would have received speedy promotion to brigadier's rank, no record of his appointment as general exists.

Notes

1. Evans, ed., CMH, VII, 394.
2. Ibid.
3. Richmond Dispatch, July 24, 1861.

Main Sources

Eliot, Ellsworth. Yale in the Civil War. New Haven, 1932.

Evans, Clement A., ed. Confederate Military History: A Library of Confederate States History. 1899; 17 volume extended edition; rpr. Wilmington, N.C. 1987.

Knight, Lucian L. Georgia's Landmarks, Memorials and Legends. Augusta, 1914.

JOHN ROBERT BAYLOR

John Robert Baylor was born on July 20, 1822, in Paris, Kentucky, the son of Dr. John and Sophie (Weidner) Baylor. The Baylors were a distinguished Virginia family; a granduncle had commanded Washington's cavalry, and Baylor University was named after an uncle. He was also a grandnephew of U.S. Senator Jesse Bledsoe. Baylor grew up on various posts where his father, an army surgeon, was stationed. From 1835 to 1837 he attended Woodward College in Cincinnati. Emigrating to Texas in 1839, he settled near Weatherford on the north Texas frontier and bought a ranch. Quickly becoming a leader in his new community, Baylor was elected state representative (serving from 1853 to 1854), battled the local Indian tribes,

Western History Collections, University of Oklahoma Library

and found time to edit a Democratic party paper, *The White Man*, in Weatherford. From 1855 to 1857 Baylor held the office of subagent to the Comanche Indian tribe. In the prewar period he garnered statewide notoriety as an Indian fighter and hater.

The Texas secession convention elected Baylor lieutenant colonel of the newly formed 2nd Texas Mounted Rifles, a state unit, and ordered him to occupy abandoned U.S. Army forts in western Texas. Brigadier General Henry Sibley promoted Baylor to full colonel on December 15, 1861, with the formal commission coming on May 29, 1862. On May 24, 1861, President Davis ordered Baylor and his regiment (the 2nd was mustered into Confederate service on May 23, 1861) to move into the southern portion of the New Mexico Territory and succor that area's pro-secessionist inhabitants.[1] On July 27, 1861, his small force of cavalry (three hundred volunteers) captured five hundred U.S. Army regulars under the flagrantly incompetent Major Isaac Lynde, Union commander at Fort Fillmore. The victory panicked the local Union garrisons, and almost caused the Union abandonment of the whole of New Mexico. On August 1, 1861, Baylor proclaimed himself provisional governor of the Arizona Territory, an action subsequently recognized officially by the Confederate government. As governor his primary concern was protecting the local inhabitants from marauding Apache Indians. From personal experience Baylor, and most frontiersmen, knew the government policy of bribing the local Indian tribes to keep the peace was futile: "[The Indians] make [peace] treaties to get blankets and presents. They never think of keeping a treaty longer than they see an opportunity to rob and murder some one."[2] Accordingly, Baylor outspokenly advocated exterminating the Indians, a policy "heartily supported by virtually everybody personally involved except, of course, the Indians."[3] On May

29, 1862, the secretary of war authorized Baylor to raise a force of five battalions of rangers, known as the Arizona Brigade, to be commanded by him as colonel and governor. Baylor returned to Texas in August, 1862, and began recruiting his brigade. In October, 1862, word of his Indian extermination policy finally reached Richmond. President Davis, horrified at Baylor's bloodthirstiness, promptly removed him from office and revoked his army commission. The former governor defended his actions in newspaper articles, attacking his critics as out of touch with frontier realities. He also kept his hand in the war; as a volunteer he participated in the January 1, 1863, recapture of Galveston, and in the summer recruited a company of state troops intended to help guard the frontier. In the fall of 1863 Baylor was elected to the Second Confederate Congress, beating a pro-administration incumbent. In Congress Baylor opposed extending the president's war powers, but otherwise supported the war effort. Seemingly in the president's good graces again, on March 25, 1865, he was reappointed colonel in the Confederate army, with authority to raise a regiment of draft-exempt men for service on the Texas frontier. The war ended before Baylor could return to Texas and begin recruiting.

After the war he practiced law in San Antonio and later ranched in Uvalde County. A huge man with a ferocious temper ("Anyone he liked was the best fellow in the world, and anyone he disliked was the damnest rascal living."[4]), Baylor was involved in several bloody postwar gunfights and personal encounters. He died on February 6, 1894, in Montell in Uvalde County. He is buried in the Church of the Ascension Cemetery in Montell.

Heitman, Wood, SHSP, and CV list him as a general, his tombstone proclaims him "general," and some accounts have him "brevetted" general. In 1863 Major General John B. Magruder, impressed by Private Baylor's gallantry during the attack on Galveston, recommended that he be promoted to general to command the Arizona Brigade. However, his highest official Confederate rank was colonel.

NOTES

1. Territorial secession conventions at Mesilla (March 16, 1861) and Tucson (March 23, 1861) voted to secede from the Union and join the Confederacy as territories.

2. Baylor in the Houston *Tri-Weekly Telegraph*, October 17, 1862, quoted in Martin H. Hall, "Planter vs. Frontiersman: Conflict in Confederate Indian Policy," *Essays on the American Civil War*, eds. William F. Holmes and Harold Hollingsworth (Austin, 1968), 62.

3. Ezra Warner and W. Buck Yearns, *Biographical Register of the Confederate Congress* (Baton Rouge, 1975), 19.

4. George W. Baylor, *John Robert Baylor* (Tucson, 1966), 35.

MAIN SOURCES

Hall, Martin H. "Planter vs. Frontiersman: Conflict in Confederate Indian Policy." In *Essays on the American Civil War*. Edited by William F. Holmes and Harold Hollingsworth. Austin, 1968.

Thompson, Jerry Don. *John Robert Baylor: Texas Indian Fighter and Confederate Soldier.* Hillsboro, 1971.

ALFRED BECKLEY

Alfred Beckley was born in Washington, D.C., on May 26, 1802, the son of John J. and Maria (Prince) Beckley. His father, a Democratic politician, was mayor of Richmond, Virginia, and clerk of the U.S. House. After the father's death in 1807 the family moved to Pittsburg and then to Frankfort, Kentucky, from where young Beckley was appointed (in 1819) to West Point. He graduated in 1823, ninth in his class of thirty-five, and was commissioned second lieutenant of artillery. Beckley's thirteen years of military service were in the artillery, at various posts. In 1835 he finally obtained clear title to a large tract of land in western Virginia, in what is now Raleigh County, West Virginia. Beck-

Courtesy Mrs. M. M. Ralsten

ley resigned from the army on October 24, 1836, in order to manage those estates. "A gentleman of fine education and excellent understanding," [1] Beckley soon became a leading citizen of the county, being its first circuit court clerk. He founded the county seat, Beckley (also known as Raleigh Court House), which was named after his father. Among other varied activities, Beckley was a Methodist preacher, a brigadier general of Virginia militia, and a delegate to the 1844 Whig Party National Convention.

On May 17, 1861, Virginia Governor John Letcher nominated Beckley to be colonel of volunteers in the Provisional Army of Virginia. The governor ordered him to organize a regiment, to be numbered the 35th Virginia Volunteers, out of his militiamen. However, the Virginia Secession Convention refused to confirm his nomination, the militiamen refused to volunteer in any numbers, and the 35th never formed. Instead, Beckley spent the next months organizing and training both his militia brigade and Confederate volunteers. In the summer of 1861 Beckley, as general of the 12th Brigade of the Virginia Militia, called out his militiamen to help repel a Union invasion of the Kanawha Valley.[2] He met with little success. The populace of the area was largely Unionist and reluctant to fight for the South, and the pro-southern element tended to join regular units instead of the militia. Under orders of Brigadier General Henry Wise, his militia guarded ferries on the New River. On August 5, 1861, Wise condemned Beckley's militia in scathing terms, calling his force "demoralized" and stating that "Gen. Beckley can raise no force of any efficiency at all." [3] The militia served through October, 1861, their "war" limited to firing a few shots at Union scouting parties. Beckley, "light of talent, but well educated," [4] was also appointed colonel of the 35th Virginia Volunteers, but that was a "paper" regiment that never completed its organization. On February 8, 1862, Beckley resigned from the Virginia militia and returned to his Raleigh home. The arduous journey took over a month. The day he arrived (March 17, 1862) he surrendered to the Union forces occupying Raleigh. In a May 22, 1862, letter to West Virginia's Governor Francis Pierpont, Beckley claimed that he came forward in good faith and laid down his arms. The "conservative" Beckley's "desire was really for the Union" and he had only gone along with his militia role out of a general loyalty to the state of Virginia.[5] However, on April 3, 1862, the Union forces arrested him. They took Beckley to Columbus, Ohio, as a military prisoner, to be held until exchanged or released. Beckley protested that he should be treated as a civilian, that he had severed all connection with the Confederacy. On June 18 he was paroled and on June 26 returned to Raleigh. Beckley took no further part in the war. His five sons, however, all served in the Confederate army.

Beckley lived in Raleigh County for the remainder of his life, farming and resuming his office of preacher. In 1872 he was made county superintendent of schools, and in 1877 was elected state representative. General Beckley died on May 26, 1888, at his home, Wildwood, and was buried in Beckley. A monument to him was erected in Beckley in 1938.

General Beckley's command of a brigade of militia which served in a campaign qualifies him to be considered a Confederate general.

Notes

1. See the Richmond *Enquirer*, November 24, 1843.

2. It is now largely forgotten, but the state of West Virginia, formed by Unionist politicians, included at least twenty-four counties that were Confederate in outlook and which had voted to ratify the Virginia secession ordinance.

3. *OR*, V, 771, 779.

4. Charles R. Williams, ed., *Diary and Letters of Rutherford Birchard Hayes* (5 vols.; Columbus, Ohio, 1922), II, 215.

5. *Ibid.*, 187.

Main Sources

Berkeley, Edmund, and Dorothy Berkeley. *John Beckley*. Philadelphia, 1973.

Eby, Cecil D., Jr. "Memoir of a West Pointer in Florida: 1825." *Florida Historical Quarterly*, XLI (1962–63), 154–64.

———. "Memoir of a West Pointer in Saint Augustine: 1824–1826." *Florida Historical Quarterly*, XLII (1963–64), 307–20.

———. "Recollections of Fort Monroe, 1826–1828: From the Autobiography of Lieutenant Alfred Beckley." *Virginia Magazine of History and Biography*, LXXII (1964), 479–89.

Warren, Harlow. *Beckley, USA*. 3 vols. N.p., 1955.

SANTOS BENAVIDES

Santos Benavides was born on November 1, 1823, in Laredo, Texas (then part of Mexico), the son of Jose Maria and Marguerita (Ramon) Benavides. Of distinguished ancestry, he was a great-grandson of Tomas Sanchez, founder of Laredo; his uncle Basilio was later a Texas state representative. He was appointed city attorney of Laredo in 1843 by the Mexican government. Adapting quickly to the new Anglo-Texan presence, Benavides became a wealthy Laredo merchant and rancher. He was known as the "Merchant Prince of the Rio Grande" for his wide-ranging business interests. In 1856 the citizens of Laredo elected him their mayor, and in 1859 they elected him chief justice of Webb County. Active in military affairs as well, Benavides earned a reputation as an Indian fighter by leading numerous forays against hostile local tribes.

Institute of Texan Cultures

Benavides went with his state when it seceded. The first two years of the war Benavides, as captain, headed up a company of Texas state cavalry, made up of mostly Mexican-American ranchers, which protected the border against incursions by Mexican and Indian bandits. He won considerable credit as a leader of rangers. In November, 1863, Benavides was authorized by the Confederate commander of the Trans-Mississippi Department, General E. Kirby Smith, to raise a cavalry regiment in west Texas to defend that state's border.[1] In 1863, praising Benavides for his "most admirable tact, skill and decision," the Confederate area commanders recommended that Benavides be made a brigadier general to command the southern frontier of Texas.[2] Major General John B. Magruder, District of Texas commander, promised that if Benavides raised a brigade he would get his generalship. Major (from May 2, 1863) and later colonel of the 33rd (Benavides') Texas Cavalry, Benavides defeated Union-Mexican forces in an attack on Laredo in May, 1864, and otherwise did yeoman service protecting both the Laredo area and the border trade. In 1864 the Texas Legislature formally thanked Benavides for his defense of the border. Later he was put in charge of the Western Division of the Western Sub-District of Texas.

After the war Benevides resumed his mercantile business, in partnership with his brother Christobal. Benavides dabbled in Texas and Mexican politics, supporting his son-in-law (General Lorenzo Garza Ayala) against the Mexican dictator Porfirio Diaz. He was often accused of using his Charcos Largo ranch as a supply depot for the rebels. Benavides was elected to the Texas House three times, representing Webb County from 1879 to 1884, and was twice an alderman of Laredo. He died on November 9, 1891, in Laredo, and is buried in the Catholic Cemetery there.

Colonel Benavides, who "did not know the meaning of fear, and was an able, skillful commander,"[3] was undoubtedly the war's most distinguished Hispanic Confederate.

The *Handbook of Texas*[4] states that Benavides received a promotion to general by the state of Texas just before war's end. A newspaper account of his death calls him "general,"[5] and an article written three years after his death states that he "was commissioned a General, but the war ended before he assumed his rank."[6] However, at least one expert who has written extensively on Benevides states flatly that he can find no record of such a promotion.[7]

NOTES

1. Benavides spurned an offer of a general's commission in the Union army from an old friend, Union Brigadier General Edmund Davis.

2. OR, Vol. XXVI, Pt. 2, p. 249.

3. Goodspeed Publishing Company, *Memorial and Genealogical Record of Southwest Texas* (1894; rpr. Easley, S.C., 1978), 477–78.

4. Walter P. Webb and Eldon S. Branda, eds., *Handbook of Texas* (3 vols.; Austin, 1952–76).

5. See the Corpus Christi *Weekly Caller,* November 13, 1891.

6. Goodspeed Publishing Company, *Memorial and Genealogical Record,* 477–78.

7. Professor Jerry Don Thompson of Laredo State University to the author, October 22, 1990.

MAIN SOURCES

Goodspeed Publishing Company, *Memorial and Genealogical Record of Southwest Texas.* 1894; rpr. Easley, S.C., 1978.

Marshall, Bruce. "Santos Benavides: 'The Confederacy on the Rio Grande.'" *Civil War,* VIII (May–June, 1990), 18–21.

Thompson, Jerry Don. *Vacqueros in Blue and Gray.* Austin, 1976.

JAMES BOGGS

James Boggs, brigadier general of Virginia militia, was born in County Down, Ireland, on April 8, 1796, the eldest of seven children of John and Margaret (Kee) Boggs.[1] His father was an Irish immigrant who moved to western Virginia when James was eleven. James Boggs became a prosperous farmer in Pendleton County, Virginia (now West Virginia), owning seventeen slaves by 1860 (he was the second largest slaveholder in the county). Boggs was also active politically before the war, serving as justice of the county (1842, 1852 to 1862), county sheriff (1843), and state representative (1861 to 1862). By 1860 his main occupation was as a merchant in Franklin, the county seat.

Courtesy Dewayne Borrer and Grace Dyer

When the war broke out Boggs was already brigadier general of the 18th Brigade of the Virginia Militia. His militiamen, called out by the governor to assemble at Strasburg, Virginia, on July 13, 1861, served in northwest Virginia on and off until April, 1862. The November, 1861, call-up of the Pendleton County militia met with special resistance in this area of divided loyalties (Boggs's own brother was a captain in the Union army). General Boggs was compelled to request that a Confederate regiment be sent to that county to force the citizens to turn out. In the winter of 1861 Stonewall Jackson, then Confederate commander in northwest Virginia, ordered the local militia, including Boggs's brigade, to rendezvous at Winchester and receive training. That December parts of the brigade were ordered to Moorefield, west of Winchester, to rid the mountainous area of Union homeguards. In early January, 1862, General Jackson's small army advanced from Winchester to attack the Union-held towns of Bath and Romney, west Virginia. Boggs's militia, concentrated along the Potomac River south of Romney, guarded Jackson's left flank during the advance. After Romney was taken, Boggs's troops were scattered along the South Branch Valley to take shelter from the winter cold. His health failing because of the inclement weather and age, General Boggs returned home to Pendleton County and died there on January 28, 1862. He is buried in Mount Hiser Cemetery in Franklin, a short distance from his home, which stands to this day.

General Boggs's command of a brigade of militia that served in a campaign qualifies him to be considered a Confederate general.

NOTE

1. Date and place of birth from Dewayne Borror of Franklin, West Virginia, from Boggs family records in his possession.

MAIN SOURCE
Morton, Oren F. *A History of Pendleton County, West Virginia.* Dayton, Va., 1910.

PINCKNEY DOWNIE BOWLES

Pinckney Downie Bowles, the son of Isaac and Emily (Holloway) Bowles, was born on July 7, 1835, in the Edgefield District of South Carolina. His father, of an old Virginia family, was a planter near Pleasant Lane, a civil engineer, and a militia officer. A graduate of the Military Academy of South Carolina, Bowles briefly attended the University of Virginia from 1855 to 1856. Admitted to the bar in 1857, he practiced law in the office of future Confederate Brigadier General Samuel McGowen. Bowles moved to Sparta in Conecuh County, Alabama, in 1859 to practice as an attorney. In 1860 he was elected colonel of the local militia regiment.

The "Conecuh Guards" (Company E of the 4th Alabama Infantry) were organized on April 17, 1861, with Bowles as first lieutenant and later captain.

Massachusetts Commandery, Military Order of the Loyal Legion and the U.S. Army Military History Institute

The 4th was ordered to northern Virginia where, on July 21, 1861, it saw action at the First Battle of Bull Run. Bowles fought at the Battle of Seven Pines (May 31 to June 1, 1862) and in the Seven Days' Battles (June 25 to July 1, 1862). On August 22, 1862, Bowles was promoted to major. He was commissioned lieutenant colonel on September 3, 1862, and colonel on October 3, 1862. Bowles and the 4th, part of Brigadier General Evander Law's brigade, compiled an enviable record, participating in many of the battles of General Robert E. Lee's Army of Northern Virginia. Curiously, the gallant Colonel Bowles was never wounded during the war, though he was always in the thick of the fighting. At First Bull Run, his canteen was shattered by a bullet; at the Battle of Spotsylvania in May, 1864, his cap was shot from his hand. When General Law was wounded at the Battle of Cold Harbor, June 3, 1864, Bowles took temporary command of the brigade. Despite postwar claims that Bowles led Law's brigade up to the final surrender at Appomattox, the *Official Records* show that another colonel of that brigade with more seniority, William F. Perry of the 44th Alabama, commanded Law's brigade on a regular basis after Cold Harbor. Perry was promoted to brigadier general in 1865.

Bowles led the 4th in the 1864–1865 siege of Petersburg, but was not included in the final surrender at Appomattox.

After the war Bowles returned to Conecuh County, built a lucrative law practice, and served as county prosecutor for ten years. From 1887 to 1898 Bowles was county probate judge. He was also a general in the United Confederate Veterans Alabama Division. On July 25, 1910, Bowles died in Tampa, Florida, at the home of his daughter. He is buried in the Evergreen, Alabama, Old Historical Cemetery.

Bowles is listed as a general in *CMH, SHSP,* Heitman, *CV,* and Wood. *SHSP* claims he was appointed brigadier general on April 2, 1865, to lead a brigade consisting of two mixed regiments and some Virginia reserves in Brigadier General James Walker's division. However, no such Virginia reserve organization is listed in Walker's division in the *OR,* and in any event the command of such a brigade would not have necessitated Bowles's promotion to general. Walker's division was not even in the same corps as Law's brigade; it was almost unheard of to bring in a non-Virginia colonel from another corps to lead a Virginia brigade. Owen's *Alabama Biography,* in its biography of Bowles written during his lifetime, states that while he was placed in brigade command (his old regiment was led by a lieutenant colonel throughout the Appomattox campaign), he was never made brigadier.[1] Given the absence of any record of his promotion, Owen would seem to be correct.

Note

1. Thomas M. Owen, *History of Alabama and Dictionary of Alabama Biography* (4 vols., Chicago, 1921).

Main Sources

Bowles, Pinckney D. Sketch. United Daughters of the Confederacy, Alabama Division Collection, W. Stanley Hoole Special Collections Library, University of Alabama, Tuscaloosa.

Evans, Clement A., ed. *Confederate Military History: A Library of Confederate States History.* 1899: 17 vol. extended collection; rpr. Wilmington, N.C. 1987.

Owen, Thomas M. *History of Alabama and Dictionary of Alabama Biography.* 4 vols. Chicago, 1921.

THOMAS H. BRADLEY

Thomas H. Bradley, a brigadier general of Arkansas state forces, was born in Williamson County, Tennessee, on July 25, 1808, the son of Thomas and Margaret Bradley, farmers in that county. He developed into one of the leading merchants of Franklin, Tennessee. In the Second Seminole War (1835 to 1836) Bradley was a major and regimental adjutant with the 1st Tennessee Volunteers. Soon after that war he removed to Crittenden County, Arkansas, where he established a large plantation on the Mississippi River about eighteen miles north of Memphis. One of the pioneer planters and largest slaveowners in that county, Bradley prospered. Like many planters Bradley (a Democrat) dabbled in politics and served one term (from 1850 to 1851) in the state house of representatives. A Unionist by conviction, Bradley was a Douglas delegate to the 1860 Democratic Convention.

Elected to the Arkansas Secession Convention, Bradley was reputedly the only delegate from eastern Arkansas to oppose secession, although he was the wealthiest delegate and largest slaveholder elected. On account of his prior military experience, Bradley was named brigadier general of Arkansas state forces by the secession convention, to command the 2nd (Eastern) Division.[1] His stint in divisional command was not a success. Because of his Unionist background, his "old age and feeble health," the troops in camp "had no confidence in Bradley."[2] He quarelled with his officers, attempting at one point to court-martial future General Pat Cleburne. The Arkansas Military Board relieved General Bradley of duty in July, 1861; one newspaper called him a "drunkard, a coward, and incompetent in every respect."[3] Enfeebled and disappointed, Bradley took no further part in the war. He relocated to Memphis, where he died on September 30, 1864. Bradley is interred in Elmwood Cemetery, Memphis.

NOTES

1. Petty politics dictated every action of the Arkansas Secession Convention. Governor Henry Rector, a Democrat and a strong secessionist, was of a different political faction than the majority of delegates, who were members of the Johnson political machine and, though Democrats and secessionists, were bitter political opponents of the governor. The Johnson Democrats allied with anti-secessionists and Whigs to dominate the proceedings. The convention established an Arkansas army and appointed generals to that army, usurping the governor's appointment powers and arguably exceeding its authority. Two of their three appointees were simultaneously anti-secessionist and anti-Rector, the third a pro-secessionist Whig, ensuring that the patronage of appointments would be removed from the governor's power. Governor Rector objected vehemently, but eventually acquiesced in the appointments. The two anti-secessionists (Bradley and N. B. Pearce) proved so unpopular with the troops that neither of them lasted long. For an overview of this subject see Michael B. Dougan, *Confederate Arkansas* (University, Tex., 1976).

2. Goodspeed Publishing Company, *Biographical and Historical Memoirs of Eastern Arkansas* (Chicago, 1890), 391; Leo Huff, "The Military Board in Confederate Arkansas," *Arkansas Historical Quarterly*, XXVI (1967), 75–95.

3. Dougan, *Confederate Arkansas*, 75.

MAIN SOURCES

Dougan, Michael B. *Confederate Arkansas*. University, Tex., 1976.

Elmwood Cemetery Association of Memphis. *Charter, Rules, Regulations, and By-Laws of the Elmwood Cemetery Association of Memphis*. Memphis, 1874.

Goodspeed Publishing Company. *Biographical and Historical Memoirs of Eastern Arkansas*. Chicago, 1890.

JOSEPH LANCASTER BRENT

Joseph Lancaster Brent was born on November 30, 1826, in Pomonkey, Charles County, Maryland, the son of William Leigh and Maria (Fenwick) Brent. His father, a lawyer and future congressman from Louisiana, was of an old Maryland family; his brother later served as attorney general of that state. Brent was reared in his native state and attended Georgetown University. After briefly practicing law in St. Martinville, Louisiana, in 1849 he moved out to California, settling in Los Angeles County. Brent was admitted to practice law there in 1850 and soon rose to high rank among California's lawyers, specializing in land claims. At one time he owned the land that is now the city of Pasadena.

Confederate Veteran, XVII (1909)

Brent served two terms in the California House, in 1856 and 1857. "Especially popular with the Mexican element," he became the Democratic leader in southern California.[1] Brent's memoirs (which cover his life from 1850 to 1862) explain the source of his political power—he represented the local Mexican-Americans in court, and they in turn followed his political advice. "I became so decidedly the leader in Los Angeles politics that . . . no one could be elected whom I did not support, and no one defeated whom I befriended."[2]

When the war started Brent sailed back to the South, but was arrested on the high seas, taken north, and paroled. In February, 1862, Brent reached Richmond, and at once was appointed captain on the staff of Major General John B. Magruder, commanding at Yorktown. On May 9, 1862, during the Peninsula campaign, Brent was promoted to major of artillery and served as Magruder's chief of ordnance. One source states that "devoted to work, his energy and administrative ability were felt in every direction."[3] After the Seven Days' Battles he transferred to Louisiana, where Major General Richard Taylor (a close personal friend) appointed him chief of artillery in Taylor's District of Western Louisiana. In this post he worked wonders equipping and organizing the artillery of Taylor's orphan command. One exploit of Brent's was commanding two makeshift gunboats that in 1863 attacked and captured the Union ironclad *Indianola*. On April 17, 1864, General E. Kirby Smith appointed Brent colonel of the newly reorganized artillery battalions of Taylor's army. In October, 1864, the command of a newly formed brigade of Louisiana cavalry in Taylor's army became vacant. The cavalry division's commander asked Brent, whom he knew to be an officer of "energy, gallantry, judgment and ability," to turn cavalryman and take charge of the brigade.[4] On October 15, 1864, General Kirby Smith assigned Brent to command of the brigade, with the rank of brigadier general. The brigade guarded northern Louisiana against Union raids for the remainder of the war. Brent was one of three Confederate commissioners who negotiated the May 26, 1865, surrender of the Trans-Mississippi Department. On June 5, 1865, he was paroled as brigadier general.

After the war Brent lived in Baltimore until 1870, in Louisiana, and in Baltimore from 1888 on, working as a lawyer and a planter and serving behind the scenes as a power in the Louisiana Democratic party. Brent was elected to represent Ascension Parish in the Louisiana House in 1874 and 1886. General Brent married a daughter of Louisiana Congressman Duncan Kenner and by that marriage became the nephew-in-law of Generals Richard Taylor and Allen Thomas. General Brent died on November 27, 1905, in Baltimore, Maryland. He is buried in Green Mount Cemetery in Baltimore.

Brent is listed as a general in *SHSP* (with a November, 1864, date of commission), *CMH*, Wood, and Heitman, though not listed as a Kirby Smith appointment by Warner. The *OR* show him as "acting brigadier general" on December 31, 1864, the same designation as A. P. Bagby and other known Kirby Smith appointments, but the record of that appointment is not in the *OR*. The best proof of his being a general is the fact that after the war Brent applied for a general's pardon. In his application for pardon (which carried endorsements from, among others, the Union governors of Louisiana, Arizona, and California) he lists himself as a brigadier general at a time when he had every inducement not to do so.[5]

NOTES

1. Harris Newmark, *Sixty Years in Southern California, 1853–1913* (Los Angeles, 1970), 47.

2. Joseph L. Brent, *Memoirs of the War Between the States* (N.p., 1940), 22.

3. See Richard Taylor, *Destruction and Reconstruction: Personal Experiences of the Late War* (1879; rpr. New York, 1955), 139.

4. General Simon B. Buckner to Brigadier General William Boggs, October 7, 1864, in Brent's Compiled Service Records of Confederate General and Staff Officers, National Archives.

5. After the war President Johnson issued a blanket pardon for the South, excepting several narrow categories of ex-rebels. The category that concerns us here is the one excluding from the general pardon (and thus from citizenship rights) Confederate military officers above the rank of colonel. Confederate generals, if they wished to regain their civil rights, had to apply to the president for an individual pardon. The pardon papers, still on file at the National Archives, make fascinating reading. The numerous assertions that, in 1861, the appli-

cants were at heart Unionists, makes one wonder how secession ordinances won any referendums. Even more fascinating is the officer's own testimony as to his true Confederate rank. Time after time officers, called generals years later, stated they were actually colonels, that the general's commission never reached them. For example, Thomas Munford of Virginia (treated later) called himself a colonel in 1865, but by 1883 was signing his letters "late Brigadier General CSA." For a detailed exposition of the pardon laws and process, see Jonathan T. Dorris, *Pardon and Amnesty Under Lincoln and Johnson* (Chapel Hill, 1953).

Main Sources

Baltimore *Sun*, November 28, 29, 30, 1905.
Barrows, H. D. "J. Lancaster Brent." *Quarterly of the Historical Society of Southern California*, VI (1905), 238–41.
Brent, Joseph L. *Memoirs of the War Between the States*. New Orleans, 1940.
Brent, Joseph L. Papers. Hill Memorial Library, Louisiana State University, Baton Rouge.
Brent, Joseph L. Papers. Louisiana State Archives, Baton Rouge.
"Career of Gen. Joseph Lancaster Brent." *Confederate Veteran*, XVII (1909), 345–47.

(Pierre) Benjamin Buisson

(Pierre) Benjamin Buisson, the oldest man to serve as a Confederate brigadier, was born on May 20, 1793, in Paris, France, the son of Jean-Francois-Claude Buisson and Marie Esther Guillotte. Appointed in 1811 to L'Ecole Polytechnic (the French military college), Buisson graduated in 1813. After a term in the Metz Artillery School, Buisson joined Napoleon's army as a lieutenant of the 6th Artillery. He fought throughout the 1814 and 1815 campaigns, winning the Legion of Honor and the St. Helena Medal. Immigrating to New Orleans, Louisiana (where a Guillotte cousin resided) in 1817, he quickly became a prominent citizen of his new community. With his engineering training, Buisson was appointed parish surveyor of New Orleans. He also worked as an architect (designing the Custom House) and civil engineer (laying out many of New Orleans' streets). Buisson published and edited the *Courier des Natchitoches* from 1824 to 1825, and the

Author's sketch of a painting in the Louisiana State Museum showing Buisson as a lieutenant in the French army

New Orleans *Journal of Commerce* from 1825 to 1829. In 1849 he wrote a book on astronomy, and in 1861 wrote a book on light infantry training. Active in the New Orleans militia, Buisson was elected commander of the crack "Orleans Battalion" of militia artillery.

At the outbreak of the war Major Buisson (to use his militia rank) was appointed president of the New Orleans commission of engineers to fortify the city and later served on the New Orleans Committee on Public Safety. When the Union fleet approached the city the governor appointed Buisson, "of great activity and fine judgment,"[1] brigadier general of militia (commission dated February 17, 1862) and placed him in command of the 1st Brigade of Louisiana Militia. This unit—1,780 strong, with many of its number of the "French class"—was mustered in for ninety days to help defend the city. "Indifferently armed" and almost without ammunition, the brigade held the Chalmette-McGehee lines south of the city upriver from Forts Jackson and St. Philip, the two forts defending the Mississippi River to the south.[2] Buisson commanded the troops on the east (Chalmette) side of the river. On the morning of April 24 Admiral David Farragut's Union fleet ran past Forts Jackson and St. Philip. The next day Farragut's fleet approached the Chalmette-McGehee lines and opened fire. Unable to harm the Union fleet, Buisson ordered his discouraged troops to take cover in the nearby woods. The demoralized militiamen dispersed and fled to Camp Moore, north of New Orleans. Artillerymen manning the cannon on the lines expended their meager supply of ammunition firing futilely at the Union warships, after which they too retreated. This sorry episode ended Buisson's Civil War career. Subsequently he resumed his career as surveyor and dabbled in astronomy. General Buisson died in New Orleans on May 30, 1874. He is buried in St. Louis Cemetery No. 2, New Orleans.

General Buisson's command of a brigade of militia that served in a campaign qualifies him to be considered a Confederate general.

NOTES

1. New Orleans *Bee*, May 31, 1874.
2. *OR*, VI, 595.

MAIN SOURCES

Conrad, Glenn R., ed. *A Dictionary of Louisiana Biography*. 2 vols. New Orleans, 1988.
Delery, Simone de la Souchere. *Napoleon's Soldiers in America*. Gretna, La., 1972.
New Orleans *Bee*, May 31, 1874.

MICHAEL JEFFERSON BULGER

Michael Jefferson Bulger was born in Columbia, South Carolina, on February 13, 1806, the son of Pierce and Sarah (Adam) Bulger. His father, a mechanic by trade, fought in the War of 1812. Moving with his family to Montgomery, Alabama, in 1823, Bulger spent several years as an apprentice to a gin maker. In 1834 Bulger moved to Coosa County and in 1838 moved to Tallapoosa County, where he engaged in farming for the remainder of his life. An active politician, he served in the state legislature from 1851 to 1857. In the 1830s he fought in the Creek War and rose to the rank of brigadier general in the state militia.

Evans, ed., *Confederate Military History,* VIII

Bulger was a delegate to the 1860 Democratic National Convention, and ran as an elector on the Douglas ticket that fall. In 1861 he was elected delegate to the state secession convention and was a leader in the fight against secession; he even refused to sign the ordinance of secession. However, he went with his state and, after some recruiting service, entered the army as a captain in the 47th Alabama. The 47th joined Taliaferro's (later Evander Law's) brigade of the Army of Northern Virginia. In the regiment's first battle, at Cedar Mountain on August 9, 1862, Bulger commanded the 47th. In that battle Bulger suffered injury: "during an attack on the flank he was wounded in the arm, but he bound his arm tightly, laid it in his bosom, and continued to command his regiment. A little later he was shot in the leg and an artery was severed, but the indomitable soldier stopped the bleeding by placing a corn cob on each side which he bound with a suspender . . . and then persisted in the fight until, about to faint from loss of blood he was compelled to desist." [1] Returning to Alabama to recover, Bulger was elected to the state senate in 1863 to fill a vacancy. After his recovery Bulger rejoined the 47th, having been promoted to major (August 23, 1862) and lieutenant colonel (September 13, 1862). A fellow colonel in Law's brigade recalled that Bulger was "unskilled in tactics and lacking in disciplinary power, but he possessed such a high order of courage that he was greatly respected by his men." [2] In the attack on Little Round Top on the second day of the Battle of Gettysburg, Bulger was shot through the lung while in the thick of the fighting. Left for dead on that battlefield, the indestructible old soldier survived and was taken prisoner. Imprisoned at Johnson's Island, Colonel Bulger (promoted as of July 10, 1863) was exchanged on March 10, 1864. His wounds prevented further active service, and he was retired to the Invalid Corps on February 14, 1865.

After the war Bulger was a farmer, ran unsuccessfully for governor, and served another term in the state legislature (elected in 1866). He lived in Tallapoosa County and Jackson's Gap, Alabama, until his death on December 14, 1900.[3] He is buried in Dadeville Cemetery.

Both *CMH* and Heitman list Bulger as a general, the former stating that he received a commission as brigadier general while convalescing. No record of such a commission exists, and it is unlikely that he would have been promoted since his (Law's) brigade was led, after Law's wounding in 1864, by W. F. Perry as senior colonel and eventually general. A fellow colonel who knew Bulger well states with certainty that *CMH* was mistaken in saying Bulger was commissioned brigadier general.

NOTES

1. Evans, *CMH*, VIII, 394.
2. William C. Oates, *The War Between the Union and the Confederacy* (New York, 1905), 217–18.
3. Date of death per tombstone, Dadeville Cemetery.

MAIN SOURCES

Evans, Clement A., ed. *Confederate Military History: A Library of Confederate States History.* 1899; 17 vol. extended edition; rpr. Wilmington, N.C., 1987.

Oates, William C. *The War Between the Union and the Confederacy.* New York, 1905.

Owen, Thomas M. *History of Alabama and Dictionary of Alabama Biography.* 4 vols. Chicago, 1921.

NAPOLEON BONAPARTE BURROW

Napoleon Bonaparte Burrow was born in 1818 in Bedford County, Tennessee, the son of Banks Mitchum and Mary (Blanchard) Burrow. His father was a farmer in Bedford and Carroll counties. Entering Nashville University in 1836, the young Burrow graduated from the law department in 1839 and commenced a legal career. He settled in Huntingdon in Carroll County, and practiced law there until the outbreak of the Mexican War. A second lieutenant of the 2nd Tennessee Volunteers, Burrow fought with great distinction in Scott's assault on Mexico City. After the war he settled in Arkansas, first in Jefferson County and later near Van Buren. In both places he practiced law and was a substantial planter and slaveholder. Burrow was also active politically as state senator from Jefferson County from 1851 to 1855, Buchanan elector in 1856, and a delegate to both 1860 Democratic conventions. By January, 1860, Burrow was a general in command of a brigade of Arkansas militia.

A prominent secessionist, Burrow was the candidate of the ultra-secessionist "Hindman" faction to the First Confederate Senate. When Arkansas seceded Burrow and his militia brigade (3rd Brigade, First Division) took over Fort Smith, Arkansas, from the federal garrison. His command was so criticized—one influential editor called his conduct there "extravagant and . . . pompously unmilitary"—that he was relieved after two weeks.[1] The Arkansas Military Board later appointed Burrow a brigadier general and sent him to Springfield, Missouri, after the Battle of Wilson's Creek, to transfer the Arkansas militia there to regular Confederate command. The militiamen, encouraged by their commander, Brigadier General N. B. Pearce, refused to transfer, and Burrow's mission ended a fiasco. Burrow spent the rest of the war raising crops for the army. Despite his ill-fated last command, Arkansas politicians retained confidence in Burrow's abilities and recommended to President Davis that he be appointed a Confederate general, a recommendation that Davis, beset by numerous petitions of a like nature, never acted upon.

After the war Burrow resumed his farming and legal careers in Van Buren. In the latter he gained great notoriety, one contemporary stating that "as a criminal lawyer . . . in the state, he stood at the head of his profession."[2] General Burrow died of pneumonia at Alma in Crawford County, Arkansas, on May 23, 1880, while returning to Van Buren from a legal case. He is buried in Alma City Cemetery.

Burrow's rank of general in the Arkansas state army qualifies him to be considered a Confederate general.

NOTES

1. Michael B. Dougan, *Confederate Arkansas* (University, Tex., 1976), 61, 65.
2. Van Buren *Argus*, May 26, 1880.

MAIN SOURCES

Blanks, James R. *Burrows Family History*. Decorah, Iowa, 1986.
Van Buren *Argus*, May 26, 1880.

FRANCIS WITHERS CAPERS

Courtesy Ellison Capers IV

Francis Withers Capers, the son of Methodist Episcopal Bishop William Capers and Susan (McGill) Capers, was born on August 8, 1819, in Savannah, Georgia. Capers attended Randolph-Macon College in Virginia from 1835 to 1836. Entering the College of Charleston, he graduated in 1840 first in his class and commenced a long and distinguished career as a teacher. From 1841 to 1843 he tutored in math at his alma mater. Upon the organization of the South Carolina Military Academy (SCMA), he was made professor of mathematics, with the rank of first lieutenant. With the illness of the two senior professors, Capers in effect launched the new school. Resigning in 1847, he was elected professor of ancient languages at Transylvania University in Kentucky. In 1853 Capers returned to SCMA to become superintendent with the rank of major. In 1859 the state of Georgia induced him to become superintendent of the newly reorganized Georgia Military Institute (GMI), at which he remained until the beginning of the war.

Major Capers' first war service was as captain of the Kennesaw Dragoons. However, Capers' administrative abilities and long experience in drill were in demand in organizing the incoming volunteers. He served as instructor in tactics at various Georgia camps of instruction. On November 11, 1861, Governor Brown appointed Capers a brigadier general to command a brigade of Georgia state troops guarding the coast. After nearly a year's service in this post Capers returned to the superintendency of GMI. In 1863 he laid out the defensive works at Resaca, Georgia, and conducted classes in artillery instruction for state army officers. In 1864, when Sherman advanced upon Atlanta, Capers and his cadets laid out and constructed fortified works. The two company cadet battalions participated in the Battle of Resaca, then were sent to guard railroad bridges in the Confederate rear. Ordered back to the front in July, the battalion helped man the trenches around Atlanta. On August 20 they were ordered to Milledgeville, the state capital. Capers' cadets fought at Ball's Ferry and throughout Sherman's March to the Sea. After the fall of Savannah, the cadets were transferred to Augusta and Milledgeville, guarding property and keeping order, until the end of the war. His superior reported that Capers' "qualifications for military command are of the highest order."[1]

In the summer of 1865, GMI now in ruins, General Capers opened a private school in Augusta, Georgia. In 1869 the College of Charleston appointed him professor of mathematics and civil engineering, a position he held until retiring in 1889. General Capers was also president of the college from 1880 to 1882. He died in Charleston on January 11, 1892, and is buried in Bethel Churchyard. His brother, Ellison Capers, was, colonel of the 24th S.C. and brigadier general of the PACS.

Capers' rank of general in the Georgia state army qualifies him to be considered a Confederate general.

NOTE

1. Charleston *News and Courier*, January 13, 1892.

MAIN SOURCES

Capers, Ellison IV. *Capers Connections: 1684–1984*. Spartanburg, 1992.
Charleston *News and Courier*, January 13, 14, 1892.
Northen, William J., ed. *Men of Mark in Georgia*. 6 vols. Atlanta, 1907–12.

JAMES HARVEY CARSON

James Harvey Carson, brigadier general of Virginia militia, was born on February 11, 1808, at Pleasant Green, the family estate near Winchester, Virginia. His father, Simon Carson, was a farmer and militia officer; his mother was Martha Williams, whose father originally owned Pleasant Green. At the age of eighteen Carson became an assistant teacher at the Winchester Academy. Carson then studied law and soon became a prominent Winchester attorney and agriculturist. In 1837 he was elected colonel of militia. Active politically, Carson served as Frederick County's state representative from 1844 to 1847 and state senator from 1859 to 1864.

Courtesy Katherine Mahood Rugg

In early 1861 Carson, brigadier general of the 16th Brigade of the Virginia Militia since 1859, called his unit into service.[1] The brigade occupied Harpers Ferry, then guarded the Shenandoah Valley while General Joseph E. Johnston's Confederate army marched to the Bull Run battlefield. By August, 1861, Carson commanded the 3rd Division of militia—2,883 strong—in the upper (northern) Shenandoah Valley. On January 2, 1862, Carson and his old brigade joined Stonewall Jackson's small army as it advanced from Winchester on Bath and Romney. The next day Carson's troops were detached from the main body to attack the Union-held town of Bath from the west while Jackson attacked from the east. The town fell to Jackson the next day; Carson's militia could not arrive in time to take part in the capture. Carson's brigade remained in Bath, in winter quarters, while the rest of the army attacked Romney. On February 1, 1862, Carson forsook the campaign field for the legislative wars. His military performance left something to be desired; one observer called him "a most estimable gentleman, but not suited for the time and the exigencies of the moment."[2] In 1862 Carson, "an intelligent, amiable, kind-hearted Christian gentleman,"[3] was elected president of the Virginia Senate. In April, 1864, he resigned his senate seat and went back to farming.

After the war Carson remained active in law and real estate, first in Frederick County and then in Leesburg, Virginia. He died at Leesburg on January 13, 1884, and is buried in the Carson graveyard at Pleasant Green.

General Carson's command of a brigade of militia that served in a campaign qualifies him to be considered a Confederate general.

Notes

1. Parts of Carson's militia brigade served through March, 1862.
2. OR, V, 898.
3. Winchester News, January 25, 1884.

Main Sources

Morton, Oren F. The Story of Winchester, in Virginia. Strasburg, Vir., 1925.
Winchester News, January 25, 1884.
Winchester Times, January 23, 1884.

REUBEN WALKER CARSWELL

Reuben Walker Carswell, a brigadier general of Georgia militia, was born on September 29, 1837,[1] in Louisville, Jefferson County, Georgia, the son of Edward Rhodes and Mary Celesta (Walker) Carswell. The elder Carswell, a state representative, was a member of a Scotch-Irish family long distinguished in Jefferson and Burke counties. After his education in his native county Carswell attended Emory University, from which he graduated in 1856.[2] Returning home, he studied law under future Confederate Major General Ambrose R. Wright and within a year was admitted to the bar. With a "genial disposition and close attention combined with able preparation,"[3] Carswell soon built a lucrative law practice with his cousin William Carswell in Louisville.

Rogers, ed., *Representative Men: North & South*, courtesy Ellamarie Calhoun

A 250-pound gourmand "with marked gifts, large culture and much magnetic humor," he was elected state representative in 1858, serving until 1860.[4]

On June 14, 1861, Carswell was commissioned second lieutenant of Company C of the 20th Georgia. In March, 1862, he was commissioned captain of Company E of the 48th Georgia, a new regiment. The 48th, a unit in the brigade of Ambrose Wright, his former law teacher, was sent to Virginia and joined the Army of Northern Virginia. Promoted lieutenant colonel of the 48th on March 22, 1862, Carswell distinguished himself in the Seven Days' Battles in June and July of 1862 and at the Battle of Chancellorsville in May, 1863. In 1863 Carswell was again elected state representative and returned to Georgia. Governor Brown appointed Carswell brigadier general of state militia in 1864. Carswell led the 1st Brigade of the Georgia Militia, opposing the Union army of Major General William T. Sherman in its advance on Atlanta and the March to the Sea. The 1st Brigade fought at Smyrna Station (July 4, 1864), the Battle of Atlanta (July 22, 1864), and manned the trenches during the subsequent siege of Atlanta. After the fall of Atlanta Governor Brown ordered the militia division furloughed for thirty days in order to let the men harvest their crops. Reassembled in October, 1864, Carswell's men skirmished with Union troops throughout the advance on Savannah. The brigade was fortunate enough to miss the Battle of Griswoldville on November 22, 1864, during which the militia division attacked a Union brigade and was bloodily repulsed. Carswell's final active service was commanding his brigade at the siege of Savannah in December, 1864. He surrendered to Union forces at Augusta, Georgia, on May 20, 1865, and was given his parole as brigadier general of the Georgia militia.

Returning home in June, 1865, Carswell resumed his law practice with moderate success. In 1880 he was elected judge of the Superior Courts of the Middle Circuit, resigning after six years because of ill health. On January 11, 1889, Carswell died at his Louisville home. He is buried in Louisville's New Cemetery.

General Carswell's command of a brigade of militia that served in a campaign qualifies him to be considered a Confederate general.

NOTES

1. William J. Northen, ed., *Men of Mark in Georgia* (6 vols.; Atlanta, 1907–12) and Robert K. Krick, *Lee's Colonels* (Dayton, 1991) give September 26, 1828, as Carswell's date of birth. A book on the Carswell family, Mildred M. Bond and George Bond, *Alexander Carswell and Isabella Brown: Their Ancestors and Descendants* (Chipley, Fla., 1977), gives a December 26, 1838, date of birth. Emory University records give the 1837 date used here (Emory University to the author, January 28, 1991). An 1837 date of birth accords with the ages given by Carswell on his 1850 and 1860 census returns.

2. Northen, ed., *Men of Mark in Georgia*, writes that Carswell entered Emory University in 1850. However, Emory University records show that Carswell entered in September, 1854, and graduated in 1856 (Emory University to the author, January 8, 1991).

3. Northen, ed., *Men of Mark*, III, 417.

4. Bond, *Alexander Carswell*, 21–22.

MAIN SOURCES

Atlanta *Constitution*, January 13, 1889.

Bond, Mildred M., and George Bond. *Alexander Carswell and Isabella Brown: Their Ancestors and Descendants*. Chipley, Fla., 1977.

Northen, William J., ed. *Men of Mark in Georgia*. 6 vols. Atlanta, 1907–12.

Rogers, Augustus C. *Representative Men, North & South*. New York, 1872.

WILLIAM RICHARD CASWELL

William Richard Caswell, a brigadier general of Tennessee state troops, was born in Rutherford County, Tennessee, on October 22, 1809. His father, William Richard Caswell, was a grandson of North Carolina Governor Richard Caswell and second cousin of Governor David Swain. His mother, Sarah Lytle, belonged to a family prominent in the founding of Murfreesboro. The younger Caswell attended the University of Nashville and removed to east Tennessee around 1830. During the 1830s and 1840s Caswell was active in the state militia. By profession he was a farmer and lawyer, serving as attorney general for the state's Twelfth District from 1843 to 1854. During the Mexican War he was briefly aide-de-camp to General Gideon Pillow. He was then elected captain of Company K (the Knoxville company), a regiment of Tennessee Mounted Volunteers. Serving from 1846 to 1847,

Caswell led that company at the Battles of Vera Cruz and Cerro Gordo. Returning home to Tennessee, Caswell resumed the life of a farmer and lawyer in Russellville (1847 to 1849), Dandridge (1849 to 1858), and Knox County (1858 to 1862). He retired from the practice of law in 1856 to become assistant cashier of the Dandridge Bank. Wealthy and influential, Caswell owned land in two states, held slaves, and served on the board of directors of the East Tennessee and Virginia Railroad.

On May 9, 1861, Caswell, an old-line Whig Unionist, was nevertheless appointed brigadier general of Tennessee state troops by Democratic Governor Isham Harris. His Civil War service was entirely in east Tennessee, where he organized regiments and hunted down Union sympathizers. Governor Harris praised him for "discharg[ing] the duties of his position well and faithfully" and urged Richmond to appoint him general in the PACS. General Felix Zollicoffer, the Confederate commander in east Tennessee, mentioned that Caswell had "politely given me great assistance."[1] In October, 1861, Caswell resigned his state commission and for the next few months sat out the war. He had, however, made bitter enemies of many east Tennesseans while arresting local "Tories." General Caswell was murdered near his home, six miles east of Knoxville, on August 6, 1862. Blame for the murder was placed on a runaway slave and a group of unidentified men, who struck from ambush. He is buried in Old Gray Cemetery in Knoxville.[2]

Caswell's rank of general in the Tennessee state army qualifies him to be considered a Confederate general.

NOTES

1. OR, Series 4, Vol. I, p. 527; OR, Vol. LII, Pt. 2, p. 173.

2. Caswell was one of only three generals in the Provisional Army of Tennessee (the others were R. C. Foster and J. L. T. Sneed) who were not subsequently appointed a brigadier general of the PACS by President Davis, despite the vigorous urgings of Governor Harris. It was, perhaps, more than coincidental that the three not appointed were all prewar Whigs, whereas those who were appointed were mostly Democrats. Governor Harris, a Democrat, was willing to reach out to his prewar political opponents—but President Davis, apparently, was not. Davis also noticeably ignored ex-Whigs in his cabinet appointments.

MAIN SOURCES

Caswell, William R. Papers. Southern Historical Collection, University of North Carolina, Chapel Hill.

Hughes, Nathaniel C., Jr., and Roy P. Stonesifer. *The Life and Wars of Gideon J. Pillow*. Chapel Hill, 1993.

Augustus Alexandria Chapman

Augustus Alexandria Chapman was born on March 9, 1803, at Union, Virginia (now West Virginia), the son of Henly and Mary (Alexander) Chapman. The father, of a widespread and prominent Virginia family, was a lawyer and state senator. Chapman attended the University of Virginia and studied law there. Admitted to the bar in 1825, he represented Monroe County in the Virginia House from 1835 to 1841 and 1857 to 1861. He was also a U.S. congressman, a Democrat, from 1843 to 1847. Chapman was described as "a gentleman of fine presence, cultivated manners, and ripe scholarship. He was an able lawyer, a finished orator, and almost invincible in courts or in political debates."[1]

The politically prominent Chapman was brigadier general of the 19th Brigade of the Virginia Militia in 1861, which consisted of six regiments from Raleigh, Mercer, Fayette, Monroe, and Giles counties. Chapman mustered in his militia in June, 1861, to repel a threatened raid. Later the militia participated, though not in the front lines, in the Kanawha (Gauley Bridge) campaign, serving from August to October, 1861. The militia, stationed at Fayette Courthouse, aided the Confederate forces of Brigadier Generals Henry Wise and John Floyd in checking the advance of Union forces up the Kanawha River. On September 3, 1861, Wise's Confederate brigade attacked Union troops at Pig Creek and Gauley Bridge. In conjunction with Wise's attack Chapman's militiamen advanced on the Union rear and drove in the Union outposts. Wise's attack failed, however, and Chapman was forced to withdraw. On September 10 General Floyd ordered Chapman to reinforce Floyd's camp at Carnifax Ferry. Before Chapman could arrive, Union forces assaulted and seized Floyd's camp. After this action the Confederate troops evacuated the area, and with the onset of winter, the campaign petered out. For the remainder of the war General Chapman served in various civil posts, including provost marshal of Monroe County, and delivered several speeches urging a more vigorous war effort.

After the war Chapman resumed his legal career and again dabbled in local politics. He died on June 7, 1876, at the train station in Hinton, West Virginia, while en route to the state Democratic convention. His body was brought back for burial in Union's Green Hill Cemetery.

General Chapman's command of a brigade of militia that served in a campaign qualifies him to be considered a Confederate general.

Note

1. Oren F. Morton, A History of Monroe County, West Virginia (Staunton, 1916), 325.

Main Sources

Monroe (W.Va.) Border Watchman, June 11, 1876.

Morton, Oren F. *A History of Monroe County, West Virginia*. Staunton, 1916.
Reynolds, Clifford, comp. *Biographical Directory of the American Congress, 1774–1961*. Washington, D.C., 1961.

WILLIAM HENRY CHASE

William Henry Chase, a major general of Florida state forces, was born at Chase's Mills near Buckfield, Massachusetts (now Maine), on June 4, 1798. His father, Thomas Chase, was of an old Massachusetts family. Many of the family, including Chase's two brothers, were army officers. His mother, Sarah Greenleaf, was a niece of Governor John Hancock, signer of the Declaration of Independence. Appointed to the United States Military Academy, the young Chase graduated thirtieth (of forty) in the class of 1815. One classmate was future Confederate General Samuel Cooper. Chase's distinguished antebellum army career included stints building forts throughout the United States. Posted

Pensacola Historical Society

to the engineer corps, he worked at Fort Niagara in New York from 1815 to 1819. From 1819 to 1828 he helped build the forts below New Orleans. From 1829 to 1834 he was engaged in the construction of Fort Pickens near Pensacola, Florida. Chase rose to the rank of major (July, 1838) and senior officer of engineers on the Gulf Coast, with responsibility for fortifications along the Caribbean. The forts were largely constructed with rented slave labor. Chase, as chief engineer, became the largest slave renter on the Gulf Coast—a factor that led him eventually to espouse the slaveholder's point of view. In 1856 President Pierce asked Chase to become the superintendent of West Point, which honor Chase declined, fearing the appointment would injure his health. Instead, Chase resigned from the army (October 31, 1856) to devote himself to his extensive business interests in the Pensacola area. One of that town's leading citizens, he was a slaveowner, civic "booster," city alderman, and president of the Alabama and Florida Railroad Company. By now a thoroughly "southern gentleman," married into a southern family, Chase wrote nationally syndicated articles promoting the power of "King Cotton."

Florida seceded from the United States on January 10, 1861. Florida's immediate military objective was to take possession of Pensacola Bay (the best harbor on the Gulf), and Union-held Fort Pickens, which dominated the entrance to the bay.

Chase, a prominent Pensacolan and senior officer in the old army, was the obvious choice to coordinate Florida's effort. Governor Madison Perry appointed him colonel of state forces to command the eight hundred Florida troops concentrated in and around Pensacola. On January 15, 1861, Chase, his eyes filled with tears in the emotion of the moment, demanded the surrender of the fort (which he had designed and constructed) and its garrison, threatening to take the fort by assault if the demand was refused. Lieutenant Adam Slemmer, who commanded a company of U.S. troops holding the fort, refused this demand and another demand three days later. Although Chase could have taken the fort by assault (as Slemmer himself admitted) and in consequence started the war, southern politicians stepped in and arranged a truce. Florida Senator Stephen Mallory worked out a deal with President Buchanan to keep the peace. Under this deal the North would not reinforce Fort Pickens, and the South would not attack it. This arrangement lasted until April, after the Lincoln administration had taken over, by which time Confederate forces under Braxton Bragg had assumed command of Chase's state troops. The war that was not started at Fort Pickens in January was started that April in Charleston Harbor, where, under similar circumstances, Confederates bombarded the Union-held Fort Sumter. Fort Pickens remained in Union hands throughout the war. On January 17, 1861, the Florida Secession Convention authorized the governor to appoint Chase a major general in the newly created "Army of Florida," which appointment the governor soon made. The convention also officially approved Chase's diplomatic handling of the Fort Pickens crisis, adopting a resolution expressing "their approval and high appreciation" of his actions.[1] Chase took no active part in the war after March, 1861.

After the war Chase was a businessman in Pensacola until his death on February 8, 1870. He was buried at Chasefield plantation on Big Lagoon, Pensacola. Because of a construction project General Chase's remains were displaced many years ago and cannot be precisely located today.

Chase's rank of general in the Florida state army qualifies him to be considered a Confederate general.

NOTE

1. Evans, *CMH*, XVI, 16.

MAIN SOURCES

Dibble, Ernest F. *Antebellum Pensacola and the Military Presence*. Pensacola, 1974.

Johnson, Robert U., and Clarence C. Buel, eds. *Battles and Leaders of the Civil War* . . . . 4 vols. 1887–88; rpr. New York, 1956.

Pensacola *Public Record*, October 28, 1939.

DAVID CLARK

General David Clark of the North Carolina militia was born on February 11, 1820, at Albin, the family plantation near Scotland Neck in Halifax County, North Carolina, the son of David and Louisa (Morfleet) Clark. The elder Clark was a wealthy planter and director of a canal company. Educated at the Episcopal Male School in Raleigh, the younger Clark entered neither professional nor public life. Residing in Littleton in Halifax County, Clark concentrated on farming and became one of the wealthiest and most progressive planters in eastern North Carolina, with many acres and large slaveholdings. A "man of wide reading, and with a great landed interest, he found ample occupation in superintending his estates and among

Courtesy North Carolina Division of Archives and History

the books of his large private library."[1] A Whig and proponent of states' rights, Clark exerted a strong influence among the people of his area.

In December, 1861, North Carolina Adjutant General James Martin ordered Clark (who before the war had been elected colonel of the lower Halifax County [15th] militia regiment) to help organize the defenses of the northeast part of the state. Clark traveled to both Raleigh and Norfolk to obtain ammunition, guns, and supplies for his men and by January 3, 1862, established a line of couriers to relay warning of any Union invasion. The Union victory at Roanoke Island (February 8, 1862) opened up the whole of northeast North Carolina to invasion from the sea, and threw the residents of this vulnerable area into a panic. In response Governor Henry Clark (no relation) ordered out the militia in the area, including Clark's 15th Regiment. Under Clark's direction the militiamen blocked the Roanoke River, felling trees across it and, at the narrowest part, deliberately sinking four vessels. By special order of the governor, dated February 20, Clark was charged with exclusive control of the obstruction and defenses of the Roanoke River, with authority to impress wagons, horses, boats, and supplies and to arrest all suspected persons. His "executive ability, great energy and zeal for the cause"[2] so impressed the governor that he promoted Clark to brigadier general and placed under him a brigade composed of four militia regiments from three different counties. In March the militia of three more counties were placed under his command. Clark kept on this duty until, at the end of April, Confederate troops were sent in to relieve the militia. Clark thereupon returned to Halifax County. He spent the rest of the war looking after his plantations, but remained semiactive in his militia duties.

After the war General Clark continued to farm his Halifax County properties. He died on October 4, 1882, at Airlie plantation in Halifax County and is buried in the Thorne-Clark burial ground at nearby Bethel Hill.

Clark is listed as a general of North Carolina state troops in Clark's *Histories of the Several Regiments and Battalions from North Carolina in the Great War, 1861–1865*, a comprehensive and authoritative contemporary work.[3]

NOTES

1. Samuel A. Ashe, *Biographical History of North Carolina from Colonial Times to the Present* (8 vols.; Greensboro, N.C., 1905), VII, 68.

2. Walter Clark, ed., *Histories of the Several Regiments and Battalions from North Carolina in the Great War, 1861–1865* (5 vols.; Raleigh, 1901), IV, 645.

3. *Ibid.* The author of this work was General Clark's son, a lieutenant colonel of state reserve forces during the war and later chief justice of North Carolina.

MAIN SOURCES

Ashe, Samuel A. *Biographical History of North Carolina.* . . . 8 vols., Greensboro, N.C., 1905.
Boddie, John B., comp. *Virginia Historical Genealogies.* Redwood City, Calif., 1954.
Brooks, Aubray L., and Hugh T. Lefler. *The Papers of Walter Clark.* 2 vols. Chapel Hill, 1950.
Clark, Walter, ed. *Histories of the Several Regiments and Battalions from North Carolina in the Great War, 1861–1865.* 5 vols. Raleigh, 1901.

JOHN BULLOCK CLARK, SR.

Missouri State Guard

State Historical Society of Missouri, Columbia

John Bullock Clark, Sr., was born on April 17, 1802, in Madison County, Kentucky, the son of Bennett and Martha (Bullock) Clark. Two of his uncles were Kentucky Governor James Clark and Virginia Congressman Christopher Clark. In 1818 the young Clark's family moved to Missouri. Clark studied law in Fayette, Howard County, and became a successful lawyer. A born politician, Clark served as county treasurer (1823 to 1825), clerk of the county courts (1824 to 1834), and state representative (1850 to 1851). He also found time to become major general in the state militia and serve as a colonel of Missouri volunteers in the Black Hawk War. In 1840 Clark was the Whig party nominee for governor but he later left that party over the slavery issue to become a proslavery Democrat. As a Democrat, Clark was elected to the U.S. House of Representatives in 1857, serving until his expulsion in 1861.

Clark was a strong secessionist and a leader in the state's secession movement. Clark's own comments deserve quoting at length: "While insisting that the best course was to stand by the union, I had, nevertheless, always said that when war did come I would go with the South. . . . That Spring [of 1861] . . . I was worth a million [dollars]. On my place there were 160 slaves, seventy of them men. My law practice was worth $10,000 to $15,000 a year. When I came back after the war was over, I hadn't a bed to sleep on. My wife had been forced to find a temporary home with friends."[1]

Appointed brigadier general of the 3rd Division[2] of the Missouri State Guard in May, 1861, Clark fought at the battle of Wilson's Creek, during which he was wounded. He was soon elected to represent Missouri in the Confederate Provisional Congress. He won election to the First Confederate Senate and the Second Confederate House. While in Congress he was a strong supporter of the administration and of more Draconian prosecution of the war. Differences with Missouri's exiled Governor Reynolds led to Clark's failure to be reelected to a second Senate term. Clark "embarrassed Governor Reynolds by his drunkenness and rowdy behavior in the Confederate capitol," his offenses including "mendacity . . . and the attempted seduction of Gen. Albert Pike's mistress." A fellow soldier, however, called him a "brave and genial old gentleman."[3] Clark was elected to the House, after Governor Reynolds stopped his reelection to the Senate, by the votes of the Missouri troops in Major General Sterling Price's army. Price, a bitter opponent of Reynolds, openly backed Clark.

Clark stayed in Richmond until the end of the war. The federal government offered a $10,000 reward for his capture, but he disguised himself, adopted an alias, and fled to Mexico. Clark remained in Mexico until he heard that the federal authorities no longer wanted him. Crossing the border into Texas, Clark was promptly arrested and imprisoned at Fort Jackson. Eventually freed by President Johnson, Clark did not return to Missouri until five years after the war. He resumed his law practice in Fayette and attempted to restore his fortunes. He made one final effort to win a nomination for the U.S. Congress, but suffered defeat at the hands of his own son, Confederate Brigadier General John B. Clark, Jr., who went on to have a long congressional career. General Clark died in Fayette on October 29, 1885, and is buried in Fayette Cemetery.

General Clark's command of a brigade of the Missouri State Guard as well as his service in a campaign qualify him to be considered a Confederate general.

NOTES

1. Walter B. Stevens, *Centennial History of Missouri* (4 vols.; St. Louis, 1921), 859–60.

2. The Missouri State Guard was not organized into the conventional brigade/division structure. Under the law of May 14, 1861, the state was divided up into nine districts (corresponding to the nine congressional districts), and a brigadier general was appointed to head each

district. The brigadier general would command any units of infantry and cavalry raised in that district. In practice, these were usually 1–8 understrength regiments, which made the district command equivalent to a brigade. Under Section 54 of the law, however, the district command was denominated a division.

3. Ezra J. Warner and W. Buck Yearns, *Biographical Register of the Confederate Congress* (Baton Rouge, 1975), 49; Richard H. Musser, "The War in Missouri: From Springfield to Neosho," *Southern Bivouac*, n.s., I (April, 1886), 683.

MAIN SOURCES

Stevens, Walter B. *Centennial History of Missouri.* 4 vols. St. Louis, 1921.

Warner, Ezra J., and W. Buck Yearns. *Biographical Register of the Confederate Congress.* Baton Rouge, 1975.

MERIWETHER LEWIS CLARK

Meriwether Lewis Clark was born on January 10, 1809, in St. Louis, Missouri, the eldest son of the famous explorer and U.S. senator William Clark and his wife, Julie Hancock. The younger Clark graduated from West Point in 1830, twenty-third in a class of forty-two. After seeing action in the Black Hawk War, he resigned from the army and returned to St. Louis to live. Clark met with success as an architect in that city, where he designed such noted structures as the Church of St. Vincent de Paul and the St. Louis Theater. In 1836 Clark was elected to represent St. Louis in the Missouri House of Representatives. During the Mexican War Clark was appointed major to command the

Missouri Historical Society, Por-C 162

Missouri artillery battalion that accompanied Doniphan's expedition to New Mexico. In 1849 President Zachary Taylor appointed him the federal surveyor general for Illinois and Missouri. By 1860 he was living a genteelly impoverished life of semiretirement in St. Louis.

No rebel firebrand, Clark deplored the fanaticism of both North and South and, with war approaching, tried to induce his son (a cadet at West Point) to stay in school. However, with the firing on Fort Sumter Clark's fulminations against the "folly" of "treason . . . to our beloved country" abated, and he joined what he now called "the glorious cause."[1] On September 17, 1861, Clark left his St. Louis home to join the southern army. Sneaking through the Union lines at great risk, he made his way to Missouri's Rebel army. In October, 1861, Clark was made brigadier general of the 9th District (Division) of the Missouri State Guard. This district comprised Union-held St. Louis; the southern sympathizers of that city who had gone south had already joined the Confederate army, or joined state guard units from other districts. The 9th Division command was thus a nominal one. Clark opted for service with the Confederate army. He was appointed major of artillery on November 11, 1861, and colonel of artillery on April 16, 1862. On December 22, 1861, he was ordered to Fort Smith, Arkansas, to take charge of supply matters there. After the Battle of Pea Ridge (March 6 and 7, 1862) he was ordered to report to Major General Earl Van Dorn, commander of the Army of the West. That April the army (which included most of the old Missouri State Guard) was transferred from Arkansas to northern Mississippi. In the next months Clark served as chief of artillery of the Army of the West, chief of artillery of General Braxton Bragg's Department No. 2 (comprising Mississippi, Alabama, and Tennessee), and as commander of an artillery brigade in the Army of the West. On November 30, 1862, Bragg relieved Clark from command of his brigade, presumably because the two did not get along; Clark complained that Bragg made him a glorified clerk. With Bragg enjoying the favor of the president, Clark's career was, to use his own words, on the shelf. The next two years Clark was assigned the sort of administrative duties that undesirable officers were given: service on a court of inquiry and inspection duty with the Confederate ordnance department in Richmond. During the winter of 1864–1865 the "brave yet gentle" Clark[2] was assigned temporarily to command Barton's brigade of reservists in the Richmond defenses. The brigade was broken up in early 1865, and Clark returned to the ordnance department. That April, when the Army of Northern Virginia evacuated Richmond, Clark followed along, and at the Battle of Sayler's Creek (April 6, 1865) Union troops captured the aged Clark and most of the Richmond garrison.

After the war Clark settled in Kentucky, where many of his and his wife's relatives were leading citizens. The Kentucky Military Institute in Frankfort hired Clark as a professor of mathematics; he eventually became commandant of cadets. The state later hired him as an architect to design a new wing for the state capitol building. He died in Frankfort on October 28, 1881, and is buried in Bellefontaine Cemetery in St. Louis.

Clark is listed as a general in Heitman. He was a general in the Missouri State Guard, but was never more than a colonel in the Confederate army. As late as March 8, 1865, Colonel Clark petitioned the government for promotion to general.

NOTES

1. Frances H. Stadler, "Letters from Mimoma," *Missouri Historical Bulletin*, XVI (April, 1960), 258.

2. Frankfort *Kentucky Yeoman*, October 29, 1881.

MAIN SOURCES

Clark, Meriwether L. Papers. Missouri Historical Society, St. Louis.
St. Louis *Republican*, October 29, November 2, 1881.
Stadler, Frances H. "Letters from Mimoma." *Missouri Historical Bulletin*, XVI (April, 1960), 237–59.

JEREMIAH CLEMENS

Jeremiah Clemens, a reluctant Confederate who soon returned to the Union fold, was born on December 28, 1814, in Huntsville, Alabama. His father, James Clemens, was a well-to-do Kentuckian who removed to Alabama; his mother was Minerva Mills.[1] Young Clemens was educated at La Grange College and at the University of Alabama. Deciding to enter the field of law, Clemens completed a law course at Transylvania University in Kentucky, returning to Alabama in 1834. Soon after graduation, Clemens was appointed a federal district attorney. He developed a promising legal career (in partnership with Senator Clement Clay) and occasionally made forays into politics. From 1839 to 1842 and from 1843 to 1844, Clemens repre-

Alabama Department of Archives and History, Montgomery

sented Madison County in the state legislature. He served in the Alabama war against the Cherokee Indians, raised a company of volunteers in the war for Texas independence, and rose to the rank of lieutenant colonel. At the outbreak of the Mexican War Clemens joined the U.S. Army as major of the newly raised 13th Infantry. Promoted to lieutenant colonel in the 9th Infantry, he served as a supply officer until his mustering-out in 1848. Returning to Alabama, Clemens lost a race for the U.S. Congress (1849) but in the same year won election (as a Democrat) to the U.S. Senate. In the Senate Clemens was famed for his eloquence in debate. When his Senate term expired Clemens dabbled in writing historical novels, with some success. Moving to Memphis in 1859, he briefly edited the Memphis *Eagle and Enquirer*. In 1860, Clemens, whose political views had altered over the years, was elected president of Tennessee's "Opposition" (Whig party) state convention. At the Constitutional Union party's national convention he was one of the Tennessee delegates.

In 1861 Clemens was elected to the Alabama Secession Convention and chosen chairman of the Committee of Military Affairs. Clemens was one of two leaders of the anti-secessionist, "cooperationist" minority. Bowing to the inevitable, Clemens signed the secession ordinance. As both a sop to the cooperationist minority and a recognition of his military experience, Clemens was appointed major general of the newly minted army of the "republic of Alabama."[2] General Clemens spent the early part of 1861 organizing Alabama forces, inspecting defenses, and badgering the War Department for arms. The organization of the PACS left Clemens without a command. Political opposition blocked his appointment to any Confederate post. His health declined and he once again soured on the southern cause. In 1862 the ex-general is said to have volunteered as a Confederate private. By mid-1862, again an avowed Unionist, Clemens removed to Philadelphia and from there called for the South to surrender. Clemens returned to Huntsville toward the close of the war, dying there on May 21, 1865. According to one source, "he was a man of genuine ability, gifted, but erratic and over-ambitious, and at times his career was seriously affected by his dissipated habits." Another source credits Clemens with inventing the popular drink the "Tom and Jerry."[3] He is buried in Maple Hill Cemetery, Huntsville.

Clemens' rank of general in the Alabama state army qualifies him to be considered a Confederate general.

NOTES

1. Family history has it that Senator Clemens was distantly related to Samuel Langhorne Clemens (Mark Twain). See Raymond M. Bell and Harriet C. Hardaway, "James Clemens of Washington County, Pennsylvania, 1734–1795, and His Family" (MS at the Huntsville Public Library, Huntsville, Ala.).

2. At the time, many thought that Clemens was appointed major general as a payoff for his having switched to support of secession.

3. See *Dictionary of American Biography* (20 vols. and supplement; New York, 1928–44), IV, 191; Maple Hill Cemetery records, including booklet, "In Memory of Yesterday: Maple Hill Cemetery."

MAIN SOURCES

Dictionary of American Biography. 20 vols. and supplement. New York, 1928–44.
Hoole, W. Stanley. "Jeremiah Clemens, Novelist." *Alabama Review,* XVIII (1965), 5–36.

JOHN THRELKELD COX

John Threlkeld Cox, colonel of the 1st Confederate Cavalry, was born of distinguished ancestry in Washington, D.C., on December 2, 1820. His father, Colonel John Cox, was a wealthy merchant and longtime mayor of Georgetown; his mother, Hannah Threlkeld, was descended from several of the first families of Maryland. The younger Cox moved to Bowling Green, Kentucky, soon after his 1841 marriage to the daughter of Kentucky's U.S. Senator Joseph Underwood.[1] Cox embarked upon a career as a civil engineer. By 1860 he had become chief engineer of a railroad and a prominent Bowling Green resident.

Cox's first Confederate service was as an engineer officer in Nashville, Tennessee, in 1861. He was captain of engineers by 1862, and in December of that year Cox transferred to field service. He was appointed colonel of the 1st Confederate Cavalry on December 17, 1862, and was formally commissioned at that rank on June 6, 1863. The 1st (later known as the 12th) Confederate Cavalry had been formed from King's 1st Kentucky Cavalry Battalion and six unattached companies from Tennessee and Alabama. At the battle of Stone's River (December 31, 1862, to January 2, 1863) Cox led the 1st in raids on the Union rear. During one charge he and his men captured the 75th Illinois Infantry en masse—the high point of his military career. Throughout 1863 and 1864 the 1st (12th) fought in the Army of Tennessee's cavalry corps. Several times in 1863 Cox exercised temporary command of Brigadier General John Wharton's cavalry brigade. However, Cox was often absent from his regiment, missing, among other engagements, the whole Atlanta campaign of 1864. Cox's abilities appear to have left something to be desired (General John Wharton, his brigade commander, once requested that Cox be relieved of command), but that did not stop him from pressing for higher rank. In 1864 Cox applied for promotion to brigadier general to command a brigade of Kentucky cavalry in Brigadier General John H. Morgan's division, promising, if promoted, to stop the Union army's advance on Atlanta with that one brigade of cavalry! By 1865 the 12th had been transferred to the cavalry corps of Lieutenant General Nathan B. Forrest. Cox and his regiment surrendered in Gainesville, Alabama, on May 11, 1865.

After the war the once-wealthy Cox returned to Bowling Green, his fortune lost. Relocating after 1870 to Washington, D.C., he found a job as a detective in the capitol police force. The "affable, courteous and popular" Cox won respect for his "faithful, energetic and efficient" services.[2] In June, 1886, he became ill with pneumonia and traveled south to Fortress Monroe to regain his health. He died on July 17, 1886, at Old Point Comfort and is buried at Rock Creek Cemetery, Washington, D.C.

Cox is called colonel and "acting brigadier general" in *SHSP*, presumably for leading a cavalry brigade for some time. Cox's obituary calls him "brevet brigadier general."[3] His service records have him a colonel as late as September, 1864, and on his 1865 parole Cox gives his rank as colonel.

NOTES

1. The two were married in 1841 at Bowling Green. Senator Underwood was already Cox's brother-in-law, having married his elder sister in 1839. Colonel Cox's nephew, Congressman Oscar Underwood, was a prominent Alabama politician and a leading contender for the Democratic presidential nomination in 1924.

2. See the *Evening Star* (Washington, D.C.), July 19, 1886.

3. *Ibid.*

MAIN SOURCES

Underwood Family Papers. Western Kentucky State University, Bowling Green.
Washington (D.C.) *Evening Star*, July 19, 20, 1886.

CHARLES COTILDA CREWS

Charles Cotilda[1] Crews was born in 1830 in Harris County, Georgia, the son of Reuben and Elizabeth (Phillips) Crews. Brought up in Ellerslie, he studied law with his father but later switched to medicine, and in 1853 graduated from Castleton Medical College in Vermont. By 1860 he was a practicing physician in Cuthbert in Randolph County, Georgia.

On January 10, 1861, nine days before Georgia seceded, Crews was appointed ensign of a local cavalry company. That October he was commissioned second lieutenant of Georgia cavalry. Crews enlisted in the Confederate army on March 4, 1862, at Cuthbert. On May 7, 1862, he was elected captain of Company C, 2nd Georgia Cavalry. The 2nd was attached to then Brigadier General Joseph Wheeler's cavalry

Massachusetts Commandery, Military Order of the Loyal Legion and the U.S. Army Military History Institute

corps of the Army of Tennessee. In the fall of 1862 Crews was captured during a raid into Kentucky. After being exchanged he was promoted to colonel of the 2nd on November 1, 1862. The "brave and faithful"[2] Crews fought in all the battles of the Army of Tennessee. During Wheeler's January 3, 1863, attack on Dover, Tennessee, Crews was shot in the hip and severely wounded. Recovering, he led a brigade of Georgia cavalry regiments as senior colonel in the Chattanooga and east

Tennessee campaigns of 1863. As early as December, 1863, his divisional commander urged that Crews be appointed brigadier general. During the Atlanta campaign Brigadier General Alfred Iverson was placed in command of the Georgia
cavalry brigade; Crews reverted to regimental command. He particularly distinguished himself in the repulse of Stoneman's July, 1864, raid on Macon, Georgia,
personally accepting the surrender of General Stoneman. By August Crews, "brave,
intelligent, prompt, and always at his post,"[3] again took command of the brigade,
now in Brigadier General William W. Allen's division. That month the division
accompanied the bulk of Wheeler's corps on a raid against the supply lines of the
Union army besieging Atlanta. The two-month raid through Georgia, Tennessee,
and Alabama damaged Wheeler's cavalry more than it damaged the enemy. By
early October the cavalry returned to Georgia to oppose Sherman's March to the
Sea. The brigade fought in numerous skirmishes during Sherman's march and in
the 1865 Carolinas campaign. On March 10, 1865, Crews was severely wounded
in the Battle of Monroe's Crossroads, North Carolina. Crews was paroled as colonel
on May 3, 1865.

　After the war Crews returned to Georgia. In 1869 he was appointed general
agent of the Bainbridge, Cuthbert & Columbus Railroad, and settled in Bainbridge.
The company folded in 1872, and in 1874 Crews removed to Texas, stopping in
Hill, Hamilton, and Bejar counties. In 1879 Crews settled in Hillsboro, New Mexico, a mining town in the arid mountains where the climate was better for his health.
There he was a physician and part-owner of one of the local mines. Crews died
in Hillsboro November 21, 1887 and is buried there.

　CMH, Wood, Heitman, SHSP, and CV all list Crews as a general. CMH says
he was promoted brigadier general before the April 26, 1865, surrender of the Army
of Tennessee. However, the report of General Johnston, the army commander,
dated April 24, 1865, terms him colonel, commanding brigade, as does General
Wheeler's April 15 report, in which Crews is said to be "still disabled from wounds."[4]

NOTES

　1. Nicholas B. Clinch (great-grandson of Colonel Crews) to author, June 3, 1994. William
J. Northen's Men of Mark in Georgia (6 vols.; Atlanta, 1907–12) gives Colonel Crews's middle
name as "Constantine."
　2. Evans, CMH, VII, 408.
　3. General Wharton to Charles C. Crews, December 31, 1863, in Compiled Service Records
of Confederate Army Volunteers, Charles C. Crews, National Archives.
　4. OR, Vol. XLVII, Pt. 3, p. 854; OR, Vol. XLVII, Pt. 1, p. 1132.

MAIN SOURCES

Northen, William J., ed. Men of Mark in Georgia. 6 vols. Atlanta, 1907–12.
"A Woman of the South." Confederate Veteran, XXVIII (1920), 396.
"The Women of the South in War Times." Confederate Veteran, XXXI (1923), 78.

ROBERT H. CUMBY

Robert H. Cumby was born on August 24, 1824, in Charlotte County, Virginia.[1] He was probably the son of Morgan and Levicy (Tanner) Cumby of that county.[2] In 1836 his family moved to Lafayette County, Mississippi, where young Cumby grew to manhood and married. Moving to Rusk County, Texas, in 1849, Cumby built up a large plantation, owning thirty slaves in 1860. He was elected to represent Rusk County in the Eighth Texas Legislature, in which he served from 1859 to 1861.

On May 7, 1861, Cumby organized an infantry company at Henderson, Texas, and was elected its captain. When orders came to join the army, the orders called for a cavalry unit, so the would-be footsloggers found horses and turned troopers. The company rode to Dallas, and there became Company B of the 3rd Texas Cavalry. The 3rd served under General Ben McCulloch in Arkansas and Missouri in 1861 and early 1862. With his Rusk County company Cumby fought at the Battles of Wilson's Creek and Pea Ridge, particularly distinguishing himself at the former (his regimental commander reported his "great gallantry"[3]). During the Pea Ridge campaign Cumby's company led the army's advance on Bentonville and made a near-suicidal charge to break up a Union ambush, but in the battle itself they were not seriously engaged. After Pea Ridge the 3rd, along with the rest of McCulloch's division, was transferred to northern Mississippi. Upon the reorganization of the 3rd on May 20, 1862, Cumby was elected colonel. However, on June 12, 1862, he resigned his commission and returned home to Texas. Disabled with chronic diarrhea, Cumby "was in bad health, and unable to assume the command."[4] In 1864 Governor Pendleton Murrah of Texas appointed Colonel Cumby brigadier general of the 4th Brigade of Texas State Troops. He commanded these reserve forces till the end of the war.

After the war General Cumby removed to Sulphur Springs in Hopkins County, Texas, where he ran a grocery store until his retirement. Cumby died in Sulphur Springs on November 19, 1881, and is buried in the City Cemetery. The town of Cumby, Texas, is named after him.

Cumby's rank of general in the Texas state army qualifies him to be considered a Confederate general.

NOTES

1. Date of birth per tombstone. An August 24, 1825, date of birth is given in Walter P. Webb and Eldon S. Branda, eds., *Handbook of Texas* (3 vols.; Austin, 1952–76), III, 215.

2. Extensive research, both in old records and in correspondence with the descendants of General Cumby's daughter, has failed to turn up anything more conclusive as to his parentage. Morgan Cumby is suggested as his father because he is one of only two adult males of that name living in Charlotte County in 1830 and Lafayette County in the 1840s, and because General Cumby's first grandson was named Morgan Cumby.

3. *OR*, III, 120.

4. Letter of June 12, 1862, in Compiled Service Records of Confederate Army Volunteers, 3rd Texas Cavalry, Robert H. Cumby, National Archives; Victor Rose, *Ross' Texas Brigade* (Louisville, 1881), 65.

MAIN SOURCES

Cater, William D., ed. *As It Was*. San Antonio, 1981.

Winfrey, Dorman H. *A History of Rusk County, Texas*. Waco, 1961.

CHARLES GUSTAVUS ULRIC DAHLGREN

Charles Gustavus Ulric Dahlgren was born on August 13, 1811, in Philadelphia, Pennsylvania.[1] His father, Bernard Ulric Dahlgren, was the first Swedish consul to the United States; his mother, Margaret Rowan, was of a prominent Pennsylvania family. His brother was Admiral John Dahlgren, USN, and his stepdaughter Sarah Dorsey was a prominent nineteenth-century novelist. Originally on course for a career in the navy like his brother, after brief service Dahlgren entered the banking business as private secretary to Nicholas Biddle, president of the Bank of the United States. Dahlgren was soon sent to establish a branch of that bank in New Orleans. After a brief period there he left to work as a cashier of the bank's Natchez, Mississippi, branch. Though his first marriage (to the widow

Massachusetts Commandery, Military Order of the Loyal Legion and the U.S. Army Military History Institute

Mary Routh Ellis, daughter of Job Routh) Dahlgren came into extensive plantation holdings in Mississippi and Louisiana, and over two hundred slaves. By 1860 Dahlgren had accumulated a huge fortune through his cotton planting and the ownership of a substantial plantation supply firm in Natchez. A big, burly man and "a tempestuous son of a tempestuous family," Dahlgren also accumulated a "fantastic record of successful duels and dead rivals" both in the navy and thereafter, along with a large collection of duelling scars.[2]

On July 8, 1861, Dahlgren was made a brigadier general of Mississippi state troops and placed in charge of the southwest Mississippi area. His 3rd Brigade (3rd and 7th Mississippi Infantry regiments), stationed at Pass Christian, helped guard the Mississippi coast against Union invasion. Although the invasion never came, local leaders vehemently denounced Dahlgren's leadership. When he ordered the brigade to evacuate Pass Christian because of lack of supplies a local newspaper said the retreat evinced "great timidity and an entire ignorance of the geography of the country." The historian of the 3rd Mississippi considered Dahlgren "indecisive and quite unimaginative as a field commander. . . . Dahlgren would continually wire either the governor or the military board for direction on nearly every decision that he would make, regardless of how minute."[3] Like other Mississippi state generals, Dahlgren fought not against the Union troops but against Confederate government efforts to muster his state volunteers into Confederate service. By November, 1861, the Confederate army had taken over the defense of the coast, and the troops of the brigade were sent elsewhere. When President Davis placed Major General Mansfield Lovell over him, Dahlgren angrily resigned his post. In January, 1862, the governor appointed him state commissioner to oversee the construction of gunboats. Later in 1862 he commanded the post of Fayette, Mississippi (though without troops, the locals failing to turn out to defend their homes); his zeal and patriotism in evacuating supplies in the face of Yankee advances was commended by General P. G. T. Beauregard, Confederate commander in Mississippi. After 1862 Dahlgren saw no more active duty.[4] He spent the remainder of the war drawing up strategic plans for the southern armies and submitting them to President Davis. When the president, inundated with other plans sent by amateur strategists, failed to adopt his plans, Dahlgren published them in the local newspapers, implicitly criticizing the plans Davis *had* adopted. This habit could not have endeared Dahlgren to the president, or helped his chances for a Confederate army commission.[5]

When the war ended, Dahlgren (his fortune swept away, his plantations confiscated) settled briefly in New Orleans. In 1870, owing to ill health, he spent several months in Nashville, the home of his second wife, then removed his family to Winchester, Virginia. In 1876 he moved again, to Brooklyn, New York, and worked in New York City as a public accountant and lawyer. He died in Brooklyn on December 18, 1888. Dahlgren is buried in the Natchez City Cemetery.

Heitman and *SHSP* list Dahlgren as a general on the strength of his command of the state troops, some of whom served in the Army of the West in 1861. His general's appointment derived from the state of Mississippi.

NOTES

1. The date of Dahlgren's birth is taken from a sketch of his life and a genealogy compiled by his son (MS in Edith Wyatt Moore Collection, Armstrong Library, Natchez, Mississippi).

2. Harnett T. Kane, *Natchez on the Mississippi* (New York, 1947), 251–53.

3. H. Grady Howell, *To Live and Die in Dixie: A History of the Third Regiment Mississippi Volunteer Infantry, C.S.A.* (Jackson, Miss., 1991), 50.

4. Dahlgren's obituary (in the Brooklyn *Daily Eagle*, December 18, 1888) claims he was promoted to major general and participated in most of the battles of the Army of Tennessee. On his 1865 pardon application Dahlgren stated that he was never more than a brigadier general of Mississippi state troops, and did not hold that rank after June, 1862. Several sources suggest that

he served on the staff of Lieutenant General Leonidas Polk (an old friend) during the Atlanta campaign. The author has not been able to verify this, though it can be shown that Dahlgren lived in Atlanta during the campaign and in southern Georgia in 1865. See Robert M. Myers, ed., *The Children of Pride* (New Haven, 1972), 1147, 1157, 1503.

    5. Dahlgren, like many other disappointed rank seekers, developed an intense dislike of President Davis. So it is ironic that Dahlgren's estranged stepdaughter Sarah Ellis Dorsey willed to Davis his last home (Beauvoir, near Biloxi) and the remainder of her extensive estate when she died in 1879.

MAIN SOURCES

Brooklyn *Daily Eagle*, December 18, 1888.

Dahlgren, Charles G. Collection. Chicago Historical Society, Chicago.

Dahlgren, Charles G. Sketch of the Life of. MS in Edith Wyatt Moore Collection, Armstrong Library, Natchez, Miss.

Geisenburger, Amanda. Collection. Armstrong Library, Natchez, Miss.

Gower, Herschel. "The Dahlgrens and Jefferson Davis." *Journal of Mississippi History*, LV (August, 1993), 179–201.

Howell, H. Grady. *To Live and Die in Dixie: A History of the Third Regiment Mississippi Volunteer Infantry, C.S.A.* Jackson, Miss., 1991.

JEFFERSON DAVIS

Jefferson Davis' place in history as president of the Confederacy is too well-known to be recounted here. As president, Davis exercised powers as commander-in-chief of the Confederate States Army—not as modern presidents do, by rubber-stamping the decisions of military authorities, but as a practical, executive head and de facto secretary of war, the holders of that office acting as mere clerks to transmit Davis' wishes.

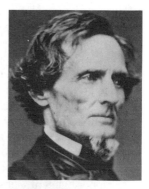

Library of Congress

    Less important, and less well known, was his role as commander-in-chief of Mississippi state forces in 1861. Then-Senator Davis, a West Point graduate with a national reputation as a hero of the Mexican War, was elected major general to command the state army on January 23, 1861, by the Mississippi Secession Convention. As Davis himself later wrote, "Mississippi had given me the position which I preferred to any other—the highest rank in her army." [1] He did not, however, exercise the practical duties of that office for long. On February 10, 1861, Davis was notified that he had been elected president of the Confederate States of America. Accordingly, he resigned his major generalship on February 12.

Davis' rank of general in Mississippi's state army qualifies him to be considered a Confederate general.

NOTE

1. Jefferson Davis, *The Rise and Fall of the Confederate Government* (2 vols.; New York, 1881), I, 230.

MAIN SOURCES

Davis, Jefferson. *The Rise and Fall of the Confederate Government*. 2 vols. New York, 1881.
Rowland, Dunbar, ed. *Jefferson Davis, Constitutionalist: His Letters, Papers and Speeches*. 10 vols. Jackson, Miss., 1923.

REUBEN DAVIS

Library of Congress

Reuben Davis, a general of Mississippi state troops, was born on January 18, 1813, in Winchester, Tennessee, the son of Reverend John Davis, a Baptist minister and farmer, and his wife Mary.[1] The family moved to northern Alabama five years later. After studying both medicine and the law, the younger Davis moved to Monroe County in Mississippi. His performance at the bar was brilliant from the beginning. In 1835 he was elected (at age twenty-two) district attorney of the Sixth Judicial District. Moving to Aberdeen, Mississippi, he received the Whig nomination for Congress in 1838. Joining the Democrats after 1840, Davis was in 1842 appointed associate justice of the Mississippi Supreme Court. During the Mexican War Judge Davis was colonel of the 2nd Mississippi Regiment, but saw no action because of ill health. Davis remained active in the state militia, rising to the rank of brigadier by 1860. He again ran for Congress in 1848 and 1851, but was unsuccessful both times. The following year he became attorney for the New Orleans, Jackson, and Great Northern railroads. In 1855 Davis was elected to the legislature, and finally achieved election to the U.S. Congress in 1857 and 1859. As congressman Davis became known as a fire-eating secessionist, a stance at odds with his earlier, more moderate views.

In 1861 Davis resigned from Congress, returning home to urge his state to se-cede. He was quickly appointed brigadier general, then major general, of the Mississippi state troops, serving with them in Kentucky in the winter of 1861. The sixty-day troops, ill-equipped and ill-fed, were all but mutinous. Davis didn't help matters by serving the troops bad whiskey for Christmas. Elected in the fall of 1861 to the Confederate Congress, Davis left the arena of martial glory for politics. In Congress he criticized war policy and openly opposed the Davis administration, a stance the effectiveness of which was somewhat negated by his missing a large num-ber of roll-call votes. Davis ran for governor of Mississippi in 1863, but because of his association with the unpopular incumbent governor (the fire-eater John Pet-tus), he was defeated.[2] Davis resigned from Congress in 1864 and did not again serve the Confederacy in an official capacity.

After the war Davis removed to Huntsville, Alabama, and had a brilliant postwar career as a criminal lawyer. His one final foray into politics was an unsuc-cessful run in 1878 for Congress on the Greenback party ticket. General Davis died October 14, 1890, in Huntsville, and is buried in the Odd Fellows Cemetery in Ab-erdeen.

Both *CMH* and *SHSP* list Davis as a Confederate general.

NOTES

1. Reuben Davis was not related to his fellow Mississippian, President Davis.
2. Even in Mississippi, prewar ultrasecessionists were unpopular after three years of war.

MAIN SOURCES

Davis, Reuben. *Recollections of Mississippi and Mississippians*. Boston, 1889.

Warner, Ezra J., and W. Buck Yearns. *Biographical Register of the Confederate Congress*. Baton Rouge, 1975.

XAVIER BLANCHARD DEBRAY

Xavier Blanchard DeBray was born on January 25, 1818, in Epinal, France.[1] Stories of his early life, written shortly after his death and based on what little he told contemporaries, are sketchy and contradictory. One authority states that he attended St. Cyr, the French military college, and afterwards served in the French diplomatic corps.[2] However, it is doubtful he did either.[3] The same authority has him immigrating to Texas in 1852 because of political differences with Emperor Napoleon III. A more modern authority cites evidence indicating that DeBray landed in New York City on September 25, 1848, and eventually settled in Texas.[4] The author believes that the old

Courtesy Larry Jones

stories contained a grain of truth—that DeBray matriculated at a national college in Paris, and that during the Revolution of 1848 he wrote political pamphlets advocating revolution, which angered the government and caused him to emigrate.[5] In San Antonio he published a Spanish language newspaper, *El Bejareño*. In 1855 he moved to Austin, edited a newspaper there, and worked as a translator in the state land office. In March, 1856, DeBray founded an academy, which flourished until 1861.

Upon his adopted state's secession, DeBray joined a Travis County company, the "Tom Green Rifles" (later Company B, 4th Texas Infantry), as first lieutenant. In the summer of 1861 Governor Edward Clark appointed DeBray an aide-de-camp on the governor's staff. On August 10, 1861, DeBray was appointed major of the 2nd Texas Infantry, and was that regiment's drillmaster. When a newly raised cavalry battalion (later formed into the 26th Texas Cavalry) lost its commander, DeBray was appointed lieutenant colonel to replace him, to rank from December 7, 1861. DeBray was elected colonel of the 26th on March 17, 1862. The 26th was a garrison unit in Texas until 1864. Its only combat action during the first three years of the war was in the January 1, 1863, retaking of Galveston. For his performance in the attack on Galveston DeBray earned the special praise of the district commander. After that battle he was assigned to command Galveston Island and often led a brigade in the Galveston garrison forces. On May 30, 1863, Major General John B. Magruder, Confederate commander of the District of Texas, appointed DeBray acting brigadier general to command the Eastern Sub-District of Texas. In the spring of 1864 the 26th was ordered to match to Louisiana to oppose the Union army advancing on Shreveport. At the Battle of Mansfield DeBray's regiment was deployed as the advance unit of the army, a fine compliment to the fighting reputation of a relatively inexperienced regiment. At the Battle of Pleasant Hill De-

Bray's regiment made a gallant mounted attack on an infantry line, but the command was literally swept away by a cross fire at close range. One-third of the regiment was struck down, and DeBray himself was injured by the fall of his mortally wounded horse. By the end of the Red River campaign DeBray had succeeded to the leadership of Hamilton Bee's Texas cavalry brigade. On April 13, 1864, five days after the Battle of Mansfield, General Kirby Smith (who considered DeBray a "superior cavalry officer"[6]) assigned DeBray to duty as brigadier general. For the rest of the war DeBray commanded a brigade of Texas cavalry in Louisiana and Texas, but saw no further action.

After the war he briefly settled in Houston, then relocated in Galveston. He worked as a teacher, an accountant, as secretary of the Produce Exchange, and briefly served on the city council. Returning to Austin by 1880, DeBray again worked as a translator in the state general land office. He died in Austin on January 6, 1895, and is buried in the State Cemetery.

CMH, Wood, Heitman, SHSP, CV, and Lonn all list DeBray as a Confederate general.

NOTES

1. Date and place of birth per General DeBray's grave marker in the State Cemetery in Austin, Texas. The author has found partial confirmation for that 1818 date in the Census of 1880, Texas, Travis County, Microfilm 247, in which DeBray was listed as age sixty-one (i.e., born in 1818 or 1819). However, the Epinal civil birth registrations 1814–20 show no DeBray births.

2. Lonn, 136–37, citing an obituary in the Austin Evening News, January 7, 1895.

3. In response to the author's queries, both St. Cyr and L'Ecole Polytechnique stated that they had no record of DeBray attending, and the French Foreign Ministry stated that they had no record of his diplomatic service. See letters, Le Directeur du Musée du Souvenir, Écoles de Saint-Cyr Coëtquidan to author, February 21, 1991; Conservateur en Chef de la Bibliothèque, École Polytechnique to author, July 28, 1994; Chef de la Division Historique, Ministère des Affairs Étrangeres to author, January 23, 1991.

4. Date of landing per DeBray's April 5, 1855, naturalization proceeding. Frustratingly, even this date is in doubt. The New York City passenger arrival lists for the period of September 18–30, 1848, show no DeBray among the arrivals.

5. The name "DeBray" appears in several surviving pamphlets and newspaper articles of the French revolution of 1848, as author and as organizer. Such activity would correspond with General DeBray's editing newspapers in Texas eight years later, as well as explain why he had to leave France that year. The Austin Evening News obituary may have been repeating a garbled version of the real story. DeBray's education level, apparent from his employment as educator, editor, and accountant, argues that he received a good education, perhaps at the College du France, the French national college, if not St. Cyr, and was of middle- or upper-class origin.

6. OR, Vol. XLI, Pt. 4, p. 1019.

MAIN SOURCES

Austin Daily Statesman, January 7, 1895.

Debray, Xavier B. A Sketch of the History of Debrays (26th) Regiment of Texas Cavalry. Austin, 1884.

Hayes, Charles W. Galveston. 1879; rpr. Austin, 1974.

WILMOT GIBBS DE SAUSSURE

Wilmot Gibbs De Saussure, general of South Carolina militia, was born in Charleston, South Carolina, on July 23, 1822, the son of Henry A. and Susan (Boone) De Saussure. The De Saussure family traces its ancestry back to the Lords of Dammartin in France in 1440 and to the Huguenot immigration to South Carolina. The general's father was a prominent lawyer; his grandfather was chancellor of South Carolina. Entering the University of South Carolina in 1838, De Saussure graduated with an A.B. in 1840 and afterward studied law. De Saussure had an antebellum career as a prominent Charleston lawyer. He was also a secretary of the South Carolina Treasury and five-time representative to the state assembly (1848 to 1849, 1854 to 1857, 1860 to 1863).

Courtesy Peter G. D. Kershaw

De Saussure began his war services as a lieutenant colonel of the 1st Regiment of Artillery of the 4th (Charleston) Brigade of the South Carolina Militia. After the tiny U.S. Army garrison evacuated Fort Moultrie on the mainland (December 26, 1861) and withdrew to Fort Sumter in Charleston Harbor, De Saussure's regiment occupied the abandoned fort. He commanded the batteries on Morris Island during the April 12 through 14, 1861, bombardment of Fort Sumter. Appointed brigadier general of militia in August, 1861, he succeeded General James Simons in command of the 4th Brigade and led that brigade throughout the war. In the summer of 1861 Governor Francis Pickens of South Carolina brought De Saussure into the cabinet as secretary of the treasury. Among other actions, De Saussure deposited state money into Richmond banks for the aid of South Carolina soldiers stationed in Virginia. On April 11, 1862, De Saussure was elected state adjutant general and inspector general of militia. During the 1863 siege of Charleston, General De Saussure commanded the fifth subdivision of the Charleston defenses, leading a mixed force of militia and Confederate troops, which guarded the rear of the city. In late 1864 and 1865 he was ordered away from the seacoast in order to oppose Major General William T. Sherman's army in its invasion of the Carolinas.

General De Saussure's postwar career was a distinguished one. Resuming his Charleston law practice, and active in civic affairs, he wrote several works on South Carolina history, became president of the Huguenot Society and president of the Sons of Cincinnati. It was said of De Saussure that "as a lawyer, a writer, a legislator, a soldier, he discharged his duty with eminent ability and entire fidelity."[1] General De Saussure died in Ocala, Florida (where he had gone to restore his shattered health), on February 1, 1886. He is buried in a family plot in Magnolia Cemetery, Charleston.

General De Saussure's command of a brigade of militia that served in a campaign qualifies him to be considered a Confederate general.

NOTE

1. Charleston *News and Courier*, February 2, 1886.

MAIN SOURCES

Charleston *News and Courier*, February 2, 4, 1886.
Gourdin, R. N. "Memorial." *Transactions of the Huguenot Society of South Carolina*, I (1889), 26–33.

JOHN JACKSON DICKISON

John Jackson Dickison was born on March 27, 1816, in Monroe County, Virginia. His father, a planter, wished his son to become a soldier. Dickison, however, grew up sickly, and when he reached age sixteen his father sent him to relatives in South Carolina to convalesce. In South Carolina he became a prosperous cotton merchant, resident in Georgetown. Active in the South Carolina militia, he served as state adjutant and inspector general of cavalry. About 1856 he removed to Marion County, Florida, near Ocala, and became a successful planter.

Florida State Archives

At the start of the war "Major" Dickison (to give his militia rank) was elected first lieutenant of the Marion Light Artillery. The company pulled garrison duty in Florida until its reorganization in 1862. In July, 1862, Dickison was authorized to raise a company of cavalry and raised what was later Company H, 2nd Florida Cavalry in August, 1862, in Marion County. Dickison soon won a reputation through his daring raids as the "Swamp Fox" and as the "Forrest of Florida." Operating mainly on the St. John's River, Dickison led numerous raids behind Union lines. He and his command captured the gunboat *Columbine* in 1864. During 1864 and 1865 he led his cavalry and local militia in repelling Union raids into central Florida, winning (among others) engagements at Palatka, No. 4, and Gainesville. It was said of Dickison that "no officer [was] more universally beloved by the officers and men under him."[1] A captain throughout most of the war, the department commander asked for Dickison's promotion to colonel, to be in charge of the whole of south Florida. The promotion to colonel was made in Richmond on April 5, 1865, but never reached Dickison; he was paroled as a captain on May 20, 1865, at Waldo, Florida.

After the war Dickison was perhaps Florida's most honored symbol of the "Lost Cause." A Democrat, he served two terms in the state legislature, representing Gadsen County from 1865 to 1866 and Lake County in 1889. From 1876 to 1880 he was Florida's state adjutant general. Less honorably, Dickison was active in the raids of the Ku Klux Klan. When the Florida Division of the UCV was formed in 1891, Dickison was named its major general and commander. He also found time to write the Florida volume of *Confederate Military History*. Dickison died on August 23, 1902, in Ocala. He is buried in West Evergreen Cemetery in Jacksonville.

Dickison is called brigadier general in *SHSP*. Although sometimes exercising a general's command, Dickison was never more than a colonel during the war, and that only briefly. His only general's rank was in the UCV. One source states that in 1863 the governor of Florida commissioned Dickison a general of state militia, but that Dickison declined the honor.[2]

Notes

1. Arch F. Blakey, *Parade of Memories: A History of Clay County, Florida* (Jacksonville, 1976), 86.

2. William E. Philpott, ed., *The Sponsor Souvenir Album and History of the United Confederate Veterans' Reunion, 1895* (Houston, 1895), 121.

Main Sources

Dickison, Mary E. *Dickison and His Men*. 1890; rpr. Gainesville, Fla., 1962.

"Gen. J. J. Dickison." *Confederate Veteran*, X (1902), 419–20.

"J. J. Dickison, Maj. Gen. U.C.V., Florida." *Confederate Veteran*, II (1894), 99.

Philpott, William E., ed. *The Sponsor Souvenir Album and History of the United Confederate Veterans' Reunion, 1895*. Houston, 1895.

Tallahassee *Florida Index*, August 29, 1902.

Weinert, Richard P. "Dickison—the Swamp Fox of Florida." *Civil War Times Illustrated*, V (December, 1966), 4–11, 48–50.

ARCHIBALD S. DOBBINS

Archibald S. Dobbins was born in 1827 near Mount Pleasant in Maury County, Tennessee, the son of David and Catherine (Gilchrist) Dobbins. His parents were common farmers; young Dobbins grew up on the family farm. In 1850 he married and removed to Arkansas, purchasing land inherited by his wife's relatives. Dobbins quickly became a wealthy planter near Helena, Arkansas, with property in Phillips County, Arkansas, and across the Mississippi River in Coahoma County, Mississippi.

Alabama Department of Archives and History, Montgomery

It appears that Dobbins spent the first year of the war raising crops for the army. In 1862 he joined Major General Thomas Hindman (an old Helena acquaintance) in Mississippi. Hindman appointed him a colonel and assigned him to duty on Hindman's staff. Dobbins accompanied Hindman when that officer returned to Arkansas. In 1863 he raised the 1st (Dobbins') Arkansas Cavalry Regiment in northeast Arkansas. This detached unit skirmished with Union garrison forces in the Helena area. Joining the main army, Dobbins led his regiment at the Battle of Helena and commanded a brigade in the Little Rock campaign. During this latter campaign Dobbins was placed under arrest for refusal to obey orders, under unique circumstances.

Dobbins' arrest stemmed from the feud between Brigadier General John S. Marmaduke and Dobbins' divisional commander, Brigadier General Lucius M. Walker. Marmaduke had unsparingly criticized Walker's performance at Helena and Little Rock as incompetent and craven. Walker (understandably) took offense and challenged Marmaduke to a duel. The duel took place almost in sight of Union forces, with results fatal to Walker. Dobbins, a close friend of the slain general and similarly a target of Marmaduke's criticism, refused to serve under Marmaduke's command. Marmaduke promptly put Dobbins under arrest for disobedience of orders. Though the army commander restored Dobbins to command of his brigade, the charges were not dropped. A court-martial found him guilty as charged, and General Holmes, the department commander, ordered Dobbins discharged from the army. The discharge was later dropped. In the fall of 1864 Dobbins led an Arkansas cavalry brigade in Price's Missouri Raid. Once again, his conduct was called into question, this time in the September 27, 1864, attack on Pilot Knob, Missouri. Dobbins' cavalry brigade was assigned to guard the sector where the Federal garrison eventually made its escape. One story has it that Dobbins was enticed by a lady to bring his troopers to her plantation for a barbecue, leaving the escape route open. The Union forces assumed that Dobbins' pickets, in the dark, mistook them for a Confederate column. Whatever the reason, the Union escape reflected poorly on both Dobbins and Price. However, Dobbins' bravery and devotion to duty (if not his skill) were unquestioned. Dobbins' brigade largely escaped the disasters that befell Price's raiders at the Battles of Westport and Mine Creek that October. During the winter of 1864 to 1865 Dobbins succeeded Acting Brigadier General Charles W. Adams as district commander in northeast Arkansas. In the spring of 1865 Dobbins commanded one of the two brigades in the North Arkansas District. He escaped the district, bound for Texas, prior to the May 11, 1865, surrender of north Arkansas. He was paroled as colonel, commanding brigade, in Galveston, Texas, July 13, 1865.

After the war Dobbins engaged in business in New Orleans. However, unsympathetic to Reconstruction, Dobbins emigrated to Brazil and tried to build a plantation there. Family sources state that his letters home ceased about 1870. He evidently died sometime after this in the Amazon wilds, probably being murdered by his native workmen.[1]

Heitman, CV, and SHSP list Dobbins as a general. However, he was paroled a colonel, he was termed "colonel, leading brigade" in the OR as late as February 2, 1865, and no record of his promotion to general exists.

NOTE

1. Dobbins' last letter to his family was written on August 29, 1869, from Itaituba, a trading post 150 miles South of Santarem. In it he relates that he is trying to construct a saw and grist mill, employing semi-savage local Indians. A 1922 letter to the Dobbins family, from Dobbins' only white companion at Itaituba, paints a picture of Itaituba as the middle of nowhere, virtually cut off from civilization, surrounded by Indians. Mrs. Dobbins believed her husband was murdered soon after his last letter—otherwise his letters home would not have stopped. The Dobbins Papers are at the University of Arkansas. Robert Dalehite, Dobbins' great-grandson, included several of these letters in an article, "Arch S. Dobbins," *Phillips County Historical Quarterly*, IV (September, 1965), 15–24.

MAIN SOURCES

Dalehite, Bob. "Arch S. Dobbins." *Phillips County Historical Quarterly*, IV (September, 1965), 15–24.

Edwards, John N. *Shelby and His Men*. Cincinnati, 1867.

HENRY KYD DOUGLAS

Henry Kyd Douglas, brigade commander, memoirist, and staff officer of Stonewall Jackson, was born on September 29, 1838, in Ireland, the son of Reverend Robert and Mary (Robertson) Douglas. The family, when Douglas was young, settled in Shepherdstown, Virginia (now West Virginia), close to the Antietam battlefield. Douglas graduated from Franklin and Marshall College in July, 1858. After teaching school in Hagerstown, Maryland, for a short time, Douglas embarked on a legal career. He studied law in Lexington, Virginia, and was admitted to the bar in 1860. Douglas practiced his profession in St. Louis, Missouri, until Virginia seceded.

Massachusetts Commandery, Military Order of the Loyal Legion and the U.S. Army Military History Institute

Enlisting as a private in Company B of the 2nd Virginia Infantry, Douglas fought in the ranks at the First Battle of Bull Run. Promoted to second lieutenant after that battle, Douglas transferred to General Thomas J. "Stonewall" Jackson's staff. He served as assistant adjutant general of Jackson's command through the fall of 1862. Promoted to captain in November, 1862, he rejoined his old company and led it at the Battles of Fredericksburg and Chancellorsville. Promoted to major in May, 1863, he joined Major General "Allegheny" Johnson's division as divisional assistant adjutant general. Douglas was wounded and captured at the Battle of Gettysburg while leading a charge on the Union right flank at Culp's Hill. Exchanged in March, 1864, Douglas was posted back as assistant adjutant general on the staffs of Generals Johnson, John B. Gordon, and Jubal Early, serving throughout the Wilderness, Petersburg, and Shenandoah Valley campaigns of 1864 and 1865. In March, 1865, Major Douglas was put in command of Brigadier General James Walker's Virginia brigade, leading it through to the surrender of Appomattox. Douglas was wounded no less than six times during the war.

Immediately after the war Douglas returned to Shepherdstown. The local Union military authorities arrested him for treason and parole violation, all because Douglas wore his Confederate uniform in public. Convicted of violation of military orders, Douglas was sent to prison for two months. Released from Fort Delaware Prison in August, Douglas settled in Winchester, Virginia, and practiced law there. By 1878 he had moved to Hagerstown, Maryland, where he prospered as a lawyer. A fellow attorney called him "the most gallant and handsomest gentleman of the Maryland bar and one of its foremost orators."[1] Douglas, a "Bourbon" Democrat, made an unsuccessful run for Congress in 1888, and in 1891 he was appointed associate judge of the Fourth Circuit. In 1892 he was appointed Maryland's adjutant general, serving four years in that post. Douglas died in Hagerstown of tuberculosis on December 18, 1903. He is buried in Shepherdstown's Elmwood Cemetery. *I Rode With Stonewall,* his memoirs of war service, remains one of the two or three best personal accounts of the war.

Douglas' memoirs note that in 1865, as adjutant general of Walker's brigade, he was promised command of the brigade and a brigadier general's rank when Walker was promoted to divisional command. Walker was in fact put in charge of a division during the last month of the war. Secretary of War John C. Breckinridge, who had served with Douglas in the Shenandoah Valley campaign, evidently recommended Douglas for promotion to brigadier general, but Richmond fell before the promotion could go through channels and the commission could be issued. Warner's *Generals in Gray* mentions Douglas as one officer who was often termed "general" postbellum.[2] However, Douglas' highest substantive Confederate rank was major.

NOTES

1. Henry C. McDougal, *Recollections: 1844–1909* (Kansas City, 1910), 68.

2. Ezra J. Warner, *Generals in Gray: Lives of the Confederate Commanders* (Baton Rouge, 1959). Although Warner did not offer any citation for the assertion that Douglas was termed "general," articles in SHSP and CV call Douglas a general. See his obituary, "Gen. H. Kyd Douglas," CV, XII (1904), 125; and X. X., "Who Was Last Soldier to Leave Burning City," *SHSP,* XXXVII (1909), 317–18 (where it is claimed that Douglas was promoted to brigadier general).

MAIN SOURCES

Douglas, Henry Kyd. *I Rode with Stonewall.* Chapel Hill, 1940.
Douglas, Henry Kyd. *The Douglas Diary: Student Days at Franklin and Marshall College, 1856–1858.* Edited by Frederick S. Klein and John H. Carrill. Lancaster, Pa., 1973.
"Gen. H. Kyd Douglas." *Confederate Veteran,* XII (1904), 125.
"Sketch of General Douglas." *The Lost Cause,* X (March, 1904), 122–23.

RICHARD GILL MILLS DUNOVANT

Richard Gill Mills Dunovant, a brigadier general of South Carolina militia, was born on May 18, 1821, in Chester, South Carolina. His father, Dr. John Dunovant, was a physician, slaveholder, and state senator; his mother was Margaret Sloan Quay. One brother, John, was a regular army officer and Confederate general killed in 1864. Dunovant himself married the sister of Congressman Preston Brooks. After graduation from South Carolina College, Dunovant studied medicine and moved to Texas, in which state he practiced until the Mexican War. At the outbreak of that war he returned to Chester and raised a company, of which he was elected captain. Later major and lieutenant colonel of South Carolina's Palmetto Regiment, his

South Caroliniana Library, University of South Carolina

account of the battles in the Valley of Mexico was published under the title *The Palmetto Regiment, South Carolina Volunteers, 1846–48.* Returning to South Carolina, Dunovant became a successful planter, owning forty-seven slaves in 1860. In 1855 the legislature elected him adjutant and inspector general of South Carolina state militia, a post he held until 1861. A secessionist, Dunovant was elected delegate to the state secession convention and signed the ordinance of secession.

On January 2, 1861, General Dunovant took over command of the 4th Brigade of militia stationed opposite Fort Sumter. At the end of that month the brigade's regular commander (General James Simons) returned to the brigade. Dunovant was then appointed commander of the newly created regular army of South Carolina. Dunovant started the war entrusted with the command of Fort Moultrie. Appointed brigadier general of South Carolina state troops, he commanded two infantry regiments on Sullivan's Island during the Fort Sumter bombardment. Later resigning his state commission when his troops were mustered into Confederate service, his "noble" self-abnegation (unusual modesty in those times) was praised by Governor Pickens.[1] Commissioned colonel of the 12th South Carolina Infantry on September 1, 1861, he commanded Fort Beauregard during the Port Royal attack. Badly outgunned by the Union fleet, Dunovant and the garrison evacuated the fort and escaped to the mainland. On April 2, 1862, Dunovant resigned his commission. Late in the war Dunovant was elected to the South Carolina General Assembly, representing Edgefield in the Forty-sixth Assembly (1864 to 1865).

After the war Dunovant lived in comparative retirement as a planter in Edgefield. General Dunovant died in Edgefield on May 12, 1898, and is buried in Baptist Cemetery there.

Dunovant's rank of general in South Carolina's state army qualifies him to be considered a Confederate general.

NOTE

1. *OR*, Vol. IV, Pt. 1, p. 317.

MAIN SOURCES

Bailey, N. Louise, ed. *Biographical Directory of the South Carolina Senate, 1776–1985*. Columbia, S.C., 1986.
Krick, Robert K. *Lee's Colonels*. Dayton, 1991.
Woodson, Mrs. A. A. "Great Generals That I Have Known." In *Recollections and Reminiscences, 1861–1865*, United Daughters of the Confederacy, South Carolina Division. 1903–1907; rpr. n.p., 1992.

THOMAS TURNER FAUNTLEROY

Thomas Turner Fauntleroy was born on October 8, 1795, in Richmond County, Virginia, the son of Joseph and Betsy (Fauntleroy) Fauntleroy.[1] During the War of 1812 Fauntleroy was commissioned a lieutenant in the U.S. Army. After that war Fauntleroy studied law in Winchester and practiced in Warrenton. In 1823 he was elected to the Virginia House of Burgesses to represent Fauquier County. In 1836 Fauntleroy rejoined the regular army as major of the 2nd Dragoons. He was promoted to lieutenant colonel of the 2nd in 1846 and colonel in 1850. Fauntleroy fought Indians in the Second Seminole War. In the Mexican War he first commanded the post of San Antonio, Texas. Later

Colorado Historical Society, F 3919

he served in Taylor's army on the Rio Grande and in Scott's army on the route to Mexico City. After the war Fauntleroy commanded Fort Leavenworth, Kansas, and Fort Union, New Mexico. Fauntleroy led several expeditions against the Apaches in company with the legendary Kit Carson.[2] The "brave and chivalric" Fauntleroy was officially thanked by the New Mexico Legislature for his efforts in those expeditions.[3] From 1859 to 1861 he commanded the Department of New Mexico.

Upon the secession of Virginia he returned to his native state. In May, 1861, Fauntleroy resigned his U.S. Army commission and was appointed by the governor brigadier general in the Provisional Army of Virginia.[4] A Richmond newspaper commented that "no officer in the country is better qualified, and in none have the people of his native State more confidence."[5] Fauntleroy was placed in command of Richmond and its defenses, succeeding future Confederate Major General John B. Magruder. From this position he was relieved, at his own request, on August 25, 1861. The old regular was never an enthusiastic Rebel,[6] and when such men as Robert E. Lee, junior to him in the old army, were given higher rank in the Virginia and Confederate armies, his enthusiasm disappeared. Fauntleroy never held Confederate rank. However, he was tendered an appointment as brigadier general of the PACS from Adjutant General Samuel Cooper on July 9, 1861, to command the Virginia militia in the Shenandoah Valley.[7] Fauntleroy declined the proferred appointment and returned to his Winchester estate. The continuing military action in that area led Fauntleroy to flee to Caroline County and finally to Charlotte County, Virginia, where he spent the last part of the war.

After the war General Fauntleroy lived with his son, Judge Thomas Fauntleroy, in Winchester. On September 12, 1883, he passed away at the home of his granddaughter in Leesburg, Virginia. He is buried in Mount Hebron Cemetery in Winchester.

Fauntleroy is listed as a general by Heitman and *SHSP*. Being tendered an appointment by the president as brigadier general of the PACS by itself would appear to qualify Fauntleroy as a general, despite his prompt refusal of the appointment.

NOTES

1. L. H. Jones, *Captain Roger Jones* . . . (Albany, 1891), 178, and Heitman, I, 415, give a 1795 birth date for General Fauntleroy. However, Fauntleroy's grave marker gives a 1796 date of birth.

2. Morris F. Taylor, "Action at Fort Massachusetts: The Indian Campaign of 1855," *Colorado Magazine*, XLII (Fall, 1865), 292–310, contains a fine article on one of Fauntleroy's campaigns against the Apache Indians.

3. *Eminent and Representative Men of Virginia and the District of Columbia of the Nineteenth Century* (Madison, Wis., 1893), 441–46.

4. On April 24, 1861, one week after Virginia seceded, that state signed a treaty with the Confederate government placing the state army under Confederate control. The Virginia state forces were transferred to Confederate command on June 8, 1861, by proclamation of Governor Letcher (General Order 25). The Virginia Provisional Army (created on April 27, 1861, by ordinance of the state convention) existed as an administrative entity for several months subsequent to the transfer.

5. Richmond *Dispatch*, April 30, 1861.

6. Several of Fauntleroy's close relatives fought for the North during the war, including his son-in-law, Union Surgeon General Joseph Barnes.

7. See OR, Vol. LI, Pt. 2, p. 159.

MAIN SOURCES

Jones, L. H. *Captain Roger Jones*. . . . Albany, 1891.
Winchester *News*, September 14, 1883.

JOHN CALVIN FISER

Courtesy V. Poindexter Fiser

John Calvin Fiser (Fizer)[1] was born on May 4, 1838, in Dyersburg, Tennessee, the son of Matthew D. Fiser, a merchant. The family moved to near Batesville, Panola County, Mississippi, when Fiser was ten. His father died soon after, and he was raised in the home of an uncle, John B. Fiser, a prominent Panola County merchant and politician. At the age of fifteen Fiser went to work as a clerk in a country store in Lafayette County. Two years later he relocated in Memphis, Tennessee, and connected himself with a mercantile establishment. By the start of the war Fiser was a rapidly rising young Memphis merchant.

Returning to Panola County on May 27, 1861, he was commissioned lieutenant of the 17th Mississippi Infantry and was made regimental adjutant on June 4. The 17th was ordered to Virginia in time to participate in the First Battle of Bull Run. Adjutant Fiser was especially praised for his "most important and effective service" that October at the Battle of Ball's Bluff. Elected lieutenant colonel of the 17th on April 26, 1862, he led the regiment at the Battles of Malvern Hill and Antietam and became a "great favorite with the soldiers."[2] Fiser especially distinguished himself at the Battle of Fredericksburg, where Barksdale's Mississippi brigade (including the 17th) delayed the advance of the whole Union army for half a day. At the Battle of Gettysburg Fiser was wounded three times, being shot once in the cheek and twice in the leg. Accompanying Longstreet's corps to Georgia, Fiser fought in the Battle of Chickamauga, and in the November 29, 1863, assault on Fort Sanders outside of Knoxville, Fiser was shot in the arm while standing atop the Union works. The wound required amputation of the arm. Fiser was promoted to colonel on February 26, 1864. Not fully recovering from the loss of the arm, the "fearless, earnest" Fiser[3] resigned his commission on June 12, 1864. In the winter of 1864, at the special request of Major General Lafayette McLaws, his old divisional commander, Colonel Fiser was transferred to South Carolina and assigned to command a brigade of Georgia reservists. His reservists fought in the Carolinas campaign of 1865, opposing Sherman's army until the end of the war.

After the war Fiser returned to Memphis. Resuming his business career, Fiser rose to a partnership in one of the South's largest cotton brokerage firms. He was also active in Democratic party politics and in veterans organizations, being elected president of the Confederate Historical Association of Memphis. Fiser died on June 14, 1876, in Memphis of the "flux" and is buried in Elmwood Cemetery.

Fiser is listed as a general in Heitman, *SHSP*, and *CV*. However, he is termed colonel, commanding brigade, throughout the OR in 1865. His small (eight-hundred-man), ragtag brigade hardly needed a full general to command it, and when on April 9, 1865, the brigade was merged with Colonel George P. Harrison's brigade[4] Harrison, not Fiser, led (as senior colonel) the combined brigade, suggesting both that Fiser wasn't a general and that there was no brigade for him to command subsequently. Fiser's obituary states that his commission as brigadier general was issued in the last days of the war, but never reached him.[5]

NOTES

1. He was born Fiser. However, soon after the war the general decided the "Fizer" spelling better corresponded with the way his name was pronounced. Three streets in Memphis are named "Fizer" after him.

2. Robert A. Moore, *A Life for the Confederacy*, ed. James W. Silver (Jackson, Tenn., 1959), 138.

3. Memphis *Appeal*, June 15, 1876.

4. See OR, Vol. XLVII, Pt. 3, p. 774.

5. See the Memphis *Appeal*, June 15, 1876.

MAIN SOURCES

Mathes, J. Harvey. *The Old Guard in Gray*. Memphis, 1897.
Memphis *Appeal*, June 15, 1876.

RICHARD FERDINAND FLOYD

Richard Ferdinand Floyd, brigadier general of Florida state forces, was born on July 7, 1810, at Fairfield plantation in Camden County, Georgia, the son of John and Isabella (Hazard) Floyd. His father was a major general in the War of 1812, a prosperous planter, and U.S. congressman. Young Floyd grew up on the family plantation in Camden County. He in turn became a planter and slave-owner, serving also as county sheriff. During the Second Seminole War Floyd commanded, as captain, a company of Georgia volunteers battling Indians in Florida. Sometime before 1850 he relocated in St. Augustine, Florida, working first as a draftsman and later running a plantation in rural St. John's County.

Floyd's first war service was as colonel and aide-de-camp to Governor John Milton of Florida, of whom he was a great favorite. Milton praised his aide as "a skilful officer, and a brave and honorable man, with a reputation as a gentleman and an officer above reproach."[1] In the fall of 1861 the governor put Floyd in command of Florida state troops stationed at Apalachicola. On November 29, 1861, the governor appointed Colonel Floyd as brigadier general and commander-in-chief of Florida state forces, consisting of militia and volunteer companies not yet in Confederate service. Floyd's only active service was in leading a brigade of Florida troops stationed at Apalachicola in the fall and winter of 1861 and 1862. Floyd's forces, little more than a regiment in strength, guarded against any Union thrust against Apalachicola and western Florida. They also suppressed the burgeoning trade between Florida planters and the Union blockading fleet by erecting batteries and blocking the Apalachicola River to outgoing vessels. Floyd was as busy keeping Floridians in Florida as he was keeping Yankees out. On March 10, 1862, the brigade disbanded. Later that same month Floyd was employed in raising guerilla forces in eastern Florida. Governor Milton, in his dispatches to Richmond, repeatedly urged that Floyd, "an accomplished gentleman and competent officer . . . of strict sobriety . . . of excellent sense and unquestioned courage," be appointed by President Davis as brigadier general of the PACS to command the District of Florida.[2] For some reason, others less favored by the governor (notably, Joseph Finegan, Florida's adjutant general) were appointed instead. Commissioned colonel of the newly organized 8th Florida Infantry on July 15, 1862, Floyd resigned his commission because of "severe illness" on October 2, 1862. The 8th served in Lee's army under other officers, and Floyd saw no further active service. Floyd lost his entire property in the war; his family became refugees.

After the war Floyd was an impecunious insurance agent in Clay County, Florida, until his death in Green Cove Springs on June 27, 1870. He is buried in Hickory Grove Cemetery, Green Cove Springs.

General Floyd's command of a brigade of militia that served in a campaign qualifies him to be considered a Confederate general.

NOTES

1. *Journal of the Proceedings of the Convention of the People of Florida* (Tallahassee, 1861), 22–23.

2. *OR*, VI, 302, 426. Governor Milton's reference to Floyd's sobriety highlights a problem both armies faced—officers too drunk to do their duty. That the governor mentioned this in an official dispatch reveals how common the problem was.

MAIN SOURCES

Census of 1870, Florida, Clay County, Microfilm, p. 333.
Daughters of the American Revolution. *Historical Collections of the Joseph Habersham Chapter, Daughters of the American Revolution*. Dalton, Ga., 1902.

JOHN SALMON FORD

John Salmon "Rip"[1] Ford was born in the Greenville District of South Carolina on May 26, 1815, the son of William and Harriet (Salmon) Ford. The family moved to Tennessee when Ford was young. In 1836 he came to Texas and began a distinguished and colorful career. According to one source, "he was one of those Renaissance men that Texas somehow produced when it couldn't produce much of anything else."[2] Ford served two years in the Texas army and upon discharge settled in San Augustine. There he practiced medicine and was elected to the Texas House of Representatives. In 1845 he moved to Austin, the state capital, and became the editor of the *Texas Democrat*. During the Mexican War he was commissioned adjutant of Colonel Jack Hays's regiment of Texas volunteers. After that war Ford helped explore the largely unknown west Texas plains, laid out a cattle trail, became captain of the Texas Rangers, and won fame as an Indian fighter. Returning to Austin, he was elected to the state senate and founded another newspaper, the *State Times*. In 1855 he helped found the Know-Nothing (American) party in Texas, but returned to the Democrats two years later. In 1859 he was commissioned an officer of Texas state troops. He defeated Indian bands in two major engagements, then was sent south to the Rio Grande River to stop Mexican border raids. "Old Rip," as he was known throughout the state, was a popular favorite there, described by one traveler as "hail-fellow-well-met with everybody, free with his money, and equally free with his six-shooter. . . . the most inveterate gambler and the hardest swearer I have ever met."[3]

In 1861 Ford was elected to the Texas Secession Convention and voted to take Texas out of the Union. On February 5, 1861, the convention appointed Ford commander of a military expedition to proceed to the Rio Grande, the sight of his prewar campaigns. Once there he was to secure all U.S. Army property in the area and guard the Mexican border. Within a month Ford organized a thousand-man force, which landed at the mouth of the Rio Grande, persuaded the U.S. Army troops on the border to surrender,[4] and repelled two Mexican raids across the border. On May 18, 1861, the convention elected Ford colonel of a newly authorized regiment of mounted men, later the 2nd Texas Mounted. For the remainder of 1861 Ford and his men guarded the border. A diplomat as well as a soldier, he initiated a trade agreement between Mexico and the Confederacy. In 1862 he was recalled to the state capital and appointed chief of conscription for Texas. On December 22, 1863, Confederate Major General John B. Magruder, who commanded the District of

Texas, ordered Ford to return to southern Texas. He organized an expeditionary force of state and Confederate troops to retake the lower Rio Grande Valley, which had been occupied by Union troops in the fall of 1863. Colonel Ford commanded the Confederate forces in the last battle of the Civil War—a southern victory at Palmito Ranch on May 13, 1865, one month after Appomattox. On May 26, 1865, he was put in charge of the Confederate Western Sub-District of the District of Texas. Ford surrendered and was paroled July 18, 1865.

After the war Ford remained in southern Texas, the site of his wartime exploits. In 1868 he became the editor of a Brownsville newspaper, and in 1874 he was elected mayor of Brownsville. From 1875 to 1879 he served in the state senate. Ford spent the later years of his life writing his reminiscences and historical articles, and promoting an interest in Texas history. He died in San Antonio on November 3, 1897, and is buried in the Confederate Cemetery in San Antonio.

Ford is listed in Heitman as a Confederate general. In 1864 Governor Pendleton Murrah of Texas appointed Ford brigadier general of District No. 1, Texas state troops. During the war Ford often commanded Confederate troops or exercised district command, either as a Confederate colonel or a Texas state general.

NOTES

1. During the Mexican War Ford served as adjutant of a regiment of volunteers. As adjutant it was Ford's duty to write the next of kin of soldiers who had been killed. He invariably began his notification letter with "Rest in Peace." As losses mounted, he shortened it to "R.I.P."

2. Houston *Post*, December 22, 1992.

3. W. J. Hughes, *Rebellious Ranger: Rip Ford and the Old Southwest* (Norman, Okla., 1964), 214.

4. From his campaigns against the Indians and Mexican border bandits, Ford knew most of the U.S. Army officers in south Texas personally. His friendship with the U.S. Army leaders helped diffuse a potentially awkward and bloody confrontation between the army and Texas troops.

MAIN SOURCES

Hughes, W. J. *Rebellious Ranger: Rip Ford and the Old Southwest.* Norman, Okla., 1964.

Oates, Stephen, ed. *Rip Ford's Texas.* Austin, 1963.

Webb, Walter P. *The Texas Rangers: A Century of Frontier Defense.* Boston, 1935.

Widener, Ralph W., Jr. "John S. "Rip" Ford, Colonel, CSA." *United Daughters of the Confederacy Magazine*, XXXVII (May, 1984), 19–23.

JEFFREY E. FORREST

Jeffrey E. Forrest, a younger brother of Lieutenant General Nathan Bedford Forrest, was born on June 10, 1838, in Tippah County, Mississippi, the son of William and Miriam (Beck) Forrest. His father, a farmer and blacksmith, died four months before Jeffrey was born, and the son was in essence raised by his older brother, the future general. Before the war Jeffrey pursued his studies in De Soto County, Mississippi, and in Memphis, Tennessee. His now wealthy brother furnished the means for the best education. At the start of the war Jeffrey Forrest was managing a livery stable in Memphis.

Wyeth, That Devil Forrest

Enlisting with his brother as a private in Company D of the 7th Tennessee Cavalry, Jeffrey was elected second lieutenant of Company C of Forrest's cavalry regiment in June, 1861. Lieutenant Forrest had a horse killed under him at the Battle of Fort Donelson and was with his brother through the escape from that fort and the Battle of Shiloh. On March 11, 1862, Forrest was elected captain of Company C. However, he declined the election and resigned his officer's commission on June 17, 1862. A young officer of great promise, Forrest soon rejoined the army and was commissioned major, then lieutenant colonel of the 8th Tennessee Cavalry. Forrest was transferred to Brigadier General Phillip D. Roddey's cavalry brigade in northern Alabama and was distinguished in various skirmishes there throughout 1863. At one skirmish at Bear's Creek, Mississippi, in October, 1863, Lieutenant Colonel Forrest was shot through both thighs. In 1864 General Forrest, by now building up a cavalry force in northern Mississippi, requested that Jeffrey and his regiment join him. Though not yet recovered from his wounds, Colonel Forrest complied and was put in command of a brigade. "Exhibiting military ability of an order which approached more nearly the genius of the great general," Colonel Forrest brilliantly led his brigade against the invading Union cavalry of General W. Sooy Smith.[1] On February 22, 1864, near Okolona, Mississippi, while leading the pursuit against Smith's raiders, Colonel Forrest was shot in the neck and mortally wounded at the head of his troopers. In 1868 his remains were transferred to Elmwood Cemetery in Memphis. He is buried in the Forrest family plot under a government grave marker which gives incorrect years of birth and death.

Although some sources say Forrest was commissioned brigadier general,[2] it appears he died a colonel.

NOTES

1. John Allan Wyeth, *That Devil Forrest: Life of General Nathan Bedford Forrest* (1899; rpr. Baton Rouge, 1989), 6.
2. Mark M. Boatner III, *Civil War Dictionary* (New York, 1988), 289; Mercer Otey, "Story of Our Great War," *CV,* IX (1901), 109.

MAIN SOURCES

Memphis *Avalanche,* May 3, 1868.
Wyeth, John Allan. *That Devil Forrest: Life of General Nathan Bedford Forrest.* 1899; rpr. Baton Rouge, 1989.

ROBERT COLEMAN FOSTER III

Robert Coleman Foster III, brigadier general of Tennessee state troops, was born in Nashville on September 12, 1818. His father, Ephraim Foster, was a prominent lawyer, Whig politician, and U.S. senator; his mother was Jane Lytle Dickenson. In 1836 Foster graduated from the University of Nashville. Reading for the law, he was admitted to the bar in Nashville and established a practice in that city. During the Mexican War Foster was captain of the "Harrison Guards," Company L of the 1st Tennessee Volunteer Infantry. The company fought with Zachary Taylor's army in northern Mexico in 1846 and the next spring participated in Winfield Scott's attack on the Mexican capital. Captain Foster rendered "highly distinguished" service leading a charge at the 1846 Battle of Monterrey "with a gallantry worthy of his name."[1] Returning to Tennessee, Foster was elected attorney general of the Sixth Judicial District in 1847, serving until his resignation in 1852. He practiced law in Nashville until the start of the war. In 1854 the University of Nashville, Foster's alma mater, appointed him a trustee; he held that position the rest of his life. Immediately before the war, Foster was active in organizing a volunteer militia company, the "Rock City Guard," in his hometown.

In the early days of the war Foster drilled army recruits in Nashville. On May 9, 1861, Governor Isham Harris of Tennessee appointed him a brigadier general of state troops to command the middle division of the Provisional Army of Tennessee. Headquartered in Nashville, Foster ("a man of great decisiveness and force of character, a stern disciplinarian, and as generous and kind of heart as he was impetuous and impulsive by nature")[2] helped organize the volunteers for the provisional army and established "Camp Cheatham" in Robertson County as a camp of instruction for the volunteers. In all over five thousand Tennesseans received their first training in camps established by Foster. Governor Harris praised highly Foster's actions in organizing the state army. In August, 1861, the provisional army began to be transferred to Confederate service. President Davis did not see fit to reappoint Foster as a general in the Confederate army. Foster was one of three generals of the provisional army (all former Whig politicians) who, despite entreaties from Tennessee politicians of all parties, was not even offered a commission in the Confederate army. Like many other disappointed commission seekers, Foster became a bitter enemy of President Davis. In December, 1861, Foster had Tennessee's Confederate congressmen withdraw his application for Confederate commission. His health broken, Foster saw no further active service. Foster fled Nashville before the 1862 Union takeover of that city and spent the remainder of the war as a refugee.

After the war Foster returned to Nashville. He practiced law and was elected, in 1866, recorder of the city. A few years later he became the secretary of a life insurance company but failed to restore his prewar fortune. Impoverished, General Foster died in Nashville on December 28, 1871, and was buried in the Mount Olivet Cemetery.

Foster's rank of general in Tennessee's state army qualifies him to be considered a Confederate general.

NOTES

1. Memphis *Avalanche*, March 27, 1862; Nashville *Republican Banner*, December 29, 1871.
2. Nashville *Republican Banner*, December 29, 1871.

MAIN SOURCES

Case Files of Applications from Former Confederates for Presidential Pardons (Amnesty Papers), 1865–67. Microfilm M1003, National Archives.
Nashville *Banner*, December 29, 30, 1871.

DANIEL GOULD FOWLE

Daniel Gould Fowle, brigadier general of North Carolina militia, was born on March 3, 1831, in Washington, North Carolina, the son of Samuel and Martha (March) Fowle. He was a descendant of George Fowle, who emigrated from England to Massachusetts in 1638. Daniel's father had moved from Massachusetts to North Carolina in 1815 and become a wealthy merchant. As a young man Fowle had a brilliant scholastic career, first in the celebrated Bingham Academy, and later at Princeton University, where he was a member of the literary society and a junior orator. Graduating from Princeton in 1851, he studied law and soon commenced a law practice in Raleigh.

Courtesy North Carolina Division of Archives and History

An opponent of secession, at the start of the war Fowle nonetheless volunteered as a private. Appointed major in the commissary branch of the state military department, he resigned his post to help raise the 31st North Carolina Infantry. Fowle was appointed lieutenant colonel of the 31st on September 9, 1861. Fowle and his regiment were captured on Roanoke Island in February, 1862. He was paroled two weeks later. In September, 1862, Fowle was defeated in the election for colonel of the 31st and subsequently severed his connection with the Confederate army. In October, 1862, he was elected to represent Wake County in the state legislature. After the legislature adjourned on March 13, 1863, Governor Zebulon Vance appointed Fowle adjutant general of North Carolina with the rank of major general. Governor Vance and Fowle worked diligently to rearm the state and reorganize its local defense troops. However, when the governor revoked one of Fowle's orders the latter, in a fit of oversensitivity, felt it was a reflection on his conduct and on August 26, 1863, resigned his post. Fowle continued with his duties through the fall of 1863, until a successor was named. The next year Fowle was reelected to the legislature.

In 1865 Reconstruction Governor Holden appointed Fowle as judge of the Superior Court. He resigned this post rather than carry out the Reconstruction orders of the military commanders in North Carolina. Fowle carried on his law practice and became prominent in the Democratic party. Elected state Democratic chairman in 1868, Fowle was an unsuccessful candidate for governor in 1880 and for Congress in 1884. In 1888 his efforts were finally rewarded with a nomination for governor by the "liberal" faction of Democrats and subsequent election. Upon taking office Fowle created a state railroad commission to protect farmers and pushed education for women. Governor Fowle died in office on April 8, 1891. He is buried in Oakwood Cemetery in Raleigh.

Fowle is listed as a general of North Carolina state troops in Clark's *Histories of the Several Regiments and Battalions from North Carolina in the Great War, 1861–1865.*[1]

NOTE

1. Walter Clark, ed., *Histories of the Several Regiments and Battalions from North Carolina in the Great War, 1861–1865* (5 vols.; Raleigh, 1901).

MAIN SOURCES

Powell, William S., ed. *Dictionary of North Carolina Biography.* 4 vols. Chapel Hill, 1979–91.
Vance, Governor Zebulon B. Letters and Telegrams, 1862–65. Microfilm T-731, National Archives.

EDWARD W. GANTT

Edward W. Gantt was born in 1829 in Maury County, Tennessee, the son of John E. Gantt. By 1850 he was a lawyer in Williamsport in Maury County. An early secessionist, Edward and his brother George[1] were delegates to the 1850 "Southern Rights" Convention in Nashville. Moving to Washington in Hempstead County, Arkansas, in 1854, Gantt became a lawyer and active Democratic politician. Gantt was elected three times as district prosecutor, elected to the U.S. Congress in 1861 (not taking his seat), and to the First Confederate Congress. Gantt had also married into a prominent Dallas County family.

U.S. Army Military History Institute and Roger D. Hunt Collection

Preferring field duty to legislative drudgery, Gantt raised the 12th Arkansas Infantry and on July 29, 1861, was elected its colonel. In the fall of 1861 the regiment was stationed at Columbus, Kentucky, as part of the Confederate garrison there. At the Battle of Belmont on November 7, 1861, the 12th was only lightly engaged, but Gantt was commended for his bravery by his brigade commander. On December 5, 1861, Gantt was ordered to New Madrid, Missouri. He took command of a brigade of two Arkansas regiments garrisoning Fort Thompson, part of the Island No. 10 defenses. Gantt, "a fine officer. . . . [who was] extremely popular with the men" but also "ambitious" and a womanizer, avidly sought promotion.[2] In early 1862 General P. G. T. Beauregard appointed Gantt acting brigadier general, with the promise to ask the president for formal appointment to that rank. The Union army of Major General John Pope began an attack on Fort Thompson on March 13, 1862. The next night the garrison was evacuated across the Mississippi River into Tennessee by order of Major General John P. McCown, the Island No. 10 commander. In the evacuation the garrison left behind thirty-three pieces of artillery and huge quantities of scarce ordnance supplies.[3] Gantt and his command surrendered on April 7, 1862, near Tiptonville, Tennessee, with the rest of the Island No. 10 garrison. Exchanged in August, 1862, Gantt returned to his home in Arkansas and awaited further assignment to duty. However, rumors had circulated about his alleged misconduct at Island No. 10 (mostly rumors about his drinking), and the Confederate authorities failed to give Gantt another assignment. In the fall of 1863 Gantt, an original secessionist,[4] experienced a change of heart and turned Union loyalist. He fled to the Union lines and from there appealed to his fellow southerners to lay down their arms. His appeals, which were widely circulated, denounced "Jefferson Davis, negro slavery, secession, and the Confederacy in good round terms."[5]

After the war Gantt, a "lawyer of ability,"[6] was a noted Arkansas "scalawag," serving the Reconstruction authorities as state prosecutor for the Little Rock area and, from 1865 to 1866, as supervisor of the Freedmen's Bureau for southwest Arkansas. In 1873 Gantt was appointed by the governor to prepare a digest of the state laws, on which he labored until his death from a heart attack on June 10, 1874, in Little Rock. He is buried in Tulip, Dallas County.

Wood, Heitman, *SHSP*, and *CV* all list Gantt as a general. For obvious reasons, his acting brigadier generalship did not lead to a corresponding PACS appointment. Contemporaries hinted that his defection from the southern cause was motivated by disappointment over lack of promotion, by cowardice, insobriety, opportunism, and immorality.

NOTES

1. George Gantt, a colonel of Tennessee cavalry, became a prominent postwar Memphis lawyer. The two brothers' war records have often been confused.

2. Eugene Nolte, "Downeasters in Arkansas: Letters of Roscoe G. Jennings to His Brother," *Arkansas Historical Quarterly*, XVIII (1959), 3–25.

3. The equipment lost included "several thousand stand of superior small-arms" and "immense quantities of property and supplies. . . . Nothing except the men escaped, and they only with what they wore." OR, VIII, 82–83.

4. Gantt stumped the state in 1860, delivering speeches for the Breckinridge-Lane presidential ticket. He belonged to the Hindman, ultrasecessionist faction of the Arkansas Democratic party.

5. Thomas S. Staples, *Reconstruction in Arkansas, 1862–1874* (New York, 1923), 12–13, citing the New York *Herald*, November 9, 1863.

6. Little Rock *Arkansas Gazette*, June 11, 1874.

MAIN SOURCES

Nolte, Eugene. "Downeasters in Arkansas: Letters of Roscoe G. Jennings to His Brother." *Arkansas Historical Quarterly*, XVIII (1959), 3–25.

Smith, Jonathan K. *Historic Tulip, Arkansas.* N.p., 1989.
————. *The Romance of Tulip.* Memphis, 1965.

ALBERT CRESWELL GARLINGTON

Albert Creswell Garlington, brigadier general of South Carolina militia, was born on June 9, 1822, in Oglethorpe County, Georgia. His father, Christopher Garlington, was a native of Lancaster County, Virginia, and a distant cousin of President Madison. His mother was Eliza Aycock of Georgia. Garlington graduated from the University of Georgia in 1842 with the highest honors. Removing to South Carolina, he was admitted to the bar in 1844. Settling in Newberry (his wife's hometown) in 1848, "he soon made a fine reputation as a lawyer and orator. He was one of the finest and most eloquent speakers I ever listened to."[1] A "secessionist fire-eater," Garlington was elected to the South Carolina House in 1850 and reelected in 1852. In 1854

Chapman and O'Neall, *The Annals of Newberry*

he lost a congressional contest to the equally avid secessionist Preston Brooks. Garlington won election to the state senate in 1856 and served through 1864. He also found time to be a director of the Greeneville and Columbia Railroad and a brigadier general of the 10th Brigade of the South Carolina Militia.

Upon secession Governor Pickens appointed Garlington one of four members of his Council of State. By action of the council, its members were each assigned a separate department. Garlington was assigned the Department of the Interior, with responsibility for coastal defenses and militia. With the transfer of the defenses and troops to Confederate authorities in April, 1861, Garlington and the council resigned. Within a few days the governor commissioned Garlington brigadier general of the 3rd Brigade of the South Carolina Volunteers. Garlington headed up a post of instruction at Columbia, South Carolina, and began training the troops. The regiments of the brigade were mustered into Confederate service that summer and left for Virginia. With the transfer Garlington's brigade command dissolved, and he joined the Confederate army. On December 19, 1861, Garlington was commissioned major of the "Holcombe Legion," a new South Carolina unit named after the governor's wife. The unit helped guard the South Carolina coast that winter, seeing action only in a skirmish on Edisto Island. Garlington resigned this commission on May 21, 1862. His services being deemed more valuable in administration, he was appointed by the governor to fill the posts of state adjutant general and inspector general. State senator through 1864, Garlington ran a strong race for governor in that year but lost. During the Carolinas campaign of 1864 and 1865 Garlington again donned a uniform and led a brigade of militia opposing Sherman's advance. His brigade evacuated Columbia, the state capital, on the approach of Sherman's army and retreated north. In late February, 1865, he disbanded the brigade.

Elected again to the state house in 1865, Garlington served there through 1867. After this Garlington settled in Atlanta, Georgia, remaining there for some years and then returning to South Carolina. For the last several years of his life he retired from law practice to live on his Newberry farm. General Garlington died at Newberry on March 27, 1885, and is buried in the Rosemont Cemetery in Newberry.

General Garlington's command of a brigade of militia that served in a campaign qualifies him to be considered a Confederate general.

NOTE

1. John A. Chapman and John B. O'Neall, *The Annals of Newberry* (1892; rpr. Baltimore, 1974), 587.

MAIN SOURCES

Chapman, John A., and John B. O'Neall. *The Annals of Newberry.* 1892; rpr. Baltimore, 1974.
Storm, Henry. Papers. William R. Perkins Library, Duke University, Durham.

JAMES ZACHARIAH GEORGE

James Zachariah George was born on October 20, 1826, in Monroe County, Georgia, the son of Joseph W. and Mary (Chamblis) George. His father died during his infancy. In 1834 the family moved to Noxubee County, Mississippi, and two years later settled in Carrollton in Carroll County. George enlisted as a private in the 1st Mississippi for the Mexican War, seeing action at the Battle of Monterrey. Discharged for ill health, he returned to Mississippi, studied law, and was admitted to the Carroll County bar. His success at the bar was rapid. In 1854 George was elected reporter to the Mississippi Supreme Court, and held this prestigious post until the start of the war.

Mississippi Department of Archives and History

Elected to the Mississippi Secession Convention, George voted for and signed that state's ordinance of secession. He was elected lieutenant, then captain (July 15, 1861) of Company C, 20th Mississippi Infantry. The 20th participated in the northwest Virginia campaigns of 1861. Transferred back to the west, the regiment was sent to Fort Donelson, Tennessee. The fort's garrison surrendered on February 16, 1862, to General U. S. Grant's investing forces. George was imprisoned in the North for the next seven months. Upon exchange, Governor Pettus of Mississippi appointed George a brigadier general of state troops, to serve until George's health improved. George headed up a slim brigade of state troops stationed in northern Mississippi, aiding Confederate cavalry in repelling Union cavalry raids. In March, 1863, Confederate Brigadier General Lloyd Tilghman arrested the indignant George for refusing to obey an order that would compromise the dignity of the state troops. The charges were soon dropped. Upon regaining his health George was elected colonel of the newly formed 5th Mississippi Cavalry. In his first battle at the head of the 5th (November 3, 1863; four days after being elected colonel), George was captured while leading a charge on Collierville, Tennessee. One authority has it that "Col. George, with a gallantry disregarding caution, dashed on ahead of his men and fell into the hands of the enemy."[1] George was kept a prisoner at the Johnson's Island, Ohio, federal prison for the balance of the war.

General George's postwar career was most distinguished. He entered into law partnership in 1872 with Wiley Harris to form the state's premier practice and moved to the state capital of Jackson. George became the chairman of the state Democratic party and in 1879 was appointed chief justice of the Mississippi Supreme Court. A prominent "Bourbon" Democrat and constitutional lawyer, George was elected to the U.S. Senate in 1880 and won reelection in 1886 and 1892. He rose to the chairmanship of the Senate Committee on Agriculture and Forestry. General George died on August 14, 1897, in Mississippi City, Mississippi, where he had gone to recover his health, and is buried in Evergreen Cemetery in Carrollton.

General George's command of a brigade of militia that served in a campaign qualifies him to be considered a Confederate general.

NOTE

1. OR, Vol. XXXI, Pt. 1, p. 252.

MAIN SOURCES

George, James Z. *The Political History of Slavery in the United States*. New York, 1915.
Goodspeed Publishing Company. *Biographical and Historical Memoirs of Mississippi*. 2 vols. Chicago, 1891.

GEORGE COUPER GIBBS

Courtesy Mrs. William Heard

George Couper[1] Gibbs was born on April 7, 1822, on St. Simons Island, Georgia, the son of George and Isabella (Kingsley) Gibbs. His father, a North Carolina native, was a merchant in North Carolina and New York City before moving to Florida. His mother was the grandaunt of the famous painter James McNeil Whistler. Gibbs grew up in Florida until reaching manhood, when he settled in New Orleans and found a job as a clerk in a mercantile establishment. During the Mexican War he served as a lieutenant in the 4th Louisiana Volunteers. In the mid-1850s he returned to Florida; the outbreak of the war found Gibbs a planter, living near St. Augustine.

In January, 1861, local militiamen seized the nearly vacant Fort Marion, which guarded St. Augustine, and Gibbs was placed in command of a company of artillerymen who temporarily garrisoned the fort. Commissioned captain in the regular Confederate army on March 20, 1861, Gibbs was placed in command of a prison guard detachment in Richmond. Promoted major in that year, on January 1, 1862, he was placed in command of the prison at Salisbury, North Carolina. In the summer of 1862 Gibbs commanded a prison post at Lynchburg, Virginia. Colonel of the 42nd North Carolina Infantry (formed from the Salisbury prison guards) from April 22, 1862, he resigned his colonelship on January 7, 1864. The regiment had seen little action in North Carolina in the meantime, and even less of Gibbs because of illness. In May of 1864 Gibbs, who because of ill health (intermittent fever and a facial ulcer) had been posted to garrison duty, was assigned to command the Macon, Georgia, officers' prison. "A most efficient officer and peculiarly suited for the position," he was nonetheless relieved from his Macon command that August.[2] In October, 1864, Gibbs was posted to command the troops at Andersonville, Georgia. Gibbs's troops, mainly Georgia reservists and local militiamen, provided the guards for the infamous Andersonville prison. Gibbs was required to furnish the commandant of the prison, Henry Wirz, with whatever troops Wirz requested. Beyond furnishing these detachments of troops, however, Gibbs had no authority over the running of the prison. In his infrequent contacts with the captive Union soldiers, Gibbs impressed the prisoners as a "cultivated, urbane and humane gentleman."[3] The number of prisoners and Confederate troops at Andersonville fluctuated wildly during his tenure there. At one time he led a brigade-sized force of 1,400 men, consisting of three regiments of Georgia reserves and a detachment of artillery. On May 4, 1865, Gibbs abandoned Andersonville to return to his Florida home. He died in St. Augustine on June 14, 1872, "after a prolonged illness brought on by the war conditions—during and after the war."[4] He is buried in the Evergreen Cemetery, St. Augustine.

Heitman, CV, and SHSP list Gibbs as a general. SHSP states that he was an acting brigadier general at Macon in 1864. The OR show Gibbs commanding the post of Macon as colonel, and show him as colonel of the 2nd Georgia Reserves (the main unit garrisoning Andersonville) as late as October 9, 1864. On March 29, 1865, he wrote a letter to his congressman asking for help in winning promotion to brigadier general and chief of Confederate prisons, and he signed himself as colonel as late as May 12, 1865.[5]

NOTES

1. Gibbs is usually listed with a middle name of Cooper. A descendant gives his middle name as Couper. He was born on the Couper plantation at St. Simons Island while his parents were visiting there and was named in honor of their host.

2. OR, VII, 373.

3. "The Treatment of Prisoners During the War Between the States," SHSP, I (1876), 189. Gibbs was a witness in the trial of Andersonville Prison commandant Major Henry Wirz. It was generally agreed that Gibbs was not to blame for the prison conditions at Andersonville. Neither was Major Wirz, but Wirz, not Gibbs, had formal responsibility for the prisoners, was made a scapegoat, and executed.

4. Margaret Gibbs Watt, The Gibbs Family of Long Ago and Near at Hand (St. Augustine, 1968), 22. Date of death per his widow's Mexican War Pension Application. See Mexican War Pension Application number C2844, filed September 26, 1887, National Archives.

5. George C. Gibbs to Congressman Samuel St. G. Rogers, March 29, 1865, in Gibbs's Compiled Service Record, 42nd North Carolina Infantry; OR, 2nd Ser., VIII, 552.

MAIN SOURCES

Jordan, Weymouth T., and Louis Manarin, comps. *North Carolina Troops*. 12 vols. Raleigh, 1966–90.

Watt, Margaret Gibbs. *The Gibbs Family of Long Ago and Near at Hand*. St. Augustine, 1968.

BENJAMIN FRANKLIN GORDON

Benjamin Franklin Gordon was born in Henry County, Tennessee, on May 18, 1826, the son of Thomas W. and Eliza (Brooks) Gordon. The family moved to Lafayette County, Missouri, in the spring of 1831. The elder Gordon, a farmer, settled in the Lexington area and was elected justice of the Lafayette County Court. During the Mexican War the younger Gordon enlisted in Doniphan's Missouri regiment, serving in that war as a private and bugler. After the war Gordon prospected for gold in California. Returning to Missouri, he became a partner in a merchandising business in Waverly and in 1858 opened his own store, selling drugs, patent medicines, and fancy groceries.

When the governor proclaimed the establishment of the Missouri State Guard in 1861, Gordon was one of the first to enlist. The records show that Gordon was adjutant of the 1st Brigade, 2nd Division. On August 10, 1861, at the Battle of Wilson's Creek, he was severely wounded. In 1862 he assisted future Major General Joseph Shelby in raising a regiment in Lafayette County. Shelby's 5th Missouri Cavalry was mustered into service on September 12, 1862; Gordon was elected the 5th's lieutenant colonel. The "knightly Gordon" served under Jo Shelby throughout the war.[1] Shelby took command of a newly recruited brigade of Missouri cavalry when the 5th was mustered in, and thus Gordon led the 5th for most of the war. Gordon saw action at the Battle of Prairie Grove on December 7, 1862, and his courageous conduct was mentioned in Shelby's report of the battle. In early 1863 Shelby's brigade and Gordon participated in Brigadier General John S. Marmaduke's two raids into Missouri. Gordon led Shelby's "Iron Brigade" during the Little Rock campaign (August through September, 1863) while Shelby was recovering from a wound. On December 15, 1863, when Shelby was promoted to brigadier general, Gordon became full colonel of the 5th. In March and April, 1864, Shelby's troops harassed Major General Frederick Steele's Union army in their advance from Little Rock to Camden, Arkansas. Gordon led more than one charge with his "usual impetuosity" during the Camden campaign.[2] At the Battle of Mark's Mills on April 25, Gordon's men were effective again and captured two artillery pieces. In July, 1864, the "brave and skillful" Gordon[3] routed the 10th Illinois Cavalry at Searcy,

Arkansas, and two weeks later routed Union forces near Helena. He led his regiment during Major General Sterling Price's Missouri Raid from August through December, 1864. At the Battle of Westport on October 23, 1864, the 5th made a successful attack, but was forced to halt when the Confederate rear collapsed. Gordon's cavalry made an about face and cut their way through the encirclement to safety. At the Battles of Mine Creek and Second Newtonia Gordon's men helped to slow down the pursuing Union force that had shattered two divisions of Price's army. After Price's Raid ended, Gordon was assigned to permanent command of Shelby's "Iron Brigade." On May 16, 1865, one month after Appomattox, General E. Kirby Smith, commander of the Confederate Department of the Trans-Mississippi, assigned Gordon to duty as brigadier general.

Upon the surrender of the Trans-Mississippi Department Shelby and Gordon fled to Mexico. Unlike Shelby, Gordon quickly returned to Missouri. He died on September 22, 1866, in Waverly, Lafayette County, and is buried in Waverly Cemetery.

Wood and Heitman list Gordon as a general.

NOTES

1. John N. Edwards, *Shelby and His Men* (Cincinnati, 1867), 299.
2. *Ibid.*, 343.
3. *OR*, Vol. XL, Pt. 1, p. 288.

MAIN SOURCES

Edwards, John N. *Shelby and His Men.* Cincinnati, 1867.
Mexican War Pension Applications. Microfilm T515, National Archives.
Young, William. *History of Lafayette County, Missouri.* 2 vols. Indianapolis, 1910.

COLTON GREENE

Colton Greene, whose antecedents are unknown, was born in 1832 in South Carolina.[1] Before 1857 he had moved to St. Louis, Missouri, and had become active in Democratic party politics. By 1860 he was a successful merchant of St. Louis, a partner in a wholesale grocery business.

Library of Congress

Active in the secessionist movement in that city, Greene was one of the organizers of the pro-southern "minutemen," who planned to seize the city and its arsenal. In the spring of 1861 he became a member of Governor Claiborne Jackson's secret strategy board, which coordinated Missouri secessionists. In April, 1861, the governor sent Greene to President Davis to obtain cannon to use in an attack on the St. Louis federal arsenal. Greene succeeded in his mission, but the cannon arrived too late. The cannon, and a brigade of Missouri militia intending to seize the arsenal, were captured by Federal troops. Greene joined the governor at Jefferson City and helped drill the eager prosouthern recruits who now flocked to the capital. That summer the governor sent Greene on confidential missions to Richmond and Arkansas to drum up support for a Confederate invasion of Missouri. At the August 10 Battle of Wilson's Creek Greene served on the staff of Brigadier General James McBride, 7th Military District commander. On October 28, 1861, the governor commissioned Greene colonel and assistant adjutant general of the 7th District. In the spring of 1862 McBride, ill and dissatisfied, resigned, and Greene, as colonel, took over the 7th Division, which he re-formed into a two-regiment brigade of volunteers. Greene led this brigade at the March 7 and 8, 1862, Battle of Pea Ridge. A very capable officer ("no braver or better officer ever drew a sword"[2]), Greene followed Sterling Price's Missouri army to Mississippi. In the summer of 1862 he received permission to return to Missouri to recruit a regiment of cavalry. Greene raised the 3rd Missouri Cavalry, of which (on November 4, 1862) he was appointed colonel. Greene spent the rest of the war as colonel of the 3rd. He led Brigadier General Marmaduke's Missouri cavalry brigade (of which the 3rd was a part) at the July 4, 1863, Battle of Helena and in the 1864 Camden expedition. Noted as a disciplinarian, Greene won the confidence of the brigade with his leadership at the Battles of Poison Spring and Jenkins' Ferry, among other engagements. In the summer of 1864 Greene was put on trial for allegedly refusing to have his men turn over their mules to the government, but a court-martial exonerated him of all charges that fall. Perhaps because of Greene's legal troubles, in August, 1864, Brigadier General John B. Clark was transferred from an infantry brigade and took over Marmaduke's brigade. Greene resumed command of the 3rd, which he led during Price's 1864 Missouri Raid. The 3rd shared in the general rout of Price's army during the raid. After the raid Clark was elevated to divisional command, and Greene once again took over the brigade.

During the war Greene's business and property in St. Louis were seized by his business partner, Stephen Hoyt (a staunch Unionist and mayor of occupied New Orleans) and others. With the end of the war the now-impoverished Greene relocated in Memphis, where "General" Greene, as he was known, became an active banker, insurance agent, and civic leader. He worked for the Memphis branch of the Knickerbocker Life Insurance Company of New York. In 1871 Greene established his own firm and prospered. He founded the State Savings Bank of Memphis, led a successful movement to construct a municipal waterworks, and organized the highly successful Memphis Mardi Gras. One source states that Greene was known as the "elegant Gen. Colton Greene, 'a gallant and conspicuous figure,' who because of his extensive European travel and command of languages had become the social arbiter (of Memphis). . . . Handsome and charming as he was, he never married, he never divulged anything about his origin except that he was born in S.C.—a mystery still talked about in Memphis."[3] A savant and a prominent society figure, he was instrumental in founding the Memphis Public Library.[4] General Greene died in Memphis on September 23, 1900, and is buried in Elmwood Cemetery.

Greene is listed as a general by Wright, SHSP, Heitman, and CV. Although he often commanded a brigade, the OR show him as colonel as late as December 31, 1864, and a dispatch calls him colonel as late as May 24, 1865. On March 27, 1865, Governor Reynolds of Missouri (who had known Greene before he war) wrote General Kirby Smith asking for Colonel Greene's promotion.[5] Petitions for Greene's promotion to general in 1865 were signed by practically all the officers in the Trans-Mississippi army. However, the OR show no indication of any promotion by either President Davis or General Kirby Smith.

NOTES

1. His obituary and tombstone state that he was born in 1832. However, on the Census of 1900, Tennessee, Shelby County, Microfilm ED 67, Sheet 6, Greene gives his birth date as July, 1838. The 1832 figure corresponds better with his life's chronology. Greene was, for example, in serious political correspondence with congressmen as early as 1857, and in 1860 headed the state executive committee of the "Breckinridge for President" campaign. The 1854-55 St. Louis Directory shows a "George C. Green" of Hoyt & Co., the firm of which Colton Greene was a partner in 1860. It is probable that the George C. Green who worked for this small firm in 1854 was the Colton Greene who was a partner in 1860, in which case Greene's real name would appear to be George Colton Greene.

2. John N. Edwards, Shelby and His Men (Cincinnati, 1867), 251.

3. Shields McIlwaine, Memphis Down in Dixie (New York, 1948), 236.

4. Interestingly, Greene's portrait, in the Cossitt Library in Memphis, has often been thought by patrons to be a portrait of Joseph Stalin! See the Memphis Commercial Appeal, September 10, 1948, for an amusing article on this topic.

5. Thomas C. Reynolds to E. Kirby Smith, March 27, 1865, Reynolds Papers, Library of Congress.

MAIN SOURCES

Greene, Colton. Collection. Memphis/Shelby County Public Library, Memphis.
Greene, Colton, to Thomas Snead, May 29, June 10, 1882. Thomas L. Snead Papers, Missouri Historical Society, St. Louis.
Memphis *Commercial Appeal*, October 2, 5, 7, 1900.

JOHN SUMMERFIELD GRIFFITH

Archives Division, Texas State Library

John Summerfield Griffith was born on June 17, 1829, in Montgomery County, Maryland, the son of Michael Berry and Lydia (Crabbe) Griffith and grandson of General Jeremiah Crabbe. The Griffiths were a prominent Maryland family whose ancestor had emigrated from Wales in 1675. Because of business losses John's father, a merchant, moved to Jefferson City, Missouri, in 1835; to Portland, Missouri, in 1837; and to San Augustine, Texas, in 1839. In 1850 the young Griffith became a clerk in a mercantile establishment. Soon setting up his own shop, Griffith prospered. In 1859 he removed to Kaufman County, Texas, where he raised livestock, cotton, and Irish potatoes.

In September, 1861, Griffith was elected captain of a volunteer cavalry company, later Company B, 6th (Stone's) Texas Cavalry. Upon the organization of the regiment, Griffith was elected lieutenant colonel. He led the regiment in a gallant charge at Chustenahlah, Indian Territory, in December, 1861, killing an Indian with his saber. The 6th fought at the Battle of Pea Ridge in Arkansas on March 7 and 8, 1862, but without Griffith, who was temporarily absent from the regiment. After Pea Ridge the 6th was transferred to Mississippi. Upon the reorganization of the regiment in May of 1862, Griffith, whose constitution was naturally delicate, declined to be a candidate for colonel. Griffith went back to Texas on recruiting duty, but returned to the 6th in the fall of 1862. As lieutenant colonel he led Lawrence S. Ross's cavalry brigade at the engagements at Oakland and Holly Springs. He is generally credited with conceiving the December, 1862, Holly Springs raid, which destroyed the main Union supply depot in the rear of Major General Ulysses S. Grant's advance upon Vicksburg, Mississippi. Griffith personally led the van of Major General Earl Van Dorn's cavalry in the successful attack on that town. Because of ill health (he was asthmatic), Colonel Griffith resigned his commission in May, 1863. Returning to Texas that June, Griffith was immediately elected to the state house and was made chairman of its Military Affairs Committee. On March 1, 1864, Governor Murrah of Texas appointed Griffith brigadier general of District No. 2 in central Texas to command state reserve forces.

The end of the war found Griffith impoverished and slaveless. However, he soon founded a successful business selling orange seed in the North. Griffith removed to Terrell, Texas, in 1874, and in 1876 he was again elected to the state house. His efforts there won him the sobriquet "Watchdog of the Treasury." General Griffith died at Terrell on August 6, 1901, and is buried in that city's Oakland Memorial Park. One source lauds Griffith as a man "unselfish in his characteristics; brave, though sagacious, as becomes a commander; patriotic in all his impulses; had health been vouchsafed to him, a career of glory . . . would have crowned his efforts with success."[1]

Griffith's rank of general in the Texas state army qualifies him to be considered a Confederate general.

NOTE

1. Victor Rose, *Ross' Texas Brigade* (Louisville, 1881), 123.

MAIN SOURCES

Raines, C. W. *Year Book for Texas, 1901*. Austin, 1902.
Rose, Victor. *Ross' Texas Brigade*. Louisville, 1881.

JOHN WARREN GRIGSBY

John Warren Grigsby was born on September 11, 1818, in Rockbridge County, Virginia, the son of Joseph and Mary Ashley Warren (Scott) Grigsby. His younger brother, Andrew Jackson Grigsby, was later colonel of the 27th Virginia and commander of the Stonewall Brigade. One cousin was future General E. F. Paxton; another cousin married into the McCormick Reaper family. A precocious youngster, J. Warren Grigsby edited a Rockbridge County paper at age sixteen.[1] At age twenty-two he was appointed U.S. Counsel in Bordeaux, France, serving abroad from 1841 to 1849. Upon his return to the U.S., Grigsby studied law and opened a practice in New Orleans. Marrying Susan

U.S. Army Military History Institute

Shelby, the granddaughter of Kentucky's legendary Governor Isaac Shelby, Grigsby removed to Kentucky and settled near Stanford in Lincoln County. There he farmed until 1861.

Like many other southern-leaning Kentuckians who respected their state's neutrality in the early months of the war, Grigsby does not appear to have been actively involved in the fighting until the Confederate invasion of Kentucky in the fall of 1862. That invasion, and the presence of a friendly army to protect them while they enlisted, prompted many Kentuckians to join the Confederate army. Assisting in raising a new cavalry regiment, the 6th Kentucky Cavalry, Grigsby was elected colonel of that regiment on September 2, 1862. The 6th was attached to Brigadier General Joseph Wheeler's cavalry corps of the Army of Tennessee, and Grigsby and Wheeler began what would be a long and close association. Grigsby was wounded in action at Milton, Tennessee, on March 20, 1863, while heading a charge against a Union battery. After this engagement his regiment was attached to the Kentucky cavalry brigade of Brigadier General John Hunt Morgan. Grigsby participated in Morgan's 1863 Ohio raid but, luckier or wiser than his chief, he escaped the capture (by swimming the Ohio River) that befell most of the brigade and returned to the South with about four hundred of Morgan's men. During the 1864 Atlanta campaign Grigsby led a brigade of Kentucky cavalry regiments in Wheeler's corps. The campaign opened with a Union division attempting on May 8, 1864, to seize Dug Gap, a mountain pass on the left flank of the Confederate main line. Unsupported, Grigsby and his troopers held off the Union attack all day, helping to save the main army's line of retreat. It was his finest hour as a Confederate. In the summer of 1864 Grigsby was relieved of his brigade command when appointed inspector general of all cavalry in the Army of Tennessee. By 1865 Grigsby was chief of staff of Wheeler's cavalry corps. A fellow trooper remembered Grigsby as "brave, determined, fearless, enterprising; he established a splendid reputation."[2]

Returning to Kentucky, Grigsby lived for a while in retirement on his Lincoln County estate, Traveler's Rest, the old Shelby homestead. He then moved to Danville, Kentucky, to practice law. Grigsby was elected, as a Democrat, to the Kentucky General Assembly in 1875. He died in office at Lexington on January 12, 1877, and is buried in Lexington Cemetery.[3] "One of the most distinguished men of Ky.," it was said of Grigsby that "in him were centered all the qualities that make a man at once noble and pure, generous, just and great."[4]

SHSP and CV list Grigsby as a general. The latter has him appointed from Kentucky in 1864. However, he is mentioned in the OR as colonel as late as April, 1865, and he was paroled in May, 1865, as colonel. Perhaps his service as inspector general led to his being called "general."

NOTES

1. Contrary to an account in *Biographical Encyclopedia of the Commonwealth of Kentucky* (Chicago, 1896), 723–24, Grigsby did not attend VMI.

2. Bennett H. Young, *Confederate Wizards of the Saddle* . . . . (1914; rpr. Boston, 1958), 68–69.

3. A biographical article on Grigsby in the Kentucky volume of *CMH* has him dying on January 12, 1872. However, the 1877 date is confirmed in a January 5, 1991, letter to the author from Margaret G. Mottley, Administrator, National Grigsby Family Society, Houston, Texas.

4. Margaret G. Mottley to the author, January 5, 1991, citing an 1878 manuscript genealogy of the Grigsby family.

MAIN SOURCES

Biographical Encyclopedia of the Commonwealth of Kentucky. Chicago, 1896.
Young, Bennett H. *Confederate Wizards of the Saddle* . . . . 1914; rpr. Boston, 1958.

WALTER GWYNN

Walter Gwynn, a major general of Virginia volunteers and brigadier general of North Carolina volunteers, was born on February 22, 1802, in Jefferson County, Virginia. His father, Humphrey Gwynn, of an old Gloucester County, Virginia, family, could trace his descent from Colonel Hugh Gwynn, who settled in Virginia before 1640. Appointed to West Point in 1818, the younger Gwynn graduated eighth in his class of forty in 1822. Gwynn served ten years in the army as an artillery lieutenant, while also working as a civil engineer for private railroad companies. Resigning in 1832 to become a private engineer, in the next three years Gwynn surveyed proposed routes for several Virginia railroad companies and served as chief engineer

Courtesy North Carolina Division of Archives and History

of the Portsmouth and Roanoke Railroad. Between 1836 and 1840 Gwynn worked as chief engineer of the Wilmington and Raleigh Railroad. In the 1840s he was employed by several Virginia railroads and served as president of the James River and Kanawha Canal Company. Subsequently chief engineer of the North Carolina Railroad, by 1861 Gwynn had established an enviable international reputation as a railroad engineer and as the founder of the southeastern railway system. One contemporary said that Gwynn "made for himself a reputation among his fellow engineers that will last for all time."[1] In 1857 Gwynn, by then a Raleigh, North Carolina, resident, largely retired from his railroad duties and moved to South Carolina.

The governor of that state seized upon the experienced Gwynn to reconnoiter the approaches to Fort Sumter in December, 1860. In March, 1861, Gwynn was commissioned major of the PACS and charged with constructing batteries at various strategic points in Charleston Harbor. For his role in the reduction of Fort Sumter, Gwynn received public praise. On April 12, 1861, Gwynn, a prewar colonel in the Virginia militia, was nominated major general of volunteers by the governor of Virginia and given command of the state forces defending Norfolk. Subsequently confirmed as brigadier general, Gwynn faithfully executed his task until relieved by regular Confederate forces on May 23, 1861.[2] At this time his Virginia commission as general expired because of the dissolution of the Virginia volunteer army. Governor John Ellis of North Carolina commissioned Gwynn brigadier general of North Carolina volunteers, to assume command of the outer coastal defenses of that state. The volunteers were disbanded on August 20, 1861, and again his command expired. On October 9, 1862, Gwynn was appointed colonel of the PACS and was directed by the secretary of war to make a survey of North Carolina coastal defenses. Gwynn served in that capacity until his resignation in 1863. He took no further active part in the war.

After Appomattox Gwynn moved back to North Carolina and performed minor surveying and archival tasks for the state. General Gwynn died in Baltimore, Maryland, on February 6, 1882, and is buried in Hollywood Cemetery, Richmond.

Gwynn is listed as a general of North Carolina state troops in Clark, *Histories of the Several Regiments and Battalions from North Carolina in the Great War, 1861–1865.*[3]

NOTES

1. William S. Powell, ed., *Dictionary of North Carolina Biography* (4 vols.; Chapel Hill, 1979–91), III, 388.

2. Douglas Southall Freeman, citing the *OR*, suggests Gwynn was relieved because he was incompetent. See Douglas S. Freeman, *Lee's Lieutenants: A Study in Command* (3 vols.; New York, 1942–44), I, 507.

3. Walter Clark, ed., *Histories of the Several Regiments and Battalions from North Carolina in the Great War, 1861–1865* (5 vols.; Raleigh, 1901).

MAIN SOURCE

Powell, William S., ed. *Dictionary of North Carolina Biography.* 4 vols. Chapel Hill, 1979–91.

JAMES HAGAN

James Hagan was born on June 17, 1822, in County Tyrone, Ireland.[1] At an early age his family emigrated to the United States, settling on a farm near Philadelphia, Pennsylvania. He grew up in Philadelphia and attended Clermont Academy there. When James was fifteen his uncle, John Hagan, a rich New Orleans merchant with business interests throughout the Southwest, took him into the family business, sending him to Mobile, Alabama, to manage the Hagan business affairs in that city. Young Hagan thus entered society with the advantages of wealth and position. During the Mexican War Hagan enlisted in Hays's Texas Rangers, a cavalry outfit. He served in Zachary

Courtesy Ann McBryde

Taylor's army, and won recognition for "conspicuous and distinguished gallantry" at the Battle of Monterrey.[2] In 1848 he was commissioned captain of the 3rd U.S. Dragoons. After that war he returned to Alabama. Abandoning the mercantile life, Hagan purchased a plantation and devoted his time to its management. In 1854 he married the beautiful and socially prestigious daughter of Alabama's attorney general.

Upon the outbreak of the war Hagan was chosen captain of a cavalry company, the "Mobile Dragoons," which helped guard the Gulf Coast. Desiring more active duty, Hagan, "a natural horseman, and reckless in his fighting," transferred to Wirt Adams' 1st Mississippi Cavalry Regiment and was commissioned that regiment's major.[3] In September, 1861, the regiment was ordered to Kentucky to join the Confederate main army and later fought in the Battle of Shiloh. On July 1, 1862, Hagan was commissioned colonel of the newly organized 3rd Alabama Cavalry. The 3rd fought in all the campaigns of the Army of Tennessee. Hagan led his regiment in General Braxton Bragg's Kentucky invasion of 1862, and at the Battle of Perryville headed a mounted charge described by his brigade commander as "one of the most brilliant of the campaign."[4] In early 1863 Hagan inherited the command of Brigadier General Joseph Wheeler's old cavalry brigade. That spring and summer Hagan's brigade screened the left front of Bragg's army. At this time General Wheeler recommended Hagan for promotion to brigadier general. General Bragg, however, blocked the promotion on the grounds that Hagan was in a state of "dissipation" (*i.e.*, he was an alcoholic). In November, 1863, suffering from wounds and dissapointed over nonpromotion, Hagan resigned his commission and returned home to Mobile. In the spring of 1864, recuperated, he requested and was granted a revocation of that resignation and returned to his regiment. During the siege of Atlanta the regiment dismounted and manned the trenches. In August, 1864, upon the elevation of Brigadier General William Allen to divisional command, Hagan received permanent command of the brigade (now consisting of five regiments and one battalion of Alabama cavalry), which he led till the end of the war. During the war the dashing Hagan was wounded three times: shot in the leg near Franklin, Tennessee, in the winter of 1862; shot through the body near Kingston, Tennessee, in November, 1863; and shot through the arm at the Battle of Monroe's Crossroads in North Carolina on March 10, 1865.

After the war Hagan returned to Mobile. The fortune left to him by his uncles he had converted to Confederate money, and he was, therefore, left penniless. In the 1870s and 1880s he worked as a manager of a plantation on the Alabama River and then returned to Mobile. In 1885 President Cleveland appointed him "crier" for the U.S. District Court in Alabama. Of Hagan one source says, "Courteous in the old-school vein, genial, convivial and simple-minded as a child, the veteran was popular with all classes and ages in Mobile. His native wit—never caustic, while ever ready—left a wealth of stories and *bons mots* to his credit; and his broken fortunes never dampened his exhaustless flow of humor and spirits."[5] Hagan died in Mobile on November 6, 1901, and is buried in Magnolia Cemetery.

CMH, Heitman, Wood, *CV*, *SHSP*, and Lonn list Hagan as a general, the first citing a February, 1865, promotion. In the April 15, 1865, report of General Wheeler, Hagan's corps commander, Wheeler called three of his colonels, including Hagan, "general."[6] A May 13, 1865, letter from General Wheeler to Hagan stated "I have been informed by the War Department that your commission as brigadier general did not reach you from the fact that it was sent to Genl Lee after his appointment as general in chief [*i.e.*, after January 23, 1865], and there was not sufficient information at his Headquarters as to the disposition of troops to enable his A.A. Genl to forward papers—I was also informed that many other papers were lost from the same cause."[7] A March, 1865, War Department memorandum confirms this promotion by mentioning Hagan as brigadier general. In his postwar pardon application, Hagan explains that he signed his May 9, 1865, parole as colonel, but that subsequently he learned he had been appointed general. Hagan was called colonel on February 28, 1865, by the secretary of war and on March 10, 1865, by the general-in-chief, in both cases *after* his alleged promotion.[8]

NOTES

1. Date of birth per Hagan's 1887 application for a Mexican War pension. During his lifetime at least three different dates were given for his birth.

2. Mobile *Daily Register,* April 20, 1898.

3. New York *Times,* November 14, 1901.

4. *OR,* Vol. XVI, Pt. 1, p. 897.

5. New York *Times,* November 14, 1901.

6. *OR,* Vol. XLVII, Pt. 1, p. 1132. The other two colonels named were Henry Ashby and Moses Hannon.

7. Letter furnished the author by Mrs. Elizabeth Carroll, Knoxville, Tennessee, great-granddaughter of General Hagan.

8. *OR,* Vol. XLVII, Pt. 2, pp. 1291, 1035.

MAIN SOURCES

Evans, Clement A., ed. *Confederate Military History: A Library of Confederate States History.* 1899; 17 vol. extended edition; rpr. Wilmington, N.C., 1987.

Hagan, James. Papers. Hill Memorial Library, Louisiana State University, Baton Rouge.

Mobile *Daily Register,* November 8, 1901.

MOSES WRIGHT HANNON

Moses Wright Hannon was born in Baldwin County, Georgia, on December 14, 1827, the son of John and Elizabeth (Wright) Hannon. His father, a Maryland native, was a planter and lawyer; his mother was an aunt to Confederate Major General Ambrose Wright. Raised in Georgia, Hannon moved to Montgomery, Alabama, in 1847 to join his older brothers. He became a wealthy merchant there and married into a prominent local family. Except for eight years spent in California, Hannon resided in Montgomery until 1861.

Courtesy Catharyn Wiley Heatly

When the war began "Wright" Hannon (as he was commonly called) was elected captain of Company B of the 1st Alabama Cavalry and was swiftly promoted to lieutenant colonel. The 1st was organized in Montgomery in late 1861. The next spring it was ordered to Corinth, Mississippi, and fought in the Battle of Shiloh. In the fall of 1862 Hannon raised the 53rd Alabama Partisan Rangers, a mounted regiment, and was commissioned its colonel on November 5, 1862.[1] The "valiant Colonel Hannon" and his regiment were stationed around the city of Tuscumbia, guarding northern Alabama from Union incursions.[2] In April, 1863, the 53rd was formally attached to the cavalry brigade of Brigadier General Phillip Roddey, which operated in northern Alabama. On August 15, 1863, Hannon's regiment was transferred to the Army of Tennessee. It saw action at the Battle of Chickamauga that September. For reasons unknown, Colonel Hannon resigned his commission on December 16, 1863; the resignation was revoked the next month. During the Atlanta campaign of 1864 Hannon commanded a small brigade (the 53rd Regiment and the 24th Battalion) of Alabama cavalry and occasionally, as senior colonel, Kelly's Division in the corps of Major General Joseph Wheeler. Hannon helped defeat a Union cavalry raid that July. In August, Hannon's brigade was detached from the main army to raid the supply lines of the Union army investing Atlanta. Taking only three hundred of the best-mounted men with him, Hannon hit Sherman's supply line near Calhoun, Georgia. Hearing of a nearby Union wagon train, Hannon smashed the train's escort and seized a herd of over a thousand cattle. With this herd, he returned to the main army defending Atlanta, whereupon General Hood, delighted with this unexpected addition to his army's meat supply, promoted him to the rank of acting brigadier general, subject to confirmation by the president. Throughout 1865 Hannon's brigade opposed Major General William T. Sherman's advance through the Carolinas. Hannon was wounded on March 10, 1865, at the Battle of Monroe's Crossroads in North Carolina and was disabled for the balance of the war.

After the war Hannon returned to Montgomery, resuming his mercantile career there and in New Orleans. In 1870 Hannon moved to Freestone County, Texas, and was a planter there at least through 1883. Sometime afterwards he removed to Leon County, Texas. Hannon died there on June 3, 1897, and is buried in Oakwood Cemetery.

CMH, CV, and SHSP list Hannon as a general, the first alleging an 1865 (month unspecified) appointment. Presumably this is based on General Wheeler's report of April 15, 1865 (See discussion under James Hagan), which says that Hannon was a general and was wounded. The OR show Hannon as a colonel as late as February 15, 1865. The promotion, if any, must have come after this date. However, there is no record of such a promotion, and even CMH acknowledges that "the commission was never received" by Hannon. In his postwar pardon application, Hannon states that he never rose above the rank of colonel; however, by 1876 he was signing letters as "brigadier general in the Confederate service," and his tombstone labels him "general."

NOTES

1. The 53rd Alabama was something of a Hannon family affair. Among the regiment's officers were no less than six Hannon cousins, plus several members of Hannon's wife's family.

2. Adam H. Whetstone, *History of the 53rd Alabama Volunteer Infantry (Mounted)* (University, Ala., 1985), 52.

MAIN SOURCES

Evans, Clement A., ed. *Confederate Military History: A Library of Confederate States History.* 1899; 17 vol. extended edition; rpr. Wilmington, N.C., 1987.

Leon County Historical Book Survey, ed. *History of Leon County, Texas.* Dallas, 1986.

Whetstone, Adam H. *History of the 53rd Alabama Volunteer Infantry (Mounted).* University, Ala., 1985.

WILLIAM HENRY HARMAN

William Henry Harman was born at Waynesboro, Virginia, on February 17, 1828, the son of Lewis and Sally (Garber) Harman. At a young age he served as second lieutenant of the 1st Virginia Infantry during the Mexican War. Returning home at the end of that war, Harman studied law. He was elected commonwealth attorney of Augusta County in 1851, serving in that post until the start of the war.

A Staunton resident, Harman was appointed brigadier general of the 13th Brigade of the Virginia militia on April 10, 1861. He helped seize Harpers Ferry, Virginia, on April 18, and his 955-man brigade defended that strategic city for ten days. On April 28 the brigade was relieved by regular Confederate forces under then Colonel Stonewall Jackson. Commissioned lieutenant colonel of the 5th Virginia Infantry on May 7, 1861 (the colonel was Kenton Harper, major general of militia over him), Harman and the 5th fought in the First Battle of Bull Run on July 21, 1861. Commissioned colonel of the 5th (part of the Stonewall Brigade) on September 11, 1861, Harman led his regiment at the Battle of Kernstown in early 1862. During the April, 1862, reorganization of the army Harman failed to win reelection as colonel. Without a command, he briefly served as a volunteer aide-de-camp to Brigadier General Edward Johnson in Jackson's 1862 Valley campaign.[1] On February 19, 1864, Harman was appointed assistant adjutant general of the PACS, a staff billet better suited to his feeble form than field duty. As colonel he led an improvised brigade of reservists at the June 5, 1864, Battle of Piedmont, where the Union army moving down the Shenandoah Valley crushed a scratch Confederate force of cavalry and reserves. Harman's "strict compliance with all orders" during that campaign earned praise from his superiors.[2] Throughout 1864 and 1865 he led a regiment of reserves in the Shenandoah Valley. At the disastrous Confederate rout at the Battle of Waynesboro on May 2, 1865, Harman was killed while trying to rally his demoralized troops. He is buried in Thornrose Cemetery in Staunton, Virginia.

General Harman's command of a brigade of militia that served in a campaign qualifies him to be considered a Confederate general.

NOTES

1. Jedidiah Hotchkiss, *Make Me a Map of the Valley* (Dallas, 1973), says that Harman led the 52nd Virginia at the Battle of McDowell on May 8, 1862. The 52nd was instead led by Colonel Michael Harman, his brother. Another brother, Major John Harman, was Stonewall Jackson's famous cursing quartermaster, reputed to be able to "swear at a mule team and make it jerk a wagon out of a mudhole as nothing else will." Robert K. Krick, *Stonewall Jackson at Cedar Mountain* (Chapel Hill, 1990), 46, citing Charles M. Blackford, *Letters from Lee's Army* (New York, 1947), 101–103.

2. Marshall M. Brice, *Conquest of a Valley* (Charlottesville, 1965), 156.

MAIN SOURCES

Staunton *Valley Virginian*, July 4, 1866.
Tyler, John G. *Encyclopedia of Virginia Biography*. 5 vols. New York, 1915.

KENTON HARPER

Kenton Harper, a general of the Virginia militia in 1861, was born in Pennsylvania in 1801, the son of George Kenton and Nancy (McClintock) Harper. His father, of a wealthy Philadelphia family with Virginia connections, was the longtime publisher of the *Franklin County Repository*. Kenton's early youth was spent as a printer in Chambersburg. In 1823 Harper bought a newspaper in Staunton, Virginia, a paper later known as the Staunton *Spectator*. Harper, who published the *Spectator* through 1849, gained a regional reputation as an editor and publisher with political influence. In 1836 he was elected to a term in the Virginia House of Delegates. During the Mexican War he was captain of the Augusta County company of the 1st Virginia Infantry. He was promoted to acting inspector general of his brigade and served as military governor of Parras in northern Mexico. After that war Harper became a farmer in Augusta County. He served in a variety of government posts—assistant to the U.S. secretary of the interior and agent to the Chickasaw Indian tribe (1851 to 1852)—as well as becoming president of a local bank.

Major general of the 5th Division of the Virginia Militia since 1860, Harper was the commander of the militia units that seized Harpers Ferry on April 18, 1861. To guard that strategic post, the whole division was called into service. Harper and his men removed the invaluable ordnance stores and machinery of the Harpers Ferry arsenal and shipped them south to safety, securing their use for the Confederacy. On April 28, 1861, Harper ("a born soldier" of "energy, skill and sagacity," but of "delicate health" [1]) and his 2,400 men were relieved of duty by Stonewall Jackson and regular Confederate troops. With the organization of the PACS, Harper was commissioned colonel of the 5th Virginia Infantry on May 7, 1861. He led the 5th, a part of the Stonewall Brigade, at First Bull Run, where his soldierly ability attracted the notice of the army commander.[2] The old militia general resigned his colonel's commission in September, 1861, in order to return home and be with his dying wife. Harper spent the balance of the war in his native Shenandoah Valley. On June 2, 1864, Harper was authorized to form a regiment from the organized reservist companies in the Shenandoah Valley. The regiment fought at the Battles of Piedmont and Waynesboro, being routed on both occasions.

Harper returned to Staunton after the war. He died of pneumonia at his home, Glen Allen, in Augusta County on December 25, 1867, and is buried in Thornrose Cemetery, Staunton.

General Harper's command of a brigade of militia that served in a campaign qualifies him to be considered a Confederate general.

NOTES

1. Staunton *Spectator*, December 31, 1867.

2. During his lifetime Harper was credited with causing General Jackson to be nicknamed "Stonewall." In response to an observation by Harper, Brigadier General Bernard Bee cried out, "There stands Jackson like a stone wall." For more on this issue see John Hennessy, "Stonewall's Nickname: Was It Fact or Was It Fiction?," *Civil War*, VIII (March–April, 1990), 10–17; Staunton *Spectator*, December 31, 1867.

MAIN SOURCES

Harper, Kenton. Papers. Southern Historical Collection, University of North Carolina, Chapel Hill.
Staunton *Spectator*, December 31, 1867.

DAVID BULLOCK HARRIS

David Bullock Harris was born in Frederick's Hall, Louisa County, Virginia, on September 28, 1814, the son of Frederick and Catherine Snelson (Smith) Harris. His father, a captain in the War of 1812, was later president of the Louisa (Virginia Central) railroad. Harris grew up at Gardner's Crossroads in that county. Appointed to West Point, he graduated seventh (of forty-three) in the class of 1833. After service in the artillery and as an engineering instructor at West Point, he resigned from the army in 1835 at the urgings of his father. Harris worked as an engineer for the James River and Kanawha Canal Company for two years, then did railroad survey work. By 1845 he had settled into the life of a tobacco farmer at Woodville, his Goochland County plantation.

Miller, ed., *Photographic History*, X

Commissioned captain of Virginia engineers on May 2, 1861, Harris served on the staff of Brigadier General Phillip Cocke at the First Battle of Bull Run. After that battle he was assigned to General P. G. T. Beauregard's staff. Harris was associated with Beauregard for the remainder of the war, planning the defenses at Centreville, Fort Pillow, Island No. 10, and Vicksburg. A "brave and efficient officer . . . [who was] admired and respected,"[1] Harris earned swift promotion to captain (February 15, 1862), major (October 3, 1862), lieutenant colonel (May 5, 1863), and colonel (October 8, 1863) of Confederate engineers. Harris' greatest contribution to the Confederacy was his work in planning and constructing the defenses of Charleston, South Carolina. Under Beauregard's general direction, Harris supervised the construction of new earthworks and the renovation of old works, constantly inspecting the many sites and making suggestions for improvements. No armchair soldier, he "threw himself constantly among the troops that were most exposed, sharing their dangers and winning their admiration by the coolest courage." General Beauregard, himself a distinguished engineer, called Harris "the only officer in his command who never made a mistake. . . . [Harris] always exceeded his most sanguine expectations."[2] Charleston remained the one major southern port that was never captured or closed by the Union navy. In 1864 Harris went with Beauregard to Virginia, where he helped plan the Petersburg defenses that proved so invulnerable to Union attack. Sent in October of that year to Charleston, Harris held the post of chief engineer of the Department of South Carolina, Georgia, and Florida. Colonel Harris died of yellow fever in Summerville, South Carolina on October 10, 1864. He is buried in Hollywood Cemetery in Richmond.

Heitman, Cullum, *SHSP*, and *CMH* all list Harris as a general. Although repeatedly recommended for promotion, and although President Davis in October, 1864, verbally promised to promote him, it appears he died a colonel before President Davis could formally appoint him. The Charleston *Mercury*, both in articles the week of his death and in his obituary, uniformly calls him colonel; there is no record of his promotion, and Colonel Alfred Roman, a fellow staff officer, stated in his book on General Beauregard that Harris died before the promotion went through.[3] Harris' association with Beauregard, an enemy of the president, is thought to have retarded his army advancement.

NOTES

1. Alfred Roman, *The Military Operations of General Beauregard in the War Between the States, 1861 to 1865* (2 vols.; New York, 1884), II, 277.

2. John Johnson, *The Defense of Charleston Harbor* (Charleston, 1890), Appendix D, xliii; "General David Bullock Harris, C.S.A.," *SHSP*, XX (1892), 397.

3. Roman, *Military Operations of General Beauregard*, II, 410.

MAIN SOURCES

Charleston *Mercury*, October 11, 12, 1864.
"General David Bullock Harris, C.S.A." *Southern Historical Society Papers*, XX (1892), 395–98.
Harris, David Bullock. Papers. William R. Perkins Library, Duke University, Durham.

JEPTHA VINING HARRIS

Jeptha Vining Harris was born in Elbert County, Georgia, on December 1, 1816, the son of General Jeptha Vining Harris of Athens and his wife Sarah Hunt.[1] His father was a prominent lawyer and planter, a state representative, and a general of militia in the War of 1812. The younger Harris graduated from the University of Georgia with a B.A. in 1836. Relocating in Lowndes County, Mississippi, in 1840, he became a wealthy antebellum slaveholder, planter, militia officer, and state senator from Lowndes County 1858 to 1861.

Vicksburg National Military Park

At the beginning of the war, Harris equipped, at his own expense, a company of Confederate Army troops. In August of 1862, he enlisted in the Mississippi state troops and was elected captain of Company D, Lowndes County Minute Men. On September 2, 1862, Governor Pettus commissioned Harris brigadier general of state troops, to command a slim brigade of drafted militia stationed at Columbus. Ordered to Vicksburg on May 7, 1863, Harris' brigade guarded the riverfront of that fortress for the next two weeks. During the siege of Vicksburg Harris' brigade held the left of the Confederate line, the two regiments being stationed just to the east of Fort Hill and to the left of Vaughn's Tennessee brigade. Harris (who was praised for his "indefatigable exertions" during the siege) and his brigade were part of the army surrendered at Vicksburg.[2] On the march home after the surrender the militiamen, who had "showed an entire willingness . . . [during] the operations in and around Vicksburg to do whatever should be required of them . . . relaxed into considerable depression. . . . Many straggled and left for their houses."[3] The brigade, demoralized by defeat and starvation like the rest of the army, dissolved. In July, 1863, Harris was exchanged; the next month the rest of his brigade was paroled and mustered out, and Harris returned to private life. On August 26, 1864, the governor recommissioned Harris a colonel and appointed him to command the post of Macon, Mississippi.

After the war General Harris returned to his farm in Lowndes County and a life of relative seclusion. He died on November 21, 1899, and is buried in Friendship Cemetery in Columbus.

Harris is listed as a Confederate general in Heitman. However, his service was entirely with Mississippi state troops, not Confederate army units.

NOTES

1. OR, Vol. XXIV, Pt. 2, p. 237, and Heitman call him John V. Harris. However, it is clear that his name was Jeptha.
2. OR, Vol. LII, Pt. 2, p. 463.

3. Harris to Mississippi Adjutant General, August 12, 1863, quoted in Jerry Causey, ed., "Selected Correspondence of the Adjutant General of Confederate Mississippi," *Journal of Mississippi History*, XLII (1981), 51; *OR*, Vol. LII, Pt. 2, p. 463.

MAIN SOURCES

Saunders, James E., and Elizabeth S. Stubbs. *Early Settlers of Alabama*. 1899; rpr. Baltimore, 1969.
University of Georgia Records. University of Georgia, Athens.

THOMAS ALEXANDER HARRIS

Thomas Alexander Harris was born in what is now Warren County, Virginia, in May, 1826. The family moved to Missouri when Harris was a boy.[1] Harris was orphaned at the age of nine, and clerked in various stores near Hannibal to survive. A military enthusiast, Harris fought in the Mormon and Iowa War at the age of twelve and was elected lieutenant colonel of a militia regiment at age seventeen. He attended West Point from 1843 to 1845, but did not graduate.[2] Instead he studied law. In 1848 Harris was appointed second lieutenant of the 12th U.S. Infantry, a regiment raised for the Mexican War. However, the day he reported for duty, peace was declared. After the war he participated in Lopez' filibustering expedition to Cuba. As colonel, Harris led another filibustering expedition into Central America. Returning to Hannibal in the 1850s, Harris became the legal counsel for the local railroad and served as city attorney. He also edited the local newspaper. Politically Harris was variously an anti-Benton Democrat, national secretary of the American party, and a Unionist who supported John Bell for president in 1860. In 1856 he made an unsuccessful run for secretary of state in Missouri on the anti-Benton ticket. In 1860 he was elected to the state house of representatives on the Bell-Everett ticket. He was chosen chairman of the house military committee.

Louisville *Courier-Journal*, April 10, 1895

Harris was traveling to Booneville to join Governor Jackson on June 21, 1861, when a messenger informed him that the governor had commissioned him brigadier general of the 2nd Division of the Missouri State Guard. Harris raised over two thousand troops in northeast Missouri that summer, often under the noses of Union occupation forces. His command joined the governor that fall in time for the siege of Lexington. Harris was one of several officers who took credit for the idea of using hemp bales as movable breastworks to attack the Lexington garrison, a stratagem that resulted in the surrender of the Union forces. After this battle he was named to the Confederate Congress, in which he served through 1864. Harris was a member of the House Military Affairs Committee. Politically he was anti-administration and opposed to all tax bills. Harris declined to run for reelection in 1864. Allegedly, Harris, "a celebrated bon vivant," was unable to run because of a broken leg suffered in a fall at a brothel.[3] After his term ended he stayed on in the capital. The government contracted with him to supply the army with needed equipment, which Harris purchased from European suppliers and shipped in via blockade runners. When Richmond fell he attempted to flee the country but was captured on May 17, 1865, in Florida. He was imprisoned at Fort McHenry in Baltimore.

Soon pardoned, Harris returned to Missouri impoverished by the war. He found employment with the Life (Insurance) Association of America, based in St. Louis. In 1870 he opened an office in Texas for them. Subsequently Harris worked for a New Orleans newspaper. He soon relocated again in Kentucky, and the governor, an old friend, appointed Harris assistant secretary of state. Harris later won election to the state legislature, representing Oldham County from 1885 to 1886. General Harris died on April 9, 1895,[4] in Pee Wee Valley, near Louisville. He is buried in Cave Hill Cemetery, Louisville.[5]

Heitman and *SHSP* list Harris as a Confederate general.

NOTES

1. Jon L. Wakelyn, *Biographical Dictionary of the Confederacy* (Westport, Conn., 1977), 218, has Harris moving to Missouri "during the late 1840s." Harris' West Point application papers make it clear that he lived in Missouri in the 1830s.

2. Harris resigned from West Point because his demerit total would not allow a furlough, which Harris desired to visit sick relatives in Virginia.

3. Ezra J. Warner and W. Buck Yearns, *Biographical Register of the Confederate Congress* (Baton Rouge, 1975), 109; Robert L. Kerby, *Kirby Smith's Confederacy: The Trans-Mississippi South, 1863–1865* (New York, 1972), 151.

4. Not April 19, 1895, the date of death given in Wakelyn, *Biographical Dictionary of the Confederacy*, 218. See Harris' obituary in the Louisville *Courier-Journal*, April 10, 1895.

5. There is a brief description of Harris, by fellow townsman Mark Twain, in Twain's *History of a Campaign That Failed*. By his first wife Harris was the brother-in-law of Union Admiral David Porter.

MAIN SOURCES

"General Thomas A. Harris." *Missouri Historical Review*, XXXVII (1942–43), 112–13.
Louisville *Courier-Journal*, April 10, 1895.
Wakelyn, Jon L. *Biographical Dictionary of the Confederacy*. Westport, Conn., 1977.

GEORGE PAUL HARRISON, JR.

George Paul Harrison, Jr., was born on March 19, 1841, at Montieth plantation near Savannah, Georgia. His father, George Paul Harrison, Sr., was a rich planter and state legislator (See George Paul Harrison, Sr.); his mother was Thurza Adelaide Guinn.

Massachusetts Commandery, Military Order of the Loyal Legion and the U.S. Army Military History Institute

The younger Harrison was a student at Georgia Military Institute when the secession crisis arose. He left school in January, 1861, to participate in the seizing of Fort Pulaski and later that month became a lieutenant of the 1st Georgia Regulars. Returning to Georgia Military Institute, Harrison graduated at the head of his class that May, and briefly served as his alma mater's commandant (at age twenty). He then rejoined the 1st Georgia, now stationed in Virginia, and served as that regiment's adjutant. In April, 1862, he was elected colonel of the 5th Georgia State Troops, a six-month regiment. On May 15, 1862, he was elected colonel of the 32nd Georgia Infantry. For the next two years the 32nd was stationed at Charleston, South Carolina. At times Harrison commanded Fort Johnson, Morris Island, and John's Island. During the July 18, 1863, Union assault on Fort Wagner (shown in the movie *Glory*), the 32nd reinforced Wagner's garrison near the end of the battle and aided in the disastrous Union defeat. While on John's Island Harrison was wounded twice in skirmishes. At the Battle of Olustee in 1864 the "brave and daring" Harrison commanded a brigade and was again wounded, receiving a citation for his gallantry.[1] In late 1864 he was put in command of the post of Florence, South Carolina, and the prison there. His humane treatment of prisoners won praise from the Union troops imprisoned there. In 1865 he led a mixed brigade of Georgia infantry and reserves in the Carolinas campaign and at the Battle of Bentonville. Harrison surrendered at Greensboro, North Carolina, on April 26, 1865.

After the war Harrison settled in Alabama, where he had a distinguished career as a lawyer and politician. Harrison served as commandant of cadets at Auburn University, then worked as a lawyer and planter. Removing to Opelika, he served as state senator from 1878 to 1884 (being president of the senate the last two years) and as U.S. congressman from 1894 to 1896. After 1896 he returned to the practice of law, serving as counsel for two railroad companies, and was again elected to the state senate in 1900 and 1902. Harrison was also major general of the Alabama Division of the United Confederate Veterans. General Harrison died on July 17, 1922, at Opelika and is buried in Rosemere Cemetery.

Harrison is listed as a general in *CMH*, Wright, Heitman, Wood, *SHSP*, and

CV. Wright has him assigned to duty by General E. Kirby Smith in the Trans-Mississippi, perhaps confusing him with another Harrison (there were many). CMH cites a winter, 1864, promotion, while Henderson's *Roster of the Confederate Soldiers of Georgia, 1861–1865* cites a February, 1865, promotion.[2] Harrison uniformly signed himself and was addressed as "colonel, commanding brigade" in the OR as late as April 19, 1865. He is perhaps confused with his father, who briefly led a brigade of state troops.[3]

NOTES

1. Evans, ed., *CMH*, VII, 421.
2. Lillian Henderson, *Roster of the Confederate Soldiers of Georgia, 1861–1865* (6 vols.; rpr. Spartanburg, 1982), III, 659.
3. There were at least four other father-son general combinations—the Lees (Robert E. and his two sons George and William), the Robertsons (Jerome and Felix), the Clarks (John B., Sr. and Jr.), and the Prices (Sterling and Edwin).

MAIN SOURCES

Northern Alabama, Historical and Biographical. Birmingham, 1888.
Owen, Thomas M. *History of Alabama and Dictionary of Alabama Biography*. 4 vols. Chicago, 1921.
Robertson, James I., Jr. "The War in Words." *Civil War Times Illustrated*, XX (October, 1981), 6.

GEORGE PAUL HARRISON, SR.

George Paul Harrison, Sr., a brigadier general of Georgia state troops, was born on October 19, 1813,[1] in Effingham County, Georgia, the son of Colonel William Harrison and his wife, Mary Keller. Colonel Harrison, who commanded a company of Georgians in the War of 1812, was said to be related to President William Henry Harrison, though histories of this distinguished Virginia family fail to disclose any relationship. The young Harrison engaged in rice planting on his plantation, Montieth, situated on the Savannah River on the border of Effingham and Chatham counties. He represented Chatham County (Savannah) in the state house in 1842, 1849 to 1850, 1853 to 1854, 1857 to 1860, and 1865 to 1866. Prior to the war Harrison had risen to the rank of brigadier

Evans, *A History of Georgia*

general in the Georgia militia, taking an active interest in state military affairs. An active Democrat, General Harrison served as county delegate to the 1858 and 1860 state party conventions.

At the outbreak of the war Governor Joseph Brown of Georgia, a lifelong friend, appointed Harrison one of three brigadier generals of Georgia troops, the commission dated September 14, 1861. The governor ordered Harrison to establish a camp of instruction on the railroads near Savannah and organize incoming companies into regiments. Harrison spent the winter of 1861 training volunteers and guarding the Georgia coast. The camp, and Harrison's command, were dissolved in 1862. In 1864, under a new militia law, he was appointed colonel in charge of the First Military District; his duties included chasing down deserters and destroying whisky stills. During Sherman's March to the Sea in 1864 Harrison's "palatial home and extensive lands were pillaged."[2] While visiting Montieth in December, 1864, Harrison was taken prisoner by Union troops. Released from prison before the close of the war, he refused to take the oath of allegiance to the federal government.

After the war General Harrison removed to Savannah and again became active in public affairs. He was elected to the state legislature in 1865, served as a delegate to the state constitutional convention, was elected clerk of the City Court of Savannah and clerk of the Superior Court of Chatham County. Harrison, "earnest in purpose, courteous in demeanor,"[3] died of a heart attack on his farm near Savannah on May 14, 1888. He is buried in Laurel Grove Cemetery, Savannah. His son, George P. Harrison, Jr., was a Confederate colonel and U.S. congressman (see George Paul Harrison, Jr.).

Harrison's rank of general in Georgia's state army qualifies him to be considered a Confederate general.

NOTES

1. Robert M. Myers, ed., *The Children of Pride* (New Haven, 1972), gives Harrison an 1814 birth date. However, a newspaper article on General Harrison's funeral (in the Savannah *Morning News*, May 17, 1888) stated that an inscription on his coffin gave his age as seventy-four years, eight months at death.

2. Myers, ed., *Children of Pride*, 1544.

3. Savannah *Morning News*, May 15, 1888.

MAIN SOURCES

Northen, William J., ed. *Men of Mark in Georgia*. 6 vols. Atlanta, 1907–12.
Savannah *Morning News*, May 15, 17, 1888.

RICHARD HARRISON

Richard Harrison was born on March 3, 1821, in Jefferson County, Alabama. His father, Isham Harrison, a planter and state representative, was a descendant of the Harrison family of Virginia and the Hampton family of South Carolina. His mother, Harriet Kelly, was a sister of Alabama's U.S. Senator William Kelly. His two brothers were both Confederate generals; a third brother was a colonel. The family moved to Monroe County, Mississippi, in 1835. Harrison studied medicine at Transylvania University in Kentucky, graduating in 1843. After graduation he practiced medicine in Aberdeen, Mississippi, and was elected state senator, representing Monroe County from 1858 to 1861.

A Memorial and Biographical History of McLennan, Falls, Bell and Coryell Counties, Texas, Courtesy Virginia Meynard

In 1861 Harrison enlisted as first lieutenant of the 11th Mississippi and served as part of the Pensacola garrison. Returning to Mississippi on April 1, 1862, he joined the newly formed 43rd Mississippi as first lieutenant. On May 15, 1862, he was elected major of the 43rd, and in January, 1863, was promoted to colonel. "Grand Old Dick Harrison" led the 43rd at the Battle of Corinth and the siege of Vicksburg.[1] At the latter the 43rd manned the Confederate lines to the north of the 3rd Louisiana redan. The 43rd lost fifty-eight men in the siege, six of whom were buried by the explosion of a Union mine. Captured there with his regiment, Harrison was soon paroled, and labored ceaselessly to reconstitute his regiment with his paroled soldiers. He fought in the Atlanta campaign, the Battle of Franklin, and the Battle of Nashville. In the 1865 Carolinas campaign he led, as colonel, Adams' Mississippi brigade, which included his old regiment. Harrison was paroled at Meridian, Mississippi, as colonel on May 16, 1865.

After the war Harrison lived in Aberdeen for a year practicing medicine, then moved to McLennan County, Texas, where his brothers lived. He practiced medicine and farmed there. Harrison also became involved in politics, serving as a member of the state Democratic committee. Colonel Harrison died on November 1, 1876, in McLennan County and is buried in First Street Cemetery in Waco.

Wood, Heitman, CV, and SHSP all have Harrison listed as a general, the first saying he was appointed from Texas in 1865. Richard Harrison was never in Texas or associated with Texas during the war. It is thought that he is being confused with his brother Thomas Harrison of the 8th Texas Cavalry, who was appointed brigadier general in 1865. A family book[2] suggests he was commissioned brigadier general in 1865 while in the Carolinas. The family history has it that he was always called "general" by his family, including his two brothers. However, Harrison stated in his own pardon application that he was only a colonel.

NOTES
1. Pat Henry, "Adams' Brigade in Battle of Franklin," *CV*, XXI (1913), 76.
2. Katherine H. Sarrafian, *The Harrison Family of Texas, 1830–1966* (Waco, 1966).

MAIN SOURCES
A Memorial and Biographical History of McLennan, Falls, Bell and Coryell Counties, Texas. Chicago, 1893.
Meynard, Virginia G. *The Venturers: The Hampton, Harrison and Earle Families of Virginia, South Carolina, and Texas.* Easley, S.C., 1981.
Sarrafian, Katherine H. *The Harrison Family of Texas, 1830–1966.* Waco, 1966.

ROBERT JOHNSON HENDERSON

Robert Johnson Henderson was born on November 12, 1822, in Newton County, Georgia, the son of Isaac P. and Ruth Shepherd (Johnson) Henderson.[1] His father, a Maryland native, was a wealthy planter and state representative. Young Henderson graduated from Franklin College (later the University of Georgia) in 1843. He had a varied antebellum career as a lawyer, judge, millowner, and planter. From 1859 to 1860 Henderson served as a state representative. At the start of the war he was a wealthy planter and slaveowner in Covington, Newton County.

Atlanta *Constitution*, February 2, 1891

Henderson was not one of the first Georgians to spring to arms. However, after the first year of the war, he felt it his duty to join the army. On March 20, 1862, he was appointed colonel of the 42nd Georgia Infantry, a regiment he helped raise. He led the 42nd, part of a Georgia brigade known variously as Barton's and Stovall's, at the Battle of Champion's Hill and the siege of Vicksburg. At the latter he was captured and paroled. In the 1864 Atlanta campaign he was wounded at the Battle of Resaca. Recovering, he led the 42nd throughout the 1865 Carolinas campaign. It was said of Henderson that "he was one of the bravest soldiers Georgia ever sent out." A fellow soldier remembered him as "a strict disciplinarian . . . a fine drill master . . . was brave in battle but not rash, and was remarkably expert in managing his command on the field of battle. . . . In short, he was a superb soldier, of splendid appearance, and a magnificent horseman."[2] At the Battle of Bentonville he led Stovall's consolidated brigade as colonel, leading his tiny unit in a charge to restore the Confederate flank and winning the special commendation of the army commander.

After the war Henderson returned to Covington, finding his farm and properties in ruins. Rebuilding his life, he became again a millowner and planter in Newton County. General Henderson died at his daughter's Atlanta home on February 3, 1891, and is buried in a family cemetery in Covington.

SHSP and *CV* list him as a general. *CMH* mentions him as a general in the body of that work, but his biography is not included in *CMH*'s biographies of Georgia generals. The omission is curious, given that his general's rank clearly shows in the OR. His obituary states that he was made a general on the battlefield of Bentonville "by Gen. Joseph E. Johnston, who witnessed a desperate charge the general led."[3] If so, this indicates that his was a promotion by army, not civil, authority. Henderson himself stated (on his pardon application) that he was recommended for promotion in March, 1865, but never received his commission. At the suggestion of his divisional commander, Henderson was induced to sign his parole as brigadier general.

NOTES

1. Henderson's place of birth per William B. Williford, *The Glory of Covington* (Atlanta, 1973), 19, which follows Henderson's pardon application. However, W. L. Calhoun, *History of the 42nd Regiment, Georgia Volunteers. . . .* (Atlanta, 1900), 42, says that Henderson was born in Jasper County, the family moving to Newton County when Henderson was young.

2. Atlanta *Constitution*, February 2, 1891; Calhoun, *History of the 42nd Regiment*, 43.

3. See the Atlanta *Constitution*, February 2, 1891. It was published while Henderson lay dying.

MAIN SOURCES

Atlanta *Constitution*, February 2, 4, 1891.
Calhoun, W. L. *History of the 42nd Regiment, Georgia Volunteers . . . .* Atlanta, 1900.
Williford, William B. *The Glory of Covington*. Atlanta, 1973.

JOHN FRANKLIN HOKE

John Franklin Hoke was born on May 30, 1820, in Lincolnton, North Carolina, the son of Colonel John and Barbara (Quickle) Hoke. Colonel Hoke, a merchant and cotton factory owner, belonged to a prominent Lincoln County family of Pennsylvania German origin. One son, William, is treated later; another son, Michael, was nominated for governor; Michael's son Robert was a Confederate major general. John F. Hoke passed through local schools and graduated from the University of North Carolina in 1841. After studying law with former governor Swain and future justice Pearson, Hoke began a law practice in Lincolnton in 1843. A prominent lawyer, Hoke served from 1850 to 1856 as a states' rights Democrat in the North Carolina Senate. In 1860, as a member of the state house, Hoke publicly advocated secession. His military career began with the Mexican War. In March, 1847, he was commissioned a first lieutenant and assigned to Company G of the 12th U.S. Infantry. Promoted to captain of the 12th in June, Hoke saw action in Mexico.

Courtesy North Carolina Division of Archives and History

In 1860 Hoke was appointed adjutant general of North Carolina, with the rank of brigadier general. In the first months of the war, he organized fourteen regiments of North Carolina volunteers. On July 10, 1861, he was commissioned colonel of the 13th (later renumbered the 23rd) North Carolina Infantry. The regiment was sent to Virginia, but arrived at Manassas too late at night to take part in the First Battle of Bull Run. Hoke led the 23rd in the May 5, 1862, Battle of Williamsburg. Upon the May 10, 1862, reorganization of the regiment, Hoke (an "upright, honorable and cultivated gentleman"[1]) failed to be reelected as colonel. Suddenly without a command, he returned to Lincolnton and was promptly elected to the state senate. In the fall of 1864 Hoke was commissioned colonel of the 1st Regiment of the North Carolina Senior Reserves, a unit of overage men assigned to guard prisoners and hunt down deserters. He served in this capacity until the end of the war, mainly at Salisbury Prison in North Carolina, seeing only minor action.

After the war Hoke was again elected, as a "Conservative," to the state house. But his elective career was over after that. He concentrated on his flourishing law practice in Lincolnton, served as a trustee of his alma mater, and engaged in several business ventures and in railroad promotion. Hoke died suddenly on October 27, 1888, while viewing a political parade from the front porch of his home. He is buried in the churchyard of St. Luke's Episcopal Church in Lincolnton.

Clark's authoritative *Histories of the Several Regiments and Battalions from North Carolina in the Great War, 1861–1865* states that Hoke was commissioned brigadier general by the state of North Carolina.[2]

NOTES

1. Walter Clark, ed., *Histories of the Several Regiments and Battalions from North Carolina in the Great War, 1861–1865* (5 vols.; Raleigh, 1901), II, 202.
   2. *Ibid.*, V, 5.

MAIN SOURCES

Jordan, Weymouth T., and Louis Manarin, comps. *North Carolina Troops*. 12 vols. Raleigh, 1966–90.
Powell, William S., ed. *Dictionary of North Carolina Biography*. 4 vols. Chapel Hill, 1979–91.

WILLIAM JAMES HOKE

William James Hoke, younger brother of John Franklin Hoke (see previous sketch), was born in Lincolnton on October 5, 1825, the son of Colonel John and Barbara (Quickle) Hoke. The younger Hoke was a merchant in Lincolnton before the war. "Beloved by all who knew him," Hoke was for many years Lincoln County clerk and master of equity.[1] He was a delegate to the 1858 Democratic state convention and a leader of the anti-Holden, more conservative wing of the state Democratic party. In 1861 he was the secretary of Lincoln County's secession vote convention.

On April 25, 1861, Hoke was commissioned captain of Company K (the "Southern Stars"), 1st (Bethel) North Carolina Infantry, a six-months regiment. The 1st was sent to Virginia where on June 10, 1861, it played a key role in the engagement at Big Bethel, the first southern land victory of the war. On January 17, 1862, Hoke was commissioned colonel of the 38th North Carolina Infantry. The 38th, part of Dorsey Pender's Brigade, fought for four years with the Army of Northern Virginia. Hoke was wounded at the June 26, 1862, Battle of Mechanicsville and did not rejoin his regiment until after the Battle of Fredericksburg. At the Battle of Chancellorsville, Hoke briefly led the brigade. On the first day of the Battle of Gettysburg, Hoke was wounded in the leg. This wound disabled him for field service. In 1864 Hoke led his regiment (and occasionally Alfred Scale's brigade) at the Battles of Spotsylvania and Cold Harbor. His old wounds acting up, he was retired to the invalid corps on June 18, 1864. Hoke's performance had, evidently, left something to be desired; Pender, his immediate superior, called him "the greatest old granny." [2] In August, 1864, Hoke was assigned to command the post of Charlotte, North Carolina, which he retained till the end of the war. He was also assigned to duty as adjutant general and inspector general of reserves. On January 12, 1865, Hoke was assigned to command a brigade of three reserve regiments, composed of detailed men, and ordered to Salisbury, North Carolina, to guard that place and the Union soldiers imprisoned there.

After the war Hoke returned to Lincoln County, making a living as a merchant and serving as Lincolntown town clerk. He died suddenly in Columbia, South Carolina on October 11, 1870, and is buried in the cemetery of St. Luke's Episcopal Church, Lincolnton.

SHSP and *CV* call him a brigadier general, in command of the post of Charlotte, presumably a reference to his leading the reservist brigade in 1865. However, Clark's *Histories of the Several Regiments and Battalions from North Carolina in the Great War, 1861–1865*, a comprehensive contemporary work that lists all North Carolina militia generals, doesn't show W. J. Hoke as general. [3] It does list his brother, which suggests that the war rank of the two Hokes may have been run together by *SHSP* and *CV*. Or W. J. Hoke's staff rank of inspector general is being misinterpreted.

Notes

1. Raleigh *North Carolina Standard*, October 13, 1870.

2. William Dorsey Pender, *The General to His Lady: The Civil War Letters of William Dorsey Pender to Fanny Pender*, ed. William W. Hassler (Chapel Hill, 1965), 251.

3. Walter Clark, ed., *Histories of the Several Regiments and Battalions from North Carolina in the Great War, 1861–1865* (5 vols.; Raleigh, 1901).

Main Sources

Charlotte *Western Democrat*, October 18, 1870.

Hoke, W. J. "Sketch of the 38th Regiment N.C. Troops." *Our Living and Our Dead*, I (1874–75), 545–51.

Hoke, William J. Papers. Southern Historical Collection, University of North Carolina, Chapel Hill.

JOHN TAYLOR HUGHES

John Taylor Hughes, the son of Samuel and Nancy (Price) Hughes, was born near Versailles, Kentucky, on July 25, 1817. In 1820 the family moved near Fayette in Howard County, Missouri. Hughes graduated from Bonne Femme College in 1844 and spent the next two years teaching school. Upon the outbreak of the Mexican War Hughes enlisted as a private in Doniphan's Regiment of Missouri Mounted Volunteers. His classic book on the Mexican War, *Doniphan's Expedition*, gained him nationwide celebrity. Returning to Missouri in 1848, Hughes was variously editor of the *Clinton County News*, plantation- and slaveowner, Clinton County school superintendent, militia colonel, and was elected state representative in 1854.

State Historical Society of Missouri, Columbia

Like most Missourians, including his distant cousin Sterling Price, Hughes did not believe in immediate secession. However, the Federal capture of a brigade of Missouri militia at Camp Jackson convinced this old-line Whig and "Conditional Unionist" to join the southern ranks. Hughes was elected colonel of the 1st Regiment of the 4th Division of the Missouri State Guard. The regiment joined the guard's main body in time to participate in the Battles of Carthage and Wilson's Creek. At Wilson's Creek Hughes led seven charges up Bloody Hill and had three horses killed beneath him. At the September 17 through 20 siege of Lexington, Missouri, Hughes was slightly wounded. During the winter of 1861 Hughes unsuccessfully attempted to penetrate into northern Missouri and bring in recruits for the guard. Friend and foe alike respected his military abilities; he was remembered by fellow soldiers as "brilliant and efficient," and "a brave, masterful man, scholarly and ambitious," and by a Union foe as "the most ambitious and daring officer in Price's army."[1] In the spring of 1862 the state guard soldiers began volunteering for the regular Confederate army, and Hughes took command of a battalion of the volunteers. At the March 7 and 8, 1862, Battle of Pea Ridge, Hughes took over command of the 2nd Brigade of Confederate Volunteers upon the wounding of General William Slack. After this battle Price's troops were transferred to Mississippi. In the summer of 1862 Hughes left Mississippi and returned to Missouri to recruit soldiers for the Confederate army. On August 11, 1862, Hughes and his recruits joined other partisan bands in an attack on Independence, Missouri. Leading the attack, which ultimately resulted in the capture of the city, Hughes was shot through the right temple and instantly killed. He is buried in Woodlawn Cemetery in Independence.

The Missouri volume of CMH and Bevier's *History of the First and Second Mis-*

souri Confederate Brigades[2] state Hughes returned from Mississippi in 1862 with a brigadier general's commission. No record of any official appointment exists, but it is possible that Major General Sterling Price, who was both commander-in-chief of the Missouri State Guard and a Confederate major general, appointed Hughes an "acting" general (whether in Confederate or Missouri State Guard service is not clear). At the time of his death Hughes was popularly known as "general."[3]

NOTES

1. John N. Edwards, *Shelby and His Men* (Cincinnati, 1867), 73; William L. Webb, *Battles and Biographies of Missourians* (Kansas City, 1900), 342–45; William E. Connelley, *Doniphan's Expedition and the Conquest of New Mexico and California* (1907; rpr. Kansas City, 1967), 55. Connelley's book contains the complete text of Hughes's *Doniphan's Expedition.*

2. Evans, ed., CMH, XII, 98; R. S. Bevier, *History of the First and Second Missouri Confederate Brigades, 1861–1865* (St. Louis, 1879), 123.

3. See the Little Rock *Arkansas Gazette*, September 13, 1862.

MAIN SOURCES

Connelley, William E. *Doniphan's Expedition and the Conquest of New Mexico and California.* 1907; rpr. Kansas City, 1967.

Evans, Clement A., ed. *Confederate Military History: A Library of Confederate States History.* 1899; 17 vol. extended edition; rpr. Wilmington, N.C., 1987.

Webb, William L. *Battles and Biographies of Missourians.* Kansas City, 1900.

SIDNEY DRAKE JACKMAN

Sidney Drake Jackman was born in Jessamine County, Kentucky, on March 7, 1826, the son of Thomas and Mary (Drake) Jackman, farmers. In 1830 Jackman's family moved from Kentucky to Missouri, finally settling in Howard County. Young Jackman had a scanty education in the local schools. At first a teacher, Jackman soon abandoned that calling "for the free life of a farmer."[1] He and his young wife bought a farm in Papinville, Missouri, near the Kansas border. In the late 1850s armed bands of antislavery Kansans raided western Missouri in retaliation for the raids into Kansas of proslavery Missourians. Caught up in the border violence, Jackman helped form a "border guard" company in Bates County and was elected its lieutenant.

Courtesy Barbara Donalson Althaus Cade

A Union man at the beginning of the war, Union army depredations in western Missouri forced him into the southern ranks. Jackman organized his neighbors into a cavalry company to protect Bates County from the Kansas "jayhawker" raiders, and was elected the company's captain. Throughout 1861 and early 1862 his company sparred with Union troops in Bates County, by now well behind the Union lines. In May, 1862, Jackman led a cavalry company in the Confederate attack on Neosho, Missouri. On August 16, 1862, Jackman, now a colonel of partisans, led a regiment-sized force that helped capture the Union forces holding Lone Jack, Missouri. By late 1862 Jackman's forces were strong enough to begin cooperating with raids into Missouri by regular Confederate forces. In September, 1862, he was elected colonel of a newly raised Missouri infantry regiment, but Jackman soon resigned this post in order to recruit a regiment of Missouri cavalry. While on recruiting duty behind Union lines Jackman was shot. He hid out with his Howard County relatives while recuperating. Recovering, he resumed his recruiting activities and, with a small band of partisans, remained in Missouri. On January 11, 1863, Jackman's band raided Columbia, Missouri, in an unsuccessful attempt to release comrades from the town jail. On April 23, 1863, Jackman kidnapped Brigadier General Thomas J. Bartholow, then encamped at Glasgow, Missouri, in circumstances reminiscent of John S. Mosby's famous capture of General Stoughton. On June 1, 1863, Jackman's twenty-man band beat off an attack by picked Union cavalry; Jackman personally shot the major who led the Union forces. By May, 1864, Jackman and his men crossed over into Arkansas. He hid out in the Boston Mountains of northwest Arkansas, skirmishing with the Union army occupation forces and organizing recruits. By June he succeeded in raising a cavalry regiment that was called "Jackman's Missouri Cavalry." The regiment was attached to Brigadier General Joseph Shelby's cavalry division. In the fall of 1864 Jackman, "a stern, able and devoted soldier,"[2] commanded as colonel a brigade of Missouri cavalry (two regiments and two battalions of mostly new recruits) in Price's Raid. During the raid Jackman led the attack and capture of Glasgow, Missouri, and its Union garrison. On the first day of the Battle of Westport (October 22 and 23, 1864), Jackman led the attack of Price's army, routing the Union forces from their position. On the second day Jackman's brigade, on the Confederate left, launched a successful attack on Westport. With the collapse of the Confederate rear the attack was halted, and Jackman's brigade was hustled back to hold off the Union pursuit. At Mine Creek Jackman's troopers guarded the army's trains and thus missed the rout, though the brigade did help blunt the Union pursuit. Jackman was twice wounded during the war.

On May 16, 1865, General Kirby Smith assigned Jackman to duty as brigadier general. The assignment orders list him as colonel of Jackman's Missouri Cavalry. At this stage of the war the soldiers of the Trans-Mississippi army, hearing that Lee had surrendered and believing that the war was lost, were deserting in droves; the army soon ceased to exist.

After the surrender of the Trans-Mississippi Department Jackman gathered his family and took the road to Mexico. He left his family in Hays County, Texas, while he went ahead to gauge the prospects of settling in northern Mexico. In 1866 he rejoined his family in Hays County. Settling near Kyle, he bought a farm and became a farmer and cattle raiser. Respected in his new community, Jackman was elected representative to the Texas Legislature in 1873. In 1885, President Cleveland appointed Jackman U.S. marshal for western Texas. He served as marshal until his death, passing away on June 2, 1886, at his Hays County ranch. He is buried in Kyle Cemetery in Hays County. It was said of Jackman that "truth, honor and duty constituted his life-creed. . . . he was profoundly loyal to friends, family and country."[3]

Wright, Wood, Heitman, *SHSP*, and CV all list Jackman as a Confederate general.

NOTES

1. Austin *Daily Statesman*, June 3, 1886.
2. John N. Edwards, *Shelby and His Men* (Cincinnati, 1867), 309.
3. Austin *Daily Statesman*, June 3, 1886.

MAIN SOURCES

"Col. Sidney Jackman." *Confederate Veteran*, XIX (1911), 436.
Dallas *Morning News*, May 23, June 5, 1886.
Edwards, John N. *Noted Guerillas*. St. Louis, 1877.
Hunter, J. Marvin. *The Trail Drivers of Texas*. Nashville, 1925.
Stovall, Frances, *et al. Clear Springs and Limestone Ledges: A History of San Marcos and Hays County*. Austin, 1986.

CLAIBORNE FOX JACKSON

Claiborne Fox Jackson, the secessionist governor of Missouri, was born in Fleming County, Kentucky, on April 4, 1807, the son of Dempsey and Mary (Pickett) Jackson. The family moved to Howard County, Missouri, where both father and son went into business and prospered. The younger Jackson, a states' rights Democrat, served as state representative from 1836 to 1854. Jackson married, in succession, three daughters of the wealthy Dr. John Sappington. His brother-in-law, Meredith Marmaduke, and his nephew, Confederate Major General John S. Marmaduke, were both governors of Missouri. In 1860 Jackson, the acknowledged leader of the secessionist, anti-Benton wing of Missouri's Democratic party, was elected governor of

State Historical Society of Missouri, Columbia

Missouri. Ironically Jackson, a secessionist, was forced by intraparty squabbles to support the Unionist Democrat Stephen Douglas in the 1860 presidential election. His support of Douglas, and his cautious political nature, caused Missouri's more rabid secessionists to distrust Jackson's sincerity when he finally attempted to maneuver the state into seceding.

Before the firing on Fort Sumter in April, 1861, Governor Jackson called for a constitutional convention for the state, which would act to take Missouri out of the Union. However, the voters, including many southern sympathizers who were not yet ready to abandon the Union, instead elected a Unionist majority to the convention. Jackson then took steps to have a pro-southern brigade of state militia seize the Federal arsenal in St. Louis, to use the equipment stored there to arm the southern partisans in the state who were already organizing for war. Quick action by Union Brigadier General Nathaniel Lyon frustrated this plan; the arms were shipped to safety in Illinois, and the militia brigade was captured. The news of the Federal action, and the violence that followed the capture of the militia, galvanized Jackson and the pro-southern majority in the Missouri General Assembly. They voted to create a Missouri State Guard, under the governor's control, to hold Missouri for the Confederacy and defend it against the federal government. Quick offensive actions by General Lyon and the Union troops forced Jackson to leave Jefferson City. Cut off from the machinery of government, Jackson became a governor in exile. He fled south with a detachment of guard troops. On July 5, 1861, Jackson led his growing army to victory at the Battle of Carthage, Missouri, defeating a Union brigade that attempted to intercept his retreat. Jackson headed up a makeshift government in southern Missouri in 1861 and early 1862. However, by the spring of 1862 the Union army had driven the southern armies from Missouri. The governor was again forced to migrate, this time to Arkansas. Heading the pro-southern Missouri government in exile, he died of cancer in Little Rock on December 6, 1862. Jackson is buried in the Sappington family burial grounds in Saline County, Missouri.

Wakelyn's *Biographical Dictionary of the Confederacy*,[1] following an article on Jackson in *Cyclopedia of American Biography*,[2] mentions that Jackson entered the Confederate army as brigadier general, but was compelled to resign because of ill health. No record of Governor Jackson's appointment exists. Moreover, Jackson was exclusively a political, not military, figure.

NOTES

1. Jon L. Wakelyn, *Biographical Dictionary of the Confederacy* (Westport, Conn.), 248.
2. *Cyclopedia of American Biography* (7 vols.; New York, 1891), III, 385.

MAIN SOURCES

National Cyclopedia of American Biography. 63 vols. New York, 1892–1984.
Wakelyn, Jon L. *Biographical Dictionary of the Confederacy*. Westport, Conn., 1977.

ALEXANDER CALDWELL JONES

Alexander Caldwell Jones was born in 1830 near Moundsville in Marshall County, Virginia (now West Virginia), across the river from Ohio. His father, Garrison Jones, was a hotel owner and state representative; his mother was Martha Houston. Jones graduated from VMI in 1850, then studied law. Attracted to the new Minnesota Territory, Jones removed to St. Paul in 1852. He quickly was elected district attorney and then Ramsey County probate judge (1854 to 1858). In 1858 Jones was appointed Minnesota's adjutant general, with the rank of brigadier general. Serving two years in that post, by 1860 Jones was a dealer in farm implements in St. Paul.

Virginia Historical Society, Richmond

Jones had been living in the North seven years when Virginia seceded. He nonetheless loyally returned to his native state to fight for the South. Commissioned major of the 44th Virginia on June 14, 1861, he was not present when the 44th was routed at Rich Mountain on July 11 of that year. During the winter of

1861 Jones commanded a portion of Brigadier General Edward Johnson's forces defending Allegheny Mountain. Jones was then detached from the 44th (to the regret of Stonewall Jackson, a hard man to please, who regarded Jones as "an officer who has inspired me with great confidence"[1]) to command partisan units in northwestern Virginia. Jones was commissioned lieutenant colonel on May 1, 1862, and rejoined the 44th (part of Jackson's Valley army) in time to participate in the Seven Days' Battles. Jones suffered a serious wound at the Battle of Gaines Mill, which limited his active duty. After convalescing he was ordered to report to the Adjutant and Inspector General's Office on December 22, 1862, and later served in the Bureau of Conscription. On June 16, 1863, Jones resigned his commission in the 44th. At his own request, Jones was then transferred to the Trans-Mississippi Department. He served on the staffs of Generals Slaughter, Walker, and Magruder as inspector general and chief of staff. From being Magruder's chief of staff Jones was assigned command, as colonel, to the Eastern Division of the Western Sub-District of Texas, and then to command a brigade of Texas infantry. General Kirby Smith, department commander, requested (on March 16, 1865) that Richmond promote Jones to general of the PACS. There is no evidence that the president made the appointment. However, Jones was paroled at Brownsville, Texas, July 24, 1865, as brigadier general.

Jones fled to Mexico after the war and served in Emperor Maximilian's army until the downfall of the empire. Returning to the states, he settled in Wheeling, West Virginia, living with his wife's family. By 1869 Jones had become the managing editor of the *National Intelligencer*, a once-influential Washington newspaper that died that year. In 1880 Jones was appointed U.S. consul in Nagasaki, Japan. In 1886, he was transferred to the China embassy, serving there eleven years. General Jones died at his post in Chungking, China, on January 13, 1898.[2]

SHSP, Wood, and CV list Jones as a general. Both his parole and a July 19, 1865, Union pass show him as a Confederate brigadier. The clear implication is that General Kirby Smith, in an unrecorded order, assigned Jones to duty as a general. The assignment would have had to come after May 15, 1865, since Jones called himself a colonel in an order on that date.

NOTES

1. Kevin C. Ruffner, *44th Virginia Infantry* (Lynchburg, Va., 1987), 92.
2. General Jones had been relieved of his embassy in October, 1897, but his successor did not arrive in Chungking until two days after his death.

MAIN SOURCES

Jones, Alexander C. Letters. Archives, Virginia Military Institute, Lexington.
Jones, Alexander C. Papers. Virginia Historical Society, Richmond.
Ruffner, Kevin C. *44th Virginia Infantry*. Lynchburg, Va., 1987.

Thomas Marshall Jones

Thomas Marshall Jones was born in Elizabeth City County, Virginia, on March 11, 1832, the son of John and Mary (Booker) Jones. His father, a wealthy farmer, was descended from Richard Jones, who immigrated to Virginia from Wales in 1620. The younger Jones attended Hampton Academy near his home before receiving an appointment to the United States Military Academy. He graduated in 1853, ranking forty-seventh in a class of fifty-two, and was commissioned lieutenant in the 8th Infantry. First posted in New York City, in a short while he was ordered to Ringgold Barracks, Texas. By 1861 Jones was acting as aide-de-camp to Major General David Twiggs, U.S. army commander in Texas.

Special Collections, United States Military Academy Library

On February 28, 1861, Jones resigned from the U.S. Army in order to enter Confederate service. On April 4, 1861, Jones was commissioned captain in the Confederate regular army and ordered to Pensacola, Florida. Major General Braxton Bragg, who led the Confederate forces there, made Jones his chief of commissary. For the next eight months Jones hunted up food and forage for Bragg's army. The only action he saw was at the November 22 and 23, 1861, bombardment of Fort McRae near Pensacola. Jones took charge of the fort when its commander was wounded and "won praise from all" for his "gallantry."[1] On January 14, 1862, he was commissioned colonel of the 27th Mississippi Infantry, a regiment in the Pensacola garrison. In the spring of 1862 General Bragg and most of the Pensacola garrison were ordered to Corinth, Mississippi, to reinforce General Albert Sidney Johnston's army. On March 9, 1862, Brigadier General Samuel Jones, Bragg's successor, put Jones in charge of the thousand troops left behind in Pensacola. On April 21, 1862, Bragg assigned Jones to duty as acting brigadier general. When Bragg's forces left for Corinth it was assumed that the reduced garrison left in Pensacola was inadequate to hold that city, and that the city would have to be evacuated. The task of evacuation was left to Jones. In the next two months the city was quietly stripped of its military stores. To provide the appearance of a substantial defense, new, mostly unarmed units were sent to Pensacola to increase Jones's command to 3,500 men. On the evening of May 9, 1862, Jones ordered his troops to burn the remaining military installations and march north. His actions in the evacuation were much criticized—the navy complained he burned naval supplies that could have been saved—but his superior praised him as "an officer of discretion and capacity."[2] The 27th rejoined General Bragg in Mississippi, where Jones reverted to his actual rank of colonel. He led a brigade of Mississippi regiments in Bragg's Kentucky campaign and the October 8, 1862, Battle of Perryville. At the December 31, 1862–January 2, 1863 Battle of Stone's River, Brigadier General J. Patton Anderson led the brigade, and Jones returned to his regiment. This battle was Jones's last field action. The night prior to the battle, Jones "had gone to the rear, complaining of being unwell, and had not returned during the action." The next day, while returning to the field from his sick bed, Jones was "slightly" wounded and again retired. His lieutenant colonel was killed that day leading the 27th. Reading between the lines of General Anderson's report of the battle, it is clear that Anderson was highly critical of Jones's conduct.[3] Angry that he had never been formally appointed brigadier general, while others junior to him in rank were being promoted, Jones resigned his colonel's commission on February 27, 1863. Immediately, Major General W. H. C. Whiting, an old army buddy who now commanded the Confederate defenses of Wilmington, North Carolina, requested that Jones be assigned to his command. But Jones was ill and unfit for immediate duty, and furloughed to Warrenton, North Carolina, where his family had fled. Recovering, Colonel Jones assumed command of Fort Caswell near Wilmington in 1863 and 1864. In the latter year he resigned his command because of failing health.

After the war the impoverished Jones settled in Fauquier County, Virginia, and bought a farm. Meeting with little success, Jones turned to the field of education, "and in this work he discovered his talent. He was a born teacher."[4] From 1874 to 1877 he was a professor of agriculture and commandant of cadets at Maryland Agricultural College, a forerunner of the University of Maryland. Returning to Virginia, he was appointed superintendent of schools in Warrenton. During the first Cleveland administration the president appointed Jones an Indian agent for the Shoshone and northern Arapahoe tribes in the Wyoming Territory. During Cleveland's second administration Jones served as superintendent of the Indian school at Santa Fe, New Mexico. Between 1898 and 1908 he worked at the Cheyenne and Arapahoe Agency in Oklahoma. In 1908 he and his family relocated to Prescott, Arizona. General Jones died on March 31, 1913, in Prescott, and is buried in that city's Masonic Cemetery.

SHSP, Cullum, and Heitman list Jones as a general. However, his substantive rank was colonel, being a general in the Army of Pensacola only by military appointment.

NOTES

1. Thomas H. Watts to Whom It May Concern, February 17, 1863, in Compiled Service Records of General and Staff Officers, Colonel Thomas Marshall Jones, National Archives.

2. OR, VI, 684.

3. OR, Vol. XX, Pt. 1, p. 764.

4. So valued was Jones as a teacher that Senator Daniel of Virginia, when asked to urge his appointment as an Indian agent, exclaimed with impatience, "Why does Tom Jones go to teach Indians? We need him here in Virginia." See United States Military Academy, Annual Reunion of the Association of Graduates (N.p., 1913), 110.

Biographical Sketches

Main Sources

Jarman, R. A. "Inventory and History Co. K 27th Miss. Infantry CSA." *Chickasaw Times Past*,
III (1985), 214–19; IV (1985), 19–24.
United States Military Academy. *Annual Reunion of the Association of Graduates.* N.p., 1913.

Wilburn Hill King

Wilburn Hill King was born on June 10, 1839, in Cul-
lodenville, Georgia, the son of Alexander and Mary
(Douglas) King. He studied both law and medicine in
Americus, Georgia. In 1860 he settled in Cass County,
Texas.

The outbreak of the war found King engaged in business in Warrensburg, Missouri. He immediately enlisted
in the Missouri State Guard and was elected lieutenant
of the "Johnson Guards." The guards entered service as
Company E of the 3rd (Price's) Infantry Regiment. As
captain King led the guards at the Battles of Carthage
and Wilson's Creek and was wounded in the latter

Archives Division, Texas State Library

battle. Upon being discharged from the guards King re-
turned to Texas and enlisted as a private in the 18th Texas Infantry. On May 13, 1862,
he was elected major of the 18th; promotions to lieutenant colonel (February 25,
1863) and colonel (to rank from August 10, 1863) followed. The 18th was attached
to McCullough's (later John G. Walker's) Texas infantry division. In the fall of 1863
the 18th was temporarily attached to Thomas Green's cavalry division, at that time
fighting in Louisiana. In his first action as colonel, at the November 3, 1863, Battle of
Bayou Bourbeau, King led his regiment, "with undaunted firmness," in a successful attack on a Union army detachment.[1] By 1864 the 18th rejoined Walker's division.
At the April 8, 1864, Battle of Mansfield, Walker's division helped smash three Union
divisions in a whirlwind assault. King was severely wounded at the end of the attack
and spent several months recuperating. On April 16, 1864, General E. Kirby Smith
assigned King to duty as brigadier general, to date from April 8. The intention was
that King would take command of the Texas brigade formerly commanded by Camille
Polignac. However, because of his Mansfield wound King was unable to assume that
command until October, 1864. In February, 1865, he was assigned to command the
newly formed 4th Brigade in Walker's old division. By the end of the war King commanded that division.

King fled to Mexico upon the collapse of the Confederacy. He briefly operated a sugar plantation in Central America, then returned to Texas and practiced law in Jefferson. Moving to Sulphur Springs in Hopkins County about 1875, he was mayor of that town, a state representative (1878 to 1881), and adjutant general of Texas (1881 to 1891). After 1891 General King retired to his Sulphur Springs home and devoted himself to the affairs of the Masonic order. General King died on December 12, 1910, in Sulphur Springs and is buried in Oakwood Cemetery in Corsicana.

Wood, Heitman, *CMH, SHSP,* and CV all list King as a general.

NOTE

1. William C. Davis, ed., *The Confederate General* (6 vols.; Harrisburg, Pa., 1991–92), VI, 187.

MAIN SOURCES

King, W. H. "Early Experiences in Missouri." *Confederate Veteran,* XVII (1909), 502.
L. M. M. [pseud.] "Service of Brig. Gen. W. H. King." *Confederate Veteran,* XVI (1908), 395.
Wheeler, L. T. "Gen. Wilbur Hill King." *Confederate Veteran,* XIX (1911), 172.

LEVIN MAJOR LEWIS

Levin Major Lewis was born in Baltimore, Maryland, on January 6, 1832, the son of John Kendall and Mary (Jones) Lewis. His father, of Welsh descent, belonged to a wealthy family of Dorchester County planters. His father died when Lewis was young; he was raised by an uncle at Vienna in Dorchester County, Maryland. Lewis attended school in Washington, D.C., and later was a cadet of the Maryland Military Academy. Lewis then attended Wesleyan University in Middletown, Connecticut, leaving in his sophomore year to study law. Lewis moved to Liberty in Clay County, Missouri, around 1854 and briefly practiced law there, but he soon abandoned that calling for the ministry.

Confederate Veteran, XV (1907)

He served as a Methodist minister in Liberty and in Missouri City. From 1856 to 1859 Lewis was the principal of Plattsburg College in Plattsburg.

At the outbreak of the war Reverend Lewis organized the "Washington Guards" and was elected its captain. In April, 1861, he was elected colonel of the 3rd Cavalry Regiment of the 5th Division of the Missouri State Guard. He served twelve months in the guard, until his term of enlistment was up, seeing little action. On June 18, 1862, he was elected captain of Company A of the 7th Missouri Infantry, a Confederate army unit being recruited behind Union lines in Missouri. In an August 16, 1862, attack on Lone Jack, Missouri, Lewis was wounded four times. The regiment broke up that fall. Lewis then became major of another 7th Missouri Infantry (later redesignated the 16th). The 7th fought at the December 7, 1862, Battle of Prairie Grove. During that winter the 7th lost its commanding officer, and Lewis (a lieutenant colonel from December 4, 1862) was promoted to colonel on March 24, 1863. In his first action as regimental commander Lewis led the 7th in an assault on Helena, Arkansas, on July 4, 1863. In the assault he was disabled by a shell fragment and captured. Imprisoned at Johnson's Island, Ohio, for a year, Lewis finally was exchanged in September, 1864, and traveled to Richmond. Governor Thomas Reynolds of Missouri, who was impressed by Lewis' energy and common sense, and by his support for President Davis, offered to appoint Lewis to the Confederate Senate. After talking it over with Missouri Congressmen Clark and Conrow, Lewis decided his duty lay with the army and returned to his regiment. On May 16, 1865, General E. Kirby Smith assigned Lewis to duty as brigadier general so that Lewis could command a Missouri infantry brigade with proper rank. He had only ten days to enjoy his hard-won rank. Although Lewis vehemently opposed the move and desired to continue fighting, the Trans-Mississippi Department surrendered on May 26, 1865.

After the war General Lewis resumed his Methodist ministry, serving in Shreveport, Louisiana; Galveston, Texas; and St. Louis. He was also active as an educator, serving as president of Arcadia Female College in Missouri; president of Arkansas Female College; professor of English at Texas A&M; and president of Marvin College in Waxahachie, Texas. In 1884 Lewis was selected to be pastor of the First Methodist Church in Dallas. He died in Los Angeles, California, where he had traveled for health reasons, on May 28, 1886, and is buried in Greenwood Cemetery, Dallas. It was said of Lewis that "he was popular and attractive, humorous and magnetic. He never became wealthy from his own financial skill; nor would he remain wealthy if it were thrust upon him. . . . He was a true orator . . . [and] a ripe scholar."[1]

Wright, Wood, and CV call Lewis a general.

NOTE

1. Dallas Morning News, May 29, 1886. The funeral of General Lewis was said to be the largest ever witnessed in Dallas.

MAIN SOURCES

Cassell, T. W. "Gen. Levin M. Lewis." Confederate Veteran, XV (1907), 346–47.
Castel, Albert. General Sterling Price and the Civil War in the West. Baton Rouge, 1968.

Dallas *Morning News*, May 29, 31, June 2, 4, 1886.
Speer, William S., ed. *The Encyclopedia of the New West*. Marshall, Tex., 1881.

PHILIP NOLAND LUCKETT

Philip Noland Luckett was born in Augusta County, Virginia, in 1824, the son of Otho Holland Williams and Elizabeth (Graham) Luckett. The Lucketts were an old Virginia-Maryland planter family, many of whom served in the U.S. Army. The elder Luckett, a soldier in the War of 1812, moved to Chillicothe, Ohio, by 1830 and became the county recorder. From that state in 1841 Philip Luckett was appointed to the United States Military Academy, but left West Point before graduating. In 1847 he emigrated to Texas and settled in Corpus Christi. Having studied medicine, he established a medical practice in that town. In 1850 Luckett served as surgeon to the Texas Ranger companies in south Texas.

In January, 1861, the voters of Webb and Nueces counties elected Luckett ("a handsome man . . . well informed and agreeable, but most bitter against the Yankees"[1]) a delegate to the state secession convention, where he supported the secession of Texas. On February 4, 1861, the convention appointed Luckett one of three commissioners to negotiate with U.S. military authorities for the surrender of Federal forces in Texas. After that mission was successfully accomplished Luckett briefly served as quartermaster and commissary general of Texas. In the fall of 1861 Luckett formed the 3rd Texas Infantry Regiment at Brownsville, Texas, and on September 4, 1861, he was commissioned its colonel. Luckett commanded the District of the Lower Rio Grande from December, 1861, through 1862, making his headquarters at Fort Brown. In the summer of 1863 the 3rd was transferred to Galveston. Sometime between June 17 and 25 in 1863, Colonel Luckett was made "Acting Brigadier General" (probably by District of Texas Commander General Magruder) and assigned to temporarily command the Eastern Sub-District of Texas in the absence of its regular commander. Luckett led a brigade-sized force guarding the Houston-Galveston area. Upon the return of the district's regular commander, Brigadier General William Scurry, Luckett returned to his regiment.[2] In April, 1864, the 3rd was attached to Walker's Texas Division. Luckett led the 3rd at the Battle of Jenkins' Ferry on April 30, 1864. After the brigade commander was killed in that battle, Luckett temporarily took over the brigade, but failed to win promotion to permanent brigade command. Luckett spent the last months of the war detached from the 3rd, as a member of the military court inquiring into the conduct of Price's Missouri Raid.

After the war Luckett, like many Trans-Mississippi Confederate leaders, fled to Mexico. Returning to Texas soon thereafter, Luckett was arrested and imprisoned at Fort Jackson, Louisiana. Finally pardoned some months later, Luckett remained in New Orleans. His ever-delicate health shattered, he was unable to engage in business. Luckett died in New Orleans of bronchial disease on May 21, 1869, and is buried in Spring Grove Cemetery, Cincinnati, Ohio.

Luckett does not appear on any of the postwar lists of Confederate generals. The omission is curious, given that his status as "acting" brigadier general is in the OR and that the same status was sufficient to get other officers listed.[3] Perhaps his service in an obscure theater and his death soon after the war caused Luckett to be forgotten. General Magruder, for one, thought highly of Luckett's abilities; in 1863 he recommended that Luckett be promoted to brigadier general of the PACS, calling him "an officer of talent. . . . [who] will make a good general."[4]

Notes

1. Arthur J. L. Fremantle, *Three Months in the Southern States: April–June, 1863* (New York, 1864), 13.

2. Luckett's regiment, which included many German-Americans, mutinied at Galveston on August 11, 1863. It was thought by many at the time that disaffection was the cause of the mutiny, but the real reason seems to have been lack of rations. Even as early as 1863 the Confederacy had trouble supplying a garrison unit in an urban area with open communications to the interior of an agricultural state as yet untouched by war. The mutiny could not have helped Luckett's chances for promotion.

3. See, for example, OR, Vol. XXVI, Pt. 2, p. 100.

4. *Ibid.*, 58.

Main Sources

New Orleans *Daily Picayune*, May 22, 1869.

Newman, Harry W. *The Lucketts of Portobacco*. Washington, D.C., 1938.

Webb, Walter P., and Eldon S. Branda, eds. *Handbook of Texas*. 3 vols. Austin, 1952–76.

HINCHIE PARHAM MABRY

Hinchie Parham Mabry was born at Laurel Hill in Carroll County, Georgia, on October 27, 1829, the son of Hinchie Parham and Linnie (Williams) Mabry.[1] His father, a native of North Carolina, was a veteran of the War of 1812. Mabry attended the University of Tennessee from 1849 to 1850, but had to leave school due to lack of funds. In 1851 Mabry moved to Jefferson, Texas, and became a merchant. He practiced law and was a state representative from 1856 to 1861.

Although an opponent of secession, Mabry raised the "Dead Shot Rangers," later Company B of the 3rd Texas Cavalry. He was elected captain of the rangers on June 13, 1861. The 3rd rode to Missouri, where on August 10, 1861, Mabry fought at the Battle of Wilson's Creek. In the fall of that year, during a scouting

Massachusetts Commandery, Military Order of the Loyal Legion and the U.S. Army Military History Institute

expedition in Missouri, Mabry was shot through the arm. Although he recovered from his wounds in time to lead his company at the March 6 and 7, 1862, Battle of Pea Ridge, he bore a crippled arm and hand the rest of his life. The 3rd was transferred to Mississippi in April, 1862. On May 8, 1862, upon the regiment's reorganization, Mabry was elected lieutenant colonel. At the September 19, 1862, Battle of Iuka, Mabry was severely wounded and captured.[2] After being exchanged in October, 1862, he was promoted to full colonel. Still suffering from his Iuka wound, Mabry returned to Texas to recuperate. In the summer of 1863 he rejoined the 3rd and was given temporary command of Brigadier General John W. Whitfield's brigade of Texas cavalry. During 1864 and 1865, Mabry led a Mississippi cavalry brigade in actions throughout northern and central Mississippi. Praised for being absolutely fearless and a strong disciplinarian, he was repeatedly recommended by his superiors for promotion. Mabry's most noted exploit was his cavalry's April, 1864, capture, near Yazoo City, Mississippi, of the Union gunboat *Petrel*. Mabry commanded a brigade in Lieutenant General Nathan B. Forrest's cavalry corps until the Army of Tennessee's 1864 invasion of Tennessee, when he was left behind to guard the army's line of supply. In March, 1865, Mabry was ordered to Louisiana to help conduct Trans-Mississippi troops to the east side of the Mississippi. On June 22, 1865, at Shreveport, Louisiana, he was paroled.

Returning to Jefferson, Mabry practiced law and was elected a judge. In 1866 he was elected delegate to the state constitutional convention. Mabry was also, less honorably, a leader in the local Ku Klux Klan affiliate (the "Knights of the Rising Sun") during Reconstruction. After one particularly notorious lynching, Mabry had to flee to Canada to escape prosecution. He relocated to Fort Worth in 1879, where he resided the rest of his life. Mabry died of an accidental pistol wound to the foot on March 21, 1884, in Sherman, Texas, and is buried in Oakwood Cemetery in Jefferson.

Wood, Heitman, *SHSP*, and *CV* list Mabry as a general. The first says he was appointed brigadier general from Texas in March, 1862. Wright's *Texas in the War, 1861–1865* suggests that he was promoted by General E. Kirby Smith, the Trans-Mississippi Department commander, in 1864.[3] It is a matter of record that Mabry was not in the Trans-Mississippi in 1864, and that he signed himself as colonel, commanding brigade, as late as January 6, 1865. It is possible, however, that Mabry received an otherwise unrecorded Kirby Smith promotion to general in the last days of the war.

NOTES

1. Though the family was of North Carolina origin, contemporary accounts, plus Mabry's own 1880 census return (Census of 1880, Texas, Tarrant County, Microfilm ED 90, Sheet 5), confirm a Georgia birthplace.

2. While Mabry was lying wounded, his captors handed him a parole paper which mentioned the "so-called Confederate states." Mabry refused to accede to the offending language and only signed when the words "so-called" were erased. It was said of him that "Gen. Mabry was a man of a high sense of honor, and firm as the Rock of Gibraltar." Sidney S. Johnson, *Texans Who Wore the Gray* (Tyler, Tex., 1907), 233.

3. Marcus J. Wright, *Texas in the War, 1861–1865*, ed. Harold B. Simpson (Hillsboro, 1965), 86.

MAIN SOURCES

Barron, Samuel B. *The Lone Star Defenders*. 1908; rpr. Washington, D.C., 1983.
Battey, F. A. & Co. *Biographical Souvenir of the State of Texas*. Chicago, 1889.
Rose, Victor. *Ross' Texas Brigade*. Louisville, 1881.
Speer, William S., ed. *The Encyclopedia of the New West*. Marshall, Tex., 1881.

ROBERT PLUNKET MACLAY

Robert Plunket Maclay was born at Armagh in Mifflin County, Pennsylvania, on February 19, 1820, the son of Samuel Plunket and Elizabeth (Johnston) Maclay.[1] Of a prominent Pennsylvania family, his grandfather and granduncle were U.S. senators; an uncle was a U.S. congressman. After early education at Lewiston Academy, he entered West Point in 1836. At graduation in 1840 he ranked thirty-second in a class of forty-two. Maclay joined the 8th Infantry as a second lieutenant and fought in the Seminole War. During the Mexican War he was an officer in General Zachary Taylor's army and was wounded in the Battle of Resaca de la Palma. Sent home to organize new recruits, Maclay rejoined the army in time to participate in the defense of Puebla.

Special Collections, United States Military Academy Library

In 1849 he was promoted to captain. For the next eleven years he was stationed at various army posts in Texas, including a stint as commandant of Fort Inge. In 1853 he married Virginia Medora Nutt (she died in 1856), whose family had large land holdings in both Louisiana and Mississippi. Maclay resigned from the army, effective December 31, 1860, in order to manage his newly acquired Louisiana plantations.

Although he was born in the North and had numerous relatives in the Union army Maclay's sympathies were with the South, with his Louisiana neighbors and in-laws. Like many of his neighbors, he accepted an officer's commission in the state militia. On December 16, 1861, he was appointed captain of Company C of the Pointe Coupee Militia Regiment. On March 1, 1862, he was appointed major and inspector general of the 6th Militia Brigade, a unit commanded by Pointe Coupee planter Charles N. Rowley. It was not until October 21, 1862, when Union naval forces began to raid Pointe Coupee Parish, that Maclay applied for service with the Confederate army. On October 31, 1862, he was appointed major of artillery and ordered to report to Lieutenant General Theophilus H. Holmes, new head of the Trans-Mississippi Department. On January 2, 1863, Holmes assigned Maclay to the staff of Major General John G. Walker, who had just taken command of a division of Texas infantry encamped in Arkansas. Maclay became Walker's assistant adjutant general and inspector general, and eventually chief of staff of the division. Throughout 1863 and 1864 the division fought in Louisiana and Arkansas, including the 1863 attack on Milliken's Bend and the 1864 Red River campaign. At the April 30, 1864, Battle of Jenkins' Ferry, Arkansas, all three brigade commanders of Walker's division were wounded, two mortally. On May 13, 1864, General Edmund Kirby Smith, who had succeeded Holmes as commander of the Trans-

Mississippi Department, assigned Major Maclay to duty as brigadier general (to rank from April 30, 1864) and put him in command of the 1st (Waul's) Brigade of Walker's division. In a later reorganization Maclay was assigned to command Brigadier General Horace Randal's old brigade. The appointments caused "very great dissatisfaction" within the division. The problem was not Maclay's lack of competence. A surgeon in Randal's brigade recorded in his letters that Maclay was "a very nice gentleman," and that he "has so far given great satisfaction to the officers and men in his brigade."[2] But it was unusual and controversial for a divisional staff major to be promoted over the heads of colonels to command a brigade. In addition, the legality of Kirby Smith's assignment to duty was open to question. By October, 1864, Smith was considering transferring another general to replace Maclay. In order to have time to sort things out, on January 31, 1865, Kirby Smith gave Maclay a sixty-day leave of absence. Maclay does not appear to have ever rejoined his brigade.

After the war he was a planter in Pointe Coupee Parish, Louisiana, and in Mississippi. His home was near New Roads, Louisiana, where he farmed and was active in the local Episcopal church. General Maclay, "a noble Christian gentleman," died on May 20, 1903, at Levy Plantation, Pointe Coupee Parish, in the home of his daughter.[3] He is buried near Fordoche, Louisiana.[4]

SHSP, Heitman, Wright, CV, and Cullum all list Maclay as a general.

NOTES

1. Date of birth furnished by General Maclay's great-granddaughter, Mrs. Cheri Caliway of Shreveport, Louisiana, from family records in her possession.

2. OR, Vol. XLI, Pt. 4, p. 1018; John Q. Anderson, ed., A Texas Surgeon in the C.S.A. (Tuscaloosa, 1957), 100, 103.

3. New Orleans Daily Picayune, May 24, 1903.

4. In 1900 General Maclay sold his plantation near New Roads. His second wife owned a plantation north of Fordoche which, on her death in 1902, descended to the general's daughter and nephew. The author believes that Maclay is buried on this plantation in an unmarked grave, along with his nephew and son-in-law.

MAIN SOURCES

Blessington, Joseph P. Campaigns of Walker's Texas Division. New York, 1875.
Maclay, Edgar S. The Maclays of Lurgan. Brooklyn, 1889.
New Orleans Daily Picayune, May 24, 1903.
United States Military Academy. Annual Reunion of the Association of Graduates. N.p., 1903.

JOHN F. MARSHALL

John F. Marshall was born in Virginia (probably Charlotte County) in 1823.[1] As a young man he moved to
Mississippi, and quickly rose to public prominence. At
the age of twenty-one he became the assistant editor
of the Jackson *Southern Reformer,* but left after a year
because of ill health. During the Polk administration
he was employed as an auditor for the Treasury Department. Returning to Jackson in 1849, Marshall
bought a half interest in the Jackson *Mississippean* and
edited that paper for two years. Active in Democratic
party politics, Marshall served as secretary of the 1845
Democratic state convention and was appointed state
printer in 1849. Moving to Austin, Texas, in 1854, he

Courtesy Bruce Marshall

took over the editorship of the Austin *State Gazette* and became the most influential editor in Texas. An ardent and voluble secessionist, he was instrumental in
preparing Texas public opinion to accept disunion. In 1858 Marshall was elected
chairman of the Texas Democratic party.

Marshall returned to Mississippi in early 1861 to be with his ailing wife, and thus
missed participating in the Texas state secession for which he had so long labored.
On October 2, 1861, President Davis, an old friend, appointed him lieutenant
colonel of the 4th Texas Infantry, a regiment whose colonel was future General
John Bell Hood. Upon Hood's promotion to brigade command (March 3, 1862),
Marshall was promoted to colonel of the 4th. According to an old friend, the intellectual Marshall, while "esteemed as a brave man, and admired as an eminent
civilian, an able editor," failed to come "up to the standard as a military man" (even
in those early days of the war)—so much so that a petition was circulated through
the regiment demanding his immediate resignation. Some in the regiment thought
his appointment smacked of political favoritism; others objected to his total lack
of military experience and his partial deafness.[2] Marshall's son-in-law, the son of
Confederate Senator W. S. Oldham, remembered Marshall's "scholarly attainments,
his erudition and his great mental endowments"—qualities that would make him
a good editor, but which would perhaps be lost on rough Texas privates.[3] Colonel
Marshall led the 4th at the Battles of Eltham's Landing and Seven Pines. At the
Battle of Gaines Mill on June 27, 1862, the Texas brigade broke the Union line and
rescued the Confederate army from impending defeat, but at a sad cost. The 4th
Texas lost fifty percent of its men and all three of its field officers charging
through a hailstorm of bullets. Among those killed was Marshall, shot from his
horse while heroically leading the charge. He is buried in Hollywood Cemetery
in Richmond.

Heitman, *SHSP*, and *CV* all list Marshall as a general. While his troops believed the promotion was imminent, there is no evidence that such a promotion had actually been made. Marshall was occasionally called (or rather miscalled) "general" before the war; perhaps the authorities misconstrued the prewar designation for the wartime rank.[4]

NOTES

1. Marshall's year of birth has been variously given as 1812 (Lynda Crist *et al.*, eds., *The Papers of Jefferson Davis* [7 vols.; Baton Rouge, 1983–91], II, 291) and 1826 (per an article by W. S. Oldham, Marshall's son-in-law, "Colonel John Marshall," *Southwestern Historical Quarterly*, XX [1916–17], 132–38). The 1823 date based on Marshall's 1860 census return (Census of 1860, Texas, Travis County: Family 735, Microfilm) and extensive correspondence with his great-grandson (Bruce Marshall of Austin, Texas) is adopted as the most authoritative and the one that best corresponds with his life's chronology. Marshall's origins were shrouded in mystery. Evidently, not even his own children knew who his parents were.

2. Mary Lasswell, ed., *Rags and Hope: The Recollections of Val C. Giles* (New York, 1961), 42–43; Larry J. Gage, "The Texas Road to Secession and War: John Marshall and the Texas State Gazette, 1860–1861," *Southwestern Historical Quarterly*, LXII (1958–59), 195–96. See also J. B. Polley, *Hood's Texas Brigade: Its Marches, Its Battles, Its Achievements* (New York, 1910), 14, 46.

3. Oldham, "Colonel John Marshall," 132.

4. Marshall was often labeled "major" (and at least once "general") before the war, but this does not mean he had military experience. All editors of antebellum newspapers seemed to be called "captain," "major," "colonel," or "general." For a jaundiced but authoritative look at United States military titles, see John Hope Franklin, *The Militant South* (Cambridge, Mass., 1956), 190–92.

MAIN SOURCES

Gage, Larry J. "The Texas Road to Secession and War: John Marshall and the Texas State Gazette, 1860–1861." *Southwestern Historical Quarterly*, LXII (1958–59), 191–226.
Marshall, Bruce. "Destiny at Gaines Mill." *Civil War*, X (March–April, 1992), 9–12.
Oldham, W. S. "Colonel John Marshall." *Southwestern Historical Quarterly*, XX (1916–17), 132–38.

John Donelson Martin

John Donelson Martin was born in Davidson County, Tennessee, on August 18, 1830, the son of James Glasgow and Catherine (Donelson) Martin.[1] His father was a wealthy Nashville merchant, nephew and intimate of President Andrew Jackson; various other Donelson relatives held distinguished positions in society and government. At the age of sixteen the younger Martin fought in the Mexican War as a private in Company D of the 3rd Tennessee Volunteers. Returning home, Martin attended the University of Pennsylvania, graduating in 1852 with a degree in medicine. He settled in Memphis and became a wealthy and prominent physician, surgeon at Memphis Hospital,

Courtesy Ann Martin Jennings

and professor at Memphis Medical College. In 1858 Martin was appointed president of the Memphis Board of Health. In 1857 he married into a prominent north Mississippi family and two years later retired from medicine to manage his Mississippi plantations.

Doctor Martin entered the war as the captain of the "Hickory Rifles," Company E of the 154th Tennessee. In May, 1861, Martin was elected major of the 154th. In July, 1861, President Davis, who had received reports praising Martin's abilities and was knowledgeable of the influence of Martin's family, authorized him to raise a regiment of infantry. Within a month the 25th Mississippi Infantry (also known as the 1st Mississippi Valley—later renamed the 2nd Confederate—a unit with companies from Tennessee and Mississippi) was organized. Martin was commissioned colonel of the 25th on January 28, 1862, to rank from August 10, 1861. He commanded a two-regiment brigade at Columbus, Kentucky, in 1861 and led his regiment at the Battle of Belmont. At Shiloh Martin took command of Brigadier General John S. Bowen's brigade upon the latter's wounding; his leadership of that brigade was so outstanding that he was recommended for promotion. The 25th/2nd was disbanded on May 8, 1862, upon the expiration of the soldiers' terms of enlistment. Martin, now without a regiment, was assigned to command the post of Meridian, Mississippi. That August President Davis placed Martin, "who possessed rare talents and untiring energy," in command of the 4th Brigade of the 1st Division, Army of the West.[2] Martin's four regiments of Mississippi and Alabama troops were heavily engaged at the Battle of Iuka, supporting the Confederate attack. On the first day of the Battle of Corinth on October 3, 1862, Colonel Martin, whose "gallant bearing . . . had won for him a place in the heart of every Mississippean," was mortally wounded leading a charge against the outer line of the Union works.[3] Originally buried in Mississippi, his remains were reinterred in 1874 in Elmwood Cemetery, Memphis.

CV has Martin appointed brigadier general from Mississippi in 1865, three years after his death. He is also called a general in *SHSP*, perhaps based on Union officers' reports of the Battle of Corinth that, quoting newspapers and prisoners, call him general. On April 29, 1862, Major General William J. Hardee promoted Martin to the rank of acting brigadier general.[4] Major General Sterling Price's report of the battle, however, makes it clear that he died a colonel.[5]

NOTES

1. The photo of General John D. Martin has long been misidentified as a photo of General James D. Martin of North Carolina, or as General Edward D. Tracy of Alabama. See, for example, William C. Davis, ed., *The Confederate General* (6 vols; Harrisburg, Pa., 1991–92), VI, 56; Ezra Warner, *Generals in Gray* (Baton Rouge, 1959), 213.

2. Memphis *Daily Appeal*, November 4, 1862.

3. *OR*, Vol. XVII, Pt. 1, p. 386.

4. Telegram in possession of John D. Martin III, Memphis, Tennessee, descendant of General Martin.

5. *OR*, Vol. XVII, Pt. 1, p. 386.

MAIN SOURCES

Law, J. G. "Diary of a Confederate Soldier." *Southern Historical Society Papers*, X (1882), 378–81.
Memphis *Appeal*, November 4, 1862.

JOHN DAVID McADOO

John David McAdoo was born in Anderson County, Tennessee, on April 4, 1824, the son of John and Mary Ann (Gibbs) McAdoo. A brother was a prominent Tennessee politician; his nephew William Gibbs McAdoo was secretary of the treasury in the Wilson administration. McAdoo attended the University of Tennessee from 1846 to 1848. In 1852 he was admitted to the Tennessee bar. McAdoo migrated to Texas in 1854, finally settling in Washington County. There he operated an extensive plantation and practiced law. In 1860 McAdoo ran (unsuccessfully) for state attorney general on the Constitutional Union (old-line Whig) party ticket.

Archives Division, Texas State Library

McAdoo's first war service was as a private in the 20th Texas Infantry. The 20th, organized in the spring of 1862, was a garrison regiment that guarded the Texas coast throughout the war. McAdoo does not appear to have risen above the rank of lieutenant and adjutant (promoted June 11, 1862) in the Confederate army. By 1863 McAdoo had transferred to state service, as lieutenant colonel and assistant adjutant general of state troops, with additional duties as chief inspector general. McAdoo was relieved as adjutant general, at his own request, on January 12, 1864. The following March Governor Murrah appointed him brigadier general of the 6th District of the Texas State Troops. On June 20, 1864, he was assigned to the command of the 3rd Frontier District in southwestern Texas, with special responsibilities for guarding the frontier against Indian raids. The area was overrun with outlaw gangs, deserters from the Confederate army, and roving bands of Indians. Under McAdoo's direction, his scattered companies of state troops restored order to the region. He then reorganized his forces (about 1,400 men were enrolled in his district) into larger, more permanent units in order to stop Indian raids. McAdoo's troops fought the Indians throughout 1864 and 1865. McAdoo eventually was put in command of the 2nd Frontier District (in central Texas) as well.

After the war McAdoo relocated in Brenham, Texas. Appointed judge of the Seventh Judicial District in 1871, he moved to Jefferson. In August, 1873, he was appointed an associate justice of the Texas Supreme Court by the Reconstruction governor. McAdoo and his colleagues (the "Semicolon Court") earned much public criticism in their decisions, particularly one overturning the results of a state election based on a semicolon in the law. McAdoo resigned from the court in January, 1874. From 1874 to 1876 he was a postmaster in Marshall, then returned to his farm near Brenham. General McAdoo died in Brenham on June 16, 1883, and is buried there in Prairie Lea Cemetery.

McAdoo's rank of general in the Texas state army qualifies him to be considered a Confederate general.

MAIN SOURCES

Smith, David P. *Frontier Defense in the Civil War*. College Station, Tex., 1992.
Webb, Walter P., and Eldon S. Branda, eds. *Handbook of Texas*. 3 vols. Austin, 1952–76.

JAMES HAGGIN MCBRIDE

James Haggin McBride, the son of William McBride and Jane Haggin, was born in 1814 near Harrodsburg, Kentucky. In his youth he engaged in manufacturing in Paris, Missouri. Relocating to Springfield, McBride soon formed a lucrative law practice and became president of the Springfield Bank. From 1850 to 1853 he lived in California. Returning to Missouri, McBride, a Democrat, was elected to the state house of representatives to represent Texas County. In 1859 he moved to Houston in Texas County and the next year was elected circuit judge.

State Historical Society of Missouri, Columbia

At the start of the war in Missouri he was appointed brigadier general of the 7th Division of the Missouri State Guard. One of McBride's staff officers remembered McBride's troops as "the most unique military body it has ever been my experience to meet. . . . The officers of the staff, who were small country lawyers, conducted their several departments somewhat after the fashion of a loosely kept county court; colonels could not drill their regiments; captains their companies; and many officers could neither read nor write. . . . While there was no such thing as military discipline in this singular army, yet perfect order was preserved in it, through the force of character of the General, his great firmness, and the patriarchal authority he exercised. He knew each man personally in his command." [1] At the Battle of Wilson's Creek on August 10, 1861, McBride (a "clear-headed, silent, courageous man" [2]) displayed great bravery as he led his division in attacks upon Bloody Hill. At the siege of Lexington (September 18 and 20, 1861) McBride's division attacked the Union garrison from positions along the banks of the Missouri River. On January 23, 1862, those Confederate volunteers not attached to the two newly formed Missouri Confederate brigades were assigned to the command of McBride, a state guard general, and denominated the 3rd Brigade of Volunteers. This mark of favor led McBride to believe he would be soon commissioned brigadier general in the Confederate army, to command the new brigade. However, Major General Sterling Price, who commanded both the state guard and the Missouri Confederate volunteers, quickly found fault with McBride's flouting of regulations and the lax discipline of his state guard division. On February 23, 1862, McBride, figuring his chances of promotion while under Price to be nil, resigned his general's commission and attempted to obtain a commission in the Confederate army. That commission never came; McBride never saw field action again. He established a camp in northern Arkansas and commenced the organization of a brigade of infantry for the regular Confederate service. Two regiments were raised, and the men sent to the main Confederate army in Little Rock. McBride, however, fell ill, and was forced to remain in northern Arkansas even after the area was occupied by Union forces. In March, 1864, he contracted pneumonia. The disease rendered him unfit for even recruiting duty, so he gathered his family and headed south. While en route he died at Bluffton in Yell County, Arkansas. He was buried near Bluffton in an unmarked grave.

General McBride's command of a brigade of the Missouri State Guard and his service in a campaign qualify him to be considered a Confederate general.

NOTES

1. Colton Greene to Thomas L. Snead, May 29, 1882, Thomas L. Snead Papers, Missouri Historical Society, St. Louis. Snead drew heavily on Greene's reminiscences to write a book on the war in Missouri.

2. *Ibid.*

MAIN SOURCES

"Biographical Sketch of General James H. McBride." Confederate Civil War Papers, Missouri Historical Society, St. Louis.

Gibson, Thomas R. "Gen. James H. McBride." *Confederate Veteran*, XXIII (1915), 375.

Greene, Colton, to Thomas L. Snead, May 29, June 10, 1882, Thomas L. Snead Papers, Missouri Historical Society, St. Louis.

Texas County, Missouri, Genealogical & Historical Society. *Texas County, Missouri Heritage*. 2 vols. Rich Hill, Mo., 1989.

HENRY KENT McCAY

Henry Kent McCay was born on January 8, 1820, in Northumberland County, Pennsylvania, the son of Robert and Sarah (Read) McCay. In 1839 he graduated from Princeton University. His older brother, Charles F. McCay, was at that time a professor at the University of Georgia in Athens, which induced the new graduate to migrate to that state. He settled in Lexington in Oglethorpe County (near Athens) and taught school for two years. While teaching he studied law under Georgia Chief Justice Lumpkin and in 1842 was admitted to the bar. Moving to Americus in Sumter County, McCay practiced law there until

Courtesy Georgia Department of Archives and History

the secession crisis. With his finished education and native abilities, his law practice was one of the most successful in southwest Georgia before the war.

By no means a states' rights advocate, McCay publicly opposed secession, running (unsuccessfully) as a "cooperationist" candidate to the Georgia Secession
Convention. But when Georgia seceded McCay went with his adopted state. On
June 5, 1861, he was commissioned second lieutenant of the 12th Georgia Infantry.
The 12th was sent to the mountains of west Virginia, where it spent the winter
of 1861 and 1862. McCay was a favorite with the men: one private wrote home
that "Leut. [sic] McCay has done a great deal for the company since we left
home. He spares no pains for the benefit of the company and is allways [sic] at
work."[1] On December 13, 1861, McCay was severely wounded during an engagement on Allegheny Mountain. On February 6, 1862, he was commissioned captain and regimental assistant quartermaster. The 12th participated in Stonewall
Jackson's Valley campaign of 1862 before joining the Army of Northern Virginia;
McCay fought gallantly in many of the battles in Virginia. On March 14, 1863, to
the regret of the whole regiment, McCay resigned his commission and returned to
Georgia. In May, 1864, he was elected lieutenant colonel of the 1st Battalion of
the Georgia Militia and served in the Atlanta campaign. A fourth brigade of militia was formed after the siege of Atlanta commenced, and McCay was appointed
brigadier general of militia to head the brigade. At the disastrous Battle of Griswoldville, his militia brigade held the center of the Confederate line; he won praise
for his "coolness and precision" while leading a charge.[2] In early December, 1864,
his brigade guarded the approaches to the important Confederate munitions
center at Augusta, Georgia. Later that month the brigade helped man the entrenchments surrounding Savannah. When the Confederate army evacuated Savannah the Georgia militia were first sent to Augusta and then scattered throughout the state.

After the war McCay resumed his law practice. In 1868 the Reconstruction governor appointed him an associate justice of the Georgia Supreme Court. He served
seven years; his "remarkable ability" and "immense learning" made him a leading
member of that court.[3] Resigning in July, 1875, Judge McCay embarked upon the
practice of law in Atlanta, again with great success. On August 4, 1882, President
Arthur appointed McCay judge of the U.S. District Court for the Northern District of Georgia. McCay was one active Republican in the Reconstruction era who
won the respect of Georgians of all political parties. He died in Atlanta on July 30,
1886, and is buried in Oakland Cemetery, Atlanta.

General McCay's command of a brigade of militia that served in a campaign
qualifies him to be considered a Confederate general.

NOTES

1. Charles R. Adams, Jr., ed., *A Post of Honor: The Pryor Letters, 1861–63* (Fort Valley, Ga.,
1989), 33.

2. Wendell O. Croom, *The War History of Company "C," Sixth Georgia Regiment* (Fort Valley, Ga., 1879), 21.

3. William J. Northen, ed., *Men of Mark in Georgia* (6 vols.; Atlanta, 1907–12), III, 433.

MAIN SOURCES

Adams, Charles R., Jr., ed. *A Post of Honor: The Pryor Letters, 1861–63*. Fort Valley, Ga. 1989.
Atlanta *Constitution*, July 31, August 2, 1886.
"Memorial." Georgia Supreme Court Law Reports, LXXXIII, 799–806.
Northen, William J., ed. *Men of Mark in Georgia*. 6 vols. Atlanta, 1907–12.

THOMAS HAMILTON MCCRAY

Thomas Hamilton McCray, the son of Henry and Mary (Moore) McCray, was born near Jonesborough in Washington County, Tennessee, in 1828. His parents, originally from South Carolina, were farmers. McCray lived in Washington County, Chatooga County, Georgia, and Monroe County, Tennessee, until reaching manhood. He then appears to have moved to Arkansas, where he operated a mill near Little Rock. Around 1856 he removed to Texas and became a manufacturer in Tellico, Ellis County, with land holdings in Navarro County. He removed to Wittsburg, in what is now Cross County, Arkansas, just before the start of the war.

Courtesy Louise Watkins

In June, 1861, McCray enlisted in the 5th Arkansas Infantry and was quickly promoted to lieutenant and regimental adjutant. Ambitious for a larger role in the war, he got himself detached from the regiment to become a mustering officer under then Brigadier General William Hardee, who commanded Confederate troops in northeast Arkansas. Utilizing his position as mustering officer, he raised a battalion later known as the 31st Arkansas Infantry. On January 25, 1862, McCray was elected major and commander of the battalion. The 31st joined Major General Earl Van Dorn's Army of the West just in time to be caught up in that army's transfer from Arkansas to Mississippi. When in May, 1862, the regiment was reorganized, McCray was elected colonel and led a brigade of the Army of Kentucky at the August 30, 1862, Battle of Richmond, Kentucky. His "gallantry and coolness" in that smashing Confederate victory won praise from his division commander.[1] As senior colonel, McCray led this brigade throughout the Kentucky campaign of 1862.

However, after the campaign a junior officer (Matthew Ector of Texas) was promoted to brigadier general over McCray's head to lead the brigade permanently. McCray believed that the promotion had been promised to him and charged that the War Department had promoted another officer of the same name (presumably Dandridge McRae of the 21st Arkansas) by mistake. In 1863 the 31st, reduced to only 125 men, was consolidated with another regiment. Now without a command, McCray was transferred back to Arkansas that August with a plan (never realized) to harass Union shipping on the Mississippi River. In 1864 McCray was ordered to his north Arkansas home grounds, behind Union lines, to organize the area's floating bands of deserters, conscripts, independent companies, and volunteers into cavalry regiments. He eventually succeeded in organizing a brigade of three regiments. In the fall of 1864 McCray's mostly unarmed command was attached to Brigadier General Joseph Shelby's division and took part in Price's raid into Missouri. The raw troops performed poorly in the assault on Fort Davidson, Missouri, on September 27, 1864, breaking for cover before they had advanced a hundred yards. At the October 22 and 23, 1864, Battle of Westport the brigade, by now fairly well armed with captured Union supplies, performed somewhat better. In the disastrous retreat after Westport, however, McCray's reluctant troopers deserted by the hundreds and the brigade essentially dissolved. McCray himself retained a nominal brigade commander's position in northern Arkansas throughout the winter of 1864 and the spring of 1865, "powerless for good or for evil," up to the final collapse of the Confederacy.[2]

After the war McCray, like many other Trans-Mississippi Confederates, fled to Mexico, but he soon returned and in 1870 was again farming near Wittsburg. Sometime after that McCray became affiliated with the McCormick reaper company and worked as a merchant for them, based in Chicago. He died on October 19, 1891, in Chicago and is buried in the Cook County Cemetery at Dunning in an unmarked "potter's field" gravesite.

Wood, Heitman, SHSP, and CV all list him as a general, the first and third stating that he was appointed brigadier general in 1863 to lead his old brigade (3rd Brigade, McCown's Division) of the Army of Tennessee. An article on Arkansas generals in Arkansas Historical Quarterly cites a November 7, 1863, date of appointment.[3] However, the OR show him as a colonel from September, 1863, to March, 1865. An 1873 newspaper article[4] calls him "colonel," thus suggesting that McCray was generally known by that rank to his contemporaries.[5]

NOTES

1. OR, Vol. XVI, Pt. 1, p. 941.

2. John N. Edwards, Shelby and His Men (Cincinnati, 1867), 313.

3. Jno. P. Morrow, Jr., "Confederate Generals from Arkansas," Arkansas Historical Quarterly, XXI (1962), 231–46.

4. In the Little Rock Arkansas Gazette, April 15, 1873, which reported that McCray had been wounded by an assailant.

5. No Confederate general presented more of a research challenge than McCray. His Compiled Service Record is scanty and in many respects contradictory; his service in Arkansas and Missouri was in areas and campaigns not covered by surviving records; no published source shed light on his prewar or postwar career. Not the least of the problems associated with McCray was that he cut himself off from his own family after the war and moved north, perhaps as a consequence of his having deserted his first and second wives.

MAIN SOURCES

Edwards, John N. *Shelby and His Men*. Cincinnati, 1867.

Sands, Sarah G. C. *History of Monroe County, Tennessee*. 3 vols. Baltimore, 1980–89.

JOHN WESLEY MCELROY

John Wesley McElroy, brigadier general of North Carolina home guard troops, was born on April 7, 1808, in Yancey County, North Carolina, the son of John and Elizabeth (Jamison) McElroy. The ancestors of the McElroys emigrated from Ireland to Pennsylvania in 1729, then drifted south into Virginia and North Carolina. Wesley McElroy (as he was called) became a prominent Burnsville merchant and farmer. He owned a number of slaves and was partner in a business to produce ginseng locally. A prominent Methodist layman, McElroy was elected Yancey County's first clerk of the Superior Court (serving from 1834 to 1846) and served on the board of trustees of the local academy. Before 1834 he had been elected colonel of the county militia regiment.

Courtesy North Carolina Division of Archives and History

In the first years of the war McElroy performed the minor duties that fell to him as colonel of the Yancey County (111th) militia. On July 7, 1863, the North Carolina General Assembly formed a new militia organization, the "home guard," to consist of men exempt from the draft. On September 26, 1863, Governor Zebulon Vance commissioned McElroy brigadier general of the newly formed 1st Brigade of the home guard. McElroy's brigade was charged with protecting the northwest border of the state against inroads from east Tennessee, which Union forces had occupied that summer. McElroy's daughter had married Governor Vance's brother, Brigadier General Robert Vance, a factor which must have aided his appointment. The 1st Brigade, which operated from a base in Yancey County, engaged in a variety of home defense tasks—guarding bridges, hunting down deserters, guarding prisoners—till the end of the war. McElroy met with little success in this thankless job. The mountainous area was overrun with "Tories," deserters, and bushwhackers. After one bushwhacker raid on Burnsville, his hometown, McElroy observed that "the County has gone up. It has got to be impossible to get any [deserter] out there unless he is dragged out" and predicted "ruin."[1]

After the war General McElroy remained in Burnsville and resumed his life as a merchant. He died on February 8, 1886, in Graham County, North Carolina, and is buried in Robbinsville Cemetery.

General McElroy, one of only two generals of the North Carolina home guard, is listed as a general in Clark's *Histories of the Several Regiments and Battalions from North Carolina in the Great War, 1861–1865.*[2]

NOTES

1. *OR*, Vol. LIII, Pt. 1, p. 326.
2. Walter Clark, ed., *Histories of the Several Regiments and Battalions from North Carolina in the Great War, 1861–1865* (5 vols.; Raleigh, 1901).

MAIN SOURCES

Bailey, Lloyd. "The McElroy Family of Yancey County." North Carolina Department of Archives and History, Raleigh.

Inscoe, John C. *Mountain Masters, Slavery, and the Sectional Crisis in Western North Carolina.* Knoxville, 1989.

McElroy, Rev. John M. *The Scotch-Irish McElroys in America.* Albany, 1901.

Peter Alexander Selkirk McGlashan

Peter Alexander Selkirk McGlashan was born on May 19, 1830, in Edinburgh, Scotland, the son of James and Mary (Selkirk) McGlashan.[1] His father, an Edinburgh merchant, had fought in the British army at the Battle of Waterloo. Immigrating to the United States in 1848, the younger McGlashan settled in Savannah and then in Thomasville, Georgia. He worked as a saddlemaker but, having a restless disposition, traveled to California to pan for gold. In the 1850s he joined the American filibusterers who were fighting in Central America.

Courtesy Georgia Department of Archives and History

In August, 1861, McGlashan enlisted as a private in the 29th Georgia Infantry. The regiment remained in Georgia that fall and winter, helping to guard the coast. In March, 1862, he was elected first lieutenant of Company E of the 50th Georgia, a newly raised infantry regiment. The 50th joined the Army of Northern Virginia that summer, after the Seven Days' Battles and became part of a brigade of Georgia regiments commanded successively by Brigadier Generals Paul Semmes, Goode Bryan, and James Simms. McGlashan was promoted to captain and, after the Battle of Gettysburg, to colonel of the 50th. He led the 50th in the Chickamauga and east Tennessee campaigns of 1863, the Wilderness and Shenandoah Valley campaigns of 1864, and in the 1864 to 1865 siege of Petersburg. McGlashan won repeated praise from his superiors for his leadership, being especially commended "for the skillful manner" in which he captured the Union skirmish line at the June 26, 1864, Battle of Fussell's Mill.[2] At the Battle of Cedar Creek that October McGlashan was severely wounded through both thighs. On several occasions in 1864 and 1865 he led, as senior colonel, Bryan's brigade, although when Bryan was invalided out of the army the senior colonel, James Simms, was given command of the brigade and eventual promotion to brigadier general. At the Battle of Sayler's Creek on April 6, 1865, both Simms and McGlashan were captured. McGlashan was not released from prison until that August.

After the war he returned to Thomasville to run a saddle and harness shop in that city. A popular citizen, he was elected mayor of Thomasville and took a lead role in Confederate veteran affairs. In 1885 he moved to Savannah and engaged in the harness business there. Late in life he held a position in the office of the Savannah city plumbing inspector. On June 13, 1908, McGlashan died of a heart attack suffered while swimming. He is buried in Laurel Grove Cemetery in Savannah.

CMH and Lonn both list McGlashan as a general. The former says he was promoted in March, 1865, to command Bryan's brigade. The latter says his was the last commission signed by President Davis before Davis left Richmond, but that McGlashan never received it. No evidence of this last-minute appointment exists, and there was no vacancy in command in Bryan's brigade to which he could have been promoted. McGlashan was a general in the United Confederate Veterans; perhaps the confusion arose because of his UCV rank.

NOTES

1. Although his year of birth has always been given as 1831 (*e.g.*, Robert K. Krick, *Lee's Colonels* [Dayton, 1991], 292), records of Edinburgh Parish, Scotland, in the Scottish Registry House, Edinburgh, list his birth on May 19, 1830.
2. *OR*, Vol. XL, Pt. 1, p. 768.

MAIN SOURCES

Lonn, Ella. *Foreigners in the Confederacy*. Chapel Hill, 1940.
Rogers, William W. *Thomas County, 1865–1900*. Tallahassee, 1973.
Savannah *Morning News*, June 14, 17, 1908.

JAMES ADDISON McMURRY

James Addison McMurry was born in 1825 in Tennessee, probably the son of Samuel McMurry of Sumner County. Entering the University of Nashville in 1841, he graduated with an A.B. degree in 1843 and became an attorney. In 1850 McMurry practiced law in Gallatin, Tennessee. By 1855 he had moved his practice to Nashville and in 1859 became a law partner of his old college classmate, future Confederate General George Maney.

At the start of the war McMurry joined the "Sewanee Rifles," a Nashville area unit officered by local lawyers. He was elected first lieutenant of that company, later Company C of the 20th Tennessee Infantry, but resigned his commission in June, 1861. On Au-

Courtesy The Huntington Library, San Marino, California

gust 5, 1861, McMurry was elected lieutenant colonel of Churchwell's 4th Tennessee Infantry of the Provisional Army (occasionally called the 34th Tennessee to be distinguished from Strahl's 4th Tennessee). The regiment was stationed in east Tennessee in 1861 and early 1862. At the April 16, 1862, reorganization of the 4th, McMurry was elected colonel and led the 4th, which was part of General E. Kirby Smith's Army of Kentucky, during General Braxton Bragg's 1862 invasion of Kentucky. In the fall of 1862 the 4th was transferred to Major General Benjamin F. Cheatham's division of the Army of Tennessee. At the Battle of Stone's River McMurry was praised for "gallantry and efficiency" by his brigade commander (and former law partner) Brigadier General George Maney.[1] As senior colonel, McMurry commanded Maney's brigade at various times in 1863. At the Battle of Chickamauga, he again led his regiment and, early in the action of September 19, "fell mortally wounded . . . while cheering his men on." General Maney's report of the battle called McMurry, "a gentleman of the noblest qualities and an officer of fine abilities and great gallantry."[2] Taken from the field, McMurry died at the Marietta, Georgia, hospital on October 2, 1863. He is buried in the Confederate Cemetery in Marietta.

McMurry is termed a general in *SHSP* for leading Maney's brigade. McMurray's *History of the Twentieth Tennessee Regiment Volunteer Infantry, C.S.A.* says Colonel McMurry was promoted to "Brigadier General while on the field of Chickamauga only a few hours before he received his death wound."[3] All the OR of his wounding and death refer to McMurry as colonel. Moreover, since his superior, General Maney, was still in brigade command, there existed no obvious vacancy to which McMurry could have been promoted.

NOTES

1. *OR*, Vol. XX, Pt. 1, p. 736.
2. *OR*, Vol. XXX, Pt. 2, pp. 96, 100.
3. W. J. McMurray, *History of the Twentieth Tennessee Regiment Volunteer Infantry, C.S.A.* (Nashville, 1904), 98.

MAIN SOURCES

Lindsley, John B. *The Military Annals of Tennessee*. Nashville, 1886.

McMurray, W. J. *History of the Twentieth Tennessee Regiment Volunteer Infantry, C.S.A.* Nashville, 1904.

Mitchell, Enoch, ed. "Letters of a Confederate Surgeon in the Army of Tennessee to His Wife." *Tennessee Historical Quarterly*, IV (1945), 341–53; V (1946), 60–81, 142–81.

GILBERT SIMRALL MEEM

Gilbert Simrall Meem was born on October 5, 1824, in Abingdon, Virginia, the son of John Gaw and Eliza (Russell) Meem. His father, a Lynchburg banker, was descended from Peter Meem, who emigrated from Holland to Pennsylvania in 1756. In 1841 John Meem purchased the Steenbergen estate near Mount Airy, Virginia. Young Meem attended Edgehill Seminary, a Princeton University prep school, but on seeing the Mount Airy property, he abandoned further schooling in order to manage the estate. Gilbert Meem became noted as a breeder of livestock. A Democrat, Meem served two years in the Virginia House of Delegates (1852 to 1854). By his marriage to Nannie Rose, daughter of Hugh Garland, he became related to Generals Samuel Garland and James Longstreet.

Museum of History and Industry, Seattle

In 1861 Meem was appointed a brigadier general to command the 7th Brigade, 3rd Division of the Virginia Militia, consisting of eight regiments from four Shenandoah Valley counties. Meem's brigade, part of James H. Carson's division, garrisoned Harpers Ferry in April, 1861. It was later left to guard Winchester when Johnston's Valley army marched to the Bull Run battlefield. The unit, portions of which were mustered in throughout 1861, varied in strength from four hundred to three thousand men. In November, 1861, Stonewall Jackson called out Meem's entire brigade to assemble at Winchester. During Jackson's January, 1862, advance on Bath and Romney, Meem's brigade marched with the main army. After Jackson ejected Union troops from both towns he ordered Meem's brigade to move south and east to Martinsburg to guard the right rear of his army. The brigade went into winter quarters there. On February 1, 1862, Meem resigned his general's commission. That resignation might have come about because of pressure from above. A letter in the OR hints that General Robert E. Lee had received "certain allegations in respect to [Meem's] habits and daily condition" (i.e., that he was an alcoholic) which would make him "not . . . a fit person for this responsibility."[1] Meem returned to managing his family estates, although he held civil positions in Shenandoah County government during the war.

The Union authorities quickly issued a pardon to the old general after the war, noting that he had "the reputation of being a good orderly citizen."[2] Meem remained in Mount Airy and continued his breeding operations. It was said that "he perhaps did more for the introduction and improvement of fine stock, esp. cattle and sheep, than anyone in the Valley of Virginia."[3] From 1871 to 1875 he served in the state senate. In 1892 he sold the Mount Airy property (Strathmore) and moved to Seattle, Washington. President Cleveland appointed Meem U.S. postmaster of Seattle, and Meem became one of that city's best-known citizens. General Meem died in Seattle on June 10, 1908, and is buried in Lake View Cemetery.

General Meem's command of a brigade of militia that served in a campaign qualifies him to be considered a Confederate general.

NOTES

1. *OR*, II, 948.
2. See Meem's postwar application for presidential pardon in the National Archives.
3. Seattle *Times*, June 10, 1908.

MAIN SOURCES

Bruce, Phillip A. *History of Virginia*. Chicago, 1924.
Seattle *Times*, June 10, 1908.
Wayland, John W. *A History of Shenandoah County*. Strasburg, Va., 1927.

WILLIAM RAPHAEL MILES

William Raphael Miles was born on March 25, 1817, near Bardstown in Nelson County, Kentucky. His parents were John and Sarah (Howard) Miles, farmers in Nelson County, both of old Maryland families. The young Miles was educated at St. Joseph's College and, after graduation, moved to Yazoo County, Mississippi. There he became a wealthy lawyer and planter. A Whig, Miles served as a state representative from 1844 to 1846, state senator from 1846 to 1848, and as a state elector-at-large for the Whig ticket in 1852. Miles was termed a "gentleman of distinguished ability . . . [and] among the foremost public speakers in the state"; it was said that "even a Democrat found it difficult to vote against William R. Miles."[1] By 1860 Miles owned

Civil War Photograph Albums, Louisiana and Lower Mississippi Valley Collections, LSU Libraries, Louisiana State University

a ten-thousand-acre plantation in the Yazoo Valley and had substantial business interests in New Orleans.

In 1861 Miles was elected to represent New Orleans in the Louisiana Secession Convention. At the convention he voted with the majority in favor of secession.

At the start of the war Miles and other New Orleans businessmen financed a privately owned and operated ship (a former river towboat renamed the *Calhoun*) to raid Union shipping. On May 16, 1861, the *Calhoun* made the first capture by a privateer in the war. Miles offered the Confederate government a plan to promote a whole fleet of privateers, based in Europe, but the Navy Department did not take up Miles's offer. In 1862 he raised and largely financed "Miles's Legion" (sometimes called the 32nd Louisiana), a mostly Louisiana unit composed of eight infantry companies, a cavalry battalion, and two artillery companies. On May 16, 1862, Miles was elected colonel of the legion. Made part of the Port Hudson garrison, the legion saw no action until 1863. In that year the legion was sent on an unsuccessful expedition to intercept Grierson's raiders. Miles led the legion at the Battle of Plains Store, where his troops made a successful assault. He commanded a brigade and the right of the Confederate line at the siege of Port Hudson. Captured there and imprisoned at Johnson's Island, he was exchanged on October 11, 1864. In 1865, as colonel, Miles commanded the post at Choctaw Bluffs, Alabama.

After the war Miles returned to Mississippi, his property in ruins, with a debt of $210,000, and no prospects of earning a livelihood. He resumed his Yazoo City law practice and for the next twenty years labored to provide for his family and discharge his debts. With his legal talents and with hard work he restored his finances and accumulated another fortune. In 1894 he retired to his plantation in Mileston in Holmes County, Mississippi. Miles died on January 1, 1900, near Mileston and is buried in the Catholic Cemetery in Yazoo City.

Wood, Heitman, *SHSP*, and *CV* list him as a general. *SHSP* states he received his commission in 1864 in order to command in northeast Mississippi. However, the *OR* show Miles as a colonel as late as April 3, 1865. In his postwar pardon application, Miles terms himself colonel of a legion, and he signed his May 17, 1865, parole as colonel.

NOTE

1. Robert Lowry and W. H. McCardle, *A History of Mississippi* (Jackson, Miss., 1891), 613; *National Cyclopedia of American Biography* (63 vols.; New York, 1892–1984), IX, 497.

MAIN SOURCES

National Cyclopedia of American Biography. 63 vols. New York, 1892–1984.
Yazoo City *Herald*, January 5, 1900.

SAMUEL PRESTON MOORE

Samuel Preston Moore, surgeon general of the Confederacy, was born on September 16, 1813, at Charleston, South Carolina, the son of Stephen West and Eleanore Screvan Gilbert Moore. His father, a native of Virginia, was a prominent Charleston banker whose family were among the first inhabitants of Maryland. Two other Moore brothers became army officers, including Louisiana General Stephen Westmore. Moore attended school in Charleston and graduated with an M.D. in 1834 from the South Carolina Medical College. He then established his practice in Little Rock, Arkansas. In 1835 Moore joined the U.S. Army as a surgeon, serving in the Mexican War and impressing future President Jefferson Davis with his abilities. After that war he worked at a variety of army posts, including a stint as a surgeon at West Point. In 1849 he was promoted to the rank of major.

Miller, ed., *Photographic History*, VII

Resigning his commission on February 25, 1861, Moore at first practiced medicine in Little Rock, Arkansas, where his relatives had property. In June, 1861, he was named surgeon general of the Confederacy and held that post for the rest of the war. Moore's war efforts won general contemporary praise for "his great work as an organizer, his remarkable executive ability" as well as his "great brusqueness of manner" and his sternness as a disciplinarian.[1] The Confederate medical corps grew to a strength of about three thousand men and was known for its innovative and devoted practice. In 1864 Moore founded the *Confederate States Medical Journal* to disseminate information to army surgeons. Moore also founded the "Association of Army and Navy Surgeons of the Confederate States," America's oldest military medical society. To ensure that physicians were properly trained and qualified, he established review boards to help weed out incompetents. He helped pioneer innovative medical practices, including the employment of dentists in the army. The lack of trained personnel and essential supplies hampered Confederate medical efforts throughout the war. Moore directed almost frantic programs to develop indigenous plant medicines and establish pharmaceutical laboratories.

After the war Moore remained in Richmond. He established a medical practice there and served six years on the Richmond School Board. Moore died in Richmond on May 31, 1889, and is buried in Hollywood Cemetery.

CV lists Moore as a brigadier general, appointed from South Carolina in 1865. The act of February 26, 1861, which organized the Confederate medical corps, provided that the surgeon general was to have the rank of colonel. Subsequent proposed legislation to give the surgeon general the rank of brigadier general of the PACS failed to become law.[2]

NOTES

1. Horace H. Cunningham, *Doctors in Gray* (Baton Rouge, 1958), 28–31.
2. See Cunningham, *Doctors in Gray*, 21–25, for a discussion of the laws regarding the surgeon generalship.

MAIN SOURCES

Butler, Thomas. "Moore Bible Record." *Pennsylvania Genealogical Magazine*, XI (March, 1932), 288–91.
Cunningham, Horace H. *Doctors in Gray*. Baton Rouge, 1958.
Farr, Warner D. "Confederate Surgeon General Samuel Preston Moore." *Houston Civil War Round Table Newsletter*, V (February, 1992).
Richmond *Dispatch*, June 1, 1889.

CHRISTOPHER HAYNES MOTT

Christopher Haynes Mott, brigadier general of Mississippi state troops in 1861, was born on June 22, 1826, in Livingston County, Kentucky, the son of Randolph Mott. While he was still a boy the family moved to Holly Springs, Mississippi, where the father ran an inn and served as town selectman. Mott received his education at St. Thomas' Hall in Holly Springs and Transylvania University in Kentucky. During the Mexican War Mott was elected first lieutenant of Company I of the 1st Mississippi Rifles, and was later appointed regimental commissary. At the Battle of Buena Vista Mott's valor was noticed by the regiment's commander, Jefferson Davis. Returning to Holly Springs after the war, Mott studied law under Roger Barton, the dean

Billups-Garth Archives, Columbus/Lowndes County Public Library

of northern Mississippi lawyers, and was admitted to the bar. In 1850 he formed a successful law partnership with his close friend L. Q. C. Lamar, later justice of the U.S. Supreme Court. In 1850 and 1851 Mott, "a worthy Democrat and a true man," represented Marshall County in the state legislature.[1] He was later elected probate judge and in 1858 was appointed a special U.S. commissioner to California.

On January 23, 1861, the Mississippi Secession Convention elected Mott one of four brigadier generals in the Mississippi state army and put him in charge of the 4th Brigade (the first and second military districts, comprising ten counties in northeast Mississippi).[2] He soon resigned this position to raise the 19th Mississippi. On

June 11, 1861, Mott was commissioned colonel of the 19th, the first regiment from Mississippi that enlisted for the war. The 19th was sent to Virginia that summer, arriving in Richmond on June 7, 1861. In the fall of 1861 the 19th joined the main Confederate army in northern Virginia and spent the remainder of the year in camp. In the regiment's first action at the May 5, 1862, Battle of Williamsburg Mott, "highly esteemed and brave, . . . fell, shot through the body while cheering on his men" during a bloody attack.[3] General James Longstreet, his division commander, in his post-battle report mourned the loss of "the gallant Mott," an "accomplished soldier, model gentleman, and devoted patriot."[4] First buried in Hollywood Cemetery in Richmond, in 1867 his remains were reinterred in Hill Crest Cemetery in Holly Springs.[5] Mott had been recommended for promotion to general by army commander General Joseph E. Johnston (who regarded Mott as one of only six colonels in his army "fully competent to command brigades"), and would have received the promotion had he lived.[6]

Mott's rank of general in Mississippi's state army qualifies him to be considered a Confederate general.

NOTES

1. Lynda Crist et al., eds., The Papers of Jefferson Davis (7 vols.; Baton Rouge, 1983–91), V, 153.

2. The others elected by the convention were Jefferson Davis as major general, and Charles Clark, Earl Van Dorn, and James Alcorn as brigadier generals.

3. OR, Vol. XI, Pt. 1, p. 597.

4. Ibid.

5. Brigadier General Daniel C. Govan, Mott's brother-in-law, is buried in the same lot.

6. OR, V, 1058.

MAIN SOURCES

Crist, Lynda, et al., eds. The Papers of Jefferson Davis. 7 vols. Baton Rouge, 1983–91.

Goodspeed Publishing Company. Biographical and Historical Memoirs of Mississippi. 2 vols. Chicago, 1891.

Mayes, Edward. Lucius Q. C. Lamar: His Life, Times, and Speeches. Nashville, 1896.

THOMAS TAYLOR MUNFORD

Thomas Taylor Munford was born on March 28, 1831, in Richmond, Virginia. His father, Colonel George Wythe Munford, was for many years Secretary of the Commonwealth. His mother, Lucy Singleton Taylor, was related to President Benjamin Harrison. The younger Munford graduated from VMI in 1852. For a time after graduation, Munford engaged in general railroad work. Until the outbreak of the war, he was mainly occupied as a planter.

On May 8, 1861, Munford was commissioned lieutenant colonel of the 30th Virginia Mounted Infantry, later renumbered the 2nd Virginia Cavalry. Munford's "career as a cavalry officer was brilliant and notable," spanning the war literally from Manassas to Appomattox.[1] At the First Battle of Bull Run he guarded

Massachusetts Commandery, Military Order of the Loyal Legion and the U.S. Army Military History Institute

the Confederate right flank with four companies of the 30th. Munford was promoted to full colonel of the 2nd to date from April 25, 1862. Munford led a two-regiment cavalry brigade attached to Ewell's division in Jackson's 1862 Valley campaign, eventually succeeding to the command of all of Jackson's cavalry. At Second Bull Run his cavalry made a successful surprise attack on Bristoe Station. He suffered two slight saber wounds at Second Bull Run and a slight musket wound at Turkey Ridge. During the Antietam campaign Munford temporarily commanded Robertson's brigade. At Brandy Station he led Fitzhugh Lee's brigade as senior colonel, but only arrived on the battlefield as the Union forces were retreating. Munford's gallantry at the Battle of Aldie was conspicuous; his three regiments took 138 prisoners. In regimental command, he fought at Gettysburg and in the Wilderness campaign of 1864. In November, 1864, upon the resignation of his brigade commander, Munford as senior colonel took over Wickham's brigade. In the spring of 1865, he was assigned the command of Fitzhugh Lee's cavalry division, which he led till war's end. At Appomattox Munford's troopers were able to slide around the Union left flank before the trap closed on the Confederate army. Refusing to surrender, he and his troopers escaped to Lynchburg, where the division disbanded.

With the war over Munford engaged in cotton planting at Lynchburg, Virginia, and in Uniontown, Alabama, and was vice president of the Lynchburg Iron, Steel & Mining Company. Colonel Munford also served two terms as president of the Board of Visitors of VMI and secretary of the Southern Historical Society. Munford died on February 27, 1918, in Uniontown. He is buried in Spring Hill Cemetery in Lynchburg.

CMH, CV, Heitman, Wright, and SHSP all list Munford as a general. CMH cites a November, 1864, appointment. In the OR for 1865 he is often mentioned as a general. In fact, his promotion to brigadier general had been recommended by General Robert E. Lee on March 23, 1865, to date from November, 1864.[2] However, there is no record of President Davis acting upon the recommendation, and Munford himself, in his postwar application for pardon, stated that he never received a commission. Wright suggests that Munford was promoted by Major General Fitzhugh Lee, commander of the army's cavalry corps, in the last days of the war.[3]

NOTES

1. Bennett H. Young, Confederate Wizards of the Saddle . . . . (1914; rpr. Boston, 1958), 510.
2. Munford-Ellis Family Papers, William R. Perkins Library, Duke University.
3. Confederate authorities were strangely reluctant to promote Colonel Munford. Munford had outranked, as colonel, all but one of the seven brigadier generals who in 1864 commanded brigades in Stuart's cavalry corps. Munford had also been senior to Colonel Williams C. Wickham of the 4th Virginia Cavalry who in 1863 had been promoted over Munford's head to command Fitzhugh Lee's brigade. Munford made no secret of his dislike of Jeb Stuart, his corps commander; he regarded Stuart as a vain, self-centered glory hog. Perhaps Stuart blackballed the competent but outspoken colonel.

MAIN SOURCES

Evans, Clement A., ed. Confederate Military History: A Library of Confederate States History. 1899; 17 vol. extended edition; rpr. Wilmington, N.C., 1987.
Munford-Ellis Family. Papers. William R. Perkins Library, Duke University, Durham, N.C.
Wert, Jeffrey. "His Unhonored Service: Colonel Tom Munford—A Man of Achievement." Civil War Times Illustrated, XXIV (June, 1985), 28–34.

JOHN EDWARD MURRAY

John Edward Murray, the son of John C. and Sarah Ann (Carter) Murray, was born in Virginia (probably Fauquier County) in March or April, 1843. In 1849 his father relocated in Pine Bluff, Arkansas, where he practiced law and became a judge. Young Murray was admitted as a cadet to the United States Military Academy on July 1, 1860. He resigned from West Point on April 21, 1861, one week after the firing on Fort Sumter, but before Arkansas had seceded.

Murray was mustered into the Confederate army on July 26, 1861. He reported to Brigadier General William Hardee, who had known him at West Point, and was assigned to drill the Arkansas regiments in Hardee's command. Transferring to line duty, Murray was commissioned lieutenant of the 15th Arkansas. On December 20, 1861, General Hardee promoted him to lieutenant colonel of the 5th Arkansas Infantry, at that time stationed in Kentucky. The 5th was part of a brigade of five Arkansas regiments in the Army of Tennessee, commanded at times by Brigadier Generals Thomas Hindman, St. John R. Liddell, and Daniel C. Govan. Being on detached duty at the time, the 5th missed the sanguinary Battle of Shiloh on April 6 and 7, 1862. At the Battles of Perryville (October 8, 1862) and Stone's River (December 31, 1862, to January 2, 1863) Murray and the 5th fought with conspicuous skill and valor. At Stone's River Murray commanded the 5th, bearing "the colors of this regiment through the hottest fight, and by his own bright example encouraged his men to despise danger."[1] In the fall of 1863 the 5th, depleted in numbers through arduous service, was consolidated with the 13th Arkansas. The colonel commanding the 5th/13th was killed early in the Battle of Chickamauga on September 19 and 20, 1863; Murray took over the consolidated regiment and led his troops in an attack that rolled up the left flank of the Union army. A Union counterattack nearly surrounded the Arkansans, who had penetrated far into the Union rear, and only Murray's quick-witted turnabout saved his men. After this performance Murray, "particularly distinguished for his skill and gallantry," was marked as one of the brightest young officers in the army.[2] On October 19, 1863, he was promoted to full colonel, and his brigade commander recommended him for further promotion. In the winter of 1863 and 1864 Murray, as colonel, occasionally commanded the brigade. During the Atlanta campaign of 1864, Murray led the 5th/13th with accustomed gallantry. At the Battle of Atlanta on July 22, 1864, Murray led a three-regiment wing of the brigade in a desperate attack. The initial rush was halted by unexpected Union fire. Murray grabbed the regimental colors and rallied his men, who entered the Union trenches. In the fierce, hand-to-hand fighting that ensued, Murray was mortally wounded. He died just past midnight on July 23 on the battlefield. First buried in a local cemetery, in July, 1867, his remains were transferred to Mount Holly Cemetery in Little Rock, Arkansas.

The Arkansas volume of CMH does not include a biography of Murray in its "generals" section, but the text mentions that he received a general's commission the day of his death. It also says Murray was the youngest colonel and brigadier general in the army.[3] No record of such an appointment exists. Further, his brigade commander (General Govan) was on duty the whole campaign, so there was no vacancy to which he could have been promoted. The Arkansas brigade was at that time much understrength and did not require an extra general.

NOTES

1. OR, Vol. XX, Pt. 1, p. 776.
2. OR, Vol. XXX, Pt. 2, p. 260.
3. The former assertion is not true. Walter Clark, for one, was lieutenant colonel of North Carolina reserves at age eighteen. If Murray had been appointed general, however, he would have been the youngest general in the Confederate army.

MAIN SOURCES

Barnhill, Floyd R. *The Fighting Fifth*. Jonesboro, Ark., 1990.
Census of 1860, Arkansas, Jefferson County: Family 81-79, Microfilm.

PATRICK HENRY NELSON

Patrick Henry Nelson was born on July 26, 1824, near Black River in the Clarendon District, South Carolina, the son of Samuel E. and Amarintha Carson McCauley Nelson. His early schooling was at Mount Zion Institute. Nelson graduated with first honors in 1844 from the College of South Carolina. In 1847 he married Emma Cantey, first cousin of Confederate General James Cantey. Nelson became a wealthy planter in the Sumter District, owning 110 slaves at his two plantations, Indigo Hill and Marston. He was also active before the war in a committee to send southern emigrants to Kansas.

South Caroliniana Library, University of South Carolina

A major general of the South Carolina militia before the war, after secession Nelson was appointed brigadier general of South Carolina volunteer forces. He commanded the 2nd Brigade of the South Carolina Volunteers on Morris Island during the Fort Sumter bombardment. Nelson was relieved of duty from Morris Island on May 22, 1861.

On February 24, 1862, he was commissioned major of the 7th ("Enfield") Battalion of the South Carolina Infantry. He was commissioned lieutenant colonel of that battalion on July 10, 1862. The 7th (considered a crack outfit by the brigade commander) generally served in garrison duty around Charleston for the next two years. Nelson led his battalion at Forts Wagner and Johnson in 1863, seeing action at the former, and also pulled guard duty at Wilmington, North Carolina, in January of that year. In 1864 Nelson and his battalion were ordered to Petersburg as part of a general movement of South Carolina garrison troops to aid General Lee. Nelson, "a gentleman of high culture and fine presence, and an excellent officer," led the 7th at the Battles of Swift Creek and Drewry's Bluff.[1] On July 24, 1864, Hagood's South Carolina brigade was ordered to assault the extreme right of the Union lines opposite Petersburg. Colonel Nelson was put in charge of the skirmish line that was to lead the assault. The attack succeeded in taking the Union entrenchments but, without support, could advance no further. The 7th was almost wiped out in the battle. The casualties included Colonel Nelson. He was reported to have run from the right of his lines to beyond the extreme left, then to have disappeared, never to be seen again. Brigadier General Johnson Hagood, the brigade commander, remembered that a "painful rumor reached us a few days afterward of his having been murdered by negro troops while being taken by the enemy to the rear. . . . Thus fell a devoted patriot, a gallant soldier, a courteous gentleman."[2]

Nelson's rank of general in South Carolina's state army qualifies him to be considered a Confederate general.

NOTES

1. Johnson Hagood, *Memoirs of the War of Secession* (Columbia, S.C., 1910), 209.
2. *Ibid.*, 278.

MAIN SOURCES

Hagood, Johnson. *Memoirs of the War of Secession*. Columbia, S.C., 1910.
Krick, Robert K. *Lee's Colonels*. Dayton, 1991.
University of South Carolina Records. University of South Carolina, Columbia.

JOHN WILLIAM O'FERRALL

John William O'Ferrall (sometimes spelled O'Ferrald or Farrell) was born on September 23, 1823, in Martinsburg, Virginia (now West Virginia), the son of John and Humric (House) O'Ferrall. His father was a War of 1812 veteran and longtime Virginia state representative; a younger half-brother was later governor of Virginia. His youth and early school years were spent in Berkeley Springs, Virginia. In 1856 he moved to Enterprise, Mississippi. There O'Ferrall, "an active, energetic businessman," became a wealthy merchant.[1]

In the spring of 1861 O'Ferrall was elected captain of the "Enterprise Guards," a company of twelve-month volunteers raised to meet the state's emergency need

Courtesy Richard C. O'Ferrall

for troops. Governor John Pettus of Mississippi sent O'Ferrall's company, among others, to help guard Pensacola, Florida. On July 8, 1861, the governor appointed O'Ferrall brigadier general of Mississippi state troops. He led the 4th Brigade of the Army of Mississippi, stationed in the southeast portion of that state, through the fall of 1861. In October, 1861, Governor Pettus ordered O'Ferrall to transfer his two regiments (1,800 men) to Confederate service, and the Army of Mississippi gradually dissolved. The two regiments were turned over to Confederate authorities in Pensacola, Florida, and O'Ferrall was out of a job. Returning to Enterprise, he resumed his career as a merchant, his house always open to feed and shelter passing troops. The governor subsequently appointed O'Farrell a captain of state troops. By January, 1864, anxious to do his part again, or perhaps just bored, General O'Ferrall wrote President Davis requesting an appointment in the quartermaster corps, or "some other honorable position" in the army.[2] He did not obtain the desired appointment, but was instead named an agent to the area tax collector.

After the war he remained in Enterprise, where he worked as a cotton weigher and insurance agent, representing twelve different insurance companies. An active Democrat, he was elected to the Enterprise city council, and in 1880 he was elected to the Board of Public Works of his congressional district. General O'Ferrall (described as "large and stately in appearance," and "one of the most prosperous citizens of Mississippi"[3]) died on December 10, 1895, in Enterprise. He and his family are buried in Enterprise Cemetery.

Heitman lists O'Ferrall as a general, but his general's rank was derived through state authority.

NOTES

1. Goodspeed Publishing Company, *Biographical and Historical Memoirs of Mississippi* (2 vols.; Chicago, 1891), II, 531.

2. Captain S. S. Freeman to President Davis, January 30, 1864, in Compiled Service Records, General and Staff Officers, John W. O'Ferrall.

3. Charles T. O'Ferrall, *Forty Years of Active Service* (New York, 1904), 125; Jackson *Clarion*, December 12, 1895.

MAIN SOURCES

Causey, Jerry, ed. "Selected Correspondence of the Adjutant General of Confederate Mississippi." *Journal of Mississippi History*, XLII (1981), 31–58.
Goodspeed Publishing Company. *Biographical and Historical Memoirs of Mississippi.* 2 vols. Chicago, 1891.

WILLIAM HENRY PARSONS

William Henry Parsons was born on April 23, 1826, in New Jersey (probably around Elizabeth), the son of Samuel and Elizabeth (Tompkins) Parsons. When very young his father removed to Montgomery, Alabama, where he operated a shoe and leather factory. Young Parsons was sent to be educated at Emory College in Georgia, but left school in 1845 to fight in the Mexican War. He enlisted in the 2nd U.S. Dragoons and fought in General Zachary Taylor's army. After the war Parsons remained in Texas, settling near Tyler. There he farmed and edited a newspaper, the Tyler *Telegraph*. Parsons moved to Johnson County in 1855, Hill County in 1858, and Waco in 1859. In Waco

Courtesy William D. Parsons

he practiced law and in 1860 founded the *Southwest*, a Waco newspaper. Active in Democratic party politics, Parsons was chosen an alternate delegate to the 1860 Democratic National Convention.

At the start of the war Parsons was appointed a colonel and aide-de-camp to the governor. In July, 1861, he was authorized to raise a mounted regiment for service against the Indians of western Texas. Parsons, known as "Wild Bill," organized the 12th Texas Cavalry in 1861 from Ellis and Hill County volunteers. In the spring of 1862 the 12th was ordered to Arkansas, where it helped defend Little Rock from Brigadier General Samuel Curtis' Federal army. By October Colonel Parsons had command of a brigade of three Texas cavalry regiments: his own 12th, the 19th, and the 21st. His brigade was stationed along the west bank of the Mississippi River and performed outpost duty, scouting, raiding, and occasionally fighting. However, for much of the war the 12th was stationed in Texas, where Parsons commanded his regiment and occasionally the brigade. It was said of Parsons, a renowned prewar secessionist orator, that "no commander west of the Mississippi could deliver more fiery, colorful, and enthusiastic speeches from the saddle," which along with his courage made him "more popular with his regiment than any Colonel in America."[1] In the 1864 Red River campaign Parsons led the 12th with "uniform steadiness," winning praise for his conduct during engagements at Blair's Landing and Yellow Bayou.[2] In March, 1865, Parsons, still a colonel, was in charge of a brigade of Texas cavalry stationed in northeast Texas.

At war's end Parsons fled the United States for British Honduras, but soon returned to Texas. Active in railroad promotion, newspapers, and politics, Parsons became a noted "scalawag," or southern-born Reconstructionist. He served as a Republican in the Texas Senate from 1870 to 1871, running unsuccessfully for senate president. Subsequently President Grant appointed him to the U.S. Centennial Commission, based in New York. While in New York Parsons also served as an immigration agent for the state of Texas. Later he received an appointment to the U.S. Customs Office in Norfolk, Virginia. In the 1880s and 1890s Parsons lived, for the most part, in New York City and Baltimore, Maryland, practicing law and selling real estate. Becoming more radical in politics, the former southern secessionist became a pamphleteer for the Knights of Labor and served as Maryland chairman of the Greenback-Labor party.[3] General Parsons died on October 2, 1907, in Chicago, Illinois, where he had lived with his son Edgar for several years. He is buried in Mount Hope Cemetery, Hastings-on-Hudson, New York.

Parsons is listed as an "acting" brigadier general in *SHSP*. Though repeatedly recommended for promotion, and in actual command of a brigade for years, Parsons never made brigadier. For much of the war Parsons and a subordinate, Colonel George W. Carter of the 21st Texas Cavalry, bickered over who was the senior colonel and thus entitled to command Parsons' brigade. Although Parsons was commissioned colonel months before Carter, the latter maintained that Parsons' original commission was as colonel of a twelve-months regiment; that Parsons' commission as colonel of a permanent, enlisted-for-the-war regiment, was later than Carter's. The government eventually decided in Carter's favor (Carter had a great deal of political influence in addition to his legal claim), but by then Carter and his regiment had transferred to another brigade. Parsons "claimed the rank of brigadier after the war and liked to be addressed as such," and was appointed major general of Texas militia during the Reconstruction era.[4]

NOTES

1. B. D. Gallaway, *The Ragged Rebel* (Austin, 1988), 20; Henry E. Ingram, comp., *Civil War Letters of George W. and Martha F. Ingram, 1861–1865* (Waco, 1973), 23.

2. *OR*, Vol. XXXIV, Pt. 1, p. 628.

3. Albert Parsons, the general's younger brother, was the anarchist leader hanged for his part in the "Haymarket Riot" murders in Chicago. During the trial General Parsons aided the counsel for his brother's defense.

4. Gallaway, *Ragged Rebel*, 71. For more on the Parsons-Carter feud, see Anne J. Bailey, *Between the Enemy and Texas: Parsons' Texas Cavalry in the Civil War* (Fort Worth, 1989), 32; OR, Vol. XXXIV, Pt. 1, p. 628. The author would like to thank Bill Parsons of Lake Forest, Illinois, descendant of General Parsons, for his kind assistance.

MAIN SOURCES

Anderson, John Q., ed. *Campaigning with Parsons' Texas Cavalry Brigade, CSA*. Hillsboro, 1967.
Bailey, Anne J. *Between the Enemy and Texas: Parsons' Texas Cavalry in the Civil War*. Fort Worth, 1989.
Gallaway, B. D. *The Ragged Rebel*. Austin, 1988.
Ingram, Henry E., comp. *Civil War Letters of George W. and Martha F. Ingram, 1861–1865*. Waco, 1973.
Parsons, William H. *Condensed History of Parsons Texas Cavalry Brigade, 1861–1865. . . .* Corsicana, Tex., 1903.
Zuber, William P. *My Eighty Years in Texas*. Austin, 1971.

NICHOLAS BARTLETT PEARCE

Nicholas Bartlett Pearce was born on July 20, 1828, in Caldwell County, Kentucky, the son of Allen and Mary (Polly) Morse Pearce. His early education included a stint at Cumberland College in Kentucky. Appointed to West Point, he graduated in 1850 twenty-sixth in a class of forty-four. Commissioned lieutenant in the 7th Infantry, Pearce was stationed in western Arkansas and Oklahoma for the bulk of his army career. In 1858 he resigned from the army in order to go into business with his father-in-law, a merchant in Osage Mills, Arkansas. He settled into his new community very quickly and soon won election to colonel of the local militia.

Special Collections, United States Military Academy Library

In May, 1861, the Arkansas Secession Convention appointed Pearce brigadier general of Arkansas state forces, to command the 1st (Western) Division. One source has it that "no more unpopular appointment could have been made by the convention," for Pearce, an opponent of secession, had "heaped abuse" on Governor Rector and "every prominent man in the state who favored secession."[1] His short tenure as general was controversial. In July, 1861, Pearce led a brigade of militia, 2,200 strong, into Missouri to help drive back a

Union army nearing the Arkansas border. At the August 10, 1861, Battle of Wilson's Creek, Pearce's brigade performed valiantly, repulsing the Union diversionary attack and then helping to defeat the main Union army. After the battle, Arkansas authorities attempted to transfer his brigade to Confederate service. Pearce resisted the transfer, and in August furloughed the men to their homes.[2] The unit was disbanded; Pearce's combat role in the war was at an end. On December 13, 1861, Pearce was appointed a major in the Confederate Commissary Department. One week later he was assigned to duty as chief commissary of western Arkansas and the Indian Territory.[3] By 1863 he was chief commissary of the District of Texas. In this post suspicious observers charged that Pearce was too intimate with war profiteers. Pearce also served on the Texas Military Board and as chief quartermaster at San Antonio, Texas. On June 21, 1865, Major Pearce was paroled at Houston, Texas.

After being paroled Pearce traveled to Washington, D.C., and obtained a pardon from President Andrew Johnson. In 1867 Pearce returned to Osage Mills, rebuilt his residence, mill, and store, and resumed his business career. In 1872 he joined the mathematics faculty at the University of Arkansas. In 1874 he resigned his teaching post and returned to Osage Mills. From 1870 to 1884 he was employed by a wholesale house in Kansas City. Later he was employed as an expert land examiner in Texas (where he had moved because of his wife's health). General Pearce died on March 8, 1894, in Dallas, at the home of his daughter-in-law, and is buried in Whitesboro, Texas.

SHSP, Heitman, Cullum, and Wright all list Pearce as a general. The latter two allege a Kirby Smith appointment. However, SHSP, which says Pearce's general rank was by state authority only, seems to be correct.

NOTES

1. Michael B. Dougan, *Confederate Arkansas* (University, Tex., 1976), 65. For another view of Pearce's popularity, see the Van Buren *Press*, May 8, 1861, which ventured that the newly appointed Pearce "had the fullest confidence of the people of this section of the state."

2. General Thomas Hindman, no political ally, tried to exonerate Pearce of this charge. In a letter to the Little Rock *Arkansas Gazette*, published October 11, 1862, Hindman stated that Pearce urged his men to transfer to Confederate service. Hindman admitted that Pearce was personally opposed to the transfer.

3. The Little Rock *Arkansas Gazette* on September 20, 1862, noted that Pearce declined an 1862 "boomlet" to run for governor, saying that "his [Pearce's] conduct, from the first of the war, has been that of a true, devoted, and gallant soldier."

MAIN SOURCES

Aldridge, Smith M. "Nicholas Bartlett Pearce," *Benton County Pioneer*, XXX (Fall, 1985), 33–39.
Dougan, Michael B. *Confederate Arkansas*. University, Tex., 1976.
"In Memory of Gen. Nicholas Bartlett Pearce." *Backtracker*, I (April, 1972), 8–9.
Reynolds, John H., and David Y. Thomas. *History of the University of Arkansas*. Fayetteville, Ark., 1910.

CHARLES W. PHIFER

Charles W. Phifer was born in 1833 in Tennessee, probably Bedford County. His father and mother, John and Ann (Phifer) Phifer, were both descended from an old North Carolina family of German (allegedly noble Austrian) descent. His father, a planter, moved to Coffeeville in Yalobusha County, Mississippi, when he was young. Phifer attended the University of Mississippi (class of 1852) and the University of North Carolina (graduating with honors in 1854) before receiving an appointment into the regular army in 1855. He served six years as a lieutenant in the 2nd Cavalry, mostly fighting Indians in Texas and displaying both gallantry and bravery.

Phifer resigned his army commission on April 1, 1861, and was commissioned a lieutenant in the Confederate cavalry. His first duty was as a mustering officer in Louisiana. Phifer was swiftly appointed major of an Arkansas cavalry battalion and led that battalion in Kentucky during the winter of 1861 and 1862. Transferring to the staff, Phifer served with Major General Earl Van Dorn, an old 2nd Cavalry friend, in early 1862. On May 25, 1862, General Van Dorn assigned Phifer to duty as acting brigadier general. He led a brigade of dismounted cavalry (later Ross's Texas cavalry brigade) at the Battles of Corinth and Hatchie Bridge. He had labored with "untiring energy" to train the "wild Texas boys" who, under Phifer's lead, fought well in the attack on Corinth.[1] However, at the Battle of Hatchie Bridge Phifer reported "ill" and did not actively participate. Either because of this, or because his sponsor, General Van Dorn, was now under a cloud (the whole South blamed Van Dorn for the defeat at Corinth), the president allowed Phifer's assignment to lapse.[2] On October 16, 1862, he was relieved of his "acting" general's rank and his brigade command. In 1863 Phifer joined the staff of Colonel Alexander W. Reynolds, another old army friend. During the siege of Vicksburg he was assistant adjutant general of Reynolds' brigade, with the rank of major. Captured there, he was paroled and served on Reynolds' staff through 1863. In early 1864 Phifer requested transfer to the Trans-Mississippi Department and active duty. The transfer order never came through, but Phifer left his staff position anyway and was listed as absent without leave for the rest of the war.

After the war General Phifer returned to Texas. He taught school in Brownwood and worked as a civil engineer. In 1880 he was living in Austin. Around 1890 he relocated to Savannah, Georgia, and found employment in various governmental positions. According to the local newspaper, General Phifer had a sad end. He was "highly educated," and genial when sober, but quarrelsome when drunk. Phifer held several governmental jobs, but lost them because of his drinking habits. His last years found him descended to the level of a common laborer. On December 25, 1896, a drunken Phifer accidentally fell down the steps of the cellar of a Savannah saloon to his death.[3] He is buried in Laurel Grove Cemetery in Savannah.

Heitman, CV, SHSP, and Wood all list Phifer as a Confederate general.

NOTES

1. Judith A. Benner, *Sul Ross, Soldier, Statesman, Educator* (College Station, Tex., 1983), 80.

2. During his command in Mississippi Van Dorn assigned several officers to duty as generals. President Davis eventually appointed all but one of these, Phifer being the exception.

3. The story of Phifer's decline and death is taken from the Savannah *Morning News*, December 27, 1896.

MAIN SOURCES

Benner, Judith A. *Sul Ross, Soldier, Statesman, Educator.* College Station, Tex., 1983.

Cockrell, Monroe F. *The Lost Account of the Battle of Corinth and Court-Martial of Gen. Van Dorn.* Jackson, Tenn., 1935.

Phifer, Charles H. *Genealogy and History of the Phifer Family.* Charlotte, 1910.

Savannah *Morning News*, December 27, 1896.

PLEASANT JACKSON PHILLIPS

Pleasant Jackson Phillips, brigadier general of Georgia militia, was born on July 3, 1819, in Harris County, Georgia, the son of General Charles and Anne (Nicks) Phillips. His father was a North Carolina native. Young Phillips grew up to be a very prosperous plantation owner and slaveholder in Harris County and president of the Bank of Brunswick. By 1860 he resided in Columbus.

Phillips, a prewar major in the militia, organized the 31st Georgia Infantry Regiment in the fall of 1861. On November 18 of that year he was unanimously elected colonel, his commission dating from November 19. Colonel Phillips was a great favorite with his men; one of his privates wrote that Phillips was "very popular with his regiment" and "busy as a bee."[1] The authorities ordered the 31st to Savannah, and throughout the winter of 1861 the regiment helped guard that city. Upon the reorganization of the army in May, 1862, Phillips was not reelected as colonel, and resigned his commission, effective May 13, 1862.[2] The next month his old regiment entrained for Virginia and fought in Lee's army till the end of the war. Returning to Columbus, Phillips resumed his militia service and was, on July 7, 1862, appointed brigadier general. In 1863 the governor appointed Phillips colonel, and district commander, in the reorganized Georgia militia. In 1864 he was appointed brigadier general of the 2nd Brigade of the Georgia Militia. The four-brigade militia division joined the Army of Tennessee before Atlanta that July and served throughout the siege of Atlanta. After Atlanta fell, Governor Brown of Georgia gave the militiamen a thirty-day furlough to allow them to harvest their crops. Recalled to duty in October, the militia division was detached from the main army and ordered to oppose, as best it could, Major General William T. Sherman's Union army in its march through Georgia. On October 22, 1864, the militia division's commander, Major General G. W. Smith, put Phillips, the senior brigadier, in temporary command of the division, with instructions not to become engaged with the advancing Union forces. Phillips spotted an isolated Union infantry brigade near Griswoldville and, in disobedience of orders, launched his inexperienced militiamen in an attack. The division was slaughtered, and Phillips came in for heavy criticism. Phillips was accused by some survivors of being drunk when ordering the fatal attack. After this battle, Phillips departed from the militia division and the war.

General Phillips returned to Columbus and reentered the banking business. He died at his residence in Wynnton on October 12, 1876, and is buried in Columbus' Linnwood Cemetery.

General Phillips' command of a brigade of militia that served in a campaign qualifies him to be considered a Confederate general.

NOTES

1. Robert G. Stephens, *Intrepid Warrior: Clement Anselm Evans* (Dayton, 1992), 77.

2. In April, 1862, the Confederate Congress passed a conscription law which, among other features, automatically extended army enlistments to three years. Since the men in the 31st (and most regiments) had volunteered for only one year, the original regimental officer elections were voided and new officers elected.

MAIN SOURCES

Bragg, William H. "A Little Battle at Griswoldville." *Civil War Times Illustrated*, XVII (July, 1979), 44–49.
Stephens, Robert G. *Intrepid Warrior: Clement Anselm Evans*. Dayton, 1992.

WILLIAM PHILLIPS

William Phillips was born on July 8, 1824, in Asheville, North Carolina, the son of George Duval and Elizabeth (Patton) Phillips. The elder Phillips, a Unionville, South Carolina, doctor and farmer, soon removed to Clarksville in Habersham County, Georgia, where he became a prominent public figure. The younger Phillips attended the University of Georgia at Athens, class of 1844. By 1850 he settled in Marietta in Cobb County, Georgia, and studied law under ex-Governor McDonald. Phillips, "by his close attention to business, genial manners, and wonderful tact," soon became one of the more prominent and successful lawyers in northern Georgia.[1] In 1854 he was appointed solicitor general of the Blue Ridge Circuit, serving until 1867. Active in Democratic party affairs, Phillips became an ally of Georgia's war governor, Joseph Brown.

Courtesy Betty Hargis Peardon

At the commencement of the war Phillips, a prewar militia captain, was appointed brigadier general of Georgia state troops by Governor Brown. Placed in command of the 4th Brigade, he organized two camps of instruction in northern Georgia, at which thousands of volunteers received their first training.[2] On August 1, 1861, Phillips resigned his state rank to become colonel of "Phillips' Legion," an organization of fifteen infantry companies, six cavalry companies, and a company of artillery. The command performed well throughout the war, serving in Lee's army. In the Kanawha Valley campaign of 1861, Phillips, "as true to his men as a man could be," contracted typhoid fever and was forced to return to Georgia.[3] In the spring of 1862, somewhat recovered, he rejoined his unit, now stationed in South Carolina. The legion returned to Virginia that summer, but Phillips, suffering a recurrence of ill health, did not accompany them. A patient in several Virginia hospitals, he formally resigned his commission (because of "paralysis") on February 13, 1863. Returning to Marietta, the general channeled his energies into managing the Marietta Paper Mills, producing writing paper as well as Confederate currency. His only other war involvement was a stint as major of a militia unit, the 9th Georgia Cavalry Battalion of the State Guard, charged with rounding up conscripts and deserters in northern Georgia. In November, 1864, Phillips was placed in command of Camp Newnan and served as commander there until the end of the war.

Broken in health (his bout with typhoid caused his right eye to go blind) and fortune (Sherman's army destroyed his paper mill), Phillips returned to Marietta after the war. He resumed his lucrative legal practice, engaged in farming, and was active in promoting local education. The remainder of his fortune was spent in the development of the Marietta and North Georgia Railroad, of which he was vice president. Phillips' only public service was as Cobb County's state representative in the 1877 to 1878 legislature. General Phillips died on September 24, 1908, at his Marietta home, and is buried in Citizen's Cemetery, Marietta.

Phillips' rank of general in Georgia's state army qualifies him to be considered a Confederate general.

NOTES

1. William J. Northen, ed., *Men of Mark in Georgia* (6 vols.; Atlanta, 1907–12), III, 248.

2. There were several bodies of Georgia state forces, organized under several different state laws. The 4th Brigade of the Georgia Volunteers was formed in mid-March, 1861, under an 1860 law authorizing the governor to raise men for the defense of the state. In early June Governor Brown offered to transfer Phillips' brigade (two infantry regiments plus other units, 2,500 strong) en masse to the Confederacy. The purpose of the offer was to obtain for Phillips a commission as brigadier general of the PACS. The president objected, wanting to keep the power to create generals out of state governors' hands. In August Brown relented and transferred the brigade anyway.

3. United Confederate Veterans: Marietta Camp 763, *Proceedings of Memorial Exercises, August 5, 1909*, 13, quoted in a November 21, 1991, letter from Betty Peardon, great-granddaughter of General Phillips, to the author.

MAIN SOURCES

Coffman, Richard M. "A Vital Unit." *Civil War Times Illustrated*, XX (January, 1982), 40–45.
Northen, William J., ed. *Men of Mark in Georgia*. 6 vols. Atlanta, 1907–12.

JOHN GALBRAITH PRATT

John Galbraith Pratt, a brigadier general of Louisiana militia, was born on March 31, 1816, in Hartford, Connecticut.[1] His father, Joseph Pratt, the postmaster of Hartford, was descended from John Pratt, an original proprietor of Hartford. His mother, Fanny Wadsworth, was also descended from an old and prominent Connecticut family. The family removed to St. Landry Parish, Louisiana, in 1845. Pratt became a merchant and sugar planter, living a life of seclusion and retirement in Opelousas until the secession crisis. An ardent states' rights Democrat, Pratt was chosen as a delegate to the 1860 Democratic Convention in Charleston.

At the start of the war Pratt was commissioned a colonel of the Opelousas regiment of militia. Five days after Fort Sumter he was elected to the rank of brigadier general to command the 1st Brigade of the 4th Division of the Louisiana Militia. In October, 1861, he was promoted to major general to command the 4th Division. Upon the reorganization of the state militia in early 1862, Pratt, reduced in rank to brigadier general, was put in command of the 9th Militia Brigade. In May, 1862, after the fall of New Orleans to a Union invasion force, Governor Thomas Moore of Louisiana called Pratt and his brigade into active service. That same month the governor ordered Pratt to establish a camp of instruction for Confederate army conscripts of south Louisiana. Named Camp Pratt in his honor, the camp (near New Iberia) housed as many as 6,800 draftees, who received their first training under his command. On August 25, 1862, the Confederate government took over operation of the camp, and Pratt returned to his militia brigade. In September, 1862, he led a mixed force of militia and Confederate cavalry in a raid along the Bayou des Allemands, engaging in two skirmishes. On September 4, Pratt's militiamen captured a Federal outpost and 182 Union soldiers. On February 19, 1863, the governor appointed Pratt, whom he called "my most intelligent brigadier," to command the district of south and east Louisiana.[2] In this post Pratt relentlessly enforced the Confederate conscription laws, using militiamen to hunt down reluctant civilians and force them to join the army. Like most conscript officers, Pratt was despised by the stay-at-homes. Because of ill health, he was soon forced to resign his militia commission and return home. On October 12, 1863, a Union patrol ran across General Pratt riding calmly through the streets of Grand Coteau in a buggy. The Union troops sent the protesting general (he claimed to be a private citizen, not a soldier) to a New Orleans prison. Later paroled, Pratt returned home. In the last months of the war Governor Henry Allen chose Pratt to prepare a public report on Union army depredations in Louisiana.

When the war ended Pratt ran for a seat in the U.S. Congress, was defeated, and returned to his native Connecticut. On July 30, 1866, in the town of Portland, Connecticut, General Pratt passed away. He is buried in Trinity Cemetery in Portland.

General Pratt's command of a brigade of militia that served in a campaign qualifies him to be considered a Confederate general.

NOTES

1. Charles B. Whittelsey, *The Ancestry and The Descendants of John Pratt* (Hartford, 1900), cited in Glenn R. Conrad, ed., *A Dictionary of Louisiana Biography* (2 vols.; New Orleans, 1988), gives an 1817 date of birth. However, his tombstone inscription and a more contemporary book on the Pratt family, F. W. Chapman, *The Pratt Family* (Hartford, 1864), agree on an 1816 date of birth.

2. OR, LIII, 813.

MAIN SOURCES

Casey, Powel A. *Encyclopedia of Forts, Named Camps, and Other Military Installations in Louisiana, 1700–1981*. Baton Rouge, 1983.

Conrad, Glenn R., ed. *A Dictionary of Louisiana Biography*. 2 vols. New Orleans, 1988.

Edmonds, David C. *Yankee Autumn in Acadiana*. Lafayette, La., 1979.

EDWIN WALLER PRICE

Edwin Waller Price was born on June 10, 1834, in Randolph County, Missouri, the eldest son of future governor and Confederate major general Sterling Price and his wife, Martha Head. After his education at the state university, the young Price bought a farm in Chariton County, Missouri, where he resided the rest of his life.

In May, 1861, Price was elected captain of a militia company raised in Chariton County. With the coming of open conflict in Missouri the younger Price joined the Missouri State Guard, commanded by his father. Elected lieutenant colonel of the 1st Regiment of the 3rd (John B. Clark's) Division, he distinguished himself at the Battles of Carthage, Wilson's Creek, and Lexington. At Carthage Price had a horse killed under him "while gallantly urging and cheering forward the forces."[1] On December 2, 1861, Price, known as "Stump" because of his short stature, was elected brigadier general of the 3rd Division to succeed Clark. During the winter of 1861 Price, "an able, gallant officer," was detached on recruiting duty.[2] In February, 1862, while leading a band of recruits back to his father, Price was captured by a Union patrol while he was resting at the home of a southern sympathizer. He was paroled, with the proviso that he remain within the limits of Chariton County until exchanged. In the summer of 1862 he was exchanged for Union Brigadier General Benjamin Prentiss, who had been captured at the Battle of Shiloh. After visiting his father, then in Mississippi, Price returned to Missouri and took the oath of allegiance to the Union. At the behest of Missouri's Union Governor Hamilton Gamble, President Lincoln issued Price a full pardon. For the rest of the war Price was an open and public Unionist. On at least two occasions he gave Union authorities information of Confederate troop movements. Despite this public posture, rumor had it that Price was spending his time secretly organizing for the South.[3] The papers of Missouri's Confederate Governor Thomas Reynolds mention two reports current at the time. One indicates that Price allowed himself to get caught, that he was a Unionist; the rumors about his being a secret agent were put out by Sterling Price to save his son's (and Price's own) reputation. The second rumor was that young Price was his father's secret agent in Missouri, organizing southern supporters there into breaking away from the Confederacy and setting up a separate state under Sterling Price. In this scenario Sterling Price's loyalty to the Confederacy was questioned. It is only fair to note that Governor Reynolds was a political opponent of Sterling Price. Yet an-

Civil War Photograph Albums, Louisiana and Lower Mississippi Valley Collections, LSU Libraries, Louisiana State University

other rumor[4] had Price deserting the southern cause because he resented how President Davis treated his father.

Despite this seeming desertion, father and son were reconciled after the war. Price even moved to St. Louis for four years to care for his father's widow. In 1871 he returned to his Chariton County farm, where he raised wheat and ran a tobacco factory. "A splendid citizen, and one of the best known and most popular men in Chariton County," Price died in St. Louis on January 6, 1908.[5] He is buried, with his father, in Bellefontaine Cemetery in St. Louis.

NOTES

1. OR, III, 31.
2. Albert Castel, *General Sterling Price and the Civil War in the West* (Baton Rouge, 1968), 192.
3. The whole, fascinating story is told in Castel's *General Sterling Price*, 132–36.
4. In the Charleston *Mercury*, November 7, 1862.
5. Benjamin L. Price, *John Price the Emigrant* (Alexandria, La., 1910), 49.

MAIN SOURCES

Castel, Albert. *General Sterling Price and the Civil War in the West*. Baton Rouge, 1968.
Shalhope, Robert E. *Sterling Price: Portrait of a Southerner*. Columbia, Mo., 1971.
Wallace, J. C. "Gen. E. W. Price." *Confederate Veteran*, XI (1903), 544.

GEORGE WASHINGTON RAINS

George Washington Rains, the son of Gabriel Manigault and Hester (Ambrose) Rains, was born in Craven County, North Carolina, in 1817. His father, a successful cabinetmaker and furniture trader, moved to Alabama soon afterward. Rains attended local schools in North Carolina and the United States Military Academy, graduating in 1842 third in a class of fifty-six. After graduation he stayed at West Point to teach engineering, chemistry, mineralogy, and geology. During the Mexican War Rains served as aide-de-camp to Lieutenant General Winfield Scott, commander of the U.S. Army, and won brevet promotions to captain and major. In 1856 he was promoted to captain, but

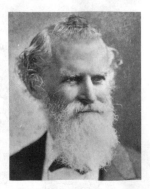

Augusta Richmond County Museum

resigned from the army in that year to become part owner and president of the large

Washington and Highland Iron Works in Newburgh, New York. An inventor like his older brother (future Confederate General Gabriel Rains), Rains received several patents for advances in steam engines and boilers.

On July 10, 1861, President Davis assigned Rains the task of building and operating a central gunpowder mill, which would supply the new nation's armies. At this time the Confederacy had only a small reserve of prewar powder and no facilities for large-scale production. Although he had considerable experience as a manufacturer, Rains had no experience manufacturing gunpowder. Equipped only with a pamphlet on how to make gunpowder, Rains built a factory in Augusta, Georgia, and performed miracles. He pioneered new methods of powder manufacture, producing large quantities of powder of a purity previously unknown. He also initiated the wholesale collection of niter (the base element of gunpowder) from caves and cesspools, and authored a book on the making of saltpeter. The Augusta powder mills supplied the armies with 2.75 million pounds of high quality gunpowder during the war, enough for all their needs. Arguably, Rains did more than any other man to keep the Confederate war machine running. On April 7, 1862, this "very clever, highly educated, and agreeable officer" was placed in charge of all munitions productions in Augusta.[1] His factories turned out cannon, ammunition, grenades, and a host of ordnance stores. His successes were rewarded with promotions to major (July 10, 1861), lieutenant colonel (May 22, 1862) and colonel (July 12, 1863). Rains's only active service was as colonel of a regiment of local defense troops, made up in large part of his factory workers and invalids, which defended Augusta during Sherman's 1864 March to the Sea. On March 14, 1865, he was put in charge of the ordnance depots and arsenals that still functioned in Alabama, Georgia, and South Carolina. On April 28, 1865, three weeks after Lee's surrender, Rains finally ceased production.

Rains remained in Augusta after the war and embarked on a career in education. From 1867 to 1884 he was a professor of chemistry at the University of Georgia, eventually becoming dean of the faculty. In 1882 he published his *History of the Confederate States Powder Works*. In 1894 Colonel Rains returned to New York and engaged in business there. He died in Newburgh on March 21, 1898, and is buried in St. George's Cemetery.

CV and Cullum list Rains as a general. CV has him appointed general from Georgia in 1865, presumably for leading local defense and reservist forces in Georgia. However, Rains's highest rank appears to have been colonel. He appears in the *OR* as a colonel as late as March 29, 1865.

NOTE

1. Florence F. Corley, *Confederate City. Augusta, Georgia, 1860–1865* (Columbia, S.C., 1960), 53.

MAIN SOURCES

Melton, Maurice. "'A Grand Assemblage': George W. Rains and the Augusta Powder Works."
Civil War Times Illustrated, XI (1973), 28–37.

Rains, George W. *History of the Confederate Powder Works*. Augusta, 1882.

Savas, Theodore P. "Bulwark of the Beleaguered Confederacy: George Washington Rains and
the Augusta Powder Works." *Civil War*, IX (September–October, 1991), 10–17, 20.

JAMES SPENCER RAINS

James Spencer Rains was born in Tennessee (proba-
bly in Warren County) on October 2, 1817, the son of
Asahel and Malvina (Duncan) Rains of Warren County.
An uncle was future Ohio Congressman Alexander
Duncan. By 1840 Rains had moved to southwest Mis-
souri, around Sarcoxie. Rains farmed in Newton and
Jasper counties, but his main interest was politics.
He served as prewar general of the militia, as Newton
County judge from 1840 to 1842, was elected in 1844
to represent Newton County in the state house, and
served in the state senate from 1854 to 1861. In 1845
President Polk appointed Rains as an agent for Indian
affairs for the Neosho Agency (in northeast Okla-
homa). In 1848 he was transferred to the Osage River
Agency in Kansas. In 1850 Rains went to California,

Civil War Photograph Albums, Louisiana
and Lower Mississippi Valley Collections,
LSU Libraries, Louisiana State University

where he was made a general in the state militia. Returning to Missouri, the
Democrat Rains, soured by secessionist ex-Whigs taking over his old party, switched
his allegiance to the American ("Know-Nothing") party. In 1860 Rains was the
"Union" (American) party's unsuccessful candidate for Congress for the Southwest
Missouri District.

On May 18, 1861, Governor Claiborne Jackson of Missouri commissioned Rains
a brigadier general in the Missouri State Guard, to head the 8th Division. Rains entered into his new duties with great energy and zeal, and recruited a large number
of men to the southern cause. It soon became apparent, however, that notwith-
standing his "undoubted courage, patriotism, and zeal" the affable and popular Rains
was not suited to military command. As one friend recalled, Rains "was profoundly
ignorant of everything pertaining to military affairs. . . . and was so good natured
that he could not say 'no' to any request, or enforce regulations that were distaste-

ful to his men."[1] Rains led the 8th at the Battles of Wilson's Creek, Lexington, and Pea Ridge, and was wounded in the latter battle. On the Confederate retreat from Pea Ridge Rains vehemently denounced Confederate army commander Major General Earl Van Dorn, in Van Dorn's presence, as the only man in the army who was "whipped."[2] Understandably, Van Dorn arrested Rains for his intemperate insult, but within three weeks Rains was reinstated in command. In April, 1862, when Van Dorn urged the Missouri State Guard to march with him to Mississippi, Rains (not surprisingly) remained behind and took command of those guard troops who wished to stay in the Trans-Mississippi theater. Major General Thomas Hindman, the new commander in Arkansas, then placed Rains (a state militia officer) in command of mixed state guard and regular Confederate forces in northwest Arkansas, Rains leading the whole with his militia rank. General Hindman reported that he accepted Missouri State Guard general officers (including Rains) "into the Confederate service, conditioned upon the approval of the Secretary of War," in order to prevent the reestablishment of a separate state guard and to unify the command structure.[3] From this command Hindman relieved him in October, 1862, alleging incompetence and insobriety. It appears that the latter charge was well-founded; the governor of Missouri reprimanded Rains on at least one occasion for an incident involving an ambulance crash. The governor did acknowledge Rains's "known ability" and recommended him for promotion to general of the PACS.[4] Rains moved to Texas, suffering from war wounds and broken in health. Recovering, in 1864 Rains reentered Missouri at the command of the governor to recruit for the Missouri State Guard. By Rains's count, he raised thousands of men there, who withdrew to Arkansas upon the failure of Price's raid into Missouri.[5]

After 1865 Rains remained in Texas, settling in Wood County and, after 1867, in Kaufman County. Rains became a prominent farmer, railroad promoter, lawyer, and civic leader. One newspaper called him "one of the most intelligent farmers in this state."[6] Once a Democrat, Rains became a Granger organizer. In 1878 he ran for lieutenant governor of Texas on the Greenback party slate. In 1880 Rains was a delegate to the National Greenback Party Convention. On May 19, 1880, General Rains died at his Kaufman County home and was buried in Lee Cemetery in Seagoville, Dallas County.

General Rains's command of a brigade in the Missouri State Guard, as well as his service in a campaign, qualify him to be considered a Confederate general.

NOTES

1. John F. Snyder to Walter B. Douglas, December 15, 1913, in John F. Snyder Papers, Missouri Historical Society, St. Louis.

2. William L. Shea and Earl J. Hess, Pea Ridge: Civil War Campaign in the West (Chapel Hill, 1992), 260.

3. Evans, ed., CMH, XIV, 107, quoting Hindman's report of operations in Arkansas.

4. Reynolds to General William R. Boggs, January 10, 1865, in Thomas C. Reynolds Papers, Library of Congress.

5. The governor, by his own admission, had no funds to pay the troops raised and no supplies to feed or equip them. It was intended that the troops be transferred to Confederate service. Rains was at this time the ranking officer of the Missouri State Guard which, since 1862, had existed only on paper. It appears that Rains's recruiting claims were, like most such claims, greatly exaggerated.

6. Dallas *Herald*, July 14, 1874.

MAIN SOURCES

Dallas *Herald*, May 20, 1880.
Snyder, J. F. to Walter B. Douglas, December 15, 30, 1913, February 21, 1914. John F. Snyder
Collection, Missouri Historical Society, St. Louis.

HORACE RANDAL

Horace Randal was born on January 4, 1833, in McNairy County, Tennessee, the son of Dr. Leonard and Sarah (Kyle) Randal.[1] His parents moved to near St. Augustine, Texas, in 1838, where his father, a doctor and army surgeon, was elected Texas congressman. Appointed to West Point in 1849, the young Randal graduated five years later, forty-fifth in a class of forty-six. Posted to the infantry, Randal transferred to the 1st Dragoons in 1855. With the 1st he fought Indians on the southwest frontier. In 1857 then Secretary of War Jefferson Davis recommended that Randal receive a brevet promotion in recognition of Randal's "gallant and meritorious conduct in affairs with the Apache Indians."[2]

Courtesy J. Tom Jones, Jr.

Lieutenant Randal was in Washington, D.C., the week before President Lincoln's inaugural. Lieutenant General Winfield Scott, who thought highly of him, allegedly offered Randal a commission as major in the regular army to keep him loyal.[3] However, Randal followed his state, resigning from the U.S. Army on February 26, 1861. On March 26, 1861, Randal was commissioned a first lieutenant in the Confederate regular army, to rank from March 16. On April 25, 1861, Randal (by now a captain) was ordered to Pensacola, where he served as quartermaster on the staff of General Braxton Bragg. In the summer of 1861 Randal resigned his commission. Randal had complained to President Davis that others, junior to him in the old army, had been promoted ahead of him. Randal intended to return to Texas and raise a regiment. However, at the request of his brother-in-law, Major General G. W. Smith, who had recently been given command of a corps in northern Virginia, Randal postponed that trip in order to serve on Smith's staff. For six weeks he acted as a volunteer aide-de-camp, while Smith begged the president to give Randal a formal appointment. President Davis was reluctant to reappoint an officer who had so recently resigned, but eventually reappointed Randal lieutenant and aide-de-camp. He was the inspector general of Smith's corps throughout the winter of 1861. An especial favorite of General Joseph E. Johnston, the army commander, Randal was often "given the most important duties and authority." A fellow staff officer remembered him as "in some respects the most remarkable man I met during the war." Randal was, among other talents, "a most remarkable horseman," continually riding at a full gallop no matter what the terrain. It was said that Randal's close friend and West Point roommate, General John B. Hood, "always predicted that he would be the cavalry leader of the war if he got a chance."[4] On December 19, 1861, Randal was authorized to organize a regiment of cavalry out of companies then being raised in Texas. On February 12, 1862, he was commissioned colonel of cavalry. Returning to Texas, he was given command of the newly recruited 28th Texas Cavalry, a unit that fought dismounted most of the war. By December Colonel Randal was in charge of a brigade of infantry in Brigadier General Henry McCulloch's division. His brigade was left in reserve during the June 25, 1863, attack on Milliken's Bend. On November 8, 1863, General Kirby Smith recommended Randal for promotion to brigadier general. However, the brigade at the time was not large enough to justify having a general to command it. At the Battle of Mansfield (April 8, 1864) Randal's brigade crushed the Union line and led the pursuit, capturing five hundred prisoners and the Union wagon train. The army commander reported that "in vigor, energy and daring Randal surpassed my expectations, high as they were of him and his fine brigade."[5] Five days after that battle General Kirby Smith assigned Randal to duty as brigadier general, the commission to date from April 8. Randal had only two weeks to enjoy this honor. While leading his brigade in a charge at the Battle of Jenkins' Ferry in Arkansas on April 30, 1864, Randal was mortally wounded. He died of his wounds on May 2.[6] First buried near the battlefield, his remains were later removed to Old Marshall Cemetery in Marshall, Texas. Randall County, Texas, is named (or rather misnamed) after General Randal.

Wright, *SHSP*, *CMH*, Heitman, Wood, and *CV* all list Randal as a general.

NOTES

1. An article on General Randal in William C. Davis, ed., *The Confederate General* (6 vols.; Harrisburg, Pa., 1991–92), VI, 192–93, gives a January 1 date of birth. A January 20, 1849, letter from Randal's father to the secretary of war (provided to the author by James T. Jones, Jr., grandnephew of General Randal) mentions the January 4 date of birth used here.

2. Lynda Crist et al., eds., *The Papers of Jefferson Davis* (7 vols.; Baton Rouge, 1983–1991), VI, 111.

3. George C. Crocket, *Two Centuries in East Texas* (Dallas, 1932), 339–41, relates that,

after Randal resigned, Senator Charles Sumner, on behalf of the Lincoln administration, offered Randal a major general's commission if Randal remained loyal. If an offer was in fact made, the rank of major seems more plausible. It would have been unprecedented for a lieutenant—even a highly regarded lieutenant—to be promoted to major general. Mark M. Boatner, III, *Civil War Dictionary* (New York, 1988), 678, has Randal commanding the U.S. Army cavalry at President Lincoln's 1861 inaugural, embellishing the story in Crocket, *Two Centuries*, 340, wherein Senator Sumner also offered Randal command of the cavalry at Lincoln's inaugural. Randal actually resigned from the U.S. Army the week before and was visiting his brother-in-law in New York the day of the inaugural.

4. Gilbert E. Govan and James W. Livingood, eds., *The Haskell Memoirs: The Personal Narrative of a Confederate Officer* (New York, 1960), 10.

5. Evans, ed., *CMH*, XV, 251.

6. Randal's tombstone says he was killed at the Battle of Jenkins' Ferry, April 30, 1864. However, the contemporary account of a member of Walker's division makes it clear that Randal lived until May 2. See Joseph P. Blessington, *Campaigns of Walker's Texas Division* (New York, 1875), 253–56.

MAIN SOURCES

Anderson, John Q., ed. *A Texas Surgeon in the C.S.A.* Tuscaloosa, 1957.
Blessington, Joseph P. *Campaigns of Walker's Texas Division*. New York, 1875.
Crockett, George C. *Two Centuries in East Texas*. Dallas, 1932.
Smith, Gustavus W. *Confederate War Papers*. New York, 1884.

JOHN COLEMAN REID

John Coleman Reid was born on December 6, 1824, in Tuscaloosa County, Alabama, the son of Thomas and Mary (Coleman) Reid. The father, of Irish descent, was a North Carolina native and a wealthy planter. The family removed to Memphis in 1830, and young Reid received his education there. At the age of nineteen he began the study of law and in 1843 was admitted to the bar of Jackson, Tennessee. Reid practiced at Purdy, Tennessee; Kingston, Tennessee (1845 to 1851); Prattville, Alabama (1851 to 1853); and Marion, Alabama (1854 to 1871). Reid served as a "Know-Nothing" state representative from Perry County from 1855 to 1857. Disgusted with politics after one term, he formed a company in 1856 to explore the newly acquired Gadsden Purchase (now southern Arizona). The expedition lasted ten months and the story of the expedition was published in 1858 under the title *Reid's Tramp*. While on the "tramp," Reid briefly joined in a filibustering expedition into Mexico, being elected first lieutenant of a company of ragged adventurers.

In the 1860 election Reid, an opponent of secession, supported the "Constitutional Union" party. After Abraham Lincoln's election, however, Reid, along with most southern Whigs, reluctantly supported secession. In April, 1861, he was elected first lieutenant of Company A of the 8th Alabama Infantry. The regiment was sent to Virginia, but saw little action. In October, 1861, Secretary of War Leroy P. Walker, an old friend from north Alabama, commissioned Reid to raise a regiment of infantry. He raised the 28th Alabama and, upon its organization in March, 1862, was elected its lieutenant colonel. The 28th joined the Army of Tennessee after the Battle of Shiloh and was attached to a brigade of Alabama and South Carolina regiments, soon to be commanded by Brigadier General Arthur M. Manigault. The 28th quickly won the reputation as "a fighting regiment that never failed to give a good account of itself," though it missed the major fighting that occurred in the summer and fall campaigns of the Army of Tennessee.[1] On November 29, 1862, Reid, "an active, energetic officer," was appointed colonel of the 28th.[2] At the Battle of Stone's River on December 31, 1862, to January 2, 1863, he was shot in the thigh, but with great courage stayed on his horse and continued in command. Reid also led his regiment at the September 19 and 20, 1863, Battle of Chickamauga. On February 10, 1864, General Joseph E. Johnston, the army commander, ordered Reid to leave the 28th and travel to northern Alabama to organize dispersed cavalry commands. He served there the remainder of the war, hunting down deserters more than fighting Yankees. In December, 1864, in the wake of General John Bell Hood's invasion of Tennessee, General P. G. T. Beauregard placed Reid in command of the post of Corinth, Mississippi, a vital supply center in the rear of Hood's army.

Reid returned to Marion, and his law practice, after the war. In 1871 he relocated to Selma, Alabama, where he made a mark as one of the city's ablest attorneys. The townspeople elected him to the city council. In 1894, the city's Confederate veterans elected him commander of the local UCV camp. Colonel Reid died in Selma on February 26, 1896, and is buried there in Live Oak Cemetery.

SHSP and CV list Reid as a general. The latter has him appointed brigadier general from Alabama in 1864. The former says he was acting brigadier general for recruiting in Alabama. Owen's History of Alabama and Dictionary of Alabama Biography[3] has him appointed brigadier general by General Johnston in the fall of 1864. This is unlikely, given that Johnston had been relieved of command that summer and thus was not in a position to promote anyone. During the war both his superiors and the Alabama Legislature recommended Reid for promotion to general. He occasionally exercised brigade command and was often called "general" after the war. However, the OR have Reid as a colonel as late as December, 1864, and his May 15, 1865, parole shows him as a colonel.

NOTES

1. R. Lockwood Tower, ed., A Carolinian Goes to War: The Civil War Narratives of Arthur Middleton Manigault (Columbia, S.C., 1983), 42.

2. OR, Vol. XLV, Pt. 1, p. 1255.
3. Thomas M. Owen, *History of Alabama and Dictionary of Alabama Biography* (4 vols.; Chicago, 1921), IV, 1424.

MAIN SOURCES

Northern Alabama, Historical and Biographical. Birmingham, 1888.
Tower, R. Lockwood, ed. *A Carolinian Goes to War: The Civil War Narratives of Arthur Middleton Manigault.* Columbia, S.C., 1983.
Walker, James H. "Those Gallant Men of the Twenty-Eighth." *United Daughters of the Confederacy Magazine,* XLI (November, 1988), 29–30.

ARTHUR EXUM REYNOLDS

Arthur Exum Reynolds as born on November 29, 1817, in Alexandria in Smith County, Tennessee, the son of Josiah and Sally (Exum) Reynolds. Educated at Clinton College, he moved to Lawrence County, Alabama, in 1838, and studied law there. He moved to Jacinto in Tishomingo County, Mississippi, in the 1840s and became a teacher, a lawyer, and a state senator from Tishomingo County from 1850 to 1858. A Whig, and a Unionist delegate at the state's secession convention, Reynolds nonetheless signed the proclamation of secession.

Courtesy The Huntington Library, San Marino, California

At the start of the war Reynolds proposed to President Davis that he raise a regiment. Davis agreed to the offer, but since the Confederate government had no arms told Reynolds that he would have to equip the regiment himself. Returning to Corinth, Reynolds, with the help of local business people, organized and equipped the 26th Mississippi Infantry. He was unanimously elected colonel on September 10, 1861. At the Battle of Fort Donelson Reynolds led the 26th in a successful charge until his horse was shot out from under him. The corpulent Reynolds, weighing over three hundred pounds, could not keep up on foot with his charging men. The 26th was caught up in the eventual Confederate surrender. The Union authorities confined Reynolds in Old Capitol Prison in Washington, D.C. After exchange on August 27, 1862, the "enterprising and gallant" Reynolds led the 26th in the Vicksburg campaign.[1] At the Battle of Champion's Hill he succeeded Brigadier General Lloyd Tilghman in command of the brigade after Tilghman was wounded, and led the brigade through the 1863 Mississippi campaigns. In August, 1863, Reynolds was detached and assigned to the Conscription Bureau. By the spring of 1864 Reynolds was back with his old regiment and was again in temporary brigade command. That summer the 26th was transferred to Davis' brigade of the Army of Northern Virginia. Reynolds missed the early battles of the Wilderness campaign, but joined Lee's army in time for the Petersburg battles. He was wounded at the Battle of Weldon Railroad on August 18, 1864. The wound sent him to the hospital for months. After partial recovery, the medical board ordered him back to Mississippi to recuperate. Reynolds was paroled at Meridian, Mississippi, on May 21, 1865.

Immediately after the war Reynolds was elected to the U.S. Congress. However, the radical Republican Congress refused to seat the ex-rebel. Subsequently he moved to Corinth, Mississippi, and practiced law there. The Reconstruction governor appointed Reynolds chancellor judge of the Eighth District in 1870. After four years, Reynolds returned to his law practice. He died in 1881 and is buried in Jacinto Cemetery.[2] It was said of him that the county "never claimed a citizen of more genuine manliness or universal popularity."[3]

SHSP, Wood, *CV*, and Heitman list Reynolds as a general. *SHSP* says he was appointed a brigadier general in March, 1865, but the final surrender came before he was assigned to a command. Brigadier General Joseph Davis, the President's nephew, led the brigade that included the 26th through to the surrender at Appomattox; it is difficult to see any brigade command vacancy Reynolds could have been promoted to fill.

NOTES

1. *OR*, Vol. XXIV, Pt. 1, p. 419.

2. Reynolds' 1880 date of death per his tombstone, which inaccurately gives him an 1816 date of birth. A biographical article in Dunbar Rowland, ed., *History of Mississippi: The Heart of the South* (4 vols.; Chicago, 1925), III, 721, followed in Robert K. Krick, *Lee's Colonels* (Dayton, 1991), 317–18, gives him an April, 1882, date of death. However, the author has examined Corinth newspapers for April and May of 1882 finding no mention of Reynolds' death. The papers of his nephew and law partner, L. P. Reynolds, at the Department of Archives and History, Jackson, Mississippi, show a tax receipt of Colonel Reynolds' dated as late as March 8, 1881.

3. Fan Alexander Cochran, *History of Old Tishomingo County, Mississippi Territory* (Oklahoma City, 1969), 310.

MAIN SOURCES

Alcorn County Historical Association. *The History of Alcorn County, Mississippi*. Dallas, 1983.
Cochran, Fan Alexander. *History of Old Tishomingo County, Mississippi Territory*. Oklahoma City, 1969.
Rowland, Dunbar, ed. *History of Mississippi: The Heart of the South*. 4 vols. Chicago, 1925.

THOMAS GRIMKÉ RHETT

Thomas Grimké Rhett was born Thomas Moore Smith on August 2, 1821, in South Carolina, the son of James and Charlotte (Haskell) Smith. Both parents were from prominent South Carolina families.[1] His father (a lawyer, planter, and state senator) and his five brothers (an uncle was future Senator Robert Barnwell Rhett) changed their name to the more aristocratic "Rhett" in 1837. Appointed at large to West Point, Rhett graduated sixth in his class of forty-one in 1845. His antebellum army career started as a second lieutenant of ordnance on July 1, 1845, working in the Washington, D.C., arsenal. Transferring to the Mounted Rifles Regiment, he was promoted to first lieutenant on April 18, 1847, and captain on September 16, 1853. Active in the Mexican War, Rhett was breveted captain in 1847 for gallant and meritorious conduct. Major and paymaster from April 7, 1858, he served as paymaster at Fort Bliss, Texas, through 1861.

Upon the surrender of the U.S. Army forces in Texas, Rhett, pursuant to the surrender terms, transferred his funds to the Texas authorities. He officially resigned from the army on April 1, 1861. In the meantime Rhett was nominated by the governor of South Carolina to be a brigadier general of South Carolina volunteers (under the act of December 17, 1860). This was before Fort Sumter, and Rhett never served as general. Commissioned a Confederate major in March, 1861, Rhett joined the staff of General P. G. T. Beauregard. On July 20, 1861, he was appointed assistant adjutant general and chief of staff to General Joseph E. Johnston, commander of the main army in northern Virginia. He served on Johnston's staff until the latter's wounding at the Battle of Seven Pines in 1862. Relieved from duty with Johnston, Rhett was transferred to the Trans-Mississippi Department and served first as chief of ordnance for the District of Arkansas. In April, 1863, Rhett was appointed chief of artillery for the Trans-Mississippi Department. The balance of the war he spent in that capacity. A fellow staff member remembers him as "a man of grand physique, spirit and capacity. He could see no wrong in one he liked and no good in one he disliked." His exile to the Trans-Mississippi can perhaps be explained by his association with General Johnston and with Senator Rhett, both vocal administration opponents.[2]

After the war Rhett refused to remain in America. Along with several other former officers, both northern and southern, he accepted an offer to join the army of the Khedive of Egypt. Rhett served as colonel of ordnance in the Egyptian army through 1873. Paralyzed by a stroke in September, 1873, Rhett resigned his commission and went to Europe. Returning to the U.S. in 1876, he lived in Baltimore with relatives until his death on July 28, 1878. He is buried in Green Mount Cemetery in Baltimore.

Rhett's rank of general in South Carolina's state army qualifies him to be considered a Confederate general.

NOTES

1. The Smiths were closely related to the Boston Smiths and Mrs. John Adams (Abigail Smith).

2. William R. Boggs, *Military Reminiscences of General Wm. R. Boggs* (Durham, 1913), 67. Boggs, who was chief of staff of the Trans-Mississippi Department, hints that Rhett was one of several staff officers exiled to the Trans-Mississippi because they were in disfavor with President Davis.

MAIN SOURCES

Barnwell, Stephen B. *The Story of an American Family*. Milwaukee, 1969.
Charleston *News and Courier*, August 2, 1878.
United States Military Academy. *Annual Reunion of the Association of Graduates*. N.p., 1879.

ELIJAH STERLING CLACK ROBERTSON

Elijah Sterling Clack Robertson was born on August 2, 1820, in Nashville, Tennessee, the son of Sterling Clack and Fanny (King) Robertson. The elder Robertson, a member of an old Tennessee family, was a Texas pioneer, legislator, and signer of the Texas Declaration of Independence. The family migrated to Texas in 1832, where his father had a huge land grant centered around Nashville (The "Robertson Colony"). Young Robertson fought in the Texas Revolution in his father's company. From 1837 to 1839 he attended Jackson College in Tennessee. Returning home, he was immediately appointed assistant clerk of the Texas Post Office Department. During the winter of 1839

Institute of Texan Cultures

and 1840 the nineteen-year-old Robertson, having risen to chief clerk, served as Texas' acting postmaster general. In 1840 he was elected secretary of the Texas Senate. In 1845 Robertson was admitted to the bar and found employment as a translator of Spanish deeds in the state land office. Moving to Bell County, near Salado, in 1852, Robertson bought a plantation and raised livestock until the secession crisis. In 1858 he was elected chief justice (county executive) of Bell County.

Robertson was elected to represent Bell County in the 1861 Secession Convention and voted for the ordinance of secession. Long active in militia affairs, Robertson, a colonel of militia since 1844, had been commissioned brigadier general of militia in April, 1860. Despite this high civil title, he never joined the Confederate army. In the summer of 1862 he briefly joined the staff of Colonel Henry McCullough (an old friend), as a volunteer aide-de-camp and purchasing agent. Other than this he held no civil or military post during the war. Robertson did, however, donate much of his personal fortune to finance the southern cause.

After the war Robertson returned to Salado and his extensive (and lucrative) land holdings. He was active in reviving Salado College and was a member of the state constitutional convention of 1875. General Robertson died on October 8, 1879, at Salado and is buried in the family cemetery near his home.

SHSP, in its list of Confederate generals, calls Robertson brigadier general "of the 27th Brigade Texas State Forces." Robertson was a prewar militia general but his highest rank in Confederate service appears to have been captain.[1]

NOTE

1. Walter P. Webb and Eldon S. Branda, eds., *Handbook of Texas* (3 vols.; Austin, 1952–76), II, 488, have PACS Brigadier General Jerome B. Robertson as a son of Sterling Clack Robertson and thus brother of Elijah Robertson. General Jerome Robertson was in fact the son of Cornelius Robertson, an immigrant from Scotland, and was not related to the Tennessee family. See Harold B. Simpson, *Touched With Valor* (Hillsboro, 1964), 2–3, where he sets forth information derived from General Robertson's great-granddaughters.

MAIN SOURCES

McLean, Malcolm D. *Papers Concerning Robertson's Colony in Texas*. 18 vols. Arlington, Tex., 1980–93.

A Memorial and Biographical History of McLennan, Falls, Bell and Coryell Counties, Texas. Chicago, 1893.

Webb, Walter P., and Eldon S. Branda, eds. *Handbook of Texas*. 3 vols. Austin, 1952–76.

REUBEN REDDICK ROSS

Reuben Reddick Ross was born on April 17, 1830, in Montgomery County, Tennessee, the son of James and Mary (Barker) Ross. His father was a professor at the Masonic College in Clarksville; his grandfather, for whom he was named, was a prominent Baptist leader. The family had farmlands in both Kentucky and Tennessee. The younger Ross studied under his father prior to an appointment to West Point. Entering in 1849, Ross graduated in 1853, fifty-first in a class of fifty-two. Commissioned a second lieutenant of infantry, Ross served less than one year in garrison at Newport Barracks, Kentucky. Ross resigned from the army on January 25, 1854, to become an engineer

Confederate Veteran, IV (1896)

for the Memphis and Tennessee Railroad, a move motivated by his desire to return to Tennessee. From 1855 to 1861 he taught school near Clarksville with his father.

When the war started Ross was appointed captain of artillery by the governor of Tennessee. He served as drillmaster for the Maury County artillery (Sparkman's Tennessee light artillery company). In November, 1861, Captain Ross was elected lieutenant colonel of the 8th Kentucky Infantry, but did not receive a commission because charges were made against him on unspecified grounds. Ross was later cleared by a court of inquiry, but the charges hampered his future promotion. Again captain of the Maury artillery, Ross was ordered to Fort Donelson, arriving on February 11, 1862, just before the naval attack. Taking charge of the heavy artillery, he personally managed the one effective cannon that almost single-handedly stopped Foote's fleet. Taken prisoner with the rest of the garrison, Ross was paroled to his Clarksville home. Traveling to Kentucky to report to the Union authorities, he was thrown into jail on trumped-up charges by Union troops. Imprisoned in various Federal camps, Ross was not exchanged until October, 1862. Ross then requested a cavalry command, but none was forthcoming. Promoted to lieutenant colonel in 1863, Ross obtained a position as acting assistant adjutant general on the staff of Brigadier General Henry B. Davidson, a West Point classmate who commanded a cavalry brigade in the Army of Tennessee. In 1864 Ross was again captured. While being carried north to prison, he jumped from a moving train near Cincinnati and, although injured in the fall, escaped and made his way south. Meeting up with Confederate cavalry under Brigadier General Hylan B. Lyon, Ross joined them. Lyon was in the middle of a raid into Kentucky, in conjunction with John Bell Hood's Tennessee campaign. Ross became involved in an action near Hopkinsville on December 16. "He and a portion of his command were cut off," and in a hand-to-hand encounter, Ross was clubbed over the head with a rifle. He survived, unconscious, for several days in a Hopkinsville house, finally dying on December 21.[1] Ross is buried in Meriwether Cemetery in Meriville, Kentucky.

CV has Ross appointed brigadier general from Texas in 1865, perhaps confusing him with General L. S. Ross of Texas. Cullum says he was made a general posthumously. SHSP has Ross leading Humes's brigade as a general. While contemporaries seemed to believe he was appointed general in some fashion, no record of such a promotion exists.

EDMUND WINCHESTER RUCKER

Edmund Winchester Rucker was born on July 22, 1835, in Rutherford County, Tennessee, the son of Edmund and Louisa (Winchester) Rucker. His father was a farmer and physician; his mother, a daughter of War of 1812 General James Winchester. Rucker grew up on his father's farms in Wilson and DeKalb counties, receiving only such meager education as the local schools could furnish. At age eighteen he left home to work with a party surveying the route of the Nashville and Decatur Railroad. Three years later Rucker removed to Memphis and began a career as an engineer. In 1858 he was appointed city engineer of Memphis.

Alabama Department of Archives and History, Montgomery

In May, 1861, a month before Tennessee seceded, Rucker enlisted as a private in Pickett's company of sappers and miners (*i.e.*, engineers). Commissioned as first lieutenant of engineers, Confederate regular army, Rucker was stationed at Columbus, Kentucky, in the summer of 1861. Promoted to captain of Tennessee artillery in late 1861, he was assigned to command a company of Illinoisans who had come downriver to fight for the South. Rucker and his artillerymen fought at the Battles of Island No. 10 and Fort Pillow. In the summer of 1862 he was promoted to major of the 16th (Rucker's) Tennessee Cavalry Battalion and sent to east Tennessee, where he commanded the posts at Kingston and Cleveland. Rucker's primary task was to round up conscripts, a task he detested. He later recalled this duty as the "meanest and damnest job a soldier . . . ever had."[1] The only action he saw in east Tennessee was during a raid into Kentucky. In 1863 Rucker's Battalion was combined with the 12th Battalion to form "Rucker's Legion." The legion was attached to Forrest's cavalry corps of the Army of Tennessee. A colonel by late 1863, Rucker led the legion in the Chickamauga campaign. In the spring of 1864, at the request of General Forrest, he was transferred from the Army of Tennessee to Mississippi and given command of a brigade of Tennessee cavalry in Brigadier General James Chalmers' division of Forrest's new cavalry command. Rucker led the brigade at the Battles of Brice's Crossroads (June 10, 1864) and Tupelo (July 14, 1864). During the latter battle Rucker was shot twice while leading a charge that tore his brigade apart. In September, 1864, upon his return to duty after convalescence, Rucker was given command of another cavalry brigade, over the heads of more senior colonels. The move caused great dissatisfaction within the brigade. One trooper, while admitting that Rucker was "a brave and competent man," protested that Rucker should not have superseded serving colonels.[2] Rucker led the brigade in General John Bell Hood's invasion of Tennessee. On the second day of the Battle of Nashville (December 15 and 16, 1864), Rucker's brigade was ordered to hold open the army's line of retreat. In a confused melee amidst rain and darkness, Rucker was shot in the arm and captured. The shattered left arm was amputated by Union surgeons that evening.

The now one-armed colonel returned to Memphis after the war. In 1869 he removed to Alabama, living mostly in Birmingham. Utilizing his engineering and railroad background, Rucker became president of the Salem, Marion & Memphis Railroad (working with his old commander, General Forrest); president of the Birmingham Sloss Steel & Iron Company; and a bank president. Rucker died on April 13, 1924, in Birmingham and is buried in Oak Hill Cemetery there.

Rucker is termed a brigadier general in *SHSP*. Long a brigade commander, he was called "general, being in command of a brigade, though he was never commissioned."[3]

NOTES

1. Edwin C. Bearss, *Forrest at Brice's Cross Roads and in North Mississippi in 1864* (Dayton, 1979), 346.

2. J. P. Young, *The Seventh Tennessee Cavalry (Confederate): A History* (Nashville, 1890), 100.

3. Thomas M. Owen, *History of Alabama and Dictionary of Alabama Biography* (4 vols.; Chicago, 1921), IV, 1472.

MAIN SOURCES

Bearss, Edwin C. *Forrest at Brice's Cross Roads and in North Mississippi in 1864*. Dayton, 1979.
"Gen. Edmund W. Rucker," *Confederate Veteran*, XXXII (1924), 163–64.
Sifakis, Stewart. *Who Was Who in the Civil War*. New York, 1988.

ALFRED ALEXANDER RUSSELL

Alfred Alexander Russell was born in 1827 in Jackson County, Alabama, the son of Lorenzo Dow and Eleanore (Duncan) Russell. The Russell family, prominent in the Doran's Cove area of Jackson County, was descended from Revolutionary War veteran Thomas Russell. Young Russell served in the Mexican War as a private in the Alabama militia. After that war he settled in Stevenson, Alabama, and practiced medicine there until the start of the Civil War.

Wyeth, *That Devil Forrest*

Elected major of the 7th Alabama Infantry on May 18, 1861, Russell and the 7th served in the garrison at Pensacola, Florida, until their twelve-month enlistments expired. He then was commissioned lieutenant colonel of the 15th Tennessee Cavalry Battalion. The 15th was combined with four Alabama companies of Bedford Forrest's command to form the 4th Alabama Cavalry, of which, on November 23, 1862, Russell was commissioned colonel.[1] It was said that "Russell's 4th Alabama was justly ranked as one of the best cavalry regiments in the service" under its "brave, grim doctor."[2] Russell participated in Forrest's west Tennessee raid of 1862, distinguishing himself for gallantry at the Battle of Lexington. In February, 1863, the 4th was transferred from Forrest's command to Wheeler's cavalry corps of the Army of Tennessee, much to the regret of General Forrest. In the Battle of Chickamauga, the Sequatchie raid, and the east Tennessee campaign, Russell commanded a brigade of Alabama cavalry in Major General Will T. Martin's division. On October 12, 1863, General Martin wrote Richmond requesting that Russell be promoted to brigadier general. Martin praised Russell as "cool in action . . . of fine judgment . . . possessing the confidence of his officers . . . a strict disciplinarian"—and, unlike Martin's other colonels, "temperate."[3] However, one of the other colonels was promoted instead. During the Atlanta campaign Russell again led the 4th. In Hood's invasion of Tennessee Russell and the 4th guarded Hood's rear along the Tennessee River Valley. In 1865 Russell rejoined General

Forrest, now in command of the cavalry of Mississippi and Alabama, and participated in the unsuccessful defense of Selma, Alabama. He was wounded twice during the war.

When the war ended Russell refused to take the oath of allegiance. After a short period hiding out in a cave in Jackson County, he fled to Mexico, settling near Cordova. Dr. Russell prospered in Mexico as a physician and owner of a coffee plantation. Several times he returned to Stevenson to visit friends, the last time in 1890, but never returned to the U.S. Family history states that he died in one of the endemic Mexican revolutions.[4] A former subordinate, writing in 1914, states that Russell died a "couple years" before.[5]

CV and SHSP have Russell appointed brigadier general from Alabama in 1864. SHSP says he was appointed as brigade commander. His superiors repeatedly recommended Colonel Russell for promotion. However, Russell is referred to in the OR as colonel as late as February 20, 1865.

NOTES

1. There were two regiments denominated 4th Alabama Cavalry—Russell's and the regiment of Colonel Phillip D. Roddey.

2. John A. Wyeth, *With Sabre and Scalpel* (New York, 1914), 198, 199. Russell had several peculiarities. For example, he never unbuttoned his coat, no matter how hot it was.

3. General Martin to Adjutant General Samuel Cooper, October 12, 1863, Compiled Service Records, Alfred A. Russell, 4th Alabama Cavalry.

4. Walter A. Russell to author, February 9, 1990.

5. Wyeth, *With Sabre and Scalpel,* 236.

MAIN SOURCE

Wyeth, John A. *With Sabre and Scalpel.* New York, 1914.

RAPHAEL SEMMES

Raphael Semmes, Confederate sailor and part-time general, was born on September 27, 1809, in Charles County, Maryland, the son of Richard Thornton and Catherine (Middleton) Semmes. He came from a distinguished Maryland family: one uncle was a congressman; a brother was Brigadier General Paul Semmes of Georgia.[1] Semmes was appointed a midshipman in the U.S. Navy on April 1, 1826, and commenced a long naval career.[2] During leaves he studied law and in 1834 was admitted to the Maryland bar. On February 9, 1837, Semmes was commissioned a lieutenant. During the Mexican War he commanded vessels blockading the Mexican coast. His brig, the *Somers*, sank, and Semmes barely escaped death. He wrote two books on the Mexican War. After that war Semmes was put in charge of lighthouse inspection along the Gulf Coast. Promoted to commander on September 14, 1855, by the outbreak of the war Semmes was in charge of the navy's Lighthouse Bureau.

Civil War Photograph Albums, Louisiana and Lower Mississippi Valley Collections, LSU Libraries, Louisiana State University

Semmes had been a resident of Mobile, Alabama, since 1849. One month after Alabama's secession, on February 15, 1861, Semmes resigned from the U.S. Navy. President Davis ordered Semmes to purchase munitions from northern suppliers before the outbreak of actual hostilities. He purchased large quantities of percussion caps and powder from compliant merchants, then returned to the Confederacy. On April 4, 1861, he was commissioned commander of the Confederate navy and assigned to head the Lighthouse Bureau. After only two weeks behind a desk, Semmes received permission to convert a former packet steamer, the *Havana*, into a commerce raider. Rechristened the *Sumter*, the ship and Semmes left New Orleans in June, 1861, for what turned out to be a six-month cruise. The *Sumter* took eighteen prizes during this time. The decrepit raider was finally run down by the U.S. Navy and blockaded in Gibraltar. Leaving his vessel there, Semmes proceeded to England to take command of the CSS *Alabama*. He was promoted to captain in 1862. Leaving England with his new ship in September, 1862, Semmes and the *Alabama* embarked on a two-year odyssey. The *Alabama* roamed the Atlantic and Indian oceans and the Gulf of Mexico, taking in all sixty-nine prizes. On June 19, 1864, the *Alabama* was finally caught by the USS *Kearsage* off Cherbourg, France, and after a short, fierce battle, the *Alabama* was sunk. Semmes was rescued by a passing English yacht and taken to that country. In November, 1864, Semmes returned to the South through Mexico. In February, 1865, Semmes was promoted to rear admiral and put in command of the James River Squadron. After the fall of Richmond, Semmes blew up his ships and shepherded his sailors westward. The city of Danville, Virginia, needed to be held and President Davis, casting about for someone to take charge of that post, chanced upon Semmes. "Old Beeswax," as he was known to his sailors, was actually a logical choice for the role since he was a known fighter of vast command experience and his sailors would be the main component of the defense force. Semmes's memoirs are somewhat vague as to his exact command status. Apparently Semmes concluded that a navy rear admiral's rank was legally equivalent to an army brigadier general, and that he could command army troops with his naval rank only. The formula he and the president finally settled upon was that he would command the Danville defenses in the capacity of an army brigadier—which implies a presidential appointment to that rank. When the Confederate army surrendered, Semmes's May 1, 1865, parole reflected that he was both rear admiral of the Confederate States Navy and brigadier general of the PACS. Being a shrewd lawyer, Semmes insisted that the latter rank be listed on his parole, to forestall any attempts to try him as a naval "pirate" for his commerce-raiding activities.

After the war Semmes returned to Mobile. He briefly served as county probate judge, but the Reconstruction authorities deprived him of that office. He also briefly taught moral philosophy at Louisiana Military Institute (the forerunner of Louisiana State University) and edited a Memphis paper. In 1868 he returned to Mobile and the practice of law. Admiral Semmes died on August 30, 1877, outside that city, and is buried in the Catholic Cemetery in Mobile.

Notes

1. The Semmes family is said to include Christopher Columbus as one of its ancestors.

2. Jon L. Wakelyn's *Biographical Dictionary of the Confederacy* (Westport, Conn., 1977) has Semmes attending West Point until 1826. However, he did not attend West Point. Admiral Semmes's son Oliver was a cadet at West Point when the war broke out, which perhaps accounts for the mistake.

Main Sources

Hoole, W. Stanley. "Admiral on Horseback: The Diary of Brigadier General Raphael Semmes, February–May, 1865." *Alabama Review*, XXVIII (1975), 129–50.

Meriwether, Colyer. *Raphael Semmes*. Philadelphia, 1913.

Roberts, W. Adolphe. *Semmes of the "Alabama."* Indianapolis, 1938.

WILLIAM PINKNEY SHINGLER

William Pinkney Shingler was born on November 11, 1827, in the Orangeburg District of South Carolina, the son of Colonel James and Eleanor (Bradwell) Shingler. His father was a wealthy plantation owner in St. James Parish. Shingler became a rice planter and large slaveowner in Christ Church Parish. He also worked as the teller of a Charleston bank and as a broker in that city. Active in the militia, by 1860 he was a lieutenant colonel of the 17th Militia, a Charleston unit. Shingler was elected to represent Christ Church Parish at the 1860 South Carolina Secession Convention, where he signed the ordinance of secession.

Shingler's first war service, around Charleston, was as an aide to Colonel Clement H. Stevens. He saw action at the First Battle of Bull Run as a member of Brigadier General Barnard Bee's staff. After that battle Shingler returned to South Carolina and helped raise a combined infantry-cavalry unit, the "Holcombe Legion." On November 21, 1861, Shingler was commissioned lieutenant colonel of the legion. The legion served in the Department of Charleston in 1861 and 1862. In March, 1862, Shingler led the legion in a skirmish with Union troops on Edisto Island near Charleston. In the summer of 1862 the legion was transferred to Richmond, Virginia, and split up; the infantry component was attached to Brigadier General Nathan G. Evans' brigade of the Army of Northern Virginia, and the cavalry component remained at Richmond and became part of that city's garrison. Shingler took charge of the legion cavalry and on October 8, 1862, he was commissioned colonel. Charged with drunkenness while on duty, Shingler was relieved from his command in April, 1863, to face a court-martial. However, he continued in command through 1864, so evidently the charges were never pursued. On March 18, 1864, the legion cavalry was combined with five detached cavalry companies to form the 7th South Carolina Cavalry, of which Shingler was given command. He led the 7th in several skirmishes and the Battle of Drewry's Bluff during the Petersburg campaign of 1864. "Slated for promotion to brigadier general," Shingler resigned his Confederate commission on May 30, 1864, after a running dispute with President Davis.[1] He then returned to South Carolina, where Governor Andrew McGrath placed him in command of South Carolina state militia.

After the war ended Shingler, "a man of character, intelligence and integrity," was elected to the state senate, where he served two years.[2] Reconstruction Governor James Orr praised him for his "intelligence and conservatism."[3] He also was appointed to various political posts. Shingler died on September 14, 1869, and is buried in Venning Cemetery near Mount Pleasant, South Carolina.

Shingler is called a general by CV and SHSP. The title must refer either to a militia rank or to the fact that he was slated for promotion. Shingler never commanded more than a regiment in the Confederate army, and he signed his pardon application as colonel CSA.

NOTES

1. Emily B. Reynolds and Joan R. Faunt, *Biographical Directory of the Senate of the State of South Carolina, 1776–1964* (Columbia, S.C., 1964), 307.

2. See Shingler's postwar application for presidential pardon at the National Archives.

3. *Ibid.*

MAIN SOURCES

Bailey, N. Louise, ed. *Biographical Directory of the South Carolina Senate, 1776–1985*. Columbia, S.C., 1986.

Krick, Robert K. *Lee's Colonels*. Dayton, 1991.

JAMES SIMONS

James Simons, a brigadier general of South Carolina militia, was born in Charleston, South Carolina, on May 9, 1813, the son of Major James Simons and his third wife, Sarah Harris. The Simons were an old Huguenot family long resident in South Carolina; his father was a merchant, Revolutionary War officer, and state representative. The younger Simons attended Pendleton Academy, the College of Charleston, and was an honor graduate of the University of South Carolina in 1833. He became a prominent Charleston lawyer and politician. He represented St. Philip and St. Michael parishes in the state house for nineteen years (from 1842 to 1861), being speaker of the house from 1850 to 1861. As both a lawyer and a represent-

South Caroliniana Library, University of South Carolina

ative Simons gained statewide respect for his "prompt and just" rulings and was "acknowledged to have been the best presiding officer the State has seen."[1] Simons, a militia officer since 1833, by 1858 had attained the rank of brigadier general of the 4th (Charleston) Brigade of the South Carolina Militia.

In January, 1861, General Simons departed for Columbia in order to resume his duties as speaker of the house. Governor Pickens, in a move of questionable legality, turned command of the 4th Brigade over to the state's adjutant general. Later that month Simons returned to Charleston and resumed command of the brigade. Simons' first war service was as a brigadier general of militia commanding on Morris Island during the Fort Sumter bombardment. Appointed to command Morris Island on April 11, he was relieved of that command by Governor Pickens on April

29. Although Pickens and Simons were political opponents, there may have been more substantive reasons for Simons' relief. Governor Pickens had grounds to believe that Simons was more devoted to politics than war. In addition, rumor had it that Simons earned the nickname "Hospital Jimmy" during the Fort Sumter bombardment with his penchant for avoiding hostile fire. On May 27, 1861, Pickens ordered Simons to keep his militia brigade in readiness for active duty. Simons complained, and the two elderly politicians wrangled for months. Claiming that "his honor had been impugned and that he had not been given command and authority commensurate with his rank," Simons "resigned his commission in a huff on July 10, 1861, and took no further active part in the war."[2] Simons carried on an ill-disguised vendetta with the governor for months afterward. He volunteered as a private in an artillery unit and remained there until failing health compelled his retirement. In February, 1862, President Davis authorized Simons to raise a legion. Throughout that spring and summer Simons attempted to organize his legion from companies being recruited in the Charleston area, but the project fizzled out. He spent the rest of the war concentrating on his law practice.

After the war Simons continued his lucrative Charleston law practice in partnership with his son. He served as a trustee of the University of South Carolina from 1863 to 1869 and was active in several civic organizations. General Simons died in Charleston on April 26, 1879, and is buried in a family plot in Magnolia Cemetery in Charleston.

General Simons' command of a brigade of militia that served in a campaign qualifies him to be considered a Confederate general.

NOTES

1. Charleston *News and Courier*, April 28, 1879.

2. R. Lockwood Tower, ed., *A Carolinian Goes to War: The Civil War Narratives of Arthur Middleton Manigault* (Columbia, S.C., 1983), 24.

MAIN SOURCES

Charleston *News and Courier*, April 28, 29, 1879.

Simons, James. Papers. Southern Historical Collection, University of North Carolina, Chapel Hill.

Simons, Admiral Robert B. *Thomas Grange Simons III*. Charleston, S.C., 1954.

GEORGE AUGUSTUS SMITH III

George Augustus Smith III was born in Georgia on November 4, 1824, the son of George A. and Agnes (Harrell) Smith. Before the war he was a candymaker in Macon. In 1861 Smith raised, in his native city, the "Brown Infantry," later Company C of the 1st Independent Georgia Battalion. The unit was ordered to Pensacola, where Smith commanded a battery of artillery. During the November 22 and 23, 1861, bombardment of Pensacola by Federal forces, he fired the first gun on the Confederate side and won praise for his steadiness and courage. Smith was elected lieutenant colonel of the 1st Georgia (Confederate), formed from the 1st Georgia Battalion on December

Valentine Museum, Richmond, Virginia

10, 1861, and commissioned colonel on September 10, 1863, to rank from November 25, 1862.[1] The 1st served as part of the garrison of Mobile, Alabama, from February, 1862, through 1863. Smith commanded Fort Gaines and often was in brigade command in the garrison. During the Atlanta campaign of 1864, Smith's regiment was transferred to the Army of Tennessee and attached to Brigadier General Clement Stevens' Georgia brigade.[2] During the June 27, 1864, Battle of Kennesaw Mountain, General Stevens placed Smith under arrest because Smith had granted a temporary front line truce so that both sides could tend to their dead and wounded. The charges were not followed up; the services of the popular and respected Colonel Smith were too valuable to lose. In the Battle of Atlanta on June 22, 1864, Smith led Stevens' Brigade (Stevens having been mortally wounded on July 20). He had his horse shot from under him, and was severely wounded in the left shoulder. After a brief convalescence, the not-yet-recovered Smith, "known for his modesty, his firmness of purpose, integrity and intelligence," followed the Army of Tennessee to the Franklin battlefield.[3] Smith was killed in the assault of November 30, 1864, falling "most gallantly while putting his regiment into the interior works of the enemy."[4] Buried first on the battlefield and later at the McGavock Confederate Cemetery, Colonel Smith's remains were reinterred in Rose Hill Cemetery, Macon, in July of 1867, in a family plot.

Smith is termed a general in *SHSP*. His tombstone inscription also terms him "Brig. Gen. C.S.A." However, the *OR* uniformly designate his rank as colonel. An obituary in the July 10, 1867, Macon *Journal and Messenger* calls him a colonel at a time when hometown newspapers were not likely to downgrade an officer's rank. He led the 3rd Brigade of the Department of the Gulf in 1863 and temporarily led a brigade in the Atlanta campaign, both times as a colonel.

NOTES

1. The 1st Georgia (Confederate) was formed from the 1st Battalion (sometimes called Vil-lipigue's or Larey's Battalion), plus companies from Mississippi, Alabama, Tennessee, and Florida in October, 1861. The regiment was sometimes called the 36th Georgia, and the "Georgia and Mississippi Regiment." It was officially designated the 1st Regiment Confederate Infantry on January 31, 1862.

2. In 1863 the "2nd Battalion" (five companies) of the regiment were ordered to join the Army of Tennessee. It participated in the Battles of Chickamauga and Missionary Ridge. The two parts of the regiment were reunited in northern Georgia in 1864 at Smith's request.

3. Macon *Journal and Messenger,* July 10, 1867.

4. *OR,* XLV, 743.

MAIN SOURCES

Census of 1860, Georgia, Bibb County, Microfilm, p. 465.
Macon (Ga.) *Journal and Messenger,* July 10, 1867.

JOHN LOUIS TAYLOR SNEED

John Louis Taylor Sneed was born on May 12, 1820, in Raleigh, North Carolina, the son of Major Junius and Julia Rowan (Taylor) Sneed. His father was a cashier of the state bank; his mother, a daughter of North Carolina Chief Justice John Louis Taylor. Sneed was admitted to the Tennessee bar in 1841. In 1843 he settled in Memphis and started a distinguished legal and political career. A Whig, Sneed served in the Tennessee General Assembly from 1843 to 1846. During the Mexican War Sneed was sergeant major, then captain, of Company G, Regiment of Tennessee Mounted Volunteers. Returning to Memphis at the conclusion of that war, Sneed was a district attorney general from 1851 to 1854 and state attorney general from 1854 to 1859. In 1858 and 1859 he ran, unsuccessfully, as an opposition (old Whig party) candidate for Congress.

Library of Congress

On May 9, 1861, Governor Isham Harris appointed Sneed brigadier general of Tennessee state forces. Sneed was placed in command of the volunteers encampment at Fort Randolph, Tennessee (near Memphis), and later led the "River Brigade" in Major General Leonidas Polk's army. Sneed's war service was brief, but praiseworthy. He even survived the daily panicking of his superior, Major General Gideon

Pillow. The Tennessee army was transferred to Confederate service in August, 1861. Sneed, however, was one of three generals in that force (all prewar Whigs) who were not, despite the governor's urgings, subsequently appointed generals in the regular Confederate army.[1] In 1862 Sneed attempted to raise a regiment of infantry, but the Federal advance ended those plans. Governor Harris later appointed Sneed to settle accounts between the Tennessee provisional army and the Confederacy.

After the war General Sneed returned to Memphis and rebuilt his legal career. A "high-toned, honorable gentleman,"[2] Sneed served as a judge of the Tennessee Supreme Court from 1870 to 1878, judge of the Court of Arbitration in 1879, judge of the Court of Referees from 1883 to 1884, and chancellor of the Eleventh Chancery Division of Tennessee from 1894 to 1900. Sneed also served as a Democratic elector in 1880, vice president of the American Bar Association in 1882, president of the Memphis law school from 1887 to 1893, and was an unsuccessful candidate for the U.S. Senate in 1887. General Sneed died on July 29, 1901, in Memphis, and is buried in Elmwood Cemetery.

SHSP and CV list General Sneed as a Confederate general.

NOTES

1. See note 2 on William R. Caswell (treated earlier).
2. Memphis *Avalanche*, June 3, 1860.

MAIN SOURCES

Green, John W. *Lives of the Judges of the Supreme Court of Tennessee, 1796–1947*. Knoxville, 1947.

Mathes, J. Harvey. *The Old Guard in Gray*. Memphis, 1897.

McBride, Robert M. *Biographical Directory of the Tennessee General Assembly*. 2 vols. Nashville, 1975.

PIERRE SOULÉ

Pierre Soulé, shepherd, French revolutionary, and U.S. senator, was born on August 31, 1801, in Castillon, France, the son of Joseph and Jeanne (Lacroix) Soulé. The elder Soulé was a lieutenant general under Napoleon and a local magistrate. Pierre, destined for the priesthood, attended the Jesuit college in Toulouse and the academy in Bordeaux. After working as a shepherd and a teacher, Soulé was admitted to the bar and set up a practice in Paris. He was sent to prison in 1825 for publishing revolutionary tracts, but he escaped and fled to England. The next year he left England for Haiti and later the United States. He worked as a gardener for a while, mastered English, studied American law, and established a law practice in New Orleans in the 1830s. The former French revolutionary, a many-sided character, soon gained success in American politics. He served a term in the Louisiana Senate, then in 1847 was elected to the U.S. Senate. Soulé served in the Senate until his resignation in 1853. Politically, he was a states' rights Democrat who nevertheless opposed secession, a stance at some variance with his youthful opinions. Soulé then served two years as a U.S. ambassador to Spain, authoring the famous Ostend Manifesto, a declaration of American expansionism. In 1855 he returned to New Orleans and his law practice, and was an active supporter of William Walker's filibustering expeditions in Central America.[1]

Picture Collection, Louisiana and Lower Mississippi Valley Collections, LSU Libraries, Louisiana State University

Soulé supported Stephen Douglas, a Unionist Democrat, in the 1860 presidential election. However, when Louisiana seceded, Soulé went with his adopted state. Early in the war he went to Europe as an agent for the Confederate government. Returning to New Orleans, Soulé was arrested for treason by Union troops in May, 1862. Confined at Fort Lafayette, he was paroled to Boston in November of that year. From there he sailed to Nassau and then to Havana, Cuba. Running the blockade in 1863, Soulé served on General P. G. T. Beauregard's staff during the siege of Charleston, South Carolina, that year. Late in the war he left the Confederacy and returned to Havana, and was in Cuba when the Confederacy collapsed.

Soulé returned, after the war, to New Orleans. Four years later his mind gave way and he was declared incompetent. Soon after, on March 26, 1870, he died in New Orleans. Senator Soulé was buried in St. Louis Cemetery No. 2 in New Orleans.

Lonn has Soulé made an "honorary" brigadier general of "special services" for his work at Charleston, citing Roman's biography of General Beauregard.[2] Confederate law did not provide for "honorary" generalships, nor for generalships of "special services." And there is no evidence that President Davis, a confirmed enemy of General Beauregard, promoted one of the general's close associates in this irregular manner. However, Soulé carried the title "general" during the war— perhaps in reference to some prewar office.[3]

NOTES

1. Among other actions, Soulé arranged for money to be loaned Walker and acted as Walker's unofficial advisor. For the full extent of Soulé's heavy involvement in Walker's schemes, see Edward S. Wallace, *Destiny and Glory* (New York, 1957), 201–204.

2. Alfred Roman, *The Military Operations of General Beauregard in the War Between the States, 1861 to 1865* (2 vols.; New York, 1884). Roman was an officer on General Beauregard's staff during the war. It is widely believed that General Beauregard actually wrote this book.

3. Edward Manigault, *Siege Train*, ed. Warren Ripley (Columbia, S.C., 1986), 76 (diary entry for November 4, 1863).

MAIN SOURCES

Dictionary of American Biography. 20 vols. and supplement. New York, 1928–44.

Moore, J. Preston. "Pierre Soulé: Southern Expansionist and Promoter." *Journal of Southern History*, XXI (1955), 203–23.

Wakelyn, Jon L. *Biographical Dictionary of the Confederacy*. Westport, Conn., 1977.

ALEXANDER EARLY STEEN

Alexander Early Steen was born in St. Louis, Missouri, in 1828, the son of Colonel Enoch Steen, U.S. Army (who remained loyal during the war), and Mary Rector, the aunt of Arkansas Governor Henry Rector. Steen was commissioned directly into the regular army in 1847, seeing Mexican War action and being breveted for gallantry at the Battles of Contreras and Churubusco. Leaving the army at the end of that war, Steen was recommissioned in 1852. He served in the 6th and 3rd infantries before the war, rising to first lieutenant, and suffering a wound fighting Indians in 1857.

State Historical Society of Missouri, Columbia

The spring of 1861 found Steen back in Missouri. He promptly entered into that state's secession movement, resigning from the army on May 10, 1861. In May Governor Claiborne Jackson of Missouri commissioned Steen a lieutenant colonel of Missouri militia. When Union troops captured his regiment at Camp Jackson, Steen was fortuitously absent, having traveled to Jefferson City (accompanied by his brother-in-law, future Confederate General Henry Little) on a mission to the governor.[1] Later in May, he was appointed as an aide to the governor and commissioned a colonel. On June 18, 1861, Steen was appointed brigadier general of the 5th Division of the Missouri State Guard. Eight days later he was appointed a captain in the regular Confederate army. A "hard driver" and a "good judge of men," Steen was the drillmaster of Major General Sterling Price's army.[2] With the state guard he fought at the Battles of Wilson's Creek and Lexington, often commanding the combined cavalry units of the state guard as well as his own division. In March, 1862, Price recommended Steen for promotion to brigadier general of the PACS, "but the appointment was denied because Steen's brigade was not fully formed."[3] The Missourians were transferred east of the Mississippi River. Steen, however, fell ill while in Memphis (he suffered from rheumatism) and did not rejoin them in their northern Mississippi campaigns. Returning to the Trans-Mississippi theater, Steen was appointed colonel of the newly formed 10th Missouri Infantry. That fall he occasionally led a brigade of four Missouri infantry regiments in the army commanded by Major General Thomas C. Hindman. At the Battle for Prairie Grove on December 7, 1862, Steen was shot through the head "while gallantly charging the enemy," and instantly killed.[4] He is buried in the National Cemetery in Fort Smith, Arkansas.

Heitman, Wood, *SHSP*, and CV list Steen as a general. *SHSP* has Steen appointed brigadier general CSA on April 1, 1862. However, the OR show him as a colonel as late as December 12, 1862. A Confederate colonel, he was promised promotion appropriate to his brigade command, but died before action on the promotion was formally taken.

NOTES

    1. Steen and Little married daughters of Colonel Pitcairn Morrison, who remained loyal during the war and was breveted to brigadier general for his war services.

    2. Hans C. Adamson, *Rebellion in Missouri, 1861* (Philadelphia, 1961), 181.

    3. Russell K. Brown, *Fallen in Battle: American General Officer Combat Fatalities from 1775* (Westport, Conn., 1988), 131. On August 20, 1862, Missouri's Confederate congressional delegation seconded Price's recommendation of Steen, calling him "an officer and soldier . . . worthy of trust" (Civil War Papers, Confederate, Missouri Historical Society, St. Louis).

    4. Amelia Martin, "United Confederate Veterans," *Fort Smith Historical Society Journal*, V (September, 1981), 4, quoting a letter by Dr. E. R. Duval to General Steen's widow written a week after the battle. For another account of his death, see John F. Howes to Mrs. Steen, December 17, 1862, Civil War Papers, Confederate, Missouri Historical Society, St. Louis. Heitman has him killed on November 27, 1862, in an engagement at Cane Hill, Arkansas. However, Steen's infantry did not participate in that engagement. The Duval and Howes letters make it clear that the general was shot while leading one of the last charges at Prairie Grove.

MAIN SOURCES

"Gen. Information in re General Early Alexander Steen," Confederate Civil War Papers, Missouri Historical Society, St. Louis.

Little, Henry. Diary. U.S. Army Military History Institute, Carlisle, Pa.

Steen, Moses D. *The Steen Family in Europe and America*. Cincinnati, 1917.

ALEXANDER WATKINS TERRELL

Alexander Watkins Terrell was born on November 3, 1827, in Patrick County, Virginia, the son of Christopher and Susan (Kennerly) Terrell. His father, a doctor, died when Terrell was six years old. The family moved to Boonville, Missouri, in 1832. Terrell attended the University of Missouri, studied law, and practiced in St. Joseph, Missouri, from 1849 to 1852. In that year he moved to Austin, Texas, practicing law there and becoming a judge.

Jake Johnson Collection, Archives Division, Texas State Library

Terrell, a close friend of Governor Sam Houston, opposed secession (like the governor) and favored a compromise of sectional differences. Nevertheless, when Texas seceded Terrell went with his state. The first two years of the war, in between his judicial duties, he served as a volunteer aide and as major of the 1st Texas Cavalry. For most of 1862 he was a captain and volunteer aide-de-camp to Brigadier General Henry McCullough, who commanded Texas troops stationed in Arkansas. Declining a colonel's commission in 1861, Terrell was thereafter repeatedly recommended for an officer's commission. Texas Governor Francis Lubbock, for one, praised Terrell's service in Arkansas "without pay or rank, which was declined by him several times." Lubbock said that Terrell "had one of the finest minds in the state."[1] On March 31, 1863, Terrell was commissioned lieutenant colonel of a cavalry battalion later built up into the 34th Texas Cavalry. Upon the formation of the regiment (June 20, 1863) Terrell was chosen colonel. In July, 1863, Terrell was temporarily assigned to command the Northern Sub-District of Texas. The 34th spent the balance of 1863 in various camps in the District of Texas. In March, 1864, the 34th, along with most of the troops in Texas, were ordered to Louisiana to oppose the Union advance on Shreveport. At the Battle of Mansfield (April 8, 1864) Terrell's troops attacked on the Union right. At the Battles of Pleasant Hill the next day his dismounted troopers seized a Union position but could advance no further. At the Battle of Mansura (May 16) Terrell led Arthur Bagby's veteran cavalry brigade. In September, 1864, Terrell was given command of a brigade of three Texas cavalry regiments, which formed the advance line of the Confederate positions in west Louisiana. But by the end of the year Brigadier General Bagby assumed command of the brigade, and Terrell returned to command of the 34th. In late April, 1865, the brigade was drawn back to Texas. Hearing of Lee's surrender at Appomattox, the troops deserted their colors. On May 14, 1865, Terrell, recognizing the war was lost, disbanded his regiment. Two days later (May 16, 1865) General Kirby Smith, who had not heard of Terrell disbanding his unit, assigned the "daring and efficient" Terrell brigadier general to succeed Bagby (promoted that day to major general) in command of the brigade.[2] By this late date there was no brigade left to command—Terrell had the title, but no troops.

After the war Terrell fled to Mexico, becoming an officer in Maximilian's army. Returning to Texas, he had a varied postbellum career as a lawyer, politician, and cotton planter. Terrell was elected four times to the state senate, serving from 1876 to 1883. He also served three terms in the state house, in the Twenty-second, Twenty-eighth, and Twenty-ninth legislatures, was elected a reporter to the Texas Supreme Court, and was an ambassador to Turkey in the Cleveland administration. General Terrell, "a delightful orator," was an unsuccessful candidate for the U.S. Senate in 1887.[3] His efforts on behalf of the state university, both in the legislature and as regent of the board of trustees, earned him the title of "Father of the University of Texas." A historian, Terrell became president of the Texas State Historical Association. He lived in Houston (1865), Robertson County (1865 to 1871), and then Austin. General Terrell died on September 9, 1912, at Mineral Wells, Texas, and is buried in the State Cemetery in Austin.

Wright and Wood list Terrell as a Confederate general.

NOTES

1. John W. Spencer, *Terrell's Texas Cavalry* (Burnet, Tex., 1982), 93–94.
2. *Ibid.*, 95.
3. Alwyn Barr, *Reconstruction to Reform: Texas Politics, 1876–1906* (Austin, 1971), 101.

MAIN SOURCES

"Judge Alexander Watkins Terrell." *Confederate Veteran*, XX (1912), 575–76.
Spencer, John W. *Terrell's Texas Cavalry*. Burnet, Tex., 1982.
Terrell, Alexander W. *From Texas to Mexico and the Court of Maximilian in 1865*. Dallas, 1933.
Webb, Walter P., and Eldon S. Branda, eds. *Handbook of Texas*. 3 vols. Austin, 1952–76.

MERIWETHER THOMPSON

Meriwether ("Jeff") Thompson, one of the more colorful figures in a colorful army, was born on January 22, 1826, at Harpers Ferry, Virginia. His father, Captain Meriwether Thompson, was a paymaster in the U.S. Army; his mother, Nancy Slaughter Broadus, was a distant relative of George Washington. Young Thompson moved to Liberty in Clay County, Missouri, in 1847 and a year later to St. Joseph. There he was a clerk, grocer, county surveyor, real estate agent, inventor, mayor of St. Joseph, and railroad president.

Civil War Photograph Albums, Louisiana and Lower Mississippi Valley Collections, LSU Libraries, Louisiana State University

An energetic and voluble secessionist, Thompson led secessionist activities in northeast Missouri and lobbied in the state capitol for secession. In July, 1861, while on his way to Richmond to offer his services to the Confederate government, Thompson was elected brigadier general of the 1st Division of the Missouri State Guard. He led an irregular force in the swamps of southeast Missouri and northeast Arkansas for much of the war, gaining fame as the "Swamp Fox." Thompson was also famous for his eccentricities, his theatrical air, and his appreciation of strong liquor. One contemporary remembered that "Gen. Thompson was a man of ability, but it was not strictly of a military order. He excelled in issuing proclamations and manifestoes. . . . His efforts, whether written or spoken, were . . . a combination of sense and bombast, of military shrewdness and personal buffoonery. They . . . gave his campaigns a decided opéra bouffe aspect."[1] On October 21, 1861, Brigadier General Joseph B. Plummer's bluecoats attacked and defeated Thompson's ragtag division in an engagement at Fredericktown, Missouri. In March, 1862, Thompson's ill-equipped, irregular forces skirmished with the Union army of Brigadier General John Pope as the latter advanced down the Mississippi River to New Madrid and Island No. 10. Largely driven out of Missouri, Thompson and a band of followers crossed the Mississippi and fought on in such diverse locales as Memphis, Tennessee, and New Orleans, Louisiana. Transferred back to northeast Arkansas in the fall of 1862, Thompson again led a number of raids against Union detachments. On August 22, 1863, near Pocahontas, Arkansas, a Union patrol captured him. Imprisoned at Johnson's Island, Ohio, Thompson was not exchanged until August 3, 1864. He immediately returned to the Trans-Mississippi. In the fall of 1864 Major General Sterling Price's cavalry corps left Arkansas for a raid into Missouri. Thompson joined the raid as a volunteer. However, on October 6, 1864, General Price ordered Thompson to take command of a crack brigade of Missouri cavalry that had lost its commander. This assignment by Price was irregular and curious—he was putting his best unit (the " Iron Brigade" formerly commanded by Brigadier General Joseph Shelby) under the control of a person who was not even a Confederate officer—and can only be explained by his great respect for Thompson's abilities. Thompson proved to be a very competent cavalry commander as he led the Iron Brigade in the Battles of Westport, Mine Creek, and Newtonia. In the winter of 1864, while in camp in Arkansas and Texas, Thompson occasionally was placed in command of Shelby's entire division. In February, 1865, Thompson was assigned to command the Northern Sub-District of Arkansas. He had hardly arrived in the district when the news of the surrender at Appomattox completely demoralized the district's southern sympathizers. On May 11, 1865, Thompson surrendered himself and his entire command.

General Thompson settled in Memphis after the war and tried his hand at running a grocery. In 1867 he moved to New Orleans and was soon appointed chief engineer of that state's Board of Public Works. That employment shattered his health. Returning to St. Joseph, he died there on September 5, 1876, and is buried in Mount Mora Cemetery in St. Joseph.

Heitman, Wood, *SHSP*, and CV all list Thompson as a Confederate general. Although Thompson commanded Confederate troops as a general, his end-of-war parole gives his correct rank—brigadier general, Missouri State Guard. During the war Thompson repeatedly petitioned President Davis for promotion to brigadier general. The president repeatedly refused.[2]

NOTES

1. Evans, ed., *CMH*, XII, 67.
2. For more on Thompson's efforts to win promotion, see Stephen Davis, "Jeff Thompson's Unsuccessful Quest for a Confederate Generalship," *Missouri Historical Review*, LXXXV (October, 1991), 53–65. Thompson is a prominent and humorous figure in Mark Twain's semi-historical novel *The Gilded Age*, Chapters 16 and 17.

MAIN SOURCES

Daily News, The. *History of Buchanan County and St. Joseph*. St. Joseph, Mo., 1899.
Davis, Stephen. "Jeff Thompson's Unsuccessful Quest for a Confederate Generalship." *Missouri Historical Review*, LXXXV (1990–91), 53–65.
Thompson, M. Jeff. *Reminiscences of General M. Jeff Thompson*. Edited by Donal J. Stanton, Goodwin F. Berquist, and Paul C. Bowers. Dayton, 1988.

James Webb Throckmorton

James Webb Throckmorton, brigadier general of Texas state troops, was born on February 1, 1825, in Sparta in White County, Tennessee, the son of Dr. William E. and Jane (Roton) Throckmorton. He moved with his father to Collin County, Texas, in 1841. Throckmorton studied medicine in Princeton, Kentucky, and then returned to Collin County to practice his profession. In 1843 Throckmorton served as sergeant of a ranger company and during the Mexican War served as a private and surgeon. Subsequently he studied law and commenced practice in McKinney, Texas. An old-line Whig, Throckmorton was elected to the state house in 1851, serving six years, and to the state senate in 1857, serving until 1861.

Institute of Texan Cultures

Elected to represent Collin County in the 1861 Texas Secession Convention, Throckmorton, "personally the most popular man in [the convention]," nevertheless was one of only seven delegates to vote against the ordinance of secession.[1] However, unlike fellow oppositionists A. J. Hamilton and E. J. Davis, Throckmorton went with his state. His first Confederate service was as lieutenant colonel of William C. Young's regiment, a state unit that occupied abandoned army forts at the beginning of the war. In September, 1861, Throckmorton was commissioned captain of Company K of Stone's 6th Texas Cavalry. He led his company at the Battles of Chustenahlah and Pea Ridge. On May 25, 1862, he was discharged from the army because of ill health. Rejoining the reorganized 6th Texas with the rank of major in February, 1863, he fought in Louisiana until again invalided and discharged on September 12, 1863. In late 1863 Throckmorton was elected to the state senate. Governor Murrah, on March 1, 1864, appointed Throckmorton brigadier general of Third District Texas state troops, with headquarters at Bonham, Texas. Major General John B. Magruder, Confederate commander in Texas, urged Throckmorton's appointment as brigadier general of the PACS, calling him "gallant and distinguished on the field." However, Magruder's recommendation was not acted upon.[2] In December, 1864, Throckmorton was assigned by the governor to head up the First Frontier District in northwest Texas. From this post "Old Leathercoat," as he was nicknamed, was relieved in April, 1865, to become commissioner to the Indians.

Throckmorton's postwar career was most distinguished. He was elected the presiding officer of the Texas Reconstruction Convention in 1866. Later that year Throckmorton was elected governor of Texas, serving until 1867, when he was removed on orders of General Phil Sheridan, commander of the Federal forces of occupation in Texas. Subsequently Throckmorton returned to Collin County and his law practice. In 1875 General Throckmorton was elected to the U.S. Congress, serving from 1875 to 1879 and 1883 to 1887, and was an unsuccessful candidate for the U.S. Senate in 1888. General Throckmorton died in McKinney on April 21, 1894, and is buried in Pecan Grove Cemetery.

Throckmorton's rank of general in the Texas state army qualifies him to be considered a Confederate general.

NOTES

1. Claude Elliott, *Old Leathercoat: The Life History of a Texas Patriot* (San Antonio, 1938), 54.
2. *OR*, Vol. XXXIV, Pt. 3, p. 779.

MAIN SOURCES

Elliott, Claude. *Old Leathercoat: The Life History of a Texas Patriot*. San Antonio, 1938.
Lynch, James D. *The Bench and Bar of Texas*. St. Louis, 1885.
Reynolds, Clifford, comp. *Biographical Directory of the American Congress, 1774–1961*. Washington, D.C., 1961.

GASPARD TOCHMAN

Gaspard (Kacper) Tochman, Polish revolutionary and southern rebel, was born in December, 1797, in Letowna, Poland. Of upper-class lineage, his uncle was General Jan Skrzynecki, who led the Polish army in the rebellion of 1830. Tochman matriculated at the prestigious University of Warsaw and after graduation practiced law in that city. During the Polish Revolution of 1830, he joined the rebels, rose to the rank of major, and for his distinguished bravery earned the Gold Cross of the Polish Legion of Honor. When the Russian army crushed the rebellion Tochman fled Poland for France. Tochman was ordered out of France four years later and, after a brief stop in England, emigrated to the United States. The New World was kind to the Old World rebel. Tochman prospered in New York and Maryland as a lawyer, involved mainly in prosecuting government claims for his fellow Poles. Lecturing extensively on Poland and editing the Polish Slavonic Literary Association *Literary Journal*, Tochman was recognized as the leading American spokesman on Poland. In 1852 he settled in Alexandria, Virginia. Active politically, Tochman was a Douglas Democrat elector for Virginia in 1860.

Originally favoring a peaceful settlement of sectional issues, Lincoln's call for troops to suppress the rebellion drove Tochman to join the southern cause.[1] Writing his old friend Jefferson Davis, Tochman offered to raise a "Polish brigade" composed of southerners of foreign birth. The offer was accepted; the secretary of war promised Tochman a brigadier generalship if he raised more than one regiment. Commissioned colonel on May 11, 1861, Tochman repaired to New Orleans and commenced a vigorous recruitment drive among that city's foreign-born citizens. By June 20 two regiments (the 14th Regiment and 3rd Battalion of the Louisiana Infantry, mostly non-Poles)—1,700 men—were raised. Tochman did not receive the promised general's commission; President Davis did not honor his secretary's promise. Subsequent congressional investigators thought it was clear that the president had not authorized a rank above colonel. Tochman suspected that objecting Louisiana politicians induced Davis' about-face. He spent the rest of the war pressing his claims to rank, pay, and reimbursement upon the Confederate Congress.[2] In September, 1864, Tochman proposed to President Davis that he be sent abroad to recruit Polish refugees, pointing out that unless this were done, those refugees might enlist in the Union army. Davis rejected the offer in favor of another émigré group.

After the war Tochman practiced law in Richmond. In 1866 he was appointed that state's European agent for the Bureau of Immigration. Tochman's plan was to establish a settlement ("New Poland"), near Spotsylvania. The plan met with some initial success; over one hundred immigrant families settled in Virginia. However, the state failed to appropriate funds to sustain the program, and after two years Tochman quit his post. He thereafter retired to his estate in Spotsylvania County. General Tochman died there on December 20, 1880, and was buried on a hill overlooking his house.

Tochman is called a general in *SHSP*, Lonn, the *Journal of the Congress of the Confederate States of America, 1861–1865*, and the Moffett Papers.[3]

NOTES

1. Tochman, writing President Davis, explained that although antislavery, he was a states' rights supporter and opposed to race-mixing, toward which he felt an aggressive northern policy was driving the country. Tochman, with a "fertile but essentially muddled brain," had earlier pressed President Lincoln to appoint him American consul to France. Frank Mocha, ed., *Poles in America* (Stevens Point, Wis., 1978), 58.

2. Tochman contributed a large sum of money to the raising of his "brigade." In March, 1865, the Confederate Congress voted to reimburse those expenses and passed a resolution thanking him for his services. President Davis, however, pocket-vetoed the reimbursement bill.

3. *Journal of the Congress of the Confederate States of America, 1861–1865* (7 vols.; Washington, D.C., 1904–1905). Andrew Moffett was a South Carolina physician and researcher who, around 1875, compiled a list of Confederate generals and their current addresses. The list, which is in the Moffet Papers at William R. Perkins Library, Duke University, evidences considerable research and widespread correspondence.

MAIN SOURCES

Crist, Lynda, *et al.*, eds. *The Papers of Jefferson Davis*. 7 vols. Baton Rouge, 1983–91.

Gerber, Rafal. *Studenci Uniwersytetu Warzawskiego 1808–1831. Slownik Biograficzny.* Wroclaw, Poland, 1977.

Mocha, Frank, ed. *Poles in America.* Stevens Point, Wis., 1978.

Uminski, Sigmund H. "Two Polish Confederates." *Polish American Studies,* XXIII (1966), 65–73.

ELISHA LEFFINGWELL TRACY

Elisha Leffingwell Tracy, general of Louisiana militia, was born on March 31, 1800, in Norwich, Connecticut, to Henry and Alice (Leffingwell) Tracy. The Tracys trace their descent from one Thomas Tracy, who came to Connecticut in 1637 and settled in Norwich. Elisha Tracy married Eliza Early of New Orleans in 1825 and moved to that city shortly thereafter. In New Orleans he became a wealthy public weigher and produce broker. The public-spirited Tracy involved himself in various civic activities, including a term as member of the New Orleans Board of Assistant Aldermen. Interested in military matters, Tracy was first an officer of the 4th Militia Regiment, then captain and later major of New Orleans' crack volunteer militia organization, the Washington Artillery. By 1852 he had risen to the rank of brigadier general, commanding the 1st Brigade of the 1st Division of the Louisiana Militia.

On April 29, 1861, Governor Thomas Moore ordered Tracy to leave his militia brigade and assume command of Camp Walker, near New Orleans, which had been established to house and train incoming Confederate volunteers. The camp was quickly transferred to northeast Louisiana, where the climate was healthier. On May 13, 1861, Tracy was assigned to command the new camp, named Camp Moore in honor of the governor. One waggish volunteer encamped there described Tracy as "a noble old man . . . with a very respectable rotundity. His head and chin resemble the summits of high mountains. . . . He acts very spry, and his short legs clamp lightly around a proud charger that must have been young twenty years ago." [1] Tracy probably returned to New Orleans that fall when Confederate General Mansfield Lovell assumed command of the camp. On January 31, 1862, Tracy was commissioned brigadier general of the newly formed 2nd Brigade of the Louisiana Militia Volunteers. On March 1, 1862, when Admiral Farragut's fleet threatened New Orleans, Tracy's militia brigade—1,500 strong—was mustered into Confederate service for ninety days. It was placed under General Lovell's command and stationed on the inner defenses of the city. Indifferently armed, lacking ammunition, food, and artillery, the militia could do little to impede the progress of the Union fleet as it steamed up the Mississippi River, and so dispersed. Tracy himself traveled to Camp Moore and without authority discharged the few militia troops who had fled there. General Tracy died on October 16, 1862, at Chatawa Station, Mississippi, just north of Camp Moore.[2] His remains were reinterred in the family tomb in St. Patrick's Cemetery No. 2 in New Orleans, in 1865.

General Tracy's command of a brigade of militia that served in a campaign qualifies him to be considered a Confederate general.

NOTES

1. See Powel A. Casey, ed., *The Story of Camp Moore* (Baton Rouge, 1985), 70.

2. The New Orleans *Times* of October 8, 1865, suggests that he died on October 6, not October 16. The author prefers the contemporary account in the *Daily Picayune*, October 22, 1862, which gives an October 16 date of death.

MAIN SOURCES

Casey, Powel A., ed. *The Story of Camp Moore*. Baton Rouge, 1985.
Conrad, Glenn R., ed. *A Dictionary of Louisiana Biography*. 2 vols. New Orleans, 1988.
New Orleans *Daily Picayune*, October 22, 1862.
Tracy, Evert E., comp. *The Tracy Genealogy*. Albany, 1898.

JAMES DEBERTY TRUDEAU

James DeBerty Trudeau, a many-sided man who became a Confederate general, was born on September 14, 1817, in Louisiana, probably St. James Parish, to Rene and Adele (Sauvé) Trudeau. His father, a planter, came from a distinguished Creole family; the general's grandfather was a governor of Louisiana. Trudeau's parents sent him to Europe to be educated, first at the College of Louis-le-Grand in France, then to a military school in Switzerland. He studied medicine, both in France and, on his return to the United States, in Philadelphia. In May, 1837, the University of Pennsylvania awarded him a medical degree. Trudeau practiced medicine in New York City in the 1840s and 1850s before returning to New Orleans to practice there. He achieved distinction as a physician, authoring

Courtesy Louisiana Historical Association Collection, Manuscripts Department, Howard-Tilton Memorial Library, Tulane University, New Orleans

articles and co-founding the New York Academy of Medicine. His real love, though, was the outdoors. A friend of John James Audubon, the celebrated ornithological artist, Trudeau frequently supplied Audubon with rare species of birds and was an accomplished painter of birds himself.[1] He spent several months traveling amongst the wild Indian tribes of the West. His love of the outdoors and hunting was such that it ruined his medical career; he was forever abandoning patients to hunt or camp.

In January, 1861, Trudeau, a socially prominent Louisianian with some military training, was appointed by the governor as artillery instructor for the militia garrisoning the local forts. Trudeau also wrote a pamphlet outlining a plan of defense of New Orleans. During the summer of 1861 Trudeau was made brigadier general of the "Louisiana Legion," a brigade-sized unit of Louisiana militia.[2] In September, 1861, at the request of Major General Leonidas Polk, who commanded the Confederate forces along the upper Mississippi River, Trudeau left his militia brigade to help lay out the fortifications of Columbus, Kentucky. The next month Polk appointed Trudeau chief of artillery for the vital post of Columbus. In February, 1862, General P. G. T. Beauregard appointed this "highly accomplished artillery officer" to command of the batteries at Island No. 10.[3] It is an illustration of the improvised nature of the Confederate army that, a year after the war began, the artillery at one of the most vital defense points in the South was commanded by a man not even a member of the Confederate army. General Polk, the district commander, thought highly of Trudeau's abilities. Polk went so far as to nominate him to be a brigadier general of the PACS, but the president did not approve. Trudeau escaped the April 7, 1862, southern surrender at Island No. 10. Shortly before the surrender Trudeau was ordered to report to General Beauregard, then assembling an army at Corinth, Mississippi. He followed Beauregard to the field of Shiloh, without an assignment, and joined Beauregard's staff as a volunteer aide. During the battle Trudeau was seriously wounded. Disabled, Trudeau returned to Louisiana. In the summer of 1863, by now partially recovered, he requested appointment in the Confederate army. Although the request was endorsed by the whole Louisiana Legislature and the Confederate commanders in Louisiana, no commission was ever issued. On November 5, 1863, Trudeau was captured at his plantation home by Union forces. By the terms of his parole he was ordered to stay on the family plantation in Ascension Parish. It appears that he broke that parole, because in 1864, still suffering from his wartime wounds, he traveled through Mississippi and reported to President Davis on conditions there.

After the war General Trudeau returned to New Orleans to resume his medical practice. As one authority has it, " To say that he stood in the front rank of his profession as physician and surgeon scarcely gives accurate comprehension of the varied intellectual powers he displayed throughout a long, active and useful life, which ended in New Orleans May 25, 1887."[4] He was interred in the Trudeau family vault, St. Louis Cemetery No. 1 in New Orleans. Trudeau's second wife, Louise Bringier, was the niece of the wives of Generals Richard Taylor and Allen Thomas.[5]

Trudeau is listed as a general in *SHSP*.

NOTES
1. Audubon named a newly discovered species of bird "Trudeau's tern." Audubon's son painted Trudeau's portrait.
2. See OR, LIII, for the long-range debate over the telegraph as to what rank Trudeau held and whether the legion actually existed. Louisiana Governor Thomas Moore, for one, wired Richmond that Trudeau, a general claiming to command a brigade, probably didn't have any men under him.
3. OR, VII, 821.
4. Stanley C. Arthur, ed., *Old Families of Louisiana* (New Orleans, 1931), 95.
5. Garry Trudeau, the creator of the *Doonesbury* comic strip, is General Trudeau's great-grandson.

MAIN SOURCES
Arthur, Stanley C., ed. *Old Families of Louisiana*. New Orleans, 1931.
Gifford, George. "James DeBerty Trudeau: Physician-Naturalist." *Bulletin of the History of Medicine*, LIV (1980), 78–94.
Malloch, Archibald. "James DeBerty Trudeau: Artist, Soldier, Physician." *Bulletin, New York Academy of Medicine*, 2nd ser., II (December, 1935), 681–99.
Seebold, Herman de B. *Old Louisiana Plantation Homes and Family Trees*. 2 vols. N.p., 1941.
Trudeau, Edward L. *An Autobiography*. Philadelphia, 1916.

WILLIAM BARTEE WADE

William Bartee Wade was born in Bedford County, Virginia, on October 9, 1823, the son of Paschall B. and Frances Barton (Alexander) Wade. The Wades were a prosperous slaveowning Bedford County family descended from Isaac Wade, a Revolutionary War veteran. In 1835 Wade's father moved to Columbus in Lowndes County, Mississippi.[1] During the Mexican War Wade enlisted in the 1st Mississippi Regiment, rising to lieutenant of Company K and distinguishing himself at the Battles of Monterrey and Buena Vista. Returning to Lowndes County, he married and became a prosperous planter. A Whig, Wade was elected state representative in 1854, serving one term. Wade was also captain of the local militia company.

U.S. Army Military History Institute and Martin Callahan Collection

Upon the secession of Mississippi Wade raised a company, the "Lowndes Southrons," which was sent along with six other companies to Pensacola, Florida.

On January 17, 1861, Wade was elected lieutenant colonel of the regiment organized from these companies. The regiment was mustered out in February, 1861, and Wade reverted to captain of the "Southrons," redesignated Company D, 10th Mississippi Infantry. The 10th served at Pensacola in 1861 and at the Battle of Shiloh. Upon the May, 1862, reorganization of the army Wade was not reelected captain. On July 17, 1862, he was elected colonel of the 8th Confederate Cavalry, formed by the consolidation of three battalions of Alabama and Mississippi cavalry. Wade led the 8th in the fight at Booneville, Mississippi, on July 1, 1862. Later the regiment was transferred to the Army of Tennessee and participated in the Kentucky campaign and the Tennessee campaigns of 1862 and 1863. Wade usually commanded a cavalry brigade in Tennessee in the latter year. Perhaps his most notable exploit was the capture, on January 13, 1863, of three steamers and a gunboat on the Cumberland River. One week after this raid Wade (now commander, as senior colonel, of a cavalary brigade) received a letter informing him that his wife was dangerously ill. He applied for immediate leave to return home, and leave was granted with the proviso that when it expired (in fifteen days) he was to report to the Army of Tennessee's conscript bureau. For the next three months Wade headed the East Mississippi subdepartment of that bureau. When Wade returned to the army, his division commander brought him before a board of examination and, when Wade flunked the exam, suspended him from command. However, the division commander failed to follow proper procedure for the suspension, and Wade won reinstatment to command.[2] He led a brigade in Kelly's division after the Battle of Chickamauga. His career with the cavalry corps of the Army of Tennessee came to an abrupt end in October, 1863, when Major General Joseph Wheeler, who commanded the cavalry corps, arrested Wade for being intoxicated while facing the enemy. Pending trial, Wade was ordered by Wheeler (who admired him as "a gallant though intemperate officer") to the rear on sick leave.[3] Wade never rejoined his regiment. In 1864 Wade, now in Virginia, led a mixed home guard/reserve force guarding bridges on the strategic South Side Railroad. Wade was then transferred to Mississippi and given command of a brigade of Chalmers' Division in Forrest's cavalry corps. He won universal praise as a "very brave and determined officer," who was "always distinguished for gallantry and good conduct in action."[4] On December 27, 1864, during the Tennessee campaign, Wade was again wounded. Reverting to regimental command, Wade led the 8th in Mississippi in 1865. He was paroled at Columbus, Mississippi, as a colonel on May 17, 1865.

After the war was over Wade returned to Columbus. In 1866 he got into an altercation with the Union occupying forces who were bothering the local belles. According to family sources, Wade shot seven Yankee soldiers before a northern bullet shattered his right arm. The townspeople carried Wade to the Gilmer Hotel where, three days later, vengeful Union soldiers took him from his sickbed and threw him out the window, killing him instantly. It was said of Wade that "after going through two wars, he died a martyr's death defending the womanhood of his home town."[5] Wade is buried in Friendship Cemetery in Columbus.

Wade is called general in *SHSP* and CV. He led, as colonel, a brigade of cavalry during the last year of the war. He was briefly a general in the state militia before the war, which rank perhaps caused the confusion.

NOTES

1. A biographical sketch of Wade, "Gen. W. B. Wade's Military Achievement," CV, XIV (1906), 17, states that he attended Virginia Military Institute as a youth. However, VMI has no record of his having attended.

2. Wade's formal protest to the board's decision and suspension can be found in the Will T. Martin Papers, University of Texas. General Martin obviously used the board as a pretext to rid himself of Wade and promote a junior officer in Wade's stead.

3. W. C. Dodson, *Campaigns of Wheeler and His Cavalry. 1862–1865* (Atlanta, 1899), 377.

4. "Gen. W. B. Wade's Military Achievements," 17.

5. *Ibid.* Particulars on Colonel Wade's death courtesy of a great-grandson, William Wade O'Neill of Oklahoma City.

MAIN SOURCES

Arnott, Mary. "The Wade Family of Virginia—Bedford County." Latter-Day Saints Library, Salt Lake City.

Bearss, Edwin C. *Forrest at Brice's Cross Roads and in North Mississippi in 1864.* Dayton, 1979.

"Gen. W. B. Wade's Military Achievements." *Confederate Veteran*, XIV (1906), 17.

JOHN ANDREAS WAGENER

John Andreas Wagener was born on July 21, 1816, at Sievern in Hanover, at that time a kingdom in the German Confederation. His parents were Johann A. Wagener, a merchant, and Rebecca Hencken. When very young he immigrated to the U.S., landing in New York. Soon thereafter, at age seventeen, he went to Charleston, South Carolina. Wagener entered the mercantile trade, and very soon became the political, business, and social leader of the (not inconsiderable) German community, not only in Charleston but through- out the state. He established and published a German language newspaper, organized a German church, or- ganized German fire companies and German lodges, and was president of the Carolina Mutual Insurance Company. It was said that "his was one of those noble natures, that never con-

Collection of City Hall, Charleston, South Carolina

sidered self; ever active, even unto self-sacrifice, to promote the welfare of his countrymen."[1] As early as 1843 Wagener was a lieutenant in a militia company, the "German Fusiliers."

By 1860 Wagener was elected major of the German artillery, another crack city militia unit. As such he and his unit participated in the bombardment of Fort Sumter. Wagener was rapidly promoted to lieutenant colonel, and on September 5, 1861, to colonel, of the 1st Regiment of the South Carolina Militia Artillery. Wagener commanded the batteries at Fort Walker during Du Pont's attack on Port Royal. Although stunned by a bursting shell and temporarily disabled, Wagener won praise for his gallant conduct. He also led the militia artillery during the siege of Charleston in 1863 and 1864. Wagener's militia regiment, 215 strong, was stationed in the city proper and acted as infantry. His two sons, the younger only fifteen years old, endured the shelling with their father. In the latter stages of the siege Wagener was promoted to brigadier general of militia.

A prewar anti-secessionist, Wagener's postwar career was devoted to reconciling South Carolina to the post-slavery order. He was a member of the 1865 Constitutional Convention, and was elected to represent Charleston in the Forty-Seventh General Assembly (1865 to 1866). In 1867 the governor appointed him state commissioner of immigration. In 1871 Wagener, a Democrat, was elected mayor of Charleston on a "Citizens' Conservative" ticket. During his two years in office, his administration was widely criticized for extravagance and corruption. Although Wagener himself was credited with honesty and integrity, the charges stuck, and he lost his bid for reelection. In 1876 Wagener lent his aid to General Wade Hampton's electoral campaign to rid the state of carpetbag rule. Wagener did not live to see the successful end of that campaign, dying at Walhalla, South Carolina, on August 27, 1876. General Wagener was first buried in Walhalla, where he had founded a German settlement. The next year his remains were reinterred in Charleston.

Wagener is listed in Lonn as a general.

NOTE

1. *Cyclopedia of the Eminent and Representative Men of the Carolinas of the Nineteenth Century* (2 vols.; Madison, Wis., 1892), I, 616.

MAIN SOURCES

Charleston *News and Courier*, August 28, 1876.
Cyclopedia of the Eminent and Representative Men of the Carolinas of the Nineteenth Century. 2 vols. Madison, Wis., 1892.
Dictionary of American Biography. 20 vols. and supplement. New York, 1928–44.

FRANCIS MARION WALKER

Francis Marion Walker was born on November 12, 1827, in Paris, Kentucky, the son of John and Tabitha (Taylor) Walker.[1] His mother died when Francis was young, and in 1843 the family moved to Hawkins County in east Tennessee, where his father operated a tavern. Walker received a meager education at local schools. Like many bright, ambitious, but impoverished young men of the time, Walker taught school part-time, both to further his education and to earn enough money to go to college and become a lawyer.

Chattanooga-Hamilton County Bicentennial Library

During the Mexican War Walker was elected second lieutenant of the 5th Tennessee Infantry Regiment. The regiment was sent to Mexico, but the war ended before it saw action. Upon discharge from the army, Walker entered Transylvania University, from which he graduated in 1850 with honors. Returning to east Tennessee, he opened a law practice in Rogersville. He relocated in Chattanooga in 1854 and practiced law there until 1861. Walker's prewar legal career was most distinguished and included stints as Chattanooga alderman (from 1858 to 1859) and attorney general of the state's Fourth District (from 1860 till the start of the war).

During the secession crisis Walker, an ardent Unionist, delivered Union speeches throughout east Tennessee. But when Tennessee joined the Confederacy, he took up arms in the state's defense. Walker entered Confederate service as captain of the "Marsh Blues," Company I of the 19th Tennessee Infantry, a Hamilton County unit. Swiftly promoted to lieutenant colonel (June 11, 1861), Walker fought at the Battles of Mill Springs and Shiloh. At the latter his regiment won a reputation as the "bloody 19th," and Walker was praised for his gallantry. Elected colonel on May 8, 1862, Walker led the 19th at the Battles of Stone's River, Chickamauga, and Chattanooga. During the Atlanta campaign he won further laurels as "an officer of great distinction, of exalted character," particularly at the Battle of Kennesaw Mountain, where the entrenched Tennesseans slaughtered a Union assault column.[2] He was repeatedly recommended for promotion by Brigadier General Otho F. Strahl, his brigade commander, and Lieutenant General William Hardee, the corps commander, among others. When Brigadier General George Maney, who commanded another Tennessee brigade in the same division, was elevated to divisional command, Walker and the 19th were transferred from Strahl's brigade to Maney's so that Walker could take command of Maney's old brigade. Colonel Walker was killed at the Battle of Atlanta on June 22, 1864, while leading the brigade in a desperate assault. It is said that his commission as brigadier general, won at Kennesaw Mountain, arrived on the day following his death.[3] Walker's remains were removed from the field and taken to Griffin, Georgia, where they were interred in Citizens Cemetery. In 1889 the body was brought to Chattanooga and reburied in a family plot in Forest Hills Cemetery.

Walker is termed brigadier general, on the basis of this posthumous promotion, in the Tennessee volume of *CMH*, although he is not given a biography in the same volume's section on Tennessee generals.

Notes

1. Zella Armstrong, *The History of Hamilton County and Chattanooga, Tennessee* (2 vols.; Chattanooga, 1931), I, 466–67, suggests that General Walker's mother was a niece of President Zachary Taylor. However, the author's search of the Taylor family tree fails to disclose the relationship. The same source also gives an 1821 date of birth for Walker. However, the 1827 date, based on family sources, is confirmed by census records.

2. Evans, ed., *CMH*, VIII, 136.

3. A biographical article in the Chattanooga *News-Free Press*, June 28, 1987, suggests that Walker was promoted to general on June 21. General Maney returning to the brigade, Walker was said to have led his old regiment in the battle. However, it appears that Maney led Cheatham's division that day and Walker led Maney's brigade—the left wing brigade of Hardee's corps during the assault.

Main Sources

Armstrong, Zella. *The History of Hamilton County and Chattanooga, Tennessee*. 2 vols. Chattanooga, 1931.

Chattanooga *Daily Times*, October 30, 31, November 1, 1889.

Walker, Francis M. Biographical Sketch. MS at Tennessee State Archives, Nashville.

Worsham, Dr. W. J. *The Old Nineteenth Tennessee Regiment*, C.S.A. Knoxville, 1902.

ABSALOM MADDEN WEST

Absalom Madden West was born on March 9, 1813, near Marion in Perry County, Alabama, the son of Anderson and Celia (Tubb) West. His father, a native of South Carolina, was a planter and county sheriff. The younger West, after a meager country schooling, migrated to Holmes County, Mississippi, in 1837. He soon became a noted and prosperous plantation owner. A Whig and a Unionist, West won election to the state house in 1847, where he took a leading part. Subsequently the voters of Holmes County elected him to the state senate, where he served from 1854 to 1861. In 1859 he was named director of the Mississippi Central Railroad, thus beginning a lifelong involvement with railroads. In 1860 West supported the anti-secessionist Democrat Stephen Douglas for president, an act at odds with the vast majority of Mississippi voters.

Courtesy L. A. Smith III

On May 22, 1861, Governor John Pettus of Mississippi, an ultrasecessionist and old political foe, appointed West brigadier general of Mississippi state troops. West took command of the 2nd Brigade of Mississippi state troops (the 4th and 6th regiments). The companies within the two regiments rendezvoused at Grenada, Mississippi, in August, 1861, at a camp site selected by General West. The next month was spent organizing the units and in drilling the soldiers. On September 21 the two regiments were ordered to Tennessee to join the Confederate army. The regiments were accepted into Confederate service, and West's troop-leading days were at an end. His abilities were more suited to staff duties. The governor appointed him successively state quartermaster general, paymaster general, and commissary general. West's "practical usefulness" and business experience made him particularly fitted to discharge these duties.[1] He also was assigned the duty of providing salt for indigent families and the families of soldiers. In 1863 he ran for governor of Mississippi, but was defeated. In 1864 West resigned his three posts to become president of the Mississippi Central Railroad.

West continued his career as a planter and railroad executive after the war. He served as president of the Mississippi Central through 1874, then as director of its successor through 1886, and in those posts oversaw the rebuilding of a railroad ruined by the war. In 1865 he was elected to the U.S. Congress, but the radical Republican Congress refused to seat even this old-time Unionist.[2] In 1870 West relocated in Holly Springs, Mississippi, but retained his farms in Holmes County. In 1876 he was an elector for the Democratic presidential ticket. At this time his political views became more reformist and radical. In 1884 West was chosen as the vice presidential nominee of the Anti-Monopoly party and of the Greenback-

233

Labor party, as running mate of ex-Union general Ben Butler. The ticket lost, but West won favorable mention for his physical size— "225 pounds with not an ounce of surplus flesh"—the "resonance of his lungs," and his "unquestioned . . . integrity." [3] This flirtation with national splinter parties did not seem to affect his political fortunes in his own county, where he was elected to the state senate in both 1878 and 1880. General West died on September 30, 1894, in Holly Springs, and is buried in Hill Crest Cemetery.

West's rank of general in Mississippi's state army qualifies him to be considered a Confederate general.

NOTES

1. Goodspeed Publishing Company, *Biographical and Historical Memoirs of Mississippi* (2 vols.; Chicago, 1891), II, 1013.

2. One could hardly expect the loyal Congress in 1865 to make fine distinctions between "old-line" traitors and "reluctant" traitors.

3. New York *Times*, June 16, 1884.

MAIN SOURCES

Goodspeed Publishing Company. *Biographical and Historical Memoirs of Mississippi*. 2 vols. Chicago, 1891.

Stone, James H. "General Absalom Madden West and the Civil War in Mississippi." *Journal of Mississippi History*, XLII (1980), 135–44.

STEPHEN M. WESTMORE

Stephen M. Westmore was born in Charleston, South Carolina, on April 2, 1806, the son of Stephen West and Eleanore Screvan (Gilbert) Moore. His father, of an old Maryland-Virginia family, was a prominent banker; his two brothers were army surgeons, one of whom was future Confederate Surgeon General Samuel P. Moore. Born Stephen West Moore, he entered West Point in 1823 and graduated four years later, thirty-fourth in a class of thirty-eight. Commissioned first lieutenant in the 7th Infantry in 1827, after twenty years of routine army service, mostly in the Indian Territory, he had only risen to the rank of captain. Westmore commanded the post of Jefferson Barracks in

New Orleans *Daily Picayune*, February 5, 1896

New Orleans and led Company I of the 7th Infantry in Texas. On April 19, 1846, Westmore resigned his commission and returned to his New Orleans home. His obituary suggests that Westmore resigned after killing a fellow officer in a duel. By an act of legislature in 1850 he had his name changed to Westmore (he and a cousin of the same name were being confused). Working first as a clerk, Westmore was appointed Louisiana's adjutant and inspector general in 1853 by his old army friend Governor Paul Hebert, serving for two years. Subsequently he was register of conveyances for the city of New Orleans.

When the war started Westmore swiftly rose to high command in the Louisiana militia. On February 20, 1862, Governor Moore commissioned Westmore brigadier general of the 3rd Brigade of Louisiana Militia Volunteers. The brigade—1,104 strong—was mustered into Confederate service on March 1, 1862. This ninety-day unit was transferred to Confederate Major General Lovell's command to help defend New Orleans. The militia, poorly armed and supplied, could do little to stop the Union naval assault on that city and dispersed. Westmore himself was captured and paroled by the Unionists. Exchanged in October, 1862, the old soldier disappears from the OR of the war after this, though it appears he lived in occupied New Orleans for a time.

After the war the wealthy Westmore lived in retirement at his New Orleans home. It was said that Westmore, a member of the Metairie Racing Club, was "reckoned the best judge of horseflesh in the South."[1] Racked with illness and pain in his later years, the general grew despondent. On February 4, 1896, General Westmore committed suicide by jumping into the Mississippi River near his home. He was buried in New Orleans.

General Westmore's command of a brigade of militia that served in a campaign qualifies him to be considered a Confederate general.

NOTE

1. New Orleans *Daily Picayune*, February 5, 1896.

MAIN SOURCES

Butler, Thomas. "Moore Bible Record." *Pennsylvania Genealogical Magazine*, XI (March, 1932), 288–91.
Casso, Evans J. *Louisiana Legacy: A History of the State National Guard*. Gretna, La., 1976.
Heitman, Francis B. *Historical Register of the United States Army, from its Organization, September 29, 1789, to September 29, 1889*. 2 vols. Washington, D.C., 1890.
New Orleans *Daily Picayune*, February 5, 1896.

FRANCIS EUGENE WHITFIELD

Francis Eugene Whitfield was born in Bossier Parish, Louisiana, on June 22, 1839, the son of Francis Edwin and Demetria (Jones) Whitfield. His father, a wealthy planter born in North Carolina, moved to Memphis, Tennessee, in 1847, and later still relocated in Corinth, Mississippi. The younger Whitfield grew up in Memphis and Corinth. He attended the University of Virginia and later the law school of Cumberland University in Tennesssee, earning high academic honors at both institutions.

At the start of the war Whitfield was elected lieutenant of the "Corinth Rifles" (later Company A of the 9th Mississippi), organized in Tishomingo County in March, 1861. The 9th, a twelve-months regiment, served in garrison at Pensacola, Florida, throughout 1861. Whitfield served as regimental adjutant. Upon the expiration of the twelve-months enlistment the 9th was reorganized for the duration of the war and Whitfield was made a major. While leading the skirmish line of the 9th at the Battle of Shiloh "with great coolness and with marked ability and skill," Major Whitfield was severely wounded in the hip.[1] Heavily involved in the assaults on the "Hornet's Nest," Whitfield personally captured Union Colonel William T. Shaw of the 14th Iowa. His Shiloh wound kept him on sick leave for months and limited his further field duty. In 1863, now lieutenant colonel, he returned to the 9th. General Braxton Bragg, the army commander, had in the meantime appointed another officer to fill the colonel's vacancy in that regiment. When Whitfield protested his supercession, Bragg had him arrested for being absent without leave. A suspicious commander always on the lookout for dereliction of duty among his subordinates, Bragg was under the impression that Whitfield had used his sick leave to travel to Richmond and intrigue against Bragg's appointee. However, Whitfield had in reality been in Richmond on medical leave. The arrest was later voided by the War Department, but Whitfield's career with the 9th was over. At the Battle of Chickamauga in September, 1863, he served as provost marshal of Polk's Corps of the Army of Tennessee. In the Atlanta campaign of 1864, he was wounded at the Battle of Resaca, which ended his field service. Upon recovery he took command of the post of Meridian, Mississippi.

After the war ended Whitfield returned to Corinth. He practiced law there and in Memphis. One of the South's "most eminent lawyers . . . courtly in bearing, patient, generous hearted and forgiving," Whitfield became general attorney for the Southern Express Company and a leader of the Memphis bar.[2] Politically active, like most lawyers of that era, Whitfield was elected to the Alcorn County Democratic Executive Committee. On March 18, 1885, while on a steamboat outing on the St. John's River in Florida, Whitfield died suddenly. He is buried in Elmwood Cemetery in Memphis.

Whitfield is called a brigadier general by *SHSP*. The basis for this is questionable, since Colonel Whitfield (as contemporaries always called him) doesn't appear to have ever commanded so much as a regiment in battle. Perhaps *SHSP* confused him with Brigadier General John W. Whitfield, who served in northern Mississippi during the war. What is certain is that Whitfield was paroled at Meridian on May 10, 1865, as colonel of the 9th Mississippi.

Notes

1. *OR*, Vol. X, Pt. 1, p. 549.
2. Memphis *Appeal*, March 24, 1885.

Main Sources

Cochran, Fan Alexander. *History of Old Tishomingo County, Mississippi Territory*. Oklahoma City, 1969.
Memphis *Appeal*, March 22, 24, 1885.
Whitfield, Emma M., comp. *Whitfield, Bryan, Smith and Related Families*. N.p., 1948(?).

EDWARD S. WILLIS

Edward S. Willis was born on August 10, 1840, in Wilkes County, Georgia, the son of Francis T. and Elizabeth (Butler) Willis. The father, a physician, was the grandson of Georgia Congressman Francis Willis, of an old Virginia family distantly related to President Washington. Young "Ned" Willis attended West Point from 1857 to 1861, resigning on February 5, 1861, after Georgia's secession.

Appointed a lieutenant in the Confederate regular army, Willis was ordered to Fort Pulaski, Georgia, in March, 1861. On July 5, 1861, he was named adjutant of the 12th Georgia. The 12th was sent into west-

Evans, ed., *Confederate Military History*, VII

ern Virginia, joining a brigade-sized force guarding Allegheny Mountain. During the winter Willis was promoted to captain and served as an aide to Brigadier General Edward Johnson, the force's commander. Around January, 1862, Willis was appointed assistant chief of artillery on the staff of Major General Thomas "Stonewall" Jackson. Willis became a popular fixture on the staff. At the Battle of Port Republic Willis and several high ranking officers of Jackson's staff were captured by a wandering patrol of Union cavalry, but Willis managed to escape later that day. In the fall of 1862 Willis, now a major, transferred back to the 12th. The commander of that regiment was killed at the Battle of Fredericksburg on December 12, 1862. The officers of the regiment, in a show of respect for the abilities of their youthful former adjutant, petitioned President Davis to appoint Willis, the junior major, as their new colonel. He was promoted lieutenant colonel on December 13, 1862, and colonel on January 22, 1863. He played a gallant and conspicuous part in Lee's army, distinguishing himself at the Battles of Chancellorsville and Gettysburg. At Chancellorsville the 12th captured a Union battery during Jackson's successful flank attack on the Union Eleventh Corps; Jackson, on his deathbed, praised Willis and urged his promotion. A postwar memoirist wrote of Willis that "it was well understood throughout the army . . . that no regiment had a better commanding officer than the Twelfth Georgia."[1] During the winter of 1863 and 1864 General Robert E. Lee, another admirer of the young Georgian, sent Willis with a two-regiment demi-brigade into the Shenandoah Valley with orders to comb the nearby mountains and round up deserters. Rejoining the main army, General Lee placed Willis in temporary command of Brigadier General John Pegram's Virginia brigade when that officer was wounded in the Wilderness. On May 30, 1864, Willis fell, hit by a shell fragment while leading his brigade in a doomed assault at Bethesda Church. He died, surrounded by his fellow officers and friends, the next night. Willis is buried in Laurel Grove Cemetery in Savannah.

He is listed as a general by CMH, Wood, and CV. The former says his general's commission arrived the day after his death. No proof of such a commission exists. However, Willis had already been recommended by General Lee for a brigadier generalship. It appears that the whole army believed that the promotion had been made, although the commission had not yet been made out.

NOTE

1. J. Tracey Power, "Edward Willis: Young and Full of Promise," *Civil War Times Illustrated*, XVIII (April, 1979), 24.

MAIN SOURCES

Power, J. Tracey. "Edward Willis: Young and Full of Promise." *Civil War Times Illustrated*, XVIII (April, 1979), 22–27.

Schaff, Morris. *The Spirit of Old West Point, 1858–1862*. Boston, 1908.

Smith, Gerald J. "For the Veteran 12th Georgia Regiment Rounding Up Deserters was 'Quite a Holiday.'" *America's Civil War*, VII (March, 1994), 16–24.

Thomas, Henry W. *History of the Doles-Cook Brigade*. Atlanta, 1903.

GILBERT JEFFERSON WRIGHT

Gilbert Jefferson Wright was born on February 18, 1825, near Lawrenceville in Gwinnett County, Georgia, the son of Littlebury and Henrietta (Austin) Wright. Educated in the local schools of that county, Wright grew up into a massive six foot four inch giant. Upon the outbreak of the Mexican War, he enlisted as a private in Company A of the 1st Georgia Infantry. Wright participated in several battles and was wounded in the neck. He recovered from the wound and rejoined the regiment, but was left with a stiff neck for the rest of his life. After the war ended, he returned to Georgia, read law, and in 1848 was admitted to the bar. Settling in Albany, Georgia, Wright soon built

Courtesy Deborah Fleming

up a lucrative practice. By no means an orator, his "unique personality . . . vigorous intellect and . . . untiring energy," it was said, "made a remarkable impression upon all with whom he come into contact."[1]

In 1861 Wright helped organize the "Albany Hussars," later Company D of the cavalry battalion of Cobb's Georgia Legion. The legion joined Lee's Army of Northern Virginia and was attached to a cavalry brigade commanded successively by Brigadier Generals Wade Hampton and Pierce M. B. Young. Commissioned lieutenant on August 10, 1861, captain in 1862, and major in 1863, "Gid" Wright fought in all the early battles in Virginia. His "bulldog courage" and "stentorian voice" were conspicuous on many a battlefield. One source relates that "he was seriously wounded several times, but before his wounds ever healed he would be again on the field of battle."[2] On October 9, 1863, he was made colonel of the legion (renamed the 9th Georgia Cavalry on July 11, 1864). Upon the May 30, 1864, wounding of General Pierce M. B. Young, Wright as senior colonel took command of Young's brigade of Georgia cavalry. He led this brigade off and on throughout 1864 and 1865. Wright's conduct at the June 11 and 12, 1864, Battle of Trevilian Station won the praise of the cavalry corps commander. In January, 1865, the brigade was transferred to South Carolina to oppose the advance of Major General William T. Sherman's Union army. At the Battle of Monroe's Crossroads, North Carolina, on March 10, 1865, Wright's brigade led the surprise attack on the Union cavalry. His troopers barely missed capturing the Union commander in his bed. The war ended for Wright with the April 26, 1865, surrender of the Army of Tennessee at Greensboro, North Carolina.

After the war Wright returned to Albany and the practice of law. An active Democrat and Reconstruction opponent, he served as mayor of Albany from 1866 to 1869. From 1875 to 1880 he served as judge of the Albany Circuit. Retiring in

1880, his health failing, Wright removed to near Forsyth in Monroe County, Georgia. There he engaged in farming until his death on June 3, 1895. He is buried in the Town Cemetery, Forsyth.

CV has Wright appointed brigadier general from Georgia in 1864. SHSP has him "acting brigadier general" of Young's brigade. One source said that a commission as brigadier general was mailed to him, but that in the rush of the last months of the war Wright failed to receive it.[3]

NOTES

1. William J. Northen, Men of Mark in Georgia (6 vols.; Atlanta, 1907–12), III, 351, 352.
2. Ibid., 353; Atlanta Constitution, June 4, 1895.
3. Northen, ed., Men of Mark in Georgia, III, 353.

MAIN SOURCES

Atlanta Constitution, June 4, 1895.
Daughters of the American Revolution, Thronateeska Chapter. History and Reminiscences of Daugherty County, Georgia. 1924; rpr. Spartanburg, 1978.
Northen, William J., ed. Men of Mark in Georgia. 6 vols. Atlanta, 1907–12.

JAMES YELL

James Yell, major general of Arkansas state forces, was born on March 10, 1811, in Bedford County, Tennessee, the son of Piercy Yell and the nephew of future Arkansas Governor Archibald Yell. The younger Yell was born in reduced circumstances, yet through his own unaided efforts practically educated himself. After gaining his majority Yell taught school for three years and served one term as Bedford County magistrate. Induced by his uncle, Colonel Yell, he moved to Arkansas in March, 1838. Settling in Pine Bluff, he began a remarkable career as a jury lawyer. Yell was styled the "Apollo of the bar because of his commanding form and handsome face."[1] He also was politically active, serving as Jefferson County's state senator from 1842 to 1845. In 1856 Yell was the Whig-American party candidate for governor, and in 1861 he was an unsuccessful candidate for a seat in the Confederate Senate. A Bell (Whig) Elector in 1860, Yell was nonetheless an active secessionist. Elected to the Arkansas Secession Convention, Yell assumed the leadership of the secessionist delegates. Ironically, he led the supporters of Governor Rector, who had been his political foe not a year before.

Yell was a general in the state militia before the war started. The secession convention elected Yell, the chairman of its military committee, as major general of the newly formed two-division "Army of Arkansas." His military career was short. He commanded five to six thousand state troops in northeast Arkansas in the summer of 1861, troops that were in training and never saw active duty. The governor soon desired to transfer Yell's troops from state to Confederate authority, but Yell protested. Yell went so far as to deliver a speech to the troops, urging them not to transfer to Confederate service unless they themselves voted so. The *Arkansas Gazette*, while admitting that Yell "is a man of personal courage," thought that Yell should be shot for his conduct, but that "his sublime ignorance entitled him to an acquittal on a plea of lunacy."[2] The Arkansas Military Board (Yell had written the bill creating the board) removed Yell from command on July 23, 1861, and he took no further active part in the war. Disillusioned, he spent his time denouncing the Confederate government as "a fraud and a failure" and used his legal talents to help arrested Unionists.[3] Much of the war he spent with relatives in Texas.

After the war he returned to his Pine Bluff home, where he died of pneumonia on September 5, 1867. It is said that his death was hastened by the burden of his debts, Yell having advanced large sums of his personal fortune to pay and equip Confederate troops. He is buried in an unmarked grave in Bellwood Cemetery in Pine Bluff, his gravesite marked by a brick sepulcher that has long since crumbled away.

Yell's rank of general in the Arkansas state army qualifies him to be considered a Confederate general.

NOTES

1. Goodspeed Publishing Company, *Biographical and Historical Memoirs of Pulaski, Jefferson, Lonoke, Faulkner, Grant, Saline, Perry, Garland, and Hot Spring Counties, Arkansas* (Chicago, 1889), 116.

2. The Little Rock *Arkansas Gazette*, in an editorial of July 20, 1861, recalled that Yell, at the outset, was told that he was in charge only until President Davis sent a Confederate general to take over. It noted that "when General Yell was sent to Pocahontas [in northeast Arkansas] every one expected to see foolish ignorance and vanity displayed in the superlative degree, and in that respect he has gone beyond the most extravagant expectations." As one might expect from the excerpt, Yell and the *Gazette* belonged to different political factions.

3. See General Yell's postwar application for pardon in the National Archives. General Yell's son, Fountain Pitts Yell (1834–64), a colonel of the 26th Arkansas Infantry, was mortally wounded at the Battle of Pleasant Hill.

MAIN SOURCES

Dougan, Michael B. *Confederate Arkansas*. University, Tex., 1976.

Goodspeed Publishing Company. *Biographical and Historical Memoirs of Pulaski, Jefferson, Lonoke, Faulkner, Grant, Saline, Perry, Garland, and Hot Spring Counties, Arkansas*. Chicago, 1889.

Hughes, William W. *Archibald Yell*. Fayetteville, Ark., 1988.

McGuyre, Ruth E. "The Yell Family of Arkansas." *Backtracker*, IV (January, 1975), 14–15.

Appendix

In addition to the 137 officers listed as Confederate generals in standard sources—the lists in the *Confederate Veteran*, the *Southern Historical Society Papers*, Heitman's *Historical Register of the United States Army*, Wood's *Confederate Handbook*, and Evans' *Confederate Military History*—there are other Confederate officers called general only in less reliable, less standard sources: in articles in the *Confederate Veteran* and the *Southern Historical Society Papers* (but not in the published lists), in newspapers, in family history books, and in various Civil War–related texts from 1865 to the present. In addition, Confederate correspondence in the *Official Records* labels as "general" dozens of state militia officers, in reference to a wartime or a prewar rank. Still other militia generals can be shown to have had their units called into service, although these generals' war service is not mentioned in the *Official Records*. While in no credible sense were these officers Confederate generals, they are listed in the brief sketches that follow.

William E. Anderson (1824–1871) was brigadier general of the Western Division of Florida Militia. As such, he sent a dispatch to the secretary of war in 1861, reported in the OR.[1] He was a prewar lawyer in Marianna, Florida, and a postwar judge.

David Rice Atchison (1807–1886) was a prewar U.S. senator from Missouri and a militia general. In 1861 Atchison joined up with Sterling Price's Missouri army and in September, 1861, led a detachment of the Missouri State Guard in a successful attack on Union forces. He signed his report of the action in the OR as "general."[2] A biography of his life states that he was tendered an appointment as general in the Missouri State Guard, but declined the appointment.[3]

John De Witt Clinton Atkins (1825–1908) was lieutenant colonel of the 5th Tennessee Infantry, a prewar and postwar U.S. congressman, and a member of the Confederate Congress. He was also a Henry County, Tennessee, editor, lawyer, and farmer. An advertisement in the CV lists him as a Confederate general.[4] He was a prewar militia general.

1. OR, LIII, 180.
2. OR, III, 195.
3. William E. Parrish, *David Rice Atchison of Missouri, Border Politician* (Columbia, Mo., 1961), 215. The report is in OR, III, 195. See also OR, VIII, 734.
4. "Portraits of Confederates Wanted," CV, IV (1896), 178.

William Tennant Austin (1809–1874) was wartime adjutant and inspector general of Texas. He is mentioned as a general in the OR. He was a prewar Galveston merchant.

Isaac Wheeler Avery (1837–1897), colonel of the 4th Georgia Cavalry, was also a noted journalist, lawyer, and historian. His own *The History of the State of Georgia* says he was made brigadier general of the PACS in February, 1865.[5] Another source says there was an unofficial report that Avery was promoted to general before the war ended.[6]

John Goff Ballentine (1825–1915) was a Pulaski, Tennessee, lawyer and postwar U.S. congressman. He served as a colonel of Ballentine's Cavalry, a Tennessee-Mississippi cavalry regiment. An obituary in the CV avers that "just before the collapse of the Confederacy, he was notified that he had been made brigadier general."[7]

Washington Barrow (1807–1866) was a prewar Nashville lawyer, editor, and U.S. congressman. The OR refer to the arrest of "General Barrow" by Union military authorities in Tennessee.[8] Barrow was a general of militia who took no part in the war.

Frederick Samuel Bass (1829–1897), a colonel of the 1st Texas Infantry, is called a general in the Moffett Papers.[9] He was a prewar teacher in Marshall, Texas. The text of CMH contains a statement that Hood's Texas brigade was, near the end of the war, commanded by "F. S. Bass . . . [who was] never promoted while in command as colonel, never received his commission until it was sent to him by the war department in June, 1897."[10]

Micajah Franklin Berry (1826–1917) was brigadier general of the 1st brigade of the Mississippi State Troops in 1862. The OR have him commanding the post of Jacinto, Mississippi, with that rank in 1862.[11] He was a prewar planter in Tippah County, Mississippi.

George William Lamb Bickley (1819–1867), a Virginia-born physician, was the founder of the "Knights of the Golden Circle," an organization that, in the years before the war, promoted filibustering expeditions. An April 9, 1861, letter in the OR mentions him as a general, referring to his self-assumed title of general of the "Knights."[12]

Luke Pryor Blackburn (1816–1887) was an agent of the Kentucky Confederate troops. An October 30, 1861, report of Brigadier General Pat Cleburne in the OR mentions that "General Blackburn" advised Cleburne on positions to take near Bowling Green, Kentucky.[13] Dr. Blackburn, a prominent Kentucky-born physician, was accused later in the war of plotting to send disease-riddled clothes to the North

5. Isaac W. Avery, *The History of the State of Georgia from 1850 to 1881* (New York, 1881), 658.
6. Charles E. Jones, *Georgia in the War, 1861–1865* (Atlanta, 1909), 41.
7. Grace M. Newbill, "Col. John Goff Ballentine," CV, XXIV (1916), 268–69.
8. OR, Ser. 2, Vol. IV, pp. 618, 670.
9. Andrew Moffett Papers, William R. Perkins Library, Duke University, Durham.
10. Evans, ed., CMH, XV, 53.
11. OR, Vol. LII, Pt. 2, p. 308.
12. OR, I, 625.
13. OR, Vol. LII, Pt. 2, p. 190.

to start a yellow fever epidemic. After the war he was elected governor of Kentucky. It is not known how he came to have the title "general."

Johan Heinrich August Heros von Borcke (1835–1895) was lieutenant colonel on Jeb Stuart's staff. He is called a general in an article in the CV on foreign-born Confederate generals.[14]

Solon Borland (1808–1864) was colonel of the 3rd Arkansas Cavalry, a prewar U.S. senator, and a Mexican War veteran. He is called a general in a biographical article.[15]

Wiles Lyde Lasham Bowen (1838–1905) was colonel of the 4th Florida Infantry. Mickle's *Well Known Confederate Veterans and Their War Records* says he was promoted brigadier general on the field for gallantry.[16] He was a postwar merchant in his native Georgia.

Cary Breckinridge (1839–1918) was colonel of the 2nd Virginia Cavalry. An obituary in the CV states that "in the last days of the struggle he was promoted to brigadier general; but never having borne that title on the field of battle, he never claimed it."[17] Breckinridge, a VMI graduate, commanded a brigade of cavalry at Appomattox.

August Buchel (1811–1864), colonel of the 1st Texas Cavalry, was a native of Germany and a soldier of fortune. The *Handbook of Texas* states that he "rose to the rank of Brigadier General before he was fatally wounded" at the Battle of Mansfield.[18]

Thomas James Butler (1811–1893), a Mobile, Alabama, merchant, was descended from a distinguished South Carolina family. Bergeron's *Confederate Mobile* says that Confederate General Samuel Jones, in late March, 1862, turned over command of the Army of Mobile to Brigadier General Thomas J. Butler, of the 9th Brigade of the Alabama Militia.[19]

James Alexander Carnes (1808–1864) was brigadier general of Tennessee militia. In 1862 a Memphis newspaper reported that his militia brigade was ordered into service to protect that city.[20] He was a prewar Memphis merchant.

Thomas Jefferson Chambers (1802–1865) was a Texas pioneer, judge, militia general, and perennial candidate for governor. Mentioned in the OR as a general, he served as a volunteer aide-de-camp on General John B. Hood's staff.

Edward Clark (1815–1880), colonel of the 14th Texas, was briefly governor of Texas in 1861. Wright's *Texas in the War, 1861–1865* says Clark was promoted to brigadier general in the Texas state army late in the war.[21] A Georgia-born lawyer and politician, he resided in Marshall, Texas.

14. H. T. Owen, "Keep the Record Straight," CV, XXIV (1916), 445–46.
15. *National Cyclopedia of American Biography* (63 vols.; New York, 1892–1984), IV, 386.
16. William E. Mickle, *Well Known Confederate Veterans and Their War Records* (New Orleans, 1907), 15.
17. "Col. Cary Breckinridge," CV, XXVI (1918), 452.
18. Walter P. Webb and Eldon S. Branda, eds., *Handbook of Texas* (3 vols.; Austin, 1952–76), I, 236.
19. Arthur P. Bergeron, *Confederate Mobile* (Jackson, Miss., 1991), 24.
20. The Memphis *Avalanche,* February 22, 1862, says Carnes's brigade was the 173rd.
21. Marcus J. Wright, *Texas in the War, 1861–1865,* ed. Harold Simpson (Hillsboro, 1965), 197.

Joseph Colton's name does not appear in the OR. An article in the CV on northern-born Confederate generals mentions a man by this name as a Massachusetts-born general.[22]

William Ayers Crawford (1829–1874) was colonel of the 1st (Crawford's) Arkansas Cavalry, a Mexican War veteran, and a prewar state representative of Saline County. The Arkansas volume of CMH mentions that the 2nd Arkansas Cavalry Brigade in the Trans-Mississippi was, on December 31, 1864, commanded by "Col. William A. Crawford (promoted to brigadier-general)."[23] Crawford did command a cavalry brigade during the last months of the war, and after the war he was appointed a brigadier general of Arkansas militia.

Lewis Gustavus DeRussy (1796–1864) is called a major general in a CV article on northern-born Confederate generals.[24] DeRussy, an old regular army officer who, during the war, served as colonel of the 2nd Louisiana Infantry and as an engineer officer, was a prewar major general in the Louisiana militia.

Charles Dimmock (ca. 1800–1863), a Massachusetts-born West Point graduate, was the head of the Virginia state arsenal. Wallace's A Guide to Virginia Military Organizations, 1861–65 notes that Governor Letcher of Virginia breveted Colonel Dimmock as brigadier general (of the Virginia State Line) for "distinguished service as Colonel of the Ordnance Department." He is also called a general in articles in the SHSP and the CV.[25]

Alfred Dockery (1797–1875), a North Carolina planter and politician, was a prewar member of the U.S. House of Representatives. He is mentioned as "General Dockery" in the OR.

Alexander Doniphan (1808–1887), Missouri's Mexican War hero, was a prominent Missouri attorney and public figure. Governor Jackson appointed Doniphan major general of the Missouri State Guard in June, 1861. However, Doniphan declined the appointment and stayed out of the war.

Richard Gordon Earle (1815–1864) was colonel of the 2nd Alabama Cavalry. He was a prewar Benton County lawyer and Mexican War veteran. The text of the Alabama volume of CMH has it that Earle "became a Confederate cavalry general and was killed in battle at Kingston, Ga."[26]

Charles LeDoux Elgee (1836–1864) was adjutant general of Louisiana, with the rank of brigadier general, in 1863. He was also captain of the Confederate cavalry and is mentioned as a general in the OR. Of a prominent Rapides Parish family, Elgee was secretary of the American embassy in Mexico before the war.

22. Owen, "Keep the Record Straight," 445–46.
23. Evans, ed., CMH, XIV, 278.
24. Owen, "Keep the Record Straight," 445–46.
25. Lee A. Wallace, A Guide to Virginia Military Organizations, 1861–65 (Lynchburg, Va., 1986), 235; W. Gordon McCabe, "Graduates of the United States Military Academy at West Point, N.Y., Who Served in the Confederate States Army, with the Highest Commission and Highest Command Attained," SHSP, XXX (1902), 34–76; John C. Shields, "The Old Camp Lee," SHSP, XXVI (1898), 241–46; Owen, "Keep the Record Straight," 445–46.
26. Evans, ed., CMH, VIII, 14.

Braxton T. Elliott is listed in the Moffett Papers as a Virginia general. He is per-haps confused with Brigadier General Stephen Elliott of South Carolina.

George M. Flournoy (1832–1889) was colonel of the 16th Texas Infantry and prewar attorney general of Texas. He is called general in Davis' *The Long Surrender*.[27]

Thompson Breckinridge Flournoy (1810–1861) was a prewar speaker of the Arkansas House and a Desha County farmer. The Richmond *Dispatch*, January 16, 1862, in a listing of Confederate generals appointed up to that date, shows that Flournoy was appointed brigadier general of the PACS between July 22 and Au-gust 29, 1861, but died in the interim. Flournoy is also called a general in the text of *CMH* and in two articles in the *CV*.[28]

C. W. Frazier is called a general in the *SHSP*'s list of Confederate generals. An article in the *CV* listing Tennessee's southern generals says that "C. W. Frazier" was appointed a brigadier general in the state's provisional army of 1861.[29] A C. W. Frazier was captain of company I of the 21st Tennessee Infantry during the war. This C. W. Frazier, later a prominent Memphis attorney, was the brother of Gen-eral John W. Frazier.

Charles Alexander Fuller (1814–1890) was colonel of the 1st Louisiana Ar-tillery regiment. The text of the Alabama volume of *CMH* mentions "Generals Fuller's and Higgins' brigades" stationed at Mobile in 1865.[30] Fuller commanded a brigade in the Army of Mobile throughout 1864 and 1865.

Milton Gholsun (1814–1883) was lieutenant colonel of the 14th Tennessee In-fantry. Krick in *Lee's Colonels* notes that Gholsun was "Brig. Genl. of Tennessee militia later in the war."[31] He was also a Montgomery County, Tennessee, planter.

Henry Liter Giltner (1829–1892) was colonel of the 4th Kentucky Cavalry and longtime brigade commander. He is called a general in Mosgrove's *Kentucky Cav-aliers in Dixie* and Willis' *Kentucky Democracy*, which say that he was commissioned a general, but so late in the war the commission never reached him.[32] Before the war he was sheriff of Carroll County, Kentucky.

Ambrosio Jose Gonzales (1818–1893) was colonel of artillery and at the end of the war acting chief of artillery of the Army of Tennessee. He is called a general in the *OR*. A Cuban revolutionary, teacher, state department clerk, and South Car-olina planter, Gonzales had been a general in a prewar Cuban Revolutionary army.

Duff Cyrus Green (1828–1865) was quartermaster general of Alabama and is called a general in the *OR*. He was a prewar U.S. Army officer and Mobile mer-chant.

---

27. Burke Davis, *The Long Surrender* (New York, 1985), 196.
28. Evans, ed., *CMH*, XIV, 291; "U.D.C. Notes," *CV*, XXXVIII (1930), 200–201; Ida E. Fowler, "Confederate Dead in the State Cemetery at Frankfort, Ky.," *CV*, XXXIV (1926), 375–76.
29. John P. Hickman, "Confederate Generals of Tennessee," *CV*, XVIII (1910), 170–72.
30. Evans, ed., *CMH*, VIII, 312.
31. Robert K. Krick, *Lee's Colonels* (Dayton, 1991), 154.
32. George D. Mosgrove, *Kentucky Cavaliers in Dixie* (Louisville, 1895), 47; George L. Willis, *Kentucky Democracy* (3 vols.; Louisville, 1935), I, 201.

John Shackelford Green (1817–1891) was colonel of the 6th Virginia Cavalry, and is misidentified as a general in Lossing's *Mathew Brady's Illustrated History of the Civil War*.[33] Green was a prewar farmer in Rappahannock County, Virginia.

William Harrison Hamman (1830–1918) was a Virginia-born Texas lawyer and postwar politician. The *Handbook of Texas* says Hamman was appointed brigadier general of Texas state troops in December, 1864.[34] He was a Robertson, Texas, lawyer.

James Harding (1830–1902) was quartermaster general of the Missouri State Guard with the staff rank of brigadier general. Called a general in the *OR*, he was a prewar Jefferson City, Missouri, engineer and postwar railroad executive.

William Giles Harding (1808–1886) was a member of the Tennessee state military board and a Nashville area farmer and famous horse breeder. A prewar general in the state militia, Harding is listed as a general in the Moffett Papers.

William Wallace Harllee (1812–1897) was colonel of Harllee's Legion and lieutenant governor of South Carolina. He is called a general in the text of *CMH, The Diary of Edmund Ruffin*, and the *Biographical Directory of the Senate of the State of South Carolina, 1776–1964*, which state that he was "commissioned Brigadier General of Harllee Legion."[35] He was also a prewar militia general.

Robert Yerby Harris (1816–1894) was a Richmond County, Georgia, planter. He participated as a general of militia in the seizure of the Augusta, Georgia, arsenal in 1861. See Candler's *The Confederate Records of the State of Georgia* for more information on this episode.[36]

Thomas Sherwood Haymond (1794–1869), a Monongalia County, Virginia, politician, was a prewar U.S. congressman and militia general. He is called a general in the *OR*.

Benjamin Wilkinson Heard (1821–1893), was a Wilkes County, Georgia, planter and politician. He is mentioned as a brigadier general of militia in Krick, *Lee's Colonels*.[37]

Adolphus Heiman (1809–1862), Prussian-born Nashville architect, was a Mexican War veteran and colonel of the 10th Tennessee Infantry. A biographical article in *Tennessee Historical Quarterly* says he was appointed brigadier general in 1862, but died before the commission reached him.[38]

Samuel Hutchinson Hempstead (1814–1862) was a Little Rock editor, lawyer,

33. Benson J. Lossing, *Mathew Brady's Illustrated History of the Civil War* (1912; rpr. New York, 1972), 360.

34. Webb and Branda, eds., *Handbook of Texas*, I, 762.

35. Evans, ed., *CMH*, VI, 855; William K. Scarborough, ed., *The Diary of Edmund Ruffin* (3 vols.; Baton Rouge, 1972–89), I, 561; Emily B. Reynolds and Joan R. Faunt, *Biographical Directory of the Senate of the State of South Carolina, 1776–1964* (Columbia, S.C., 1964), 232.

36. Allen Candler, ed., *The Confederate Records of the State of Georgia* (4 vols.; Atlanta, 1909–11), II, 132.

37. Krick, *Lee's Colonels*, 447.

38. John G. Frank, "Adolphus Heiman: Architect and Soldier," *Tennessee Historical Quarterly*, V (1946), 35–57.

district attorney, and solicitor general. He is called "Gen. S. H. Hempstead" in a February 12, 1861, letter in the OR.[39]

Charles Frederick Henningsen (1815–1877) was colonel of the 59th Virginia Infantry. He is called a general in a CV article on foreign-born Confederate generals.[40] The Belgian-born Henningsen, a widely-traveled soldier of fortune, was a general in William Walker's Nicaraguan army.

Henry Washington Hilliard (1808–1892) was colonel of Hilliard's Alabama Legion, a prewar Whig politician, U.S. congressman, and diplomat. He was also a Montgomery, Alabama, lawyer. Hilliard is called a general in a biographical article in *Cyclopedia of American Biography*.[41]

George M. Holt (*ca.* 1831–1863) was brigadier general of Arkansas militia in 1862 and is mentioned as a general in the OR. He was a prewar physician and colonel of Saline County militia.

Warwick Hough (1836–1915) was adjutant general of the Missouri State Guard with the staff rank of brigadier general. He is called a general in the OR. He was a lawyer and postwar judge.

Thomas B. Howard (1820–1904) was brigadier general of the 1st Brigade of the Texas Militia and is mentioned as a general in the OR. Before the war he was a Texas soldier and state representative from Fort Bend County.

William Hudson (1829–1904) was brigadier general of the 21st Brigade of the Texas Militia in 1862 and is mentioned as a general in the OR. He was a north Texas land locator and cattle breeder.

Alfred Iverson, Sr. (1798–1873) was a prewar U.S. senator from Georgia and is called a general in a biographical article in Northen's *Men of Mark in Georgia*. Northen confuses Senator Iverson with his son, who *was* a general.[42]

David Flavel Jamieson (1810–1864), a South Carolina lawyer and planter, was president of the South Carolina Secession Convention and South Carolina's secretary of war. He is mentioned as a general in the OR.

Joseph McAfee Jayne (1823–1885) was colonel of the 48th Mississippi Infantry. An article in the SHSP says he was appointed brigadier general just before the war ended.[43] He was a prewar Rankin County, Mississippi, politician and farmer.

Benjamin P. Jett (1808–1865) was brigadier general of the 1st Brigade of the 1st Division of the Arkansas Militia. The OR show a May 1, 1861, letter from him, signed "general," tendering his brigade to the Confederate government.[44] A resident of Washington, Arkansas, Jett was speaker of the Arkansas House of Representatives before the war.

---

39. OR, I, 642.
40. Owen, "Keep the Record Straight," 445–46.
41. *Cyclopedia of American Biography* (7 vols.; New York, 1891), II, 114.
42. William J. Northen, *Men of Mark in Georgia* (6 vols.; Atlanta, 1907–12), III, 435.
43. "Youngest General of the Confederate Army," SHSP, XXXV (1907), 55–58.
44. OR, I, 689.

William A. Johnson (1828–1891) was colonel of the 4th Alabama Cavalry and sometime brigade commander in Bedford Forrest's cavalry. He is called a general in a biographical article written by a descendant, with the general's commission coming too late in the war to be effective.[45] Johnson was a steamboat operator in northern Alabama before the war.

George H. Johnston is called a general in the Moffett Papers. No officer of this name achieved field rank in either regimental or staff command. A George D. Johnston was brigadier general in the PACS. This officer is probably listed twice, as George D. and (mistakenly) as George H., in the Moffett Papers.

Hilary Pollard Jones (1833–1913) was colonel of artillery in Lee's army, and a prewar teacher in Taylorsville, Virginia. He is called a general in Du Bellet's *Some Prominent Virginia Families*.[46]

James Jones (1805–1865) was a South Carolina lawyer and chairman of the Board of Visitors of the South Carolina Military Academy. He was a wartime colonel of the 14th South Carolina Infantry but is mentioned by a prewar title of general in the OR.

Paul Juge (18?–?) was a New Orleans, Louisiana, wine importer. A French-born naturalized citizen, Juge commanded the "Foreign Brigade," an organization of foreign-born New Orleans residents, which policed the streets of that city in 1862. He is mentioned as a general several times in the OR.

Charles A. Labuzan (*ca.* 1807–1869), a New Orleans real estate broker, was brigadier general of Louisiana militia commanding at Camp Lewis, near New Orleans, in 1861. He is called a general in the OR.

Levi Welbourne Lawler (1816–1892), a Mobile, Alabama, merchant, was a state representative during the war. The OR reprint a letter from Alabama Governor Thomas Watts in which Watts mentions "Gen. Lawler."[47] Lawler had been elected brigadier general of militia prior to 1850.

John Lawson Lewis (1800–1886), mayor of New Orleans before the war, was major general and commander-in-chief of Louisiana militia in 1862. He is mentioned as a general in the OR.

Tennent Lomax (1820–1862) was colonel of the 3rd Alabama Infantry. He is called a general in the text of CMH and in the *National Cyclopedia of American Biography*. He was a prewar editor and Mexican War veteran. Evidently due to receive a promotion, he was killed in action at the Battle of Seven Pines. Brewer's *Alabama: Her History, Resources, War Record and Public Men* says the commission as brigadier general was sent to Lomax the day he was killed.[48]

William E. Mann (1817–1866) was brigadier general of the 1st Brigade of the

---

45. Sons of Confederate Veterans, *Sons of Confederate Veterans, Ancestor Album* (Houston, 1986), 113–14.

46. Louise P. Du Bellet, *Some Prominent Virginia Families* (2 vols.; 1907; rpr. Baltimore, 1976), I, 179.

47. OR, Vol. XXXII, Pt. 3, p. 763.

48. Evans, ed., CMH, VIII, 680; *National Cyclopedia of American Biography*, VII, 97; Willis Brewer, *Alabama: Her History, Resources, War Record and Public Men* (Montgomery, 1872), 476.

North Carolina Militia. He was also an Elizabeth City publisher and sheriff. A report in the OR mentions that "General Mann" promised to call out his militia brigade in 1862.[49]

David Bell Martin (1830–1892) was brigadier general of the 10th Brigade of the Texas Militia. Mentioned as general in the OR, he was later colonel of the PACS and commandant of conscripts in Texas. Before the war Martin worked as a Cherokee County merchant. He was the cousin of U.S. Senator John Bell of Tennessee.

Mathias Martin (1812–1893) was colonel of the 23rd Tennessee Infantry. Speer's *Sketches of Prominent Tennesseans* mentions that he was elected major general of the 3rd Division of the Tennessee Militia in 1861, but declined the post.[50] He was a Maury County, Tennessee, planter.

Robert Campbell Martin (1813–1881) was brigadier general of the 5th Brigade of the Louisiana Militia in 1862 and is mentioned as a general in the OR. He was a Lafourche Parish, Louisiana, planter and state senator.

Zebulon Montgomery Pike Maury (1814–1862) was brigadier general of Tennessee militia. Graf's *The Papers of Andrew Johnson* shows that General Maury was captured at Fort Donelson and imprisoned.[51] Maury was a Williamson County, Tennessee, farmer and son of the founder of Maury County.

Hugh McLeod (1814–1862), a West Point graduate, was colonel of the 1st Texas Infantry. He is called by his prewar militia title of general in the OR. A New York–born Galveston resident, McLeod had been Texas' secretary of war.

Colin John McRae (1812–1877) was a Confederate agent in Europe and a Confederate congressman. Before the war he was a merchant in Mississippi and Alabama. McRae is called by a prewar militia rank of general in the OR.

Duncan Kirkland McRae (1820–1888) was colonel of the 5th North Carolina Infantry and occasional brigade commander. He is listed in the Moffett Papers as a general, where he is confused with Colonel Thomas H. McCray. Before the war he worked as a lawyer and politician.

Thomas Dwight Merrick (1813–1866) was major general of Arkansas militia and colonel of the 10th Arkansas Infantry. A February 6, 1861, letter of Arkansas Governor Rector, printed in the OR, mentions Merrick as "general of the 1st Div. Arkansas militia."[52] He was a prewar merchant and mayor of Little Rock.

Alexander B. Montgomery (1831–1904) was lieutenant colonel of the 3rd Georgia Infantry. Before the war he held the rank of prewar lieutenant in the U.S. Army. Jones's *Georgia in the War, 1861–1865* repeats an unofficial report that Montgomery was made a brigadier general.[53]

49. OR, IX, 191, 192.
50. William S. Speer, *Sketches of Prominent Tennesseans* (Nashville, 1888), 261.
51. Leroy P. Graf, Paul Bergeron, and Ralph Haskins, eds., *The Papers of Andrew Johnson* (10 vols.; Knoxville, 1967–92), V, 321.
52. OR, I, 640.
53. Jones, *Georgia in the War*, 23.

Jesse Morin (1808–1884) was a Platte County, Missouri, lawyer, politician, and Mexican War veteran. In 1861 Governor Jackson of Missouri appointed Morin brigadier general of the 5th District of the Missouri State Guard. After considerable soul-searching Morin declined the appointment, and sat out the war.

Rufus Polk Neely (1808–1901) was colonel of the 4th Tennessee Cavalry. He is listed as a general in the Moffett Papers. A militia general, Neely was often called "general" in recognition of his militia rank.[54] He was also a railroad president and state representative.

Ebenezer B. Nichols (1814–1872) was colonel of the 9th Texas Infantry. A Galveston merchant, he is called by his militia rank of general in the *OR*.

Robert Ould (1820–1881) was a colonel and Confederate commissioner of prisoner exchanges. He is called a general in Thompson's *Reminiscences of General M. Jeff Thompson*.[55] Before the war, he was the district attorney for the District of Columbia and a militia general.

S. B. Palmer is called a general in the *SHSP*'s list of Confederate generals. The listing is probably a misprint for PACS General J. B. Palmer.

Lawrence Parker is called a general in an article in the *CV*, appointed from North Carolina in 1863. He was probably mistaken for General Lawrence Baker.[56]

William Johnson Pegram (1841–1865) was colonel of artillery in Lee's army. Pegram is listed as a general in the Moffett Papers and in an article in the *SHSP*.[57] There was talk late in the war of his taking over an infantry brigade, but he was killed at the Battle of Five Forks before any promotion could take place.

Davidson Bradfute Penn (1836–1902) was colonel of the 7th Louisiana Infantry and postwar lieutenant governor of Louisiana. He is listed as a general in the Moffett Papers. After the war Penn was also adjutant general of the Lousiana militia.

Theodore H. Phillips (1827–1884), a Jackson County, Arkansas, sheriff and planter, was brigadier general of the 8th Brigade of the Arkansas Militia. He is mentioned as a general in the *OR*.

Trusten Polk (1811–1876) was colonel and presiding judge on the military court of General Theophilus Holmes and prewar governor of Missouri. He is called a general in Davis' *The Long Surrender*.[58]

John Smith Prather (1835–1920) was lieutenant colonel of the 8th Confederate Cavalry. Avery's *History of Georgia* and an article in the *CV* call Prather a "Brevet Brigadier General."[59] After the war Prather edited an Atlanta newspaper.

54. See, for example, the Memphis *Appeal*, April 10, 1873.
55. M. Jeff Thompson, *Reminiscences of General M. Jeff Thompson*, eds. Donal J. Stanton, Goodwin F. Berquist, and Paul C. Bowers (Dayton, 1988), 233.
56. Telamon Cuyler, "Surviving Confederate Generals," *CV*, XV (1907), 118.
57. "Youngest General of the Confederate Army," *SHSP*, XXXV (1907), 57.
58. Davis, *The Long Surrender*, 196.
59. Avery, *History of Georgia*, 659; "Col. John S. Prather," *CV*, XXVIII (1920), 229.

James Fowler Pressley (1835–1877) was colonel of the 10th South Carolina Infantry. A South Carolina Military Academy graduate, Pressley was a postwar physician. He is called a general in the text of *CMH* and in May and Faunt, *South Carolina Secedes.*[60]

Bushrod Washington Price (1808–1903) was brigadier general of the 24th Brigade of the Virginia Militia in 1860 and 1861. A December 15, 1860, report of the adjutant general of Virginia, printed in the *OR*, mentions him as a general.[61] A Moundsville, Virginia, merchant and farmer, Price was a prewar state representative and postwar West Virginia state senator.

Samuel R. Pyles (1811–1862) was elected major general of the 2nd Division of the Florida Militia in 1861. He is mentioned as a general in the *OR* and was an Alachua County, Florida, planter.

Paul Jones Quattlebaum (1836–1883), a West Point graduate, was a lieutenant colonel and staff officer during the war. He is called a general in the text of *CMH*. An article in the *South Carolina Historical and Genealogical Magazine* calls him a colonel, but adds: "It is said that he was promoted to the rank of Brigadier General just before the close of the war."[62]

Richard Carlton Walker Radford (1822–1886) was colonel of the 2nd Virginia Cavalry. He is listed as a general in the Moffett Papers. Radford commanded a brigade in the "Virginia State Line," a reserve/home guard organization formed in 1862.

Alexis Theodore Rainey (1822–1891) was colonel of the 1st Texas Infantry. He is listed as a general in the Moffett Papers. Rainey occasionally commaded a brigade in Texas in the last years of the war. Rainey became a Palestine, Texas, lawyer and legislator.

(Thomas) Beverly Randolph (1792–1867) was appointed brigadier general of the Missouri State Guard in May, 1861, but declined the appointment because of advanced age. A West Point graduate, Randolph was a colonel of Virginia volunteers in the Mexican War and a Wentzville, Missouri, planter.

Robert Barnwall Rhett (1800–1876) was a South Carolina politician and secessionist. A photograph of him in La Bree's *The Confederate Soldier in the Civil War* shows him in a general's uniform and is labeled "Brigadier General Rhett."[63] In reality, he never served in the Confederate army.

William Harvie Richardson (1795–1876) was wartime adjutant general of Virginia and a prewar Virginia political figure and agriculturalist. He is called a major general in the *OR*.

Asa Rogers (1802–1887) was major general of the 2nd Division of the Virginia

60. Evans, ed., *CMH*, VI, 545; John A. May and Joan R. Faunt, *South Carolina Secedes* (Columbia, S.C., 1960), 195.

61. *OR*, Ser. 4, Vol. I, p. 382.

62. Evans, ed., *CMH*, VI, 806; Paul Quattlebaum, "Quattlebaum: A Palatine Family in South Carolina," *South Carolina Historical and Genealogical Magazine*, XLVIII (1947), 169.

63. Benjamin La Bree, ed., *The Confederate Soldier in the Civil War* (1895; rpr. Paterson, N.J., 1959), 18.

Militia. A Loudon County farmer, he also served as a state senator. The capture of "General Rogers" by Union forces is noted in the OR.[64]

William Peleg Rogers (1817–1862), colonel of the 2nd Texas Infantry, was killed at the Battle of Corinth. He is called a general in the OR in reference to a militia title. He was a prewar lawyer and politician.

Charles Andrew Ronald (1827–1898) was colonel of the 4th Virginia Infantry and briefly commander of the Stonewall Brigade. He is called a general in an advertisement and an article in the CV.[65] Ronald was a Blacksburg lawyer and Mexican War veteran.

Charles Needham Rowley (1806–1869) was brigadier general of the 6th Brigade of the Louisiana Militia. He is mentioned as a general in the OR. Before the war Rowley was state adjutant general and a Pointe Coupee Parish, Louisiana, planter.

Nathan George Shelley (1825–1898), brigadier general of the 26th Brigade of the Texas Militia, was an Austin lawyer and attorney general of Texas for much of the war. His brother was PACS Brigadier General Charles M. Shelley. The OR contain communications to "General N. G. Shelley" when Shelley was in Richmond seeking arms for Texas.[66]

Sidney Sherman (1805–1873), a Texas founder, was a politician and militia general. He owned a hotel in Galveston, Texas. The Texas Secession Convention appointed him commandant of Galveston in early 1861. He is mentioned as a general in the OR.

William Shields (1808–?) was a Lexington, Missouri, banker and minor politician. The OR mention that "General Shields" was, in 1861 and 1862, actively raising funds for the Missouri State Guard.[67]

William Ferguson Slemons (1830–1918) was a Monticello, Arkansas, lawyer and colonel of the 2nd Arkansas Cavalry. He led a cavalry brigade during Price's 1864 Missouri Raid. Speer's *The Encyclopedia of the New West* says that after Slemons' capture at Mine Creek in 1864, "he was commissioned brigadier-general, but never served as such."[68]

Charles Edward Smedes (1824–1898) was a Vicksburg, Mississippi, corn merchant and brigadier general of militia at Vicksburg in 1862. An article in the text of CMH calls him a general.[69]

Francis Henney Smith (1812–1890), superintendent of VMI, teacher, and West Point graduate, was briefly colonel of the 9th Virginia Infantry. He is called a gen-

---

64. OR, V, 514.
65. "Portraits of Confederates Wanted," CV, IV (1896), 178; W. L. Cabell, "Confederate Generals Yet Living," CV, II (1893), 28.
66. OR, Vol. XXXIV, Pt. 3, p. 793; Vol. LIII, p. 985.
67. OR, VIII, 726.
68. William S. Speer, ed., *The Encyclopedia of the New West* (Marshall, Tex., 1881), 246–48.
69. Evans, ed., CMH, IX, 441; see also the Vicksburg *Daily Whig*, May 15, 1862, for a mention of Smedes as a general.

eral, and brevet major general, in the OR in reference to his being a general of Virginia state forces.

John Blair Smith (1820–1864) was brigadier general of the 10th Brigade of the Louisiana Militia in 1862. He is mentioned as a general in the OR. Smith was a Natchitoches, Louisiana, lawyer and Mexican War veteran.

Darwin Massey Stapp (1815–1875) was brigadier general of Texas militia and signed a letter, which is reprinted in the OR, as such. [70] Stapp was a prewar Indianola, Texas, farmer.

James Wellborn Starnes (1817–1863) was colonel of the 4th Tennessee Cavalry. He is called a general in a book on the Starnes family. [71] A prewar physician, Williamson County planter, and Mexican War veteran, Starnes commanded a brigade under Bedford Forrest.

Vernon King Stevenson (1812–1884) was quartermaster general of Tennessee and the West in 1861 and prewar president of the Nashville and Chattanooga Railroad. An October 31, 1861, letter in the OR mentions "General V. K. Stevenson." [72]

Jesse R. Stubbs (1825–1870), a Martin County lawyer, state senator, and railroad president, is said to have served in the North Carolina militia after the fall of Roanoke Island in 1862. He is called a general in Clark's *Histories of the Several Regiments and Battalions from North Carolina in the Great War, 1861–1865*. [73]

Clement L. Sulivane (1838–1920), a young Marylander born in Mississippi, served as lieutenant on the staff of Major General Earl Van Dorn (his uncle) before being transferred to the adjutant general's office in Richmond. As captain, he commanded a brigade of local defense troops in the Appomattox campaign. An article in the SHSP quotes Sulivane as saying that both he and Henry Kyd Douglas were issued commissions as brigadier generals at the end of the war. [74] However, in a later article Sulivane called himself colonel. He worked postwar as an editor in Maryland. [75]

Joseph M. Taylor (1826–1892) was a Brooksville, Florida, lawyer and state senator who was elected brigadier general of Florida militia in 1861. He is mentioned as a general in the OR..

Nathaniel Terry (ca. 1799–1871) was brigadier general of the 20th Brigade of the Texas Militia and is called a general in the OR. Terry, a Fort Worth planter and politician, had served as president of the Alabama Senate.

Waddy Thompson, Jr. (1798–1868), a prewar U.S. congressman and minister

70. OR, IV, 123, 129.

71. Mrs. Avis Stearns Van Wagenen, *Genealogy and Memoirs of Charles and Nathaniel Stearns, and Their Descendents* (2 vols.; Syracuse, 1901), II, 131.

72. OR, Vol. LII, Pt. 2, p. 191.

73. Walter Clark, ed., *Histories of the Several Regiments and Battalions from North Carolina in the Great War, 1861–1865* (5 vols.; Raleigh, 1901), I, xiii.

74. X. X., "Who Was Last Soldier to Leave Burning City," SHSP, XXXVII (1909), 317–18.

75. Clement L. Sulivane, "The *Arkansas* at Vicksburg in 1862," CV, XXV (1917), 496.

to Mexico, was brigadier general of South Carolina militia. He is mentioned as "General Waddy Thompson" in a letter to General Beauregard in the OR.[76] A Greenville resident, Thompson took no active part in the war.

Robert Barr Todd (1826–1901), a Morehouse, Louisiana, lawyer and postwar judge, was brigadier general of the 11th Brigade of the Louisiana Militia in 1862. He is mentioned as a general in the OR.

Tullius Cicero Tupper (1809–1866) was major general of Mississippi militia from March, 1862, to his resignation in 1863. He is mentioned as general in the OR. The Vermont-born Tupper was a Canton, Mississippi, lawyer and Episcopal layman.

Thomas Eugene Vick (1831–1866), brigadier general of all militia in northern Louisiana in 1863, is mentioned as a general in the OR. A grandson of the founder of Vicksburg, he was a prewar physician in Thibodaux, Louisiana. Vick was major of the 4th Louisiana Infantry in 1862.

E. G. Walker is listed in the Moffett Papers as a general. He is probably confused with Major General John G. Walker.

Nathaniel W. Watkins (1796–1875), half-brother of Henry Clay, was a long-time Missouri Whig leader and Cape Girardeau lawyer. He was appointed brigadier general of the 1st District of the Missouri State Guard on May 17, 1861, and resigned this position in July, 1861.

Hugh Parks Watson (1813–1866) was adjutant general of Alabama Militia and is called a general in the OR. Watson was a Mexican War veteran and Montgomery, Alabama, resident.

A. B. Watts (18?–?) was commissioned brigadier general of Mississippi state troops from Rankin County on October 15, 1863. The OR show an April 19, 1864, letter from Watts to Lieutenant General Leonidas Polk, Confederate commander in Mississippi, concerning stopping citizens from trading with Union forces.[77] This is probably the A. B. Watts who belonged to a pioneer Wayne County family with Rankin County connections, and who lived after the war in Meridian, Mississippi.

Samuel Davies Weakley (1812–1897) was a Florence, Alabama, railroad executive and cotton mill owner. A prewar militia general, he served during the war as a volunteer aide to General Pillow. He is mentioned as a general in the OR in connection with his heading a committee to raise five thousand troops to reinforce the Tennessee River defenses.

William Graham Webb (1824–1902) was brigadier general of the 22nd Brigade of the Texas Militia. Mentioned as a general in the OR, Webb was a La Grange, Texas, lawyer.

Washington Curran Whitthorne (1825–1891) was militia general and wartime

76. Governor Milledge Bonham of South Carolina to General P. G. T. Beauregard, in OR, Vol. XXVIII, Pt. 2, p. 456.
77. OR, Vol. XXXII, Pt. 3, p. 797.

adjutant general of Tennessee. He is called a general in the OR. Whitthorne was a prewar speaker of the Tennessee House and postwar U.S. congressman.

Charles Jones Williams (1821–1862) was colonel of the 1st Georgia Infantry. As brigadier general of militia, he participated in the seizure of the Augusta arsenal in 1861. He is called a general in the OR. A Columbus resident, Williams served in the Mexican War and the Georgia General Assembly.

James Willie (1823–1863) was a Brenham, Texas, lawyer and prewar state attorney general. He is called "general" James Willie in the OR in Colonel Earl Van Dorn's May 16, 1861, report of operations in Texas.[78] Willie was serving as Van Dorn's volunteer aide at the time.

Henry Wilson of Louisiana is listed in the Moffett Papers as a general. No officer with that name served in a Louisiana Confederate unit. Henry Wilson (1792–1872), a Pennsylvania-born U.S. Army colonel and Mexican War veteran, resigned from the army in 1861 and settled in New Orleans. A garbled report of his death may have led Moffett to list him as a Confederate general.

Richard H. Winter (1822–1870) was brigadier general of Mississippi state troops at Grenada in 1862. He is mentioned as a general in the OR. Winter was a prewar planter and banker in Madison County, Mississippi.

John T. Withers (1827–1892) was a colonel and staff officer, and assistant adjutant general in the Confederate war office. He is called "General Withers, assistant secretary of war" in the text of CMH.[79] Withers was a prewar U.S. Army officer and a postwar banker.

William Temple Withers (1825–1889), a Mexican War veteran and prewar lawyer, was colonel of the 1st Mississippi Artillery. He is called a general in a history of the Withers family and in an obituary article in the Louisville *Courier-Journal*, which says he was called "general" because his artillery regiment command was the equivalent of a general's brigade command, even though his actual rank was colonel.[80]

M. H. Wright is listed as acting brigadier general in the SHSP's list of Confederate generals. This listing would appear to be a misspelling of Brigadier General Marcus J. Wright. A Moses Hanibal Wright of Tennessee (1836–1886) was colonel and commander at several Confederate arsenals. He was a West Point graduate and postwar broker.

Robert L. Wright (1813–1865) was brigadier general of the 8th Brigade of the Virginia Militia. The capture of "General Wright" by Union forces is noted in the OR.[81] Wright was a Loudon County, Virginia, farmer and state representative.

Hugh Franklin Young (1808–1888) was brigadier general of the 15th Brigade

78. OR, I, 672, 633.

79. Evans, ed., CMH, VIII, 396.

80. Franz V. Recum, *Withers, America* (New York, 1949), 83; Louisville *Courier-Journal*, June 17, 1889.

81. OR, V, 514.

of the Texas Militia in 1862. Mentioned as a general in the OR, Young was a pre-war county judge in Grayson County, Texas.

Charles Thornton Zachry (1828–1906) was colonel of the 27th Georgia Infantry. Avery's *The History of the State of Georgia from 1850 to 1881* says Zachry was appointed brigadier general of the PACS in March, 1865.[82] He was a Henry County, Georgia, planter and politician.

82. Avery, *History of Georgia*, 660.

BIBLIOGRAPHY

NOTE: Any Civil War research must start with the *Official Records* of the war, the massive 128-volume compilation of war communications and reports. On a more particularized basis, the resources of the National Archives—most notably, the compiled Confederate army service records and the U.S. census returns—provide a start for the research of any one officer.

UNPUBLISHED SOURCES

Alabama Census, 1866.

Alcorn, James L. Papers. Southern Historical Collection, University of North Carolina, Chapel Hill.

Allen, William G. Memoirs. Confederate Collection, Tennessee State Archives, Nashville.

Andrea, Leonardo, and Louise White. "Floyd Family of Virginia, North and South Carolina and Georgia." Daughters of the American Revolution Library, Washington, D.C.

Arnott, Mary. "The Wade Family of Virginia—Bedford County." Latter-Day Saints Library, Salt Lake City.

Atkins, John D. C. Collection. Chicago Historical Society, Chicago.

Bagby Family Tree. Virginia Historical Society, Richmond.

Bailey, Lloyd. "The McElroy Family of Yancey County." North Carolina Department of Archives and History, Raleigh.

Barnes, Thomas. Papers. Tennessee State Archives, Nashville.

Barnes, Thomas. Will. Will Book N, p. 548, Hancock County Probate Records, Sparta, Ga.

Bates, Edward. Papers. Missouri Historical Society, St. Louis.

Baylor, John R. Letters. Edward C. Wharton Papers, Hill Memorial Library, Louisiana State University, Baton Rouge.

Bell, Raymond M., and Harriet C. Hardaway. "James Clemens of Washington County, Pennsylvania, 1734–1795, and His Family." Huntsville Public Library, Huntsville, Ala.

Bellefontaine Cemetery Records. St. Louis.

Bowles, Pinckney D. Record of Probate Proceeding, August 31, 1910. Conecuh County Probate Records. Evergreen, Ala.

Bowles, Pinckney D. Sketch. United Daughters of the Confederacy, Alabama Division Collection, W. Stanley Hoole Special Collections Library, University of Alabama, Tuscaloosa.

Bradley, Thomas. Will. Will Book 9, pp. 288, 300, Williamson County Probate Records. Franklin, Tenn.

Bradley, Thomas H. Will. Will Book B, p. 213, Crittenden County Probate Records. Marten, Ark.

Brent, Joseph L. Papers. Hill Memorial Library, Louisiana State University, Baton Rouge.

Brent, Joseph L. Papers. Louisiana State Archives, Baton Rouge.

Case Files of Applications from Former Confederates for Presidential Pardons (Amnesty Papers), 1865–67. Microfilm M1003, National Archives.

Caswell, William R. Papers. Southern Historical Collection, University of North Carolina, Chapel Hill.

Cave Hill Cemetery Records. Louisville.

Chase, William H. Papers. Western Reserve Historical Society, Cleveland.

Chicago, Record and Index of Persons Registered and Poll List of Voters, 1888–1890. Illinois Regional Archives, Northeastern Illinois University, Chicago.

Citadel, The. Records. The Citadel, Charleston, S.C.

City Cemetery Records. Tennessee State Archives, Nashville.

Civil War Papers, Confederate. Missouri Historical Society, St. Louis.

Clark, Meriwether L. Papers. Missouri Historical Society, St. Louis.

Clemens, Jere. File. *Civil War Times Illustrated* Collection, U.S. Army Military History Institute, Carlisle, Penn.

Coffee, John. Papers. Tennessee State Archives, Nashville.

College of Charleston Records. College of Charleston, Charleston, S.C.

Compiled Service Records, Confederate. Unfiled Papers and Slips. Microfilm M347, National Archives.

Compiled Service Records of Confederate Army Volunteers. Microfilms M311 (Alabama), M317 (Arkansas), M251 (Florida), M266 (Georgia), M319 (Kentucky), M320 (Louisiana), M321 (Maryland), M269 (Mississippi), M322 (Missouri), M270 (North Carolina), M267 (South Carolina), M268 (Tennessee), M323 (Texas), M324 (Virginia), National Archives.

Compiled Service Records of Confederate General and Staff Officers and Non-Regimental Enlisted Men. Microfilm M331, National Archives.

Compiled Service Records of Confederate Soldiers Who Served in Organizations Raised Directly by the Confederate States Government. Microfilm M258, National Archives.

Crockett Papers. Tennessee State Archives, Nashville.

Dahlgren, Charles G. Collection. Chicago Historical Society, Chicago.

Dahlgren, Charles G. Sketch of the Life of. MS in Edith Wyatt Moore Collection, Armstrong Library, Natchez, Miss.

Dahlgren Family Correspondence. In possession of Herschel Gower, Dallas.

Dahlgren Family. Genealogy. MS in possession of John Berg, New York.

Dahlgren Family Papers. Tennessee Historical Society, Nashville.

Dispatches from U.S. Consuls in Chinkiang, China, 1864–1902. Microfilm M103, National Archives.

Donelson, Andrew J. Papers. Library of Congress.

Douglas, Henry Kyd. Collection. Chicago Historical Society, Chicago.

Edinburgh Parish Records. Edinburgh, Scotland.

Elmwood Cemetery Records. Memphis.

Emory University Records. Emory University, Atlanta.

Engineer Department Records of the United States Military Academy, 1812–67. Microfilm M91, National Archives.

Florida Confederate Widows' Pension Applications. Florida State Archives, Tallahassee.

Foster-Woods Papers. Tennessee State Archives, Nashville.

Freestone County Land Records. Fairfield, Tex.

Friendship Cemetery Records. Columbus, Miss.

Geisenburger, Amanda. Collection. Armstrong Library, Natchez, Miss.

Genealogical Notebooks of Alice C. Tonge. MS at Georgia Department of Archives and History, Atlanta.

Georgia Adjutant General's Office. Book of Commissions. Georgia Department of Archives and History, Atlanta.

Georgia State Military Records. Georgia Department of Archives and History, Atlanta.

Gordon, Benjamin F. Family Correspondence. In possession of Leslie Gray, Glenview, Ill.

Gordon Family History. MS by Lutie Gordon Jordon in possession of Mrs. Edward Long, Kansas City.

Green Mount Cemetery Records. Baltimore.

Greene, Colton. Collection. Memphis/Shelby County Public Library, Memphis.

Greene, Colton. Will. Shelby County Probate Records (1900), No. 15, p. 550. Memphis.

Greenwood Cemetery Records. Dallas.

Grigsby Family. Genealogy. MS of the National Grigsby Society, Dallas.

Hagan, James. Papers. Hill Memorial Library, Louisiana State University, Baton Rouge.

Hagan, John. Papers. Hill Memorial Library, Louisiana State University, Baton Rouge.

Hale Collection of Connecticut Newspapers, Tombstone Inscriptions, etc. Copy at Newberry Library, Chicago.

Hannon, Moses. Papers. In possession of Catharyn Heatly, Dallas.

Harper, Kenton. Papers. Southern Historical Collection, University of North Carolina, Chapel Hill.

Harris, David Bullock. Papers. Duke University, Durham.

Harris, Robert Y. Letters of Administration Book 11, p. 74. Richmond County Probate Records. Augusta.

Hempstead, Stephen. Papers. Missouri Historical Society, St. Louis.

Hoke, William J. Papers. Southern Historical Collection, University of North Carolina, Chapel Hill.

Hoke, William J. Will. Lincoln County Wills. Copy WB-4/64, North Carolina Department of Archives and History, Raleigh.

Hollywood Cemetery Records. Richmond.

Indian Affairs, Records of the Superintendent—Southern Superintendency, 1832–70. Microfilm M640, National Archives.

Jackman, Thomas. Will. Will Book 3, p. 106, Howard County Probate Records. Fayette, Mo.

Jones, Alexander C. Letters. Archives, Virginia Military Institute, Lexington, Va.

Jones, Alexander C. Papers. Virginia Historical Society, Richmond.

Little, Henry. Diary. U.S. Army Military History Institute, Carlisle, Penn.

Louisiana Confederate Pensions. Louisiana State Archives, Baton Rouge.

Louisiana State Government Records, 1850–88. Microfilm M359, National Archives.

Magnolia Cemetery Records. Mobile.

Maple Hill Cemetery Records. Huntsville, Ala.

Martin, William T. Papers. University of Texas, Austin.

McMurray, James A. Estate Inventory. Davidson County Will Book, 1861–65, pp. 298–99. Tennessee State Archives, Nashville.

Mexican War Pension Applications. Microfilm T515, National Archives.

Mexican War Service Records. Microfilms M278, M638, M863, National Archives.

Minnesota, Records of the Office of the Adjutant General. Minneapolis.

Mississippi Register of Commissions. Mississippi Department of Archives and History, Jackson.

Mississippi State Troops Register of Commissions, 1861–65. Record Group 109, Chap. 8, Vol. 6, National Archives.

Moffett, Andrew. Papers. William R. Perkins Library, Duke University, Durham.

Monroe County Court Records. Madisonville, Tenn.

Moore, Samuel P. File. Aztec Club Archives, U.S. Army Military History Institute, Carlisle, Penn.

Mount Hebron Cemetery Records. Winchester, Va.

Munford-Ellis Family. Papers. William R. Perkins Library, Duke University, Durham.

New Mexico Census, 1885.

Newton County Court Records. In U.S. Work Projects Administration Records, Western Historical Manuscripts Collection, State Historical Society of Missouri, Columbia, Mo.

Old Gray Cemetery Records. Knoxville.

Parsons, William H. Papers. In possession of William D. Parsons, Lake Forest, Ill.

Pendleton County Historical Society Grave Register. Franklin, W. Va.

Phifer, John. Will. Yalobusha County Probate Papers, Box 61. Coffeeville, Miss.

Phillips, Theodore. Will. Jackson County Administration Bonds and Letters, 1875–1913, p. 45. Newport, Ark.

Pierce, Franklin, and James Buchanan. Letters of Application and Recommendation During Administration. Microfilm M967, National Archives.

Postmasters, Records of Appointment, 1832–September 30, 1971. Microfilm M841, National Archives.

Price, Sterling. Order Books and Notes. Gunther Collection, Chicago Historical Society, Chicago.

Provisional Army of Tennessee and Invalid Corps Register of Officers, 1864–65. Record Group 109, Chap. 1, Vol. 197, National Archives.

Rainoshek, Dennis W., ed. "A List of Confederate Soldiers Buried in Galveston, Texas: Compiled Principally Before 1900." Eugene C. Barker Texas History Center, University of Texas at Austin.

Rains, George W. Papers. Southern Historical Collection, University of North Carolina, Chapel Hill.

Randolph-Macon College Records. Randolph-Macon College, Lynchburg, Va.

Reynolds, L. P. Papers. Mississippi Department of Archives and History, Jackson.

Reynolds, Thomas C. Papers. Library of Congress.

Rock Creek Cemetery Records. Washington, D.C.

Ross Family Papers. Small Collections, Tennessee State Archives, Nashville.

Ross, Reuben R. Diaries, Memoirs. Tennessee State Archives, Nashville.

Schaumburg, W. C. File. Lewis Leigh Collection, U.S. Army Military History Institute, Carlisle, Penn.

Seminole War Compiled Service Records. Tennessee State Archives, Nashville.

Semmes, Raphael. Folder. Walter Fleming Collection, Hill Memorial Library, Louisiana State University, Baton Rouge.

Simons, James. Papers. Southern Historical Collection, University of North Carolina, Chapel Hill.

Smith, Edmund Kirby. Papers. Southern Historical Collection, University of North Carolina, Chapel Hill.

Smith, Ira. File. Civil War Times Illustrated Collection, U.S. Army Military History Institute, Carlisle, Penn.

Snead, Thomas L. Papers. Missouri Historical Society, St. Louis.

Snyder, John F. Collection. Missouri Historical Society, St. Louis.

Spring Grove Cemetery Records. Cincinnati.

Steen, A. E. Letters. Western Historical Manuscript Collection, State Historical Society of Missouri, Columbia, Mo.

Stewart, Robert. Papers. Western Historical Manuscript Collection, State Historical Society of Missouri, Columbia, Mo.

Storm, Henry. Papers. William R. Perkins Library, Duke University, Durham.

Sykes, Columbus. Letters. Kennesaw Mountain National Battlefield Park Library, Kennesaw, Ga.

Tennessee Special Census, 1891.

Texas Commanding Officers' Service Records. Card File at Texas State Archives, Austin.

Texas State Troops Register, December 5, 1863. Record Group 109, Chap. 1, Vol. 104 1/2, National Archives.

Tupper, Tullius C. File. Mississippi Department of Archives and History, Jackson.

Underwood Family Papers. Western Kentucky State University, Bowling Green.

United Daughters of the Confederacy, Missouri Division, Records of Missouri Confederate Veterans. Western Historical Manuscript Collection, State Historical Society of Missouri, Columbia, Mo.

United States Census Returns, 1790–1920. Microfilms M19, M32, M33, M252, M407, M432, M593, M637, M653, M704, T9, T623, T624, T625, National Archives.

United States Military Academy Cadet Application Papers, 1805–1866. Microfilm M688, National Archives.

United States Military Academy Records. Archives, West Point.

United States Patents 26855, 27549.

University of Georgia Records. University of Georgia, Athens.

University of Nashville Records. Tennessee State Archives, Nashville.

University of South Carolina Records. University of South Carolina, Columbia, S.C.

University of Tennessee Records. University of Tennessee, Knoxville.

University of Virginia Records. University of Virginia, Charlottesville.

United States Consular Officers, 1789–1938. List. Microfilm M587, National Archives.

Vance, Governor Zebulon B. Letters and Telegrams, 1862–65. Microfilm T731, National Archives.

Virginia Forces' Records, 1861. Microfilm M998, National Archives.

Walker, Francis M. Biographical Sketch. MS at Tennessee State Archives, Nashville.

Warner, Ezra. Collection. Chicago Historical Society, Chicago.

West, Absalom M. Papers. In possession of Mr. and Mrs. L. A. Smith, Holly Springs, Miss.

Whitfield, Francis E. Will. Alcorn County Probate Records, Book I, Vol. A, p. 400. Corinth, Miss.

Wilson, Henry. Papers. Hill Memorial Library, Louisiana State University, Baton Rouge.

Wright, Gilbert J. Letters. United Daughters of the Confederacy, "Confederate Letters, Diaries and Reminiscences." Bound typescript at Georgia Department of Archives and History, Atlanta.

Wright, Marcus J. Papers. Southern Historical Collection, University of North Carolina, Chapel Hill.
Wright, Robert L. Will. Will Book 2P, p. 423, Loudon County Probate Records. Leesburg, Va.

NEWSPAPERS

Albany (Ga.) *Herald*, June 8, 1895.
Asheville *News*, November 8, 1855.
Atlanta *Constitution*, July 31, August 2, 1886, January 13, 1889, February 2, February 4, 1891, December 18, 1892, June 14, 1895, February 24, 1901.
Atlanta *Journal*, June 15, 1907, May 16, 1931.
Austin *Daily Statesman*, May 27, May 29, June 3, 1886, January 7, 1895.
Baltimore *American*, August 2, 1866, July 31, 1886.
Baltimore *Sun*, November 28–30, December 10, 1905.
Birmingham *News*, April 14–15, 1924.
Boston *Columbia Centinel*, July 4, 1827.
Brooklyn *Daily Eagle*, December 18, 1888.
Cambridge (Md.) *Democrat & News*, June 5, 1886.
Charleston *Mercury*, November 7, 1862, October 1, October 11–12, 1864.
Charleston *News and Courier*, August 28, 1876, August 2, 1878, April 28–29, 1879, March 30, 1885, February 2, February 4, 1886, January 13–14, 1892, May 14, 1898.
Charlotte *Western Democrat*, October 18, 1870.
Chattanooga *Daily Times*, October 30–31, November 1, 1889.
Chattanooga *News-Free Press*, June 1, 1956, June 28, 1987.
Chicago *Knights of Labor*, November 2, 1886.
Chicago *Tribune*, May 30, August 17, 1884, October 1, 1894.
Cincinnati *Commercial*, May 24, 1869.
Columbus (Ga.) *Enquirer*, October 13, 1876.
Corinth *Sub-Soiler and Democrat*, 1882–83, March 27, 1885.
Corpus Christi *Weekly Caller*, November 13, 1891.
Dallas *Herald*, February 9, 1867, September 11, 1869, May 28, 1870, July 4, 1874, May 20, 1880, February 23, 1921.
Dallas *Morning News*, May 23, May 29, May 31, June 2–5, 1886, February 23, 1921, October 11, 1925.
Dallas *Texas Baptist and Herald*, November 3, 1892.
Dallas *Weekly Herald*, March 27, November 13, 1884.
Frankfort *Kentucky Yeoman*, October 29, 1881.
Galveston *Daily News*, November 22, 1901.
Greenville (Miss.) *Times*, October 22, 1908.
Hillsboro (N.M.) *Sierra County Advocate*, 1892–98.

Houston *Post*, December 22, 1992.
Jackson (Miss.) *Clarion*, October 1, 1894, December 12, 1895.
Jefferson City *Inquirer*, April 3, 1845, May 7, 1859.
Jefferson City *State Tribune*, April 5–7, 1902.
Knoxville *Register*, July 8, 1862.
Knoxville *Whig*, 1860–61.
Little Rock *Arkansas Gazette*, 1850–79, October 9, 1908.
Louisville *Courier-Journal*, March 25, 1869, March 9, 1875, January 15, 1877, October 29, 1881, January 9, July 20, 1886, June 17, 1889, April 10, 1895.
Louisville *Daily Journal*, August 3, 1861.
Lynchburg *News*, March 1, 1918.
Macon (Ga.) *Journal and Messenger*, July 10, 1867.
Memphis *Appeal*, 1858–62, September 1, September 3, September 7, 1869, April 10, 1873, June 15, 1876, March 22, March 24, 1885.
Memphis *Avalanche*, 1860–62, April 1, April 3, 1867, May 3, 1868.
Memphis *Commercial Appeal*, October 2, October 5, October 7, 1900, June 22, 1908, September 10, 1948, May 20, 1979.
Memphis *Evening Scimitar*, October 1, 1900, June 22, 1908.
Mobile *Daily Register*, April 24, 1898, November 8, November 12, 1901.
Monroe (W.Va.) *Border Watchman*, June 11, 1876.
Nashville *Banner*, October 16, 1862, November 24, 1865, December 29–30, 1871, June 22, 1908.
Nashville *Daily American*, December 16–17, 1886.
Nashville *Dispatch*, June 5, 1862, Decemmber 13, 1863.
Nashville *Union and American*, March 3, 1873.
Natchez *Courier*, February 6, 1861.
Natchez *Democrat*, December 20, December 22, December 25, 1888.
New Orleans *Bee*, May 31, 1874, May 26, 1887.
New Orleans *Daily Picayune*, October 22, 1862, May 22, 1869, May 26, 1887, August 10, 1893, February 5, 1896, May 24, 1903, July 10, 1910.
New Orleans *Times*, October 8, 1865, February 22, 1872.
New Orleans *Times-Democrat*, November 14, 1901, December 19, 1903.
New York *Times*, November 2, December 4, 1865, May 25, July 19, 1880, June 16, August 17, October 1, 1894, January 14, 1898.
New York *Tribune*, November 20, 1841, December 19, 1888, February 6, 1901.
Pensacola *Public Record*, October 28, 1939.
Raleigh *News and Observer*, October 5, 1882.
Raleigh *North Carolina Standard*, October 13, 1870.
Richmond *Dispatch*, 1860–65, September 2, 1876, December 23, 1880, December 16, 1882, June 13, 1889.
Richmond *Enquirer*, November 24, 1843.
St. Louis *Globe-Democrat*, January 7, 1908.

St. Louis *Missouri Republican*, July 18, July 25, 1885.
St. Louis *Republican*, October 29, November 2, 1881.
Savannah *Morning News*, May 15, May 17, 1888, December 27, 1896, June 14, June 17, 1908.
Seattle *Times*, June 10, 1908.
Shiner (Tex.) *Gazette*, February 24, March 3, 1921.
Staunton *Spectator*, December 31, 1867.
Staunton *Valley Virginian*, July 4, 1866.
Stevenson (Ala.) *Chronicle*, July 29, 1890.
Tallahassee *Florida Index*, August 29, 1902.
Van Buren *Argus*, May 26, 1880.
Van Buren *Press*, 1861–62.
Vicksburg *Daily Herald*, February 19, March 10, 1867.
Vicksburg *Daily Whig*, May 15, 1862.
Washington (Ark.) *Telegraph*, December 21, 1864.
Washington (D.C.) *Evening Star*, March 30, 1880, July 19–20, 1886.
Winchester *News*, September 14, 1883, January 25, 1884.
Winchester *Times*, January 23, 1884.
Yazoo City *Herald*, January 5, 1900.

DIRECTORIES

Austin City Directory, 1877–78.
Baltimore City Directory, 1893, 1900.
Business Directory of the Principal Southern Cities, 1866, 1867.
Chicago City Directory, 1880–92.
District of Columbia Directory, 1870, 1885.
Galveston City Directory, 1866–67, 1870, 1872, 1874, 1896–97.
Kentucky State Gazetteer and Business Directory, 1859, 1860.
Little Rock, Hot Springs, Pine Bluff City Directory, 1883–84.
Memphis City Directory, 1855–56, 1860, 1877, 1900, 1907.
Missouri State Gazetteer and Business Directory, 1860.
Mobile City Directory, 1880.
Montgomery City Directory, 1859–60.
Nashville City Directory, 1853, 1855–56, 1860–61, 1865, 1867.
New Orleans City Directory, 1846, 1855, 1858, 1867, 1876, 1880, 1884.
New York City Directory, 1842–80.
St. Louis City Directory, 1851–60.
Savannah City Directory, 1892–97.
Seattle City Directory, 1897, 1903, 1907, 1910.
Southern Business Directory and General Commercial Advertiser, 1854.
Southern Business Guide, 1879–80.

Books

Abel, Annie H. *The American Indian as Participant in the Civil War*. Cleveland, 1919.

Acklen, Jeanette, ed. *Tennessee Records: Vol. 2—Bible Records and Marriage Bonds*. Nashville, 1933.

Adams, Charles R., Jr., ed. *A Post of Honor: The Pryor Letters, 1861–63*. Fort Valley, Ga., 1989.

Adamson, Hans C. *Rebellion in Missouri, 1861*. Philadelphia, 1961.

Agee, Helene B. *Facets of Goochland (Virginia) County's History*. Richmond, 1962.

Alcorn County Historical Association. *The History of Alcorn County, Mississippi*. Dallas, 1983.

Allen, Irene. *Saga of Anderson*. New York, 1957.

Allibone, Samuel A. *A Critical Dictionary of English Literature and British and American Authors. . . .* 3 vols. 1891; rpr. Detroit, 1965.

Alvord, Idress. *Head—Descent of Henry Head (1695–1770) in America*. Columbia, Mo., 1948.

Anderson, John Q., ed. *A Texas Surgeon in the C.S.A.* Tuscaloosa, 1957.

———, ed. *Brokenburn: The Journal of Kate Stone, 1861–65*. Baton Rouge, 1955.

———, ed. *Campaigning with Parsons' Texas Cavalry Brigade, CSA*. Hillsboro, 1967.

Appler, A. C. *The Younger Brothers*. New York, 1955.

Arizona State Genealogical Society. *Arizona Death Records*. 2 vols. Tucson, 1976.

Armstrong, Zella. *The History of Hamilton County and Chattanooga, Tennessee*. 2 vols. Chattanooga, 1931.

———, comp. *Notable Southern Families*. 7 vols. Chattanooga, 1918–40.

Arthur, John P. *Western North Carolina: A History*. Raleigh, 1914.

Arthur, Stanley C., ed. *Old Families of Louisiana*. New Orleans, 1931.

Ashe, Samuel A. *Biographical History of North Carolina from Colonial Times to the Present*. 8 vols. Greensboro, N.C., 1905.

Avery, Isaac W. *The History of the State of Georgia from 1850 to 1881*. New York, 1881.

Avrich, Paul. *The Haymarket Tragedy*. Princeton, 1984.

Bailey, Anne J. *Between the Enemy and Texas: Parsons' Texas Cavalry in the Civil War*. Fort Worth, 1989.

Bailey, N. Louise, ed. *Biographical Directory of the South Carolina Senate, 1776–1985*. Columbia, S.C., 1986.

Baker, Gary R. *Cadets in Gray*. Columbia, S.C., 1989.

Ballard, Margaret. *A University Is Born*. Union, W.Va., 1935.

Barbour, Lucius. *Families of Early Hartford, Connecticut*. Baltimore, 1977.

Barfield, Louise. *History of Harris County, Georgia, 1827–1961*. Columbus, Ga., 1961.

Barnes, Robert, and Catherine Barnes. *Genealogies of Pennsylvania Families*. 3 vols. Baltimore, 1982.

Barnhill, Floyd R. *The Fighting Fifth*. Jonesboro, Ark., 1990.

Barnwell, Stephen B. *The Story of an American Family*. Milwaukee, 1969.

Barr, Alwyn. *Polignac's Texas Brigade*. Houston, 1964.

———. *Reconstruction to Reform: Texas Politics, 1876–1906*, Austin, 1971.

Barron, Samuel B. *The Lone Star Defenders*. 1908; rpr. Washington, D.C., 1983.

Bartlett, Napier. *Military Record of Louisiana*. New Orleans, 1875.

Bate, W. N. *General Sidney Sherman*. Waco, 1974.

Battey, F. A. & Company. *Biographical Souvenir of the State of Texas*. Chicago, 1889.

Bay, William Van Ness. *Reminiscences of the Bench and Bar of Missouri*. St. Louis, 1878.

Baylor, George W. *John Robert Baylor*. Tucson, 1966.

Beach, Ursula S. *Along the Wariota; or, A History of Montgomery County, Tennessee*. Clarksville, Tenn., 1964.

Bearss, Edwin C. *Forrest at Brice's Cross Roads and in North Mississippi in 1864*. Dayton, 1979.

———. *Fort Smith, Little Gibraltar on the Arkansas*. Norman, Okla., 1969.

Bell, Landon C. *Cumberland Parish, Lunenberg County, Virginia, 1746–1816*. Richmond, 1930.

Benner, Judith A. *Sul Ross: Soldier, Statesman, Educator*. College Station, Tex., 1983.

Bentley, Elizabeth, comp. *Virginia Marriage Records*. Baltimore, 1982.

Bergeron, Arthur W. *Confederate Mobile*. Jackson, Miss., 1991.

———. *Guide to Louisiana Confederate Military Units, 1861–1865*. Baton Rouge, 1989.

Berkeley, Edmund, and Dorothy Berkeley. *John Beckley*. Philadelphia, 1973.

Berry, Lloyd E. *Hudson Berry and His Descendants*. Pelzer, S.C., 1956.

Bettersworth, John K. *Confederate Mississippi*. Baton Rouge, 1943.

Bevier, R. S. *History of the First and Second Missouri Confederate Brigades, 1861–1865*. St. Louis, 1879.

Biographical Encyclopedia of the Commonwealth of Kentucky. Chicago, 1896.

Blackford, Charles M. *Letters from Lee's Army*. New York, 1947.

Blackwell, Robert V., comp. *Roster and Record of Events for the 9th Battalion Cavalry, Georgia State Guards, 3 August 1863 to 3 February 1864*. N.p., n.d.

Blakey, Arch F. *Parade of Memories: A History of Clay County, Florida*. Jacksonville, 1976.

Blanks, James R. *Burrows Family History*. Decorah, Iowa, 1986.

Blessington, Joseph P. *Campaigns of Walker's Texas Division*. New York, 1875.

Boatner, Mark M. III. *The Civil War Dictionary*. New York, 1988.

Boddie, John B., comp. *Historical Southern Families*. 23 vols. Baltimore, 1967–1980.

———. *Virginia Historical Genealogies*. Redwood City, Calif., 1954.

Boddie, John T. *Boddie and Allied Families*. N.p., 1918.

Boggs, William R. *Military Reminiscences of General Wm. R. Boggs*. Durham, 1913.

Bond, Mildred M., and George Bond. *Alexander Carswell and Isabella Brown: Their Ancestors and Descendants*. Chipley, Fla., 1977.

Booth, Andrew B., ed. *Records of Louisiana Confederate Soldiers and Louisiana Confederate Commands*. 3 vols. 1920; rpr. Spartanburg, 1984.

Bradley, Stephen E., ed. *North Carolina Militia Officers Roster: As Contained in the Adjutant-General's Officers Roster*. Wilmington, N.C., 1992.

Bragg, William H. *Joe Brown's Army: The Georgia State Line, 1862–1865*. Macon, 1987.

Brent, Joseph L. *Memoirs of the War Between the States*. New Orleans, 1940.

Brewer, Willis. *Alabama: Her History, Resources, War Record and Public Men*. Montgomery, 1872.

Brice, Marshall M. *Conquest of a Valley*. Charlottesville, 1965.

Britton, Wiley. *The Civil War on the Border*. 2 vols. New York, 1891.

Brooks, Aubray L., and Hugh T. Lefler. *The Papers of Walter Clark*. 2 vols. Chapel Hill, 1950.

Brooks, U. R. *Butler and His Cavalry in the War of Secession, 1861–1865*. Columbia, S.C., 1909.

Brown, John H. *History of Texas*. St. Louis, 1892.

Brown, John Howard. *Lamb's Biographical Dictionary of the United States*. 7 vols. Boston, 1900.

Brown, Russell K. *Fallen In Battle: American General Officer Combat Fatalities from 1775*. Westport, Conn., 1988.

Browning, Charles H. *Americans of Royal Descent*. Philadelphia, 1891.

Brownlow, W. G. *Sketches of the Rise, Progress, and Decline of Secession*. 1862; rpr. New York, 1968.

Bruce, Phillip A. *History of Virginia*. Chicago, 1924.

Buenger, Walter L. *Secession and the Union in Texas*. Austin, 1984.

Buresh, Lumir F. *October 25th and the Battle of Mine Creek*. Kansas City, 1977.

Burton, E. Milby. *The Siege of Charleston, 1861–1865*. Columbia, S.C., 1970.

Cabaniss, Jim R. *Civil War Journal and Letters of Washington Ives, 4th Fla., C.S.A.* Tallahassee, 1987.

Calhoun, W. L. *History of the 42nd Regiment, Georgia Volunteers . . . .* Atlanta, 1900.

Candler, Allen, ed. *The Confederate Records of the State of Georgia*. 4 vols. Atlanta, 1909–11.

———, ed. *Cyclopedia of Georgia*. 3 vols. Atlanta, 1906.

Capers, Ellison IV. *Capers Connections 1684–1984*. Spartanburg, 1992.

Carroll, James M. *A History of Texas Baptists*. Dallas, 1923.

Cartmell, T. K. *Shenandoah Valley Pioneers and Their Descendants*. Winchester, Va., 1909.

Casey, Powel A. *Encyclopedia of Forts, Named Camps, and Other Military Installations in Louisiana, 1700–1981*. Baton Rouge, 1983.

———, ed. *The Story of Camp Moore*. Baton Rouge, 1985.

Casso, Evans J. *Louisiana Legacy: A History of the State National Guard*. Gretna, La., 1976.

Castel, Albert. *General Sterling Price and the Civil War in the West*. Baton Rouge, 1968.

Cater, William D., ed., *As It Was*. San Antonio, 1981.

Cauthen, Charles E. *South Carolina Goes to War, 1860–1865*. The James Sprunt Studies in History and Political Science, XXXII. Chapel Hill, 1950.

———, ed. *Journals of the South Carolina Executive Councils of 1861 and 1862*. Columbia, S.C., 1956.

Central Georgia Genealogical Society, Inc. *First Hundred and Ten Years of Houston County, Georgia*. Chelsea, Mich., 1983.

Century Review, 1805–1905, Maury County, Tennessee. 1905; rpr. Easley, S.C., 1980.

Chance, Joseph E. *The 2nd Texas Infantry*. Austin, 1984.

Chapman, John A. *History of Edgefield County, from the Earliest Settlements to 1897*. Newberry, S.C., 1897.

Chapman, John A., and John B. O'Neall. *The Annals of Newberry*. 1892; rpr. Baltimore, 1974.

Chapman, Rev. F. W. *The Pratt Family*. Hartford, 1864.

Chappelear, Nancy, and John K. Gott. *Early Fauquier County, Virginia Marriage Bonds, 1759–1854*. Washington, D.C., 1965.

Chase, John C., and George W. Chamberlain, comps. *Seven Generations of the Descendants of Aquila and Thomas Chase*. Derry, N.H., 1928.

Cisco, Walter B. *States Rights Gist*. Shippensburg, Pa., 1991.

Civil War Centennial Commission. *Tennesseans in the Civil War*. 2 vols. Nashville, 1964.

Claggett, Brice M. *A Sketch of the Floyd Family of the Eastern Shore of Virginia*. Washington, D.C., 1964.

Clark, Walter, ed. *Histories of the Several Regiments and Battalions from North Carolina in the Great War, 1861–1865*. 5 vols. Raleigh, 1901.

Clayton, William W. *History of Davidson County, Tennessee*. Philadelphia, 1880.

Cochran, Fan Alexander. *History of Old Tishomingo County, Mississippi Territory*. Oklahoma City, 1969.

Cockrell, Monroe F. *The Lost Account of the Battle of Corinth and Court-Martial of Gen. Van Dorn*. Jackson, Tenn., 1935.

Coleman, Kenneth, and Charles S. Gurr, eds. *Dictionary of Georgia Biography*. 2 vols. Athens, 1983.

Colonial Dames of America, National Society of the. *Alabama Portraits Prior to 1870*. Mobile, 1969.

Comstock, Jim, ed. *The West Virginia Heritage Encyclopedia*. Richwood, W.Va., 1976.

Connelley, William E. *Doniphan's Expedition and the Conquest of New Mexico and California*, 1907; rpr. Kansas City, 1967.

Conrad, Glenn R., ed. *A Dictionary of Louisiana Biography*. 2 vols. New Orleans, 1988.

Conrad, Howard L., ed. *Encyclopedia of the History of Missouri*. 6 vols. New York, 1901.

Corley, Florence F. *Confederate City: Augusta, Georgia, 1860–1865*. Columbia, S.C., 1960.

Craighead, Erwin. *Mobile: Fact and Tradition*. Mobile, 1930.

Crenshaw, Pauline S. *From Then Until Now*. Montgomery, 1932.

Crist, Lynda, *et al.*, eds. *The Papers of Jefferson Davis*. 7 vols. Baton Rouge, 1983–91.

Crocket, George C. *Two Centuries in East Texas*. Dallas, 1932.

Croom, Wendell O. *The War History of Company "C," Sixth Georgia Regiment*. Fort Valley, Ga., 1879.

Crute, Joseph H. *Confederate Staff Officers: 1861–1865*. Powhatan, Va., 1982.

Cullum, George W. *Biographical Register of the Officers and Graduates of the U.S. Military Academy*. 8 vols. Boston, 1891–1940.

Cunningham, Horace H. *Doctors in Gray*. Baton Rouge, 1958.

Cyclopedia of American Biography. 7 vols. New York, 1891.

Cyclopedia of the Eminent and Representative Men of the Carolinas of the Nineteenth Century. 2 vols. Madison, Wis., 1892.

Dahlgren, M. V. *Memoir of Admiral John A. Dahlgren*. Boston, 1882.

Daily News, The. *History of Buchanan County and St. Joseph*. St. Joseph, Mo., 1899.

Daniel, H. H. *History of Clarke County, Mississippi. Wills, 1834–1900, Land Grants & Cemetery Records, 1834–1915*. Bay Springs, Miss., 1978.

Daniel, Larry J. *Cannoneers in Gray: The Field Artillery of the Army of Tennessee, 1861–1865*. University, Ala., 1984.

Daniell, L. E. *Personnel, Texas State Government, with Sketches of Representative Men of Texas*. San Antonio, 1892.

Daughters of the American Revolution. *Historical Collections of the Joseph Habersham Chapter, Daughters of the American Revolution*. Dalton, Ga., 1902.

Daughters of the American Revolution, Gov. Treutlen Chapter. *History of Peach County, Georgia*. Atlanta, 1972.

Daughters of the American Revolution, Thronateeska Chapter. *History and Reminiscences of Daugherty County, Georgia*. 1924; rpr. Spartanburg, 1978.

Daughters of the Republic of Texas. *Founders and Patriots of the Republic of Texas: Lineages of the Members of the Daughters of the Republic of Texas*. Austin, 1963.

Davidson, Chalmers G. *The Last Foray: The South Carolina Planters of 1860: A Sociological Study*. Columbia, S.C., 1971.

Davis, Burke. *The Long Surrender*. New York, 1985.

———. *Sherman's March*. New York, 1980.

Davis, Jefferson. *The Rise and Fall of the Confederate Government*. 2 vols. New York, 1881.

Davis, Jess. *A History of Alachua County, 1824–1969*. Gainesville, Fla., 1969.

Davis, Reuben. *Recollections of Mississippi and Mississippians*. Boston, 1889.

Davis, Robert S. *A Researcher's Library of Georgia History, Genealogy, and Records Sources*. 2 vols. Easley, S.C., 1987–91.

Davis, William C., ed. *The Confederate General*. 6 vols. Harrisburg, Pa., 1991–92.

Davis, Winfield. *History of Political Conventions in California, 1849–1892*. Sacramento, 1893.

Day, James M., comp. *The Texas Almanac, 1857–1873*. Waco, 1967.

De Cordova, Jacob. *Texas: Her Resources and Her Public Men*. 1858; rpr. Waco, 1969.

De Shield, James T. *They Sat in High Places*. San Antonio, 1940.

Debray, Xavier B. *A Sketch of the History of Debrays (26th) Regiment of Texas Cavalry*. Austin, 1884.

Deen, Braswell D., and William Henwood. *Georgia's Appellate Judiciary: Profiles and History*. Norcross, Ga., 1987.

Delery, Simone de la Souchere. *Napoleon's Soldiers in America*. Gretna, La., 1972.

Dethloff, Henry C. *A Centennial History of Texas A&M University, 1876–1976*. College Station, Tex., 1975.

Dibble, Ernest F. *Antebellum Pensacola and the Military Presence*. Pensacola, 1974.

Dickison, Mary E. *Dickison and His Men*. 1890; rpr. Gainesville, Fla., 1962.

Dictionary of American Biography. 20 vols. and supplement. New York, 1928–44.

Dodson, W. C. *Campaigns of Wheeler and His Cavalry, 1862–1865*. Atlanta, 1899.

Dorris, Jonathan T. *Pardon and Amnesty under Lincoln and Johnson*. Chapel Hill, 1953.

Dougan, Michael B. *Confederate Arkansas*. University, Tex., 1976.

Douglas, Henry Kyd. *The Douglas Diary: Student Days at Franklin and Marshall College, 1856–1858*. Edited by Frederick S. Klein and John H. Carrill. Lancaster, Pa., 1973.

————. *I Rode with Stonewall*. Chapel Hill, 1940.

Douglass, Robert S. *History of Southeast Missouri*. Chicago, 1912.

Dowdey, Clifford. *Lee's Last Campaign*. New York, 1960.

Driver, Robert J. *Fifty Second Virginia Infantry*. Lynchburg, Va., 1986.

Du Bellet, Louise P. *Some Prominent Virginia Families*. 2 vols. 1907; rpr. Baltimore, 1976.

Dufour, Charles. *The Night the War Was Lost*. Garden City, N.Y., 1960.

Duke, Basil W. *A History of Morgan's Cavalry*. 1906; rpr. Bloomington, 1960.

————. *Reminiscences of General Basil W. Duke, C.S.A.* New York, 1911.

Durden, Marion L. *A History of Saint George Parish, Colony of Georgia, Jefferson County, State of Georgia*. Swainsboro, Ga., 1983.

Durkin, Joseph T. *Stephen R. Mallory, Confederate Navy Chief*. Chapel Hill, 1954.

Dyer, John P. *"Fightin' Joe" Wheeler*. Baton Rouge, 1941.

Early, Ruth. *Campbell Chronicles and Family Sketches*. Lynchburg, Va., 1927.

Easterby, J. H. *The History of the College of Charleston*. Charleston, S.C., 1935.

Edgar, Walter, ed. *Biographical Directory of the South Carolina House of Representatives*. 4 vols. Columbia, S.C., 1974.

Edmonds, David C. *Yankee Autumn in Acadiana*. Lafayette, La., 1979.

Edmunds, John B., Jr. *Francis W. Pickens and Politics of Destruction*. Chapel Hill, 1986.

Edwards, Jennie, comp. *John N. Edwards*. Kansas City, 1889.

Edwards, John N. *Noted Guerillas*. St. Louis, 1877.

————. *Shelby and His Men*. Cincinnati, 1867.

Egle, William H. *Pennsylvania Genealogies*. 1896; rpr. Baltimore, 1969.

Eliot, Ellsworth. *West Point in the Confederacy*. New York, 1941.

————. *Yale in the Civil War*. New Haven, 1932.

Elliott, Claude. *Old Leathercoat: The Life History of a Texas Patriot*. San Antonio, 1938.

Ellis County Historical Workshop. *History of Ellis County, Texas*. Waco, 1972.

Ellis, William, ed. *Norwich University, 1819–1911*. 3 vols. Montpelier, 1911.

Elmwood Cemetery Association of Memphis. *Charter, Rules, Regulations, and By-laws of the Elmwood Cemetery Association of Memphis*. Memphis, 1874.

Eminent and Representative Men of Virginia and the District of Columbia of the Nineteenth Century. Madison, Wis., 1893.

Evans, Clement A., ed. *Confederate Military History: A Library of Confederate States History*. 1899; 17 volume extended edition; rpr. Wilmington, N.C., 1987.

Evans, Lawton B. *A History of Georgia: For Use in Schools*. New York, 1888.

Farmer, Garland R. *The Realm of Rusk County*. Henderson, Tex., 1951.

Ferguson, John L. *Arkansas and the Civil War*. Little Rock, 1965.

Filson Club, The. *Early Kentucky Settlers: The Records of Jefferson County, Kentucky*. Baltimore, 1988.

Folmar, John K., ed. *From That Terrible Field: Civil War Letters of James M. Williams, Twenty-First Alabama Infantry Volunteers*. University, Ala., 1981.

Foote, Henry S. *The Bench and Bar of the South and Southwest*. St. Louis, 1876.

Fox, William F. *Regimental Losses in the . . . Civil War*. Albany, 1898.

Freeman, Douglas S. *Lee's Lieutenants: A Study in Command*. 3 vols. New York, 1942–44.

————. *Robert E. Lee: A Biography*. 4 vols. New York, 1936.

Fremantle, Arthur J. L. *Three Months in the Southern States: April–June, 1863*. New York, 1864.

Frye, Dennis E. *2nd Virginia Infantry*. Lynchburg, Va., 1984.

Furber, George C. *The Twelve Months Volunteer; or, Journal of a Private in the Tennessee Regiment of Cavalry*. Cincinnati, 1849.

Gallagher, Gary W. *Fighting for the Confederacy*. Chapel Hill, 1989.

Gallaway, B. D. *The Ragged Rebel*. Austin, 1988.

Gandolfo, Henri. *Metairie Cemetery: An Historical Memoir*. New Orleans, 1981.

Gandrud, Pauline M. J. *Alabama Records*. Easley, S.C., 1981.

Garber, Virginia A. *The Armistead Family, 1635–1910*. Richmond, 1910.

Gardner, Charles K. *A Dictionary of All Officers . . . in the Army of the United States*. New York, 1853.

Garrett, Jill K., ed. *Confederate Soldiers and Patriots of Maury County, Tennessee*. Columbia, Tenn., 1970.

Garrett, William. *Reminiscences of Public Men in Alabama*. Atlanta, 1872.

Gehrig, Pearl S., and T. Berry Smith. *History of Chariton and Howard Counties*. Topeka, 1923.

Geiser, Samuel W. *Men of Science in Texas, 1820–1880*. Dallas, 1958–59.

George, James Z. *The Political History of Slavery in the United States*. New York, 1915.

Georgia Supreme Court. *Georgia Reports*. Vols. II, LXV, LXXXIII.

Gerber, Rafal. *Studenci Uniwersytetu Warzawskiego 1808–1831: Słownik Biograficzny*. Wroclaw, Poland, 1977.

Gongaware, George J. *The History of the German Friendly Society of Charleston, South Carolina, 1766–1916*. Richmond, 1935.

Goodspeed Publishing Company. *Biographical and Historical Memoirs of Eastern Arkansas*. Chicago, 1890.

———. *Biographical and Historical Memoirs of Louisiana*. 2 vols. Chicago, 1892.

———. *Biographical and Historical Memoirs of Mississippi*. 2 vols. Chicago, 1891.

———. *Biographical and Historical Memoirs of Pulaski, Jefferson, Lonoke, Faulkner, Grant, Saline, Perry, Garland, and Hot Spring Counties, Arkansas*. Chicago, 1889.

———. *Biographical and Historical Memoirs of Southern Arkansas*. Chicago, 1890.

———. *History of Laclede, Camden, Dallas, Webster, Wright, Texas, Pulaski, Phelps and Dent Counties, Missouri*. Chicago, 1889.

———. *History of Newton, Lawrence, Barry and McDonald Counties*. Chicago, 1888.

———. *History of Tennessee—History of Carroll, Henry and Benton Counties*. Nashville, 1887.

———. *History of Tennessee—History of Gibson, Obion, Dyer, Weakley and Lake Counties*. Nashville, 1887.

———. *Memorial and Genealogical Record of Southwest Texas*. 1894; rpr. Easley, S.C., 1978.

Govan, Gilbert E., and James W. Livingood, eds. *The Haskell Memoirs: The Personal Narrative of a Confederate Officer*. New York, 1960.

Gower, Herschel, and Jack Allen, eds. *Pen and Sword: The Life and Journals of Randall W. McGavock*. Nashville, 1959.

Graf, Leroy P., Paul Bergeron, and Ralph Haskins, eds. *The Papers of Andrew Johnson*. 10 vols. Knoxville, 1967–92.

Graham, Thomas. *The Awakening of St. Augustine*. St. Augustine, Fla., 1978.

Grant, Daniel L. *Alumni History of the University of North Carolina, 1795–1924*. Durham, 1924.

Green, John W. *Lives of the Judges of the Supreme Court of Tennessee 1796–1947*. Knoxville, 1947.

Greenleaf, James E., comp. *Genealogy of the Greenleaf Family*. Boston, 1896.

Gregorie, Anne K. *History of Sumter County*. Sumter, S.C., 1954.

Griffith, Romulus R. *Genealogy of the Griffith Family*. Baltimore, 1892.

Grigsby, William H. *Genealogy of the Grigsby Family in Part, Including a Brief Sketch of the Porter Family*. N.p., 1878.

Groves, Joseph A. *The Alstons and Allstons of North and South Carolina*. Atlanta, 1901.

Grzelonski, Bogdan. *Poles in the United States of America, 1776–1865*. Warsaw, Poland, 1976.

Gwin, Jesse B. *History of the Gwin Family*. Fairfax, Va., 1961.

Hagood, Johnson. *Memoirs of the War of Secession*. Columbia, S.C., 1910.

Haiman, Miecislaus. *Polish Past in America, 1608–1865*. Chicago, 1939.

Hall, Martin H. *The Confederate Army of New Mexico*. Austin, 1978.

Hallum, John. *Biographical and Pictorial History of Arkansas*. Albany, 1887.

———. *The Diary of an Old Lawyer*. Nashville, 1895.

Halstead, Murat. *Caucuses of 1860: A History of the National Political Conventions*. Columbus, Ohio, 1860.

Hamilton, J. G. de R., Max Williams, and Mary R. Peacock, eds. *The Papers of William Alexander Graham*. 8 vols. Raleigh, 1957–93.

Hardy, Stella P. *Colonial Families of the Southern States of America*. 1958; rpr. Baltimore, 1974.

Harris, Joel C. *Memoirs of Georgia*. Atlanta, 1895.

Hartzler, Daniel D. *Marylanders in the Confederacy*. Silver Spring, Md., 1986.

Harwell, Richard B., ed. *The Confederate Reader*. New York, 1957.

Hayden, Horace E. *Virginia Genealogies*. 1891; rpr. Baltimore, 1966.

Hayes, Charles W. *Galveston*. 1879; rpr. Austin, 1974.

Heartsill, William W. *Fourteen Hundred and 91 days in the Confederate Army* . . . . Marshall, Tex., 1876.

Hebert, Donald J. *South Louisiana Records*. 12 vols. Cecilia, La., 1978–85.

Heitman, Francis B. *Historical Register of the United States Army, from Its Organization, September 29, 1789, to September 29, 1889*. 2 vols. Washington, D.C., 1890.

Hempstead, Fay. *History of Arkansas*. St. Louis, 1890.

Henderson, Harry M. *Texas in the Confederacy*. San Antonio, 1955.

Henderson, Lillian. *Roster of the Confederate Soldiers of Georgia, 1861–1865*. 6 vols. 1959–64; rpr. Spartanburg, 1982.

Herndon, Dallas T. *Annals of Arkansas*. Hopkinsville, Ky., 1947.

Hewitt, Lawrence L. *Port Hudson: Confederate Bastion on the Mississippi*. Baton Rouge, 1987.

Hilliard, Henry W. *Politics and Pen Pictures at Home and Abroad*. New York, 1892.

History of Clay and Platt Counties, Missouri. St. Louis, 1885.

The History of Clinton County, Missouri. St. Joseph, Mo., 1881.

History of Howard and Cooper Counties, Missouri. St. Louis, 1883.

Hollowak, Thomas L., comp. *Marriages and Deaths in the "Baltimore Sun," 1837–1850*. Baltimore, 1978.

Horn, Robert C. *Tap Roots: Epitaphs in East-Central Alabama Cemeteries*. 4 vols. Dadeville, Ala., 1982–85.

Hotchkiss, Jedediah. *Make Me a Map of the Valley.* Dallas, 1973.

Howard, Goldena. *Ralls County, Missouri.* New London, Mo., 1980.

Howard, McHenry. *Recollections of a Maryland Confederate Soldier, 1861–1866.* 1914; rpr. Dayton, 1975.

Howell, H. Grady. *To Live and Die in Dixie: A History of the Third Regiment Mississippi Volunteer Infantry, C.S.A.* Jackson, Miss., 1991.

Hughes, Nathanial C., Jr., and Buckner Hughes. *Quiet Places: The Burial Sites of Civil War Generals in Tennessee.* Knoxville, 1992.

Hughes, Nathaniel C., Jr., and Roy P. Stonesifer. *The Life and Wars of Gideon J. Pillow.* Chapel Hill, 1993.

Hughes, Thomas P., and Jewel B. Standefer. *Alcorn County, Mississippi Cemetery Records.* Memphis, 1971.

Hughes, W. J. *Rebellious Ranger: Rip Ford and the Old Southwest.* Norman, Okla., 1964.

Hughes, William W. *Archibald Yell.* Fayetteville, Ark., 1988.

Hunt, Roger, and Jack Brown. *Brevet Brigadier Generals in Blue.* Gaithersburg, Md., 1990.

Hunter, J. Marvin. *The Trail Drivers of Texas.* Nashville, 1925.

Index of Probate Cases of Texas: Hays County . . . . San Antonio, 1942.

Ingenthron, Elmo. *Borderland Rebellion: A History of the Civil War on the Missouri-Arkansas Border.* Branson, Mo., 1980.

Ingram, Henry E., comp. *Civil War Letters of George W. and Martha F. Ingram, 1861–1865.* Waco, 1973.

Inscoe, John C. *Mountain Masters, Slavery, and the Sectional Crisis in Western North Carolina.* Knoxville, 1989.

Isbell, Sarah L. W. *General John Floyd of the War of 1812 . . . .* N.p., 1966.

Jackson, Ronald V., ed. *Arkansas Tax Lists, 1830 to 1839.* Bountiful, Utah, 1980.

Jackson, Walter M. *The Story of Selma.* Birmingham, 1954.

Jennings, Thelma. *The Nashville Convention, Southern Movement for Unity, 1848–1851.* Memphis, 1980.

Johnson, John. *The Defense of Charleston Harbor.* Charleston, S.C., 1890.

Johnson, Brig. Gen. Richard W. *A Soldiers Reminiscences in Peace and War.* Philadelphia, 1886.

Johnson, Robert U., and Clarence C. Buel, eds. *Battles and Leaders of the Civil War . . . .* 4 vols. 1887–88; rpr. New York, 1956.

Johnson, Rossiter. *Campfire and Battlefield: A Pictorial Narrative of the Civil War.* 1894; rpr. New York, 1958.

Johnson, Sidney S. *Texans Who Wore the Gray.* Tyler, Tex., 1907.

Johnston, David E. *A History of Middle New River Settlements.* Huntington, W. Va., 1906.

Johnston, Frontis, ed. *The Papers of Zebulon B. Vance.* Raleigh, 1963.

Jones, Charles E. *Georgia in the War, 1861–1865.* Atlanta, 1909.

Jones, Frank S. *The History of Decatur County, Georgia.* N.p., 1971.

Jones, L. H. *Captain Roger Jones . . . .* Albany, 1891.

Jones, Terry L. *Lee's Tigers: The Louisiana Infantry in the Army of Northern Virginia.* Baton Rouge, 1987.

Jordan, David M. *Winfield Scott Hancock: A Soldier's Life.* Bloomington, 1989.

Jordan, Thomas, and J. P. Pryor. *The Campaigns of Lieut.-Gen. N. B. Forrest, and of Forrest's Cavalry.* New Orleans, 1868.

Jordan, Weymouth T., and Louis Manarin, comps. *North Carolina Troops.* 12 vols. Raleigh, 1966–90.

Journal of the Congress of the Confederate States of America, 1861–1865. 7 vols. Washington D.C., 1904–1905.

Journal of the Proceedings of the Convention of the People of Florida. Tallahassee, 1861.

Journal of the State Convention . . . . Jackson, Miss., 1861.

Julich, Louise M. *A Roster of Revolutionary War Soldiers and Patriots in Alabama.* Montgomery, 1979.

Kane, Harnett T. *Natchez on the Mississippi.* New York, 1947.

Keating, John M. *History of the City of Memphis and Shelby County, Tennessee.* Syracuse, 1888.

Keller, Helen. *The Story of My Life.* New York, 1904.

Kemp, Louis W. *The Signers of the Texas Declaration of Independence.* Houston, 1944.

Kennamer, John R. *History of Jackson County.* Winchester, Tenn., 1935.

Kentucky Adjutant General's Office. *Report of the Adj. Gen. of the State of Kentucky: Confederate Kentucky Volunteers, War, 1861–1865.* 2 vols. Frankfort, 1915–18.

Kerby, Robert L. *Kirby Smith's Confederacy: The Trans-Mississippi South, 1863–1865.* New York, 1972.

Kerr, Homer L., ed. *Fighting with Ross' Texas Cavalry Brigade, CSA: The Diary of George L. Griscom, Adjutant, 9th Texas Cavalry Regiment.* Hillsboro, 1976.

King, Clinton, ed. *Marriages of Mobile County, Alabama, 1813–55.* Baltimore, 1985.

Knight, Lucian L. *Georgia's Landmarks, Memorials and Legends.* Augusta, 1914.

Krick, Robert K. *Lee's Colonels.* Dayton, 1991.

———. *Stonewall Jackson at Cedar Mountain.* Chapel Hill, 1990.

La Bree, Benjamin, ed. *The Confederate Soldier in the Civil War.* 1895; rpr. Paterson, N.J., 1959.

Lamar, Howard R., ed. *The Readers' Encyclopedia of the American West.* New York, 1977.

Lasswell, Mary, ed. *Rags and Hope: The Recollections of Val C. Giles: Four Years with Hood's Brigade, Fourth Texas Infantry, 1861–1865.* New York, 1961.

Lawson, Lewis A. *Wheeler's Last Raid.* Greenwood, Fla., 1986.

Lea, Tom. *The King Ranch.* Boston, 1957.

Leiding, Harriet K. *Charleston: Historic and Romantic.* Philadelphia, 1936.

Leon County Historical Book Survey, ed. *History of Leon County, Texas.* Dallas, 1986.

Lerski, Jerzy J. *A Polish Chapter in Jacksonian America: The United States and the Polish Exiles of 1831*. Madison, Wis., 1958.

Levin, H., ed. *The Lawyers and Lawmakers of Kentucky*. Chicago, 1897.

Lindsley, John B. *The Military Annals of Tennessee*. Nashville, 1886.

Lonn, Ella. *Foreigners in the Confederacy*. Chapel Hill, 1940.

Lossing, Benson J. *Mathew Brady's Illustrated History of the Civil War*. 1912; rpr. New York, 1972.

Louisiana Supreme Court. *Louisiana Reports*. Vol. III.

Lowry, Robert, and W. H. McCardle. *A History of Mississippi*. Jackson, Miss., 1891.

Lubbock, Francis R. *Six Decades in Texas*. Austin, 1900.

Lucas, Silas E., ed. *Obituaries from Early Tennessee Newspapers, 1794–1851*. Easley, S.C., 1978.

Lynch, James D. *The Bench and Bar of Texas*. St. Louis, 1885.

MacDowell, Dorothy K. *Descendants of William Capers and Richard Capers and Related Families*. Columbia, S.C., 1973.

MacKenzie, George M. *Colonial Families of the United States of America*. 7 vols. 1912; rpr. Baltimore, 1966.

Maclay, Edgar S. *The Maclays of Lurgan*. Brooklyn, 1889.

Maddox, Jack P. *The Virginia Conservatives, 1867–1879*. Chapel Hill, 1970.

Maddox, Joseph T., and Mary Carter. *40,000 Early Georgia Marriage Records*. Albany, Ga., 1976.

Manning, Francis M., and W. H. Booker. *Martin County History*. Williamston, N.C., 1971.

Marlin, John H., comp. *Columbus, Geo., from Its Selection as a "Trading Town" in 1827 to Its Partial Destruction by Wilson's Raid in 1865*. Columbus, Ga., 1874.

Marszalek, John F., ed. *The Diary of Miss Emma Holmes, 1861–1866*. Baton Rouge, 1979.

Marten, James. *Texas Divided: Loyalty and Dissent in the Lone Star State, 1856–1874*. Lexington, Ky., 1990.

Massey, John. *Reminiscences*. Nashville, 1916.

Mathes, J. Harvey. *The Old Guard in Gray*. Memphis, 1897.

Maury, Dabney. *Recollections of a Virginian*. New York, 1894.

May, John A., and Joan R. Faunt. *South Carolina Secedes*. Columbia, S.C., 1960.

Mayes, Edward. *Lucius Q. C. Lamar: His Life, Times, and Speeches*. Nashville, 1896.

McBride, Robert M. *Biographical Directory of the Tennessee General Assembly*. 2 vols. Nashville, 1975.

McCain, William D. *The Story of Jackson: A History of the Capital of Mississippi, 1821–1954*. Jackson, Miss., 1953.

McCormick, Henrietta H., comp. *Genealogies and Reminiscences*. Chicago, 1897.

McDonald, Annette S. *A Source Book on the Early History of Cuthbert and Randolph County, Georgia*. Compiled by William B. Williford. Atlanta, 1982.

McDougal, Henry C. *Recollections, 1844–1909*. Kansas City, 1910.

McElroy, Rev. John M. *The Scotch-Irish McElroys in America*. Albany, 1901.

McGhan, Judith, comp. *Virginia Vital Records*. Baltimore, 1982.

McIlwaine, Shields. *Memphis Down in Dixie*. New York, 1948.

McLean, Malcolm D. *Papers Concerning Robertson's Colony in Texas*. 18 vols. Arlington, Tex., 1980–93.

McMurray, W. J. *History of the Twentieth Tennessee Regiment Volunteer Infantry, C.S.A.* Nashville, 1904.

Meier, Matt S., and Feliciano Rivera. *Dictionary of Mexican American History*. Westport, Conn., 1981.

A Memorial and Biographical History of Ellis County, Texas. 1892; rpr. Fort Worth, 1972.

A Memorial and Biographical History of McLennan, Falls, Bell and Coryell Counties, Texas. Chicago, 1893.

Memorial Record of Alabama. 2 vols. Madison, Wis., 1893.

Mering, John V. *The Whig Party in Missouri*. Columbia, Mo., 1967.

Meriwether, Colyer. *Raphael Semmes*. Philadelphia, 1913.

Meynard, Virginia G. *The Venturers: The Hampton, Harrison and Earle Families of Virginia, South Carolina, and Texas*. Easley, S.C., 1981.

Mickle, William E. *Well Known Confederate Veterans and Their War Records*. New Orleans, 1907.

Miller, Charles A., comp. *The Official and Political Manual of the State of Tennessee*. 1890; rpr. Spartanburg, 1974.

Miller, Francis T., ed. *Photographic History of the Civil War*. 10 vols. New York, 1911.

Miller, Thomas L. *Bounty and Donation Land Grants of Texas, 1835–1888*. Austin, 1967.

Mims, Wilbur F. *War History of the Prattville Dragoons*. N.p., n.d.

Mitchell, Thorton W. *North Carolina Wills: A Testator Index, 1665–1900*. Raleigh, 1987.

Mocha, Frank, ed. *Poles in America*. Stevens Point, Wis., 1978.

Monaghan, Jay. *Civil War on the Western Border*. Boston, 1955.

————. *Swamp Fox of the Confederacy: The Life and Military Services of M. Jeff Thompson*. Tuscaloosa, 1956.

Moore, Robert A. *A Life for the Confederacy*. Edited by James W. Silver. Jackson, Tenn., 1959.

Moneyhon, Carl H. *Republicanism in Reconstruction Texas*. Austin, 1980.

Morton, John W. *The Artillery of . . . Forrest's Cavalry*. Nashville, 1909.

Morton, Oren F. *A History of Monroe County, West Virginia*. Staunton, 1916.

————. *A History of Pendleton County, West Virginia*. Dayton, Va., 1910.

————. *A History of Rockbridge County*. Staunton, 1920.

————. *The Story of Winchester, in Virginia*. Strasburg, Va., 1925.

Mosgrove, George D. *Kentucky Cavaliers in Dixie*. Louisville, 1895.

Murray, Lois S. *Baylor at Independence*. Waco, 1972.

Myers, Robert M., ed. *The Children of Pride*. New Haven, 1972.

Nash, Charles E. *Biographical Sketches of Gen. Pat Cleburne and Gen. T. C. Hindman*. Little Rock, 1898.

National Cyclopedia of American Biography. 63 vols. New York, 1892–1984.

Neal, Lois S. *Abstracts of Vital Records from Raleigh, North Carolina, Newspapers*. Spartanburg, 1980.

Newman, Harry W. *The Lucketts of Portobacco*. Washington, D.C., 1938.

Newmark, Harris. *Sixty Years in Southern California, 1853–1913*. Los Angeles, 1970.

Nicolson, Frank W., ed. *Alumni Record of Wesleyan University*. Middletown, Conn., 1931.

Nisbet, James C. *Four Years on the Firing Line*. Chattanooga, 1914.

Northen, William J., ed. *Men of Mark in Georgia*. 6 vols. Atlanta, 1907–12.

Northern Alabama: Historical and Biographical. Birmingham. 1888.

Nott, Charles C. *Sketches of Prison Camps*. New York, 1865.

Nunn, W. C. *Texas Under the Carpetbaggers*. Austin, 1962.

Oates, Stephen, ed. *Rip Ford's Texas*. Austin, 1963.

Oates, William C. *The War Between the Union and the Confederacy*. New York, 1905.

O'Ferrall, Charles T. *Forty Years of Active Service*. New York, 1904.

O'Flaherty, Daniel. *General Jo Shelby, Undefeated Rebel*. Chapel Hill, 1954.

Opie, John N. *A Rebel Cavalryman with Lee Stuart and Jackson*. Chicago, 1899.

Owen, Thomas M. *History of Alabama and Dictionary of Alabama Biography*. 4 vols. Chicago, 1921.

Paddock, Buckley B., ed. *History and Biographical Record of North and West Texas*. 4 vols. Chicago, 1922.

Parker, James B. *The Vick Family*. N.p., 1988.

Parrish, William E. *David Rice Atchison of Missouri, Border Politician*. Columbia, Mo., 1961.

Parsons, Lucy D. *Life of Albert R. Parsons*. Chicago, 1903.

Parsons, William H. *Condensed History of Parsons Texas Cavalry Brigade, 1861–1865*. Corsicana, Tex., 1903.

Patrick, Rembert. *Aristocrat in Uniform: General Duncan L. Clinch*. Gainesville, Fla., 1963.

———, ed. *The Opinions of the Confederate Attorneys General, 1861–1865*. Buffalo, 1950.

Patton, John S. *Jefferson, Cabell, and the University of Virginia*. New York, 1908.

Paxton, W. M. *Annals of Platte County, Missouri*. Kansas City, 1897.

Pender, William Dorsey. *The General to His Lady: The Civil War Letters of William Dorsey Pender to Fanny Pender*. Edited by William W. Hassler. Chapel Hill, 1965.

Pereyra, Lillian. *James Lusk Alcorn: Persistent Whig*. Baton Rouge, 1966.

Perkins, E. F. *History of Marion County, Missouri*. St. Louis, 1884.

Peyton Society of Virginia, comp. *The Peytons of Virginia*. Stafford, Va., 1976.

Phelan, Macum. *A History of the Expansion of Methodism in Texas, 1867–1902*. Dallas, 1937.

Phifer, Charles H. *Genealogy and History of the Phifer Family*. Charlotte, 1910.

Philpott, William E., ed. *The Sponsor Souvenir Album and History of the United Confederate Veterans' Reunion, 1895*. Houston, 1895.

Polk, Cynthia Brown (Martin). *Some Old Colonial Families of Virginia*. Memphis, 1915.

Polley, J. B. *Hood's Texas Brigade: Its Marches, Its Battles, Its Achievements*. New York, 1910.

Pope, Thomas H. *The History of Newberry County, South Carolina*. Columbia, S.C., 1973.

Powell, William S., ed. *Dictionary of North Carolina Biography*. 4 vols. Chapel Hill, 1979–91.

Price, Benjamin L. *John Price the Emigrant*. Alexandria, La., 1910.

Pyne, Frederick W. *The John Pyne Family in America*. Baltimore, 1992.

Quarles, Garland R. *Some Old Homes in Frederick County, Virginia*. Winchester, Va., 1967.

――――. *Some Worthy Lives*. Winchester, Va., 1988.

Raines, C. W. *Year Book for Texas, 1901*. Austin, 1902.

Rains, George W. *History of the Confederate Powder Works*. Augusta, 1882.

Ray, Worth S. *Tennessee Cousins*. Baltimore, 1977.

Recum, Franz V. *Withers, America*. New York, 1949.

Reese, Lee F., comp. *The Ashby Book*. 2 vols. San Diego, 1976–78.

Reese, Michael. *Autographs of the Confederacy*. New York, 1981.

Register of Graduates and Former Cadets, United States Military Academy, 1802–1948. New York, 1948.

Reid, John C. *Reid's Tramp . . . .* Selma, 1858.

Researchers, The. *Kentucky Marriages in the Counties of Allen, Warren, Barren, Through 1850*. Indianapolis, 1981(?).

Reynolds, Clifford, comp. *Biographical Directory of the American Congress, 1774–1961*. Washington, D.C., 1961.

Reynolds, Emily B., and Joan R. Faunt. *Biographical Directory of the Senate of the State of South Carolina, 1776–1964*. Columbia, S.C., 1964.

Reynolds, John H., and David Y. Thomas. *History of the University of Arkansas*. Fayetteville, Ark., 1910.

Richardson, Simon P. *The Lights and Shadows of Itinerant Life*. Nashville, 1901.

Richardson, Willard, and David Richardson. *The Texas Almanac for 1859*. Galveston (?), 1859 (?).

――――. *The Texas Almanac for 1860*. Galveston (?), 1860 (?).

Rietti, John C. *Military Annals of Mississippi: Military Organizations Which Entered the Service of the Confederate States of America, from the State of Mississippi*. 1896; rpr. Spartanburg, 1976.

Riley, Benjamin F. *History of Conecuh County, Alabama*. Columbus, Ga., 1881.

Riley, E. D. *The Evergreen Old Historical Cemetery . . . .* Brewton, Ala., 1971 (?).

Rising, Marsha H., comp. *Genealogical Data from Southwest Missouri Newspapers*. Springfield, Mo., 1985.

Ritter, Charles F., and Jon L. Wakelyn. *American Legislative Leaders, 1850–1910.* New York, 1989.

Roberts, Bobby, and Carl Moneyhon. *Portraits of Conflict: A Photographic History of Arkansas in the Civil War.* Fayetteville, Ark., 1987.

Roberts, W. Adolphe. *Semmes of the "Alabama."* Indianapolis, 1938.

Robertson, Fred L., comp. *Soldiers of Florida in the Seminole Indian, Civil, and Spanish American Wars.* Live Oak, Fla., 1903.

Robertson, James I., Jr., ed. *Proceedings of the Advisory Council of the State of Virginia, April 21–June 19, 1861.* Richmond, 1977.

Robertson, John B. *Reminiscences of a Campaign in Mexico.* Nashville, 1849.

Robson, Charles. *Representative Men of the South.* Philadelphia, 1880.

Rogers, Augustus C., ed. *Representative Men: North & South.* New York, 1872.

Rogers, William W. *Thomas County, 1865–1900.* Tallahassee, 1973.

Roman, Alfred. *The Military Operations of General Beauregard in the War Between the States, 1861 to 1865.* 2 vols. New York, 1884.

Rose, Victor. *Ross' Texas Brigade.* Louisville, 1881.

Ross, James. *Life and Times of Elder Reuben Ross.* Philadelphia, 1882.

Rowland Dunbar. *Military History of Mississippi, 1803–1898.* 1908; rpr. Spartanburg, 1978.

———, ed. *Courts, Judges and Lawyers of Mississippi.* Jackson, Miss., 1935.

———, ed. *Encyclopedia of Mississippi History.* 2 vols. Atlanta, 1907.

———, ed. *History of Mississippi: The Heart of the South.* 4 vols. Chicago, 1925.

———, ed. *Jefferson Davis, Constitutionalist: His Letters, Papers and Speeches.* 10 vols. Jackson, 1923.

Ruby, James S., ed. *Blue and Gray: Georgetown University and the Civil War.* Washington, D.C., 1961.

Ruffner, Kevin C. *44th Virginia Infantry.* Lynchburg, Va., 1987.

Rushing, Anthony C. *Ranks of Honor.* Little Rock, 1990.

Russell, Elizabeth. *Persimmon Hill.* Norman, Okla., 1948.

Salmans, Levi B. *History of the Descendants of John Jacob Rector.* Guanajuato, Mexico, 1936.

Sands, Sarah G. C. *History of Monroe County, Tennessee.* 3 vols. Baltimore, 1980–89.

Sarrafian, Katherine H. *The Harrison Family of Texas, 1830–1966.* Waco, 1966.

Saunders, James E., and Elizabeth S. Stubbs. *Early Settlers of Alabama.* 1899; rpr. Baltimore, 1969.

Scarborough, William K., ed. *The Diary of Edmund Ruffin.* 3 vols. Baton Rouge, 1972–89.

Schaff, Morris. *The Spirit of Old West Point, 1858–1862.* Boston, 1908.

Scharf, J. Thomas. *History of Saint Louis City and County.* 2 vols. Philadelphia, 1883.

Schrantz, Ward L. *Jasper County Missouri in the Civil War.* Carthage, Tenn., 1923.

Seebold, Herman de B. *Old Louisiana Plantation Homes and Family Trees.* 2 vols. N.p., 1941.

Semmes, Raphael. *Memoirs of Service Afloat*. Baltimore, 1869.

Shalhope, Robert E. *Sterling Price: Portrait of a Southerner*. Columbia, Mo., 1971.

Shea, William L., and Earl J. Hess. *Pea Ridge: Civil War Campaign in the West*. Chapel Hill, 1992.

Sherrill, William L. *Annals of Lincoln County, North Carolina*. Charlotte, 1927.

Sifakis, Stewart. *Who Was Who in the Civil War*. New York, 1988.

Simon, John Y. *The Papers of Ulysses S. Grant*. 18 vols. Edwardsville, Ill., 1967–91.

Simons, Admiral Robert B. *Thomas Grange Simons III*. Charleston, S.C., 1954.

Simpson, Harold B. *Cry Comanche: The 2nd U.S. Cavalry in Texas, 1855–1861*. Hillsboro, 1979.

———. *Touched with Valor*. Hillsboro, 1964.

Slaughter, Philip. *A History of Bristol Parish, Virginia*. Richmond, 1879.

Smith, Clifford N. *Federal Land Series*. 4 vols. Chicago, 1972–82.

Smith, Daniel E., ed. *Mason Smith Family Letters*. Columbia, S.C., 1930.

Smith, David P. *Frontier Defense in the Civil War*. College Station, Tex., 1992.

Smith, Gustavus W. *Confederate War Papers*. New York, 1884.

Smith, Jonathan K. *Historic Tulip, Arkansas*. N.p., 1989.

———. *The Romance of Tulip*. Memphis, 1965.

Smith, Walter B. *American Diplomats and Counsels of 1776–1865*. Washington, D.C., 1986.

Smith, William R. *Reminiscences of A Long Life*. Washington, D.C., 1889.

Sons of Confederate Veterans. *Sons of Confederate Veterans, Ancestor Album*. Houston, 1986.

Speer, Ocie. *Texas Jurists*. Austin, 1936.

Speer, William S., ed. *The Encyclopedia of the New West*. Marshall, Tex., 1881.

———. *Sketches of Prominent Tennesseans*. Nashville, 1888.

Spence, Wilma C., comp. *Tombstones and Epitaphs of Northeastern North Carolina*. Baltimore, 1973.

Spencer, Elizabeth R. *They Are Here: Cemeteries of Clay County, Florida*. . . . Orange Park, Fla., 1973.

Spencer, John W. *Terrell's Texas Cavalry*. Burnet, Tex., 1982.

Sprunt, James. *Chronicles of the Cape Fear River*. Wilmington, N.C., 1914.

Stanley, J. Randall. *History of Jackson County*. Marianna, Fla., 1950.

Staples, Thomas S. *Reconstruction in Arkansas, 1862–1874*. New York, 1923.

Steen, Moses D. *The Steen Family in Europe and America*. Cincinnati, 1917.

Stephens, Jim. *Reflections: A Portrait Biography of the Kentucky Military Institute*. Georgetown, Ky., 1991.

Stephens, Robert G. *Intrepid Warrior: Clement Anselm Evans*. Dayton, 1992.

Stevens, Walter B. *Centennial History of Missouri*. 4 vols. St. Louis, 1921.

———. *History of the Fourth City, 1763–1909*. 3 vols. Chicago, 1903.

Still, William N., Jr., ed. *Odyssey in Gray: A Diary of Confederate Service, 1863–1865*. Richmond, 1979.

Stone, Letta B. *The West Family Register*. Washington, D.C., 1928.

Stovall, Frances, et al. Clear Springs and Limestone Ledges: A History of San Marcos and Hays County. Austin, 1986.

The Supplement to the Official Records. Vol. I. Wilmington, N.C., 1994.

Swinburn, Susan S., comp. History in Headstones. Van Buren, Ark., 1970.

Sword, Wiley. Embrace an Angry Wind. New York, 1992.

Tally-Frost, Stephanie. Cemetery Records of Leon County, Texas. Corpus Christi, 1967.

Taylor, Richard. Destruction and Reconstruction: Personal Experiences of the Late War. 1879; rpr. New York, 1955.

Temple, Sarah. The First Hundred Years: A Short History of Cobb County, in Georgia. Atlanta, 1935.

Terrell, Alexander W. From Texas to Mexico and the Court of Maximilian in 1865. Dallas, 1933.

Texas Supreme Court. Texas Reports. Vols. XXXVIII, CXL.

Texas County, Missouri, Genealogical & Historical Society. Texas County, Missouri Heritage. 2 vols. Rich Hill, Mo., 1989.

Thomas, David Y. Arkansas in War and Reconstruction, 1861–1874. Little Rock, 1926.

Thomas, Mrs. Henry K. Cemetery Records of Lafayette County, Missouri. Chillicothe, Mo., 1991.

Thomas, Henry W. History of the Doles-Cook Brigade. Atlanta, 1903.

Thompson, Jerry Don. John Robert Baylor: Texas Indian Fighter and Confederate Soldier. Hillsboro, 1971.

———. Vacqueros in Blue and Gray. Austin, 1976.

———. Warm Weather & Bad Whisky: The 1886 Laredo Election Riot. El Paso, 1991.

Thompson, M. Jeff. Reminiscences of General M. Jeff Thompson. Edited by Donal J. Stanton, Goodwin F. Berquist, and Paul C. Bowers. Dayton, 1988.

Thrall, Homer S. A Brief History of Methodism in Texas. Nashville, 1889.

Thrapp, Dan L. Encyclopedia of Frontier Biography. 3 vols. Glendale, Calif., 1988.

Threlkeld, Hansford L. Threlkeld Genealogy. Morganfield, Ky., ca. 1932.

Tillman, Stephen F. The Rennolds-Reynolds Family of England and Virginia, 1530–1948. Washington, D.C., 1948.

Tixier, Victor. Tixier's Travels on the Osage Prairies. Edited by John F. McDermott. Norman, Okla., 1940.

Tower, R. Lockwood, ed. A Carolinian Goes to War: The Civil War Narratives of Arthur Middleton Manigault. Columbia, S.C., 1983.

Tracy, Evert E., comp. The Tracy Genealogy. Albany, 1898.

Trelease, Allen W. White Terror: The Ku Klux Klan Conspiracy and Southern Reconstruction. New York, 1971.

Trudeau, Edward L. An Autobiography. Philadelphia, 1916.

Tupper, Eleanor. Tupper Genealogy, 1578–1971. North Conway, N.J., 1972.

Tyler, Lyon G. Encyclopedia of Virginia Biography. 5 vols. New York, 1915.

Underwood, Lucien, comp. *The Underwood Families of America*. Lancaster, Pa., 1913.

United Daughters of the Confederacy, Missouri Division. *Reminiscences of the Women of Missouri During the Sixties*. Jefferson City, 1901.

United Daughters of the Confederacy, Tennessee Chapter. *Confederate Patriot Index, 1924–1978*. 2 vols. Columbia, Tenn., 1978.

U.S. *Biographical and Portrait Gallery of Eminent Self-Made Men, Missouri Volume, The*. New York, 1878.

United States Military Academy. *Annual Reunion of the Association of Graduates*. N.p., various dates.

United States Navy Department. *The War of the Rebellion . . . Official Records of the Union and Confederate Navies*. 30 vols. Washington, D.C., 1894–1922.

United States War Department. *War of the Rebellion . . . Official Records of the Union and Confederate Armies*. 128 parts in 70 vols. Washington, D.C., 1880–1901.

University of Georgia. *Catalogue of the Trustees, Officers, Alumni and Matriculates of the University of Georgia at Athens, Georgia, from 1785 to 1906*. Athens, 1906.

University of Mississippi. *Historical Catalogue, 1849–1909*. Nashville, 1910.

Upton, Emory. *Military Policy of the United States*. Washington, D.C., 1907.

Van Ravenswaay, Charles. *St. Louis: An Informal History of the City and Its People*. St. Louis, 1991.

Van Wagenen, Mrs. Avis Stearns. *Genealogy and Memoirs of Charles and Nathaniel Stearns, and Their Descendants*. 2 vols. Syracuse, 1901.

Virginia General Assembly. *The General Assembly of Virginia, 1619–1978*. Richmond, 1978.

Waddell, Joseph A. *Annals of Augusta County, Virginia*. Richmond, 1886.

Wakelyn, Jon L. *Biographical Dictionary of the Confederacy*. Westport, Conn., 1977.

Wallace, Edward S. *Destiny and Glory*. New York, 1957.

Wallace, Lee A. *A Guide to Virginia Military Organizations, 1861–65*. Lynchburg, Va., 1986.

———. *5th Virginia Infantry*. Lynchburg, Va., 1988.

Warner, Ezra J. *Generals in Gray: Lives of the Confederate Commanders*. Baton Rouge, 1959.

Warner, Ezra J., and W. Buck Yearns. *Biographical Register of the Confederate Congress*. Baton Rouge, 1975.

Warner, George E. *History of Ramsey County and the City of St. Paul*. Minneapolis, 1881.

Warner, Beers and Company. *History of Franklin County, Pennsylvania*. Chicago, 1887.

Warren, Harlow. *Beckley, USA*. 3 vols. N.p., 1955.

Warren, Mary B. *Marriages and Deaths, 1820 to 1830, Abstracted from Extant Georgia Newspapers*. Danielsville, Ga., 1968.

Watson, L. E. *Fight and Survive*. Conway, Ark., 1974.

Watt, Margaret Gibbs. *The Gibbs Family of Long Ago and Near at Hand*. St. Augustine, 1968.

Wayland, John W. *A History of Shenandoah County*. Strasburg, Va., 1927.

———. *Virginia Valley Records*. Strasburg, Va., 1930.

Webb, Walter P. *The Texas Rangers: A Century of Frontier Defense*. Boston, 1935.

Webb, Walter P., and Eldon S. Branda, eds. *Handbook of Texas*. 3 vols. Austin, 1952–76.

Webb, William L. *Battles and Biographies of Missourians*. Kansas City, 1900.

Weinert, Richard P. *The Confederate Regular Army*. Shippensburg, Pa., 1991.

West, Richard S. *Lincoln's Scapegoat General: A Life of Benjamin F. Butler, 1818–1893*. Cambridge, Mass., 1965.

West Virginia Historical Records Survey. *Calendar of Francis Harrison Pierpont Letters and Papers in West Virginia Depositories*. Charleston, S.C., 1940.

Western Historical Company. *History of Boone County, Missouri*. St. Louis, 1882.

Wheeler, John H. *Reminiscences and Memoirs of North Carolina and Eminent North Carolinians*. 1884; rpr. Baltimore, 1966.

Wherry, Adolphus. *History of the First Methodist Church of Dallas, Texas, 1846–1946*. Dallas, 1947.

Whetstone, Adam H. *History of the 53rd Alabama Volunteer Infantry (Mounted)*. University, Ala., 1985.

White, Virgil D. *Index of U.S. Marshals, 1789–1960*. Waynesboro, Tenn., 1988.

Whitfield, Emma M., comp. *Whitfield, Bryan, Smith and Related Families*. N.p., 1948(?).

Whitley, Edythe, ed. *Marriages of Maury Co., Tennessee, 1808–52*. Baltimore, 1982.

———. *Red River Settlers: Records of the Settlers of Northern Montgomery, Robertson, and Sumner Counties, Tennessee*. Baltimore, 1980.

Whittelsey, Charles B. *The Ancestry and the Descendants of John Pratt*. Hartford, 1900.

Who's Who in America, 1910–1911. Chicago, 1912.

Who Was Who in America. Chicago, 1967.

Williams, Alfred B. *Hampton and His Red Shirts*. Charleston, S.C., 1935.

Williams, Charles R., ed. *Diary and Letters of Rutherford Birchard Hayes*. 5 vols. Columbus, Ohio, 1922.

Williams, J. Fletcher. *A History of the City of St. Paul and of the County of Ramsey, Minnesota*. St. Paul, Minn., 1876.

Williford, William B. *The Glory of Covington*. Atlanta, 1973.

Willingham, Jean S., and Berthenia C. Smith. *Bibb County, Georgia, Early Wills and Cemetery Records*. Macon, 1961.

Willis, George L. *Kentucky Democracy*. 3 vols. Louisville, 1935.

Wills, Brian S. *A Battle from the Start*. New York, 1992.

Wiltshire, Betty C. *Mississippi Index of Wills, 1800–1900*. Bowie, Md., 1989.

Winfrey, Dorman H. *A History of Rusk County, Texas*. Waco, 1961.

Winkler, Ernest W., comp. *Check List of Texas Imprints, 1846–1860.* Austin, 1949.

——, comp. *Check List of Texas Imprints, 1861–1876.* Austin, 1963.

Winters, John D. *The Civil War in Louisiana.* Baton Rouge, 1963.

Wood, Robert C. *Confederate Handbook.* New Orleans, 1900.

Wood, Sue, and Ronnie Howser, eds. *Fairview Cemetery, Gainesville, Cooke County, Texas.* Gainesville, Tex., 1985.

Woodard, W. S. *Annals of Methodism in Missouri.* Columbia, Mo., 1893.

Woods, James M. *Rebellion and Realignment: Arkansas's Road to Secession.* Fayetteville, Ark., 1987.

Woodson, W. H. *History of Clay County, Missouri.* Topeka, 1920.

Wooten, Dudley G., ed. *A Comprehensive History of Texas, 1685 to 1897.* 2 vols. Dallas, 1898.

Worsham, Dr. W. J. *The Old Nineteenth Tennessee Regiment, C.S.A.* Knoxville, 1902.

Wright, Marcus J. *Arkansas in the War, 1861–1865.* Batesville, Ark., 1963.

——. *Texas in the War, 1861–1865.* Edited by Harold Simpson. Hillsboro, 1965.

——, comp. *General Officers of the Confederate Army.* New York, 1911.

Wulfeck, Dorothy. *Marriages of Some Virginia Residents, 1607–1800.* 7 vols. Naugatuck, Conn., 1961–67.

Wyeth, John Allan. *That Devil Forrest: Life of General Nathan Bedford Forrest.* 1899; rpr. Baton Rouge, 1989.

——. *With Sabre and Scalpel.* New York, 1914.

Wytrwal, Joseph A. *Poles in American History and Tradition.* Detroit, 1969.

Young, Bennett H. *Confederate Wizards of the Saddle . . . .* 1914; rpr. Boston, 1958.

Young, J. P. *The Seventh Tennessee Cavalry (Confederate): A History.* Nashville, 1890.

Young, William. *History of Lafayette County, Missouri.* 2 vols. Indianapolis, 1910.

Zuber, William P. *My Eighty Years in Texas.* Austin, 1971.

ARTICLES

Abercrombie, Irene. "The Battle of Prairie Grove." *Arkansas Historical Quarterly,* II (1943), 309–15.

"Abstract of Austin City Directory 1872–73." *Austin Genealogical Society,* XIV (December, 1973), 71–110.

Acheson, Sam, and Julie A. H. O'Connell, eds. "George Washington Diamond's Account of the Great Hanging at Gainesville, 1862." *Southwestern Historical Quarterly,* LXVI (1962–63), 331–414.

Alderson, William T., ed. "The Civil War Reminiscences of John Johnston, 1861–1865." *Tennessee Historical Quarterly,* XIV (June, 1955), 142–75.

Aldridge, Smith M. "Nicholas Bartlett Pearce." *Benton County Pioneer,* XXX (Fall, 1985), 33–39.

"Alfred Beckley." *Confederate Veteran,* XXXIV (1926), 386.

Allardice, Bruce S. "Soldier and Jurist—General John David McAdoo." *Houston Civil War Round Table Newsletter*, IV (January, 1991).

Anders, Leslie. "Fighting the Ghosts at Lone Jack." *Missouri Historical Review*, LXXIX (1984–85), 332–56.

Andrews, W. H. "Hardships of Georgia Regulars." *Confederate Veteran*, XVII (1909), 230–32.

Angelotti, Mrs. Frank M. "The Polks of North Carolina and Tennessee." *New England Historic and Genealogical Register*, LXXVII (1923), 133–45, 213–27, 250–70; LXXVIII (1924), 3–53, 159–77, 318–30, 449.

Bacon, Walter R. "Pioneer Courts and Lawyers of Los Angeles." *Quarterly of the Historical Society of Southern California*, VI (1905), 211–22.

Baker, Thomas. "The Early Newspapers of Memphis, Tennessee, 1827–1860." *West Tennessee Historical Society Papers*, XVII (1963), 20–46.

Barjenbruch, Judith. "The Greenback Political Movement: An Arkansas View." *Arkansas Historical Quarterly*, XXXVI (1977), 107–22.

Barrick, Nona, and Mary H. Taylor. "Mesilla Entrada." *New Mexico Magazine*, XXXIX (July, 1961), 20–23, 38.

———. "Murder in Mesilla." *New Mexico Magazine*, XXXVIII (November, 1960), 3–5, 34.

Barrows, H. D. "J. Lancaster Brent." *Quarterly of the Historical Society of Southern California*, VI (1905), 238–41.

Barton, Henry W. "Five Texas Frontier Companies During the Mexican War." *Southwestern Historical Quarterly*, LXVI (1962–63), 17–30.

"Battle of Bethel." *Southern Historical Society Papers*, XXIX (1901), 197–207.

Bearss, Edwin C. "The Federals Raid Van Buren and Threaten Fort Smith." *Arkansas Historical Quarterly*, XXVI (1967), 123–42.

———. "Fort Smith Serves General McCulloch as a Supply Depot." *Arkansas Historical Quarterly*, XXIV (1965), 315–47.

Belcher, James R., and Ronald L. Heinemann. "Heros von Borcke, Knight-Errant of the Confederacy." *Virginia Cavalcade*, XXXV (Autumn, 1985), 86–95.

Bell, Raymond M. "Mark Twain's Clemens Ancestry." *Pennsylvania Genealogical Magazine*, XXXIV (1985), 1–25.

"Bivouac 18, A.C.S., and Camp 28, U.C.V." *Confederate Veteran*, V (1897), 566.

"Borcke." *Genealogisches Handbuch Des Adels*, Adelige Hauser A, II (1955), 104–25.

Bragg, William H. "A Little Battle at Griswoldville." *Civil War Times Illustrated*, XVIII (July, 1979), 44–49.

Brent, Joseph L. "Capture of the Indianola." *Southern Historical Society Papers*, I (1876), 91–99.

Bridges, C. A. "The Knights of the Golden Circle: A Filibustering Fantasy." *Southwestern Historical Quarterly*, XLIV (1940–41), 287–302.

Brough, Charles H. "Historic Homes." *Arkansas Historical Association Publications*, I (1906), 286–301.

Brownson, Mrs. J. M. "Colonel Anderson's Sword." *Confederate Veteran*, XXXIII (1925), 288.

Butler, Thomas. "Moore Bible Record." *Pennsylvania Genealogical Magazine*, XI (March, 1932), 288–91.

Cabell, W. L. "Confederate Generals Yet Living." *Confederate Veteran*, II (1893), 28.

Cannon, Devereaux D., Jr. "Flags of the Rock City Guards." *Tennessee Historical Quarterly*, XLVII (1988), 191–97.

"Capt. Ed B. Ross." *Confederate Veteran*, XX (1912), 176–77.

"Capt. John Pembroke Jones." *Confederate Veteran*, XVIII (1910), 533.

"Capt. William Dunovant." *Confederate Veteran*, X (1902), 422–23.

"The Capture of Memphis by Gen. Nathan B. Forrest." *Southern Historical Society Papers*, XXXVI (1908), 180–96.

"Career of Gen. Joseph Lancaster Brent." *Confederate Veteran*, XVII (1909), 345–47.

Carrigan, Alfred H., and Jesse Cypert. "Reminiscences of the Secession Convention." *Arkansas Historical Association Publications*, I (1906), 305–23.

Casey, Powell A. "Early History of the Washington Artillery of New Orleans." *Louisiana Historical Quarterly*, XXIII (1940), 471–84.

Cassell, T. W. "Gen. Levin M. Lewis." *Confederate Veteran*, XV (1907), 346–47.

Castel, Albert, ed. "The Diary of General Henry Little, C.S.A." *Civil War Times Illustrated*, XI (October, 1972), 4–11, 41–47.

Causey, Jerry, ed. "Selected Correspondence of the Adjutant General of Confederate Mississippi." *Journal of Mississippi History*, XLIII (1981), 31–58.

Childs, J. Rives. "Hancock Family of Lower Norfolk, Henrico and Bedford Counties." *Virginia Magazine of History and Biography*, XXXII (1924), 413–16; XXXIII (1925), 97–112, 212–15, 316–21, 416–19.

Coffin, James P. "Col. Henry M. Ashby." *Confederate Veteran*, XIV (1906), 121.

Coffman, Richard M. "A Vital Unit." *Civil War Times Illustrated*, XX (January, 1982), 40–45.

"Col. A. E. Reynolds." *Old Timer Press* (June, 1983), 6.

"Col. Cary Breckinridge." *Confederate Veteran*, XXVI (1918), 452.

"Col. Clement Sulivane." *Confederate Veteran*, XXIX (1921), 31.

"Col. John S. Prather." *Confederate Veteran*, XXVIII (1920), 229.

"Col. Sidney Jackman." *Confederate Veteran*, XIX (1911), 436.

Conrad, James L. "Training in Treason." *Civil War Times Illustrated*, XXX (September–October, 1991), 22–29, 62–64.

Crenshaw, Ollinger. "The Knights of the Golden Circle." *American Historical Review*, XLVII (1941–42), 23–50.

"C.S.A. Generals Killed or Died of Wounds." *Confederate Veteran*, XV (1907), 236.

Cuyler, Telamon. "Surviving Confederate Generals." *Confederate Veteran*, XV (1907), 118–19.

Dalehite, Bob. "Arch S. Dobbins." *Phillips County Historical Quarterly*, IV (September, 1965), 15–24.

Darden, David. "Alabama Secession Convention." *Alabama Historical Quarterly*, III (1941), 269–451.

Davis, Stephen. "Jeff Thompson's Unsuccessful Quest for a Confederate Generalship." *Missouri Historical Review*, LXXXV (1990–91), 53–65.

———. "Profile—I Am a Rip-Squealer and My Name Is Fight: M. Jeff Thompson of Missouri." *Blue & Gray*, IV (April–May, 1987), 28–39.

"Death of General Merriweather Lewis Clark." *Vedette* (November 15, 1881), 11.

DeHaven, Mabel. "Hannibal, Missouri." *Kansas City Genealogist*, XX (Spring, 1980), 169–73.

Dellinger, Paul. "Lincoln County Information for 1867–8." *Eswau Huppeday*, VII (February, 1987), 49–57.

Deyton, Jason B. "The Toe River Valley to 1865." *North Carolina Historical Review*, XXIV (1947), 423–36.

Dirck, Brian. "Untempered Steel." *Civil War*, VIII (September–October, 1990), 12–15, 70–71.

Douglas, H. T. "Hood's Messmates at Yorktown." *Confederate Veteran*, XIX (1911), 78–79.

Eby, Cecil D., Jr. "Memoir of a West Pointer in Florida, 1825." *Florida Historical Quarterly*, XLI (1962–63), 154–64.

———. "Memoir of a West Pointer in Saint Augustine, 1824–1826." *Florida Historical Quarterly*, XLII (1963–64), 307–20.

———. "Recollections of Fort Monroe, 1826–1828: From the Autobiography of Lieutenant Alfred Beckley." *Virginia Magazine of History and Biography*, LXXII (1964), 479–89.

Edgar, Thomas H. "Col. Charles D. Anderson." *Confederate Veteran*, X (1902), 31.

"Edward Bagby of Virginia." *Confederate Veteran*, XXVII (1919), 453–54.

Embree, D. A. "Fighting the Kansas Jayhawkers." *Confederate Veteran*, XIX (1911), 73.

Farr, Warner D. "Confederate Surgeon General Samuel Preston Moore." *Houston Civil War Round Table Newsletter*, V (February, 1992).

"Flag of the 28th Alabama Regiment." *Confederate Veteran*, XXVII (1919), 311.

Folk, Edgar E. "W. W. Holden and the Election of 1858." *North Carolina Historical Review*, XXI (1944), 294–318.

Folkes, Thomas M. "Mississippi Troops Who Served in Virginia, 1861–1865." *Southern Historical Society Papers*, XXXV (1907), 58–59.

Forrest, Robert J. "Mythical Cities of Southwestern Minnesota." *Minnesota History*, XIV (1933), 243–62.

Fowler, Ida E. "Confederate Dead in the State Cemetery at Frankfort, Ky." *Confederate Veteran*, XXXIV (1926), 375–76.

Frank, John G. "Adolphus Heiman: Architect and Soldier." *Tennessee Historical Quarterly*, V (1946), 35–57.

Friend, John H., Jr. "The Controversial Surrender of Fort Gaines, August, 1864." *Gulf Coast Historical Review*, II (Spring, 1987), 96–104.

Frizzell, Robert W. "'Killed by Rebels': A Civil War Massacre and Its Aftermath." *Missouri Historical Review*, LXXI (1976–77), 369–95.

Gage, Larry J. "The Texas Road to Secession and War: John Marshall and the Texas State Gazette, 1860–1861." *Southwestern Historical Quarterly*, LXII (1958–59), 191–226.

Gann, J. M. "Inquiry for Relatives." *Confederate Veteran*, XVII (1909), 621.

"Gen. A. P. Bagby." *Confederate Veteran*, XXIX (1921), 146.

"Gen. Arthur Pendleton Bagby." *Confederate Veteran*, XXXII (1924), 172.

"Gen. Edmund W. Rucker." *Confederate Veteran*, XXXII (1924), 163–64.

"Gen. H. Kyd Douglas." *Confederate Veteran*, XII (1904), 125.

"Gen. J. J. Dickison." *Confederate Veteran*, X (1902), 419–20.

"Gen. James William Barnes." *Texas Historical and Biographical Magazine*, II (1892), 172–79.

"Gen. Rufus P. Neely." *Confederate Veteran*, IX (1901), 509–10.

"Gen. W. B. Wade's Military Achievements." *Confederate Veteran*, XIV (1906), 17.

"General David Bullock Harris, C.S.A." *Southern Historical Society Papers*, XX (1892), 395–98.

"General Rufus Polk Neely." *Illinois Central Magazine*, IV (November, 1915), 9–16.

"General Thomas A. Harris." *Missouri Historical Review*, XXXVII (1942–43), 112–13.

Gibson, Thomas R. "Gen. James H. M'Bride." *Confederate Veteran*, XXIII (1915), 375.

Gifford, George. "James DeBerty Trudeau: Physician-Naturalist." *Bulletin of the History of Medicine*, LIV (1980), 78–94.

Gilbert, Benjamin F. "California and the Civil War: A Bibliographical Essay." *California Historical Society Quarterly*, XL (1961), 289–307.

Gilley, Billy H. "Tennessee Opinion of the Mexican War as Reflected in the State Press." *East Tennessee Historical Society Publications*, XXVI (1954), 7–26.

Goodrich, James. "In the Earnest Pursuit of Wealth: David Waddo in Missouri and the Southwest, 1820–1878." *Missouri Historical Review*, LXVI (1971–72), 155–84.

Gourdin, R. N. "Memorial." Transactions of the Huguenot Society of South Carolina, I (1889), 26–33.

Gower, Herschel. *"Belle Meade: Queen of Tennessee Plantations."* Tennessee Historical Quarterly, XXII (1963), 203–22.

———. "The Dahlgrens and Jefferson Davis." *Journal of Mississippi History*, LV (August, 1993), 179–201.

Guinn, J. M. "Pioneer School Superintendents of Los Angeles." *Quarterly of the Historical Society of Southern California*, IV (1897), 76–81.

Hale, Douglas. "The Third Texas Cavalry: A Socioeconomic Profile of a Confederate Regiment." *Military History of the Southwest*, XIX (1989), 1–26.

Hall, Martin H. "The Court-Martial of Arthur Pendleton Bagby, C.S.A." *East Texas Historical Journal*, XIV (1981), 60–65.

———. "Planter vs. Frontiersman: Conflict in Confederate Indian Policy." In

Essays on the American Civil War. Edited by William F. Holmes and Harold Hollingsworth. Austin, 1968.

Hanks, C. J. "Caleb P. Warren." *Confederate Veteran,* XXIX (1921), 107.

Harding, James. "Personal Reminiscences of Service with the Missouri State Guard." *St. Louis Missouri Republican,* July 18, 25, 1885.

Hassler, William W. "'Willie' Pegram: General Lee's Brilliant Young Virginia Artillerist." *Virginia Cavalcade,* XXIII (Autumn, 1973), 12–19.

Heistand-Moore, Eleanor M. "Marriages Performed by the Rev. David Denny, D.D. of Path Valley and Chambersburg, Pennsylvania, 1794–1844." *Publications of the Genealogical Society of Pennsylvania,* VIII (March, 1921), 65–75.

Heite, Edward F. "Judge Robert Ould." *Virginia Cavalcade,* XIV (Spring, 1965), 10–19.

Hemming, Charles. "Confederate Dead of Florida." *Southern Historical Society Papers,* XXVII (1899), 109–29.

Hennessy, John. "Stonewall's Nickname: Was It Fact or Was It Fiction?" *Civil War,* VIII (March–April, 1990), 10–17.

"Henry Alexander De Saussure." *South Carolina Historical and Genealogical Magazine,* V (1904), 67–68.

Henry, Pat. "Adams' Brigade in Battle of Franklin." *Confederate Veteran,* XXI (1913), 76–77.

Hess, Earl J. "Civilians at War: The Georgia Militia in the Atlanta Campaign." *Georgia Historical Quarterly,* LXVI (1982), 332–45.

Hickman, John P. "Confederate Generals of Tennessee." *Confederate Veteran,* XVIII (1910), 170–72.

Highshaw, Mary W. "A History of Zion Community in Maury County, 1806–1860." *Tennessee Historical Quarterly,* V (1946), 1–34, 111–40, 222–33.

"Historical and Genealogical Notes: Gwynn." *William and Mary College Quarterly,* XVIII (1910), 60–62.

Hoke, W. J. "Sketch of the 38th Regiment N.C. Troops." *Our Living and Our Dead,* I (1874–75), 545–51.

———. "What Lincoln County Did in the Late War." *Our Living and Our Dead,* I (1874–75), 429–34.

Holladay, Florence M. "The Powers of the Commander of the Confederate Trans-Mississippi Department, 1863–1865." *Southwestern Historical Quarterly,* XXI (1918), 277–98, 333–59.

Hoole, W. Stanley. "Admiral on Horseback: The Diary of Brigadier General Raphael Semmes, February–May, 1865." *Alabama Review,* XXVIII (1975), 129–50.

———. "Jeremiah Clemens, Novelist." *Alabama Review,* XVIII (1965), 5–36.

Huff, Leo. "The Military Board in Confederate Arkansas." *Arkansas Historical Quarterly,* XXVI (1967), 75–95.

Hulston, John K., and James W. Goodrich. "John Truesdale Coffee: Lawyer, Politician, Confederate." *Missouri Historical Review,* LXXVII (1982–83), 272–95.

Hunter, Lloyd A. "Missouri's Confederate Leaders After the War." *Missouri Historical Review*, LXVII (1972–73), 371–96.

Huske, Benjamin R. "More Terrible than Victory." Edited by Walker Brown. *Civil War Times Illustrated*, XX (October, 1981), 28–33.

"In Memory of Gen. Nicholas Bartlett Pearce." *Backtracker*, I (April, 1972), 8–9.

Inge, Mrs. F. A. "Corinth, Miss., in Early War Days." *Confederate Veteran*, XVII (1909), 442–44.

"J. J. Dickison, Maj. Gen. U.C.V., Florida." *Confederate Veteran*, II (1894), 99.

Jarman, R. A. "Inventory and History Co. K 27th Miss. Infantry CSA." *Chickasaw Times Past*, III (1985), 214–19; IV (1985), 19–24.

Jensen, Evalyn R. "Navy Gunboat Falls Prey to Rebel Cavalry." *United Daughters of the Confederacy Magazine*, XL (January, 1987), 32.

Jervey, Elizabeth H. "Marriage and Death Notices from the City Gazette of Charleston, 1824." *South Carolina Historical and Genealogical Magazine*, LVIII (1957), 48–55, 114–16, 183–85, 266–70.

Johannson, Jane Harris, and David H. Johannson. "Two 'Lost' Battle Reports: Horace Randal's and Joseph L. Brent's Reports of the Battles of Mansfield and Pleasant Hill, 8 and 9 April 1864." *Military History of the West*, XXIII (Fall, 1993), 169–80.

Johnson, Evans C. "Henry W. Hilliard and the Civil War Years." *Alabama Review*, XVII (1964), 102–12.

Johnson, Louise R., and Julia Rosa. "Inscriptions from the Churchyard of Prince George Winyah, Georgetown, South Carolina." *South Carolina Historical and Genealogical Magazine*, XXXI (1930), 184–208, 292–313.

Johnson, Michael P. "A New Look at the Popular Vote for Delegates to the Georgia Secession Convention." *Georgia Historical Quarterly*, LVI (1972), 259–75.

Johnson, Norman K. "Personality." *America's Civil War*, III (January, 1991), 10–14, 18–20, 72–74.

Jones, Charles C. "A Roster of General Officers, Heads of Departments, Senators, Representatives, Military Organizations, &c., &c., in Confederate Service During the War Between the States." *Southern Historical Society Papers*, vols. I and II (printed as vols. IA and IIA; 1876–77).

————. "The Siege and Evacuation of Savannah, Georgia, in December, 1864." *Southern Historical Society Papers*, XVII (1889), 60–85.

Jones, Charles E. "General Officers of the Regular C.S. Army." *Confederate Veteran*, XVI 1908 45–48.

————. "Necrology of Confederate Generals." *Confederate Veteran*, XVI (1908), 45–48.

Jones, Lewis P. "Ambrosio Jose Gonzales, a Cuban Patriot in Carolina." *South Carolina Historical and Genealogical Magazine*, LVI (1955), 67–76.

"Judge Alexander Watkins Terrell." *Confederate Veteran*, XX (1912), 575–76.

"Justices of the Peace for Bedford County, Tennessee." *Bedford County Historical Quarterly*, IV (Spring, 1978), 7–9.

King, W. H. "Early Experiences in Missouri." *Confederate Veteran*, XVII (1909), 502.

Kirkpatrick, Arthur. "Missouri's Delegation in the Confederate Congress." *Civil War History*, V (1959), 188–98.

L. M. M. [pseud.] "Service of Brig. Gen. W. H. King." *Confederate Veteran*, XVI (1908), 395.

"Lafayette County, Mississippi—1845 Tax Roll Index." *Mississippi Genealogical Exchange*, XXVIII (Winter, 1982), 158–65.

Law, J. G. "Diary of a Confederate Soldier." *Southern Historical Society Papers*, X (1882), 378–81.

Lester, John H. "Titles in the U.C.V." *Confederate Veteran*, XVII (1909), 54.

"Letter of Colonel Edward Willis." *Southern Historical Society Papers*, XLI (1916), 161–65.

"Letters of John Floyd, 1813–1838." *Georgia Historical Quarterly*, XXXIII (1949), 228–69.

Lewis, Samuel E. "Dr. Samuel P. Moore." *Southern Historical Society Papers*, XXIX (1901), 273–79.

Longest, Doy Payne. "John Allan Wyeth: Soldier, Surgeon, Scribe, Southerner." *United Daughters of the Confederacy Magazine*, XXXII (March, 1979), 21–23.

Luckey, John H. "Adopted Texan—Captain Isaac Newton Brown, C.S.A." *Houston Civil War Round Table Newsletter*, VI (October, 1992).

Malloch, Archibald. "James DeBerty Trudeau: Artist, Soldier, Physician." *Bulletin, New York Academy of Medicine*, 2nd ser., II (December, 1935), 681–99.

Marchman, Watt. "The Florida Historical Society, 1856–1861, 1879, 1902–1940." *Florida Historical Quarterly*, XIX (1940–41), 3–65.

Marsh, Helen C. "Bedford County Extracts from *The Correspondence of James K. Polk*, Volume III." *Bedford County Historical Quarterly*, III (Fall, 1977), 89–96.

———. "Bedford County Marriages." *Bedford County Historical Quarterly*, I (Summer, 1975), 44–49.

Marshall, Bruce. "Destiny at Gaines Mill." *Civil War*, X (March–April, 1992), 9–12.

———. "Santos Benavides: 'The Confederacy on the Rio Grande.'" *Civil War*, VIII (May–June, 1990), 18–21.

Martin, Amelia. "United Confederate Veterans." *Fort Smith Historical Society Journal*, V (September, 1981), 2–4.

Martin, Roscoe C. "The Greenback Party in Texas." *Southwestern Historical Quarterly*, XXX (1926–27), 163–77.

Mattox, Henry E. "Chronicle of a Mississippi Soldier: The Civil War Letters of Samuel H. Davis of Kemper County." *Journal of Mississippi History*, LII (1990), 199–214.

Maury, Dabney H. "Recollections of Campaign Against Grant in North Mississippi in 1862–63." *Southern Historical Society Papers*, XIII (1885), 285–311.

McBrien, D. D., ed. "Letters of an Arkansas Confederate Soldier." *Arkansas Historical Quarterly*, II (1943), 58–70, 171–89, 268–86.

McCabe, W. Gordon. "Graduates of the United States Military Academy at West Point, N.Y., Who Served in the Confederate States Army, with the Highet Commission and Highest Command Attained." *Southern Historical Society Papers*, XXX (1902), 34–76.

McCaslin, Richard B. "Conditional Confederates: The Eleventh Texas Cavalry West of the Mississippi River." *Military History of the Southwest*, XXI (1991), 87–99.

McCoy, Raymond. "Victory at Fort Fillmore." *New Mexico Magazine*, XXXIX (August, 1961), 20–23, 35.

McDonald, Homer C. "Act #59 State of Louisiana—Senate & House Representatives at New Orleans—December 1874." *New Orleans Genesis*, XXII (1983), 107–12.

McGuyre, Ruth E. "The Yell Family of Arkansas." *Backtracker*, IV (January, 1975), 14–15.

McInvale, Morton R. "'All the Devils Could Wish for': The Griswoldville Campaign, November, 1864." *Georgia Historical Quarterly*, LX (1976), 117–30.

Meek, Melissa. "The Life of Archibald Yell." *Arkansas Historical Quarterly*, XXVI (1967), 11–23.

Melton, Maurice. "'A Grand Assemblage': George W. Rains and the Augusta Powder Works." *Civil War Times Illustrated*, XI (1973), 28–37.

"Members of House of Representatives Representing Hays County, 1846–1971." *Hays County Historical and Genealogical Quarterly*, V (September, 1971), 3–5.

Merrifield, J. K. "Col. Hugh Garland—Captured Flags." *Confederate Veteran*, XXIV (1916), 551–52.

Mitchell, Enoch, ed. "Letters of a Confederate Surgeon in the Army of Tennessee to His Wife." *Tennessee Historical Quarterly*, IV (1945), 341–53; V (1946), 60–81, 142–81.

Mitchell, Leon, Jr. "Camp Groce, Confederate Military Prison." *Southwestern Historical Quarterly*, LXVII (1963–64), 15–21.

"Montgomery County, Alabama, Cemetery Records." *Alabama Genealogical Register*, IX (1967), 197–206.

Moore, J. Preston. "Pierre Soule: Southern Expansionist and Promoter." *Journal of Southern History*, XXI (1955), 203–23.

Morris, George R. "The Battle of Bayou Des Allemands." *Confederate Veteran*, XXXIV (1926), 14–16.

Morrow, Jno. P., Jr. "Confederate Generals from Arkansas." *Arkansas Historical Quarterly*, XXI (1962), 231–46.

Mudd, Joseph A. "The Cabell Descendants in Missouri." *Missouri Historical Review*, IX (1914–15), 75–93.

———. "What I Saw at Wilson's Creek." *Missouri Historical Review*, VII (1912–13), 89–105.

Muir, Andrew F. "Inventions Patented by Texans, 1846–1861." *Southwestern Historical Quarterly*, LXII (1958–59), 522–24.

Mundie, Jim. "The Confederate Governor of Arizona and the Two-Term Vice President of the United States." *Houston Civil War Round Table Newsletter*, III (December, 1989).

Musser, Richard H. "The War in Missouri: From Springfield to Neosho." *Southern Bivouac*, n.s., I (April, 1886), 678–85; I (May, 1886), 745–52.

Nelson, Guy, Jr. "Baylor University at Independence: The War Years, 1861–1865." *Texana*, II (Summer, 1964), 87–111.

Ness, George T., Jr. "Missouri at West Point." *Missouri Historical Review*, XXXVIII (1943–44), 162–69.

Newbill, Grace M. "Col. John Goff Ballentine." *Confederate Veteran*, XXIV (1916), 268–69.

Nolte, Eugene. "Downeasters in Arkansas: Letters of Roscoe G. Jennings to His Brother." *Arkansas Historical Quarterly*, XVIII (1959), 3–25.

Norvell, James R. "The Reconstruction Courts of Texas, 1867–1873." *Southwestern Historical Quarterly*, LXII (1958–59), 141–63.

Oates, Stephen B. "The Prairie Grove Campaign, 1862." *Arkansas Historical Quarterly*, XIX (1966), 119–41.

Oldham, W. S. "Colonel John Marshall." *Southwestern Historical Quarterly*, XX (1916–17), 132–38.

Organ, Minnie. "History of the Newspaper Press of Missouri." *Missouri Historical Review*, IV (1909–10), 111–33, 149–66, 252–308.

Otey, Mercer. "Story of Our Great War." *Confederate Veteran*, IX (1901), 107–10.

Owen, H. T. "Keep the Record Straight." *Confederate Veteran*, XXIV (1916), 445–46.

Patterson, Mrs. R. L. "The Burrow and Campbell Family." *Bedford County Historical Quarterly*, V (Winter, 1979), 95–97.

Payne, John M. "University of Virginia Companies." *Confederate Veteran*, XL (1932), 256–58.

Pilcher, J. E. "Dr. Samuel Preston Moore, Surgeon General of the Confederate Army, 1861–1865." *Journal of the Association of Military Surgeons*, XVI (1905), 211–15.

"A Plan to Escape in 1863, from the Federal Prison on Johnson's Island." *Southern Historical Society Papers*, XIX (1891), 283–89.

"Portraits of Confederates Wanted." *Confederate Veteran*, IV (1896), 178.

Power, J. Tracey. "Edward Willis: Young and Full of Promise." *Civil War Times Illustrated*, XVIII (April, 1979), 22–27.

Prucha, F. Paul. "Fort Ripley: The Post and the Military Reservation." *Minnesota History*, XXVIII (1947), 205–24.

Quattlebaum, Paul. "Quattlebaum: A Palatine Family in South Carolina." *South Carolina Historical and Genealogical Magazine*, XLVIII (1947), 1–11, 84–94, 167–76, 219–26; XLIX (1948), 41–56, 104–18, 170–86, 231–45.

Read, C. W. "Reminiscences of the Confederate Navy." *Southern Historical Society Papers*, I (1876), 331–62.

"Reunion Committee." *Confederate Veteran*, XXXII (1924), 83.

Richardson, Hila A. "Raleigh County, West Virginia, in the Civil War." *West Virginia History*, X (1948–49), 213–98.

Riedel, Mildred H. "The Church of the Ascension—Frankfort, Kentucky." *Kentucky Ancestors*, XII (October, 1976), 59–61.

Ritter, Ben. "Miss Sallie Conrad. Kyd Douglas' Inspiration." *Blue & Gray*, II (January, 1985), 51–54.

"River Batteries at Fort Donelson." *Confederate Veteran*, IV (1896), 393.

Rivers, Flournoy. "The Flournoy Family." *Virginia Magazine of History and Biography*, IV (1896–97), 97–101.

Robertson, James I., Jr. "The War in Words." *Civil War Times Illustrated*, XX (October, 1981), 6.

Robinson, Mary F. "A Sketch of James Lusk Alcorn." *Journal of Mississippi History*, XII (1950), 28–45.

Roher, Walter. "Confederate Generals—The View from Below." *Civil War Times Illustrated*, XVIII (July, 1979), 10–13.

Roper, James. "The Founding of Memphis." *West Tennessee Historical Society Papers*, XXIII (1969), 5–29.

Rushing, Anthony C. "Rackensacker Raiders: Crawford's 1st Arkansas Cavalry." *Civil War Regiments*, I (1991), 44–75.

Salley, A. S., Jr. "Captain William Capers and Some of His Descendants." *South Carolina Historical and Genealogical Magazine*, II (1901), 273–98.

———. "Historical Notes: More on Landgrave Smith's Family." *South Carolina Historical and Genealogical Magazine*, XXX (1930), 255–58.

Savas, Theodore P. "Bulwark of the Beleaguered Confederacy: George Washington Rains and the Augusta Powder Works." *Civil War*, IX (September–October, 1991), 10–17, 20.

Scammel, J. M. "Military Units in Southern California, 1853–1862." *California Historical Society Quarterly*, XXIX (1950), 229–49.

"The Schirmer Diary." *South Carolina Historical and Genealogical Magazine*, LXXIX (1978), 72–74, 166, 250–52; LXXX (1979), 88–90, 192, 265–66; LXXXI (1980), 92–93.

Scroggs, Jack B. "Arkansas in the Secession Crisis." *Arkansas Historical Quarterly*, XII (1953), 179–224.

Shadel, Dana. "Henry Kyd Douglas: Reconstructed Rebel." *Maryland Historical Magazine*, LXXXVIII (Summer, 1994), 203–209.

Sheffield, G. M. G. "The Louisiana Brents." *Maryland Historical & Genealogical Bulletin*, XXI (October, 1950), 52.

Shephard, Edward. "Early Springfield." *Missouri Historical Review*, XXIV (1929–30), 50–65.

Shields, John C. "The Old Camp Lee." *Southern Historical Society Papers*, XXVI (1898), 241–46.

Simpson, Harold B. "West Pointers in the Texas Confederate Army." *Texas Military History*, VI (1967), 55–88.

"Sketch of General Douglas." *The Lost Cause*, X (March, 1904), 122–23.

Smith, David P. "The Elm Creek Raid, 1864: State and Confederate Defense and Response." *Military History of the Southwest*, XIX (1989), 120–36.

Smith, Gerald J. "For the Veteran 12th Georgia Regiment Rounding Up Deserters Was 'Quite a Holiday.'" *America's Civil War*, VII (March, 1994), 16–24.

Smith, Harold T. "The Know-Nothings in Arkansas." *Arkansas Historical Quarterly*, XXXIV (1975), 291–303.

Snyder, J. F. "The Democratic State Convention in Missouri in 1860." *Missouri Historical Review*, II (1907–1908), 112–30.

"Some Officials of the City Government of Pensacola." *Florida Historical Quarterly*, III (January, 1925), 31–33.

Spence, Philip B. "General Polk and His Staff." *Confederate Veteran*, IX (1901), 121–23, 248.

Squires, C. W. "The Boy Officer of the Washington Artillery." *Civil War Times Illustrated*, XIV (May, 1975), 10–23; XIV (June, 1975), 18–29.

Stadler, Frances H. "Letters from Mimoma." *Missouri Historical Bulletin*, XVI (April, 1960), 237–59.

Stephens, E. W. "Little Bonne Femme Church." *Missouri Historical Review*, XIV (1919–20), 193–200.

Sterky, H. E., and L. Y. Trapp, eds. "One Year of the War: Civil War Diary of John Withers, Assistant Adjutant-General of the Confederate Army." *Alabama Historical Quarterly*, XXIX (1967), 133–84.

Stevenson, William R. "Robert Alexander Smith: A Southern Son." *Alabama Historical Quarterly*, XX (1958), 35–60.

Stone, James H. "General Absalom Madden West and the Civil War in Mississippi." *Journal of Mississippi History*, XLII (1980), 135–44.

Stonebreaker, John B. "Munford's Marylanders Never Surrendered to Foe." *Southern Historical Society Papers*, XXXVII (1909), 309–12.

Sulivane, Clement L. "The *Arkansas* at Vicksburg in 1862." *Confederate Veteran*, XXV (1917), 496.

Sullivan, David M. "John Albert Pearson, Jr.: Arkansas Soldier and Confederate Marine." *Arkansas Historical Quarterly*, XLV (1986), 250–60.

"Surviving Confederate Generals." *Confederate Veteran*, VII (1899), 420.

Taylor, Morris F. "Action at Fort Massachusetts: The Indian Campaign of 1855." *Colorado Magazine*, XLII (Fall, 1965), 292–310.

Terry, W. C. "Data About Third Texas Cavalry." *Confederate Veteran*, XX (1912), 521.

Thomas, John L. "Some Historic Lines in Missouri." *Missouri Historical Review*, III (1908–1909), 5–33, 210–33, 251–74.

Thomas, L. P. "Reminiscences of Forty-Second Georgia." *Confederate Veteran*, XII (1904), 14–15.

———. "Their Last Battle: Fight at Bentonville, N.C., Between Sherman and Johnston." *Southern Historical Society Papers*, XXIX (1901), 215–22.

"Thomas R. R. Cobb . . . Extracts from Letters to His Wife, February 3, 1861–December 10, 1862." *Southern Historical Society Papers*, XXVIII (1900), 280–301.

Thomas, Wm. M. "The Slaughter at Petersburg, June 18, 1864." *Southern Historical Society Papers*, XXV (1897), 222–30.

Thompson, Jerry D. "A Stand Along the Border: Santos Benavides and the Battle for Laredo." *Civil War Times Illustrated*, XIX (August, 1980), 26–33.

———. "Colonel Santos Benavides, C.S.A." *Houston Civil War Round Table Newsletter*, III (May, 1990).

Thompson, Joseph C. "The Great-Little Battle of Pilot Knob." *Missouri Historical Review*, LXXXIII (1988–89), 139–60, 271–94.

Todd, George T. "Commands in Hood's Texas Brigade." *Confederate Veteran*, XX (1912), 281–82.

"The Treatment of Prisoners During the War Between the States." *Southern Historical Society Papers*, I (1876), 113–221.

Tullos, Tom. "History of Genl. James Wellborn Starnes of Williamson County." *Williamson County Historical Society*, XXII (Spring, 1991), 71–82.

Turner, Charles W. "William H. Richardson: Friend of the Farmer." *Virginia Cavalcade*, XX (Winter, 1971), 14–20.

"U.D.C. Notes." *Confederate Veteran*, XXXIV (1926), 151–53.

"U.D.C. Notes." *Confederate Veteran*, XXXVIII (1930), 200–201.

Uminski, Sigmund H. "Two Polish Confederates." *Polish American Studies*, XXIII (1966), 65–73.

Utley, J. S. "Graves of Eminent Men." *Arkansas Historical Association Publications*, II (1907), 254–95.

Walker, James H. "Those Gallant Men of the Twenty-Eighth." *United Daughters of the Confederacy Magazine*, XLI (November, 1988), 29–30.

Wallace, J. C. "Gen. E. W. Price." *Confederate Veteran*, XI (1903), 544.

Wallace, Laura B. "Kyle Cemetery." *Hays County Historical and Genealogical Quarterly*, VI (December, 1972), 8.

Walz, Robert R. "Arkansas Slaveholdings and Slaveholders in 1850." *Arkansas Historical Quarterly*, XII (1953), 38–74.

Warren, Mrs. J. E. "Bankhead Family." *William and Mary Quarterly*, 2nd ser., IX (1929), 303–14.

Waterman, George S. "Afloat-Afield-Afloat: Notable Events of the Civil War." *Confederate Veteran*, IX (1901), 24–29.

Waters, W. Davis. "'Deception Is the Art of War': Gabriel J. Rains, Torpedo Specialist of the Confederacy." *North Carolina Historical Review*, LXVI (1989), 31–60.

Weinert, Richard P. "Dickison—the Swamp Fox of Florida." *Civil War Times Illustrated*, V (December, 1966), 4–11, 48–50.

Welsh, Donald H. "A Union Band Director Views Camp Rolla, 1861." *Missouri Historical Review*, LV (1960–61), 307–43.

Wert, Jeffrey. "His Unhonored Service: Colonel Tom Munford—A Man of Achievement." *Civil War Times Illustrated*, XXIV (June, 1985), 28–34.

Wheeler, L. T. "Gen. Wilbur Hill King." *Confederate Veteran*, XIX (1911), 172.

White, P. J. "Gen. Thomas T. Munford." *Confederate Veteran*, XXVI (1918), 221, 229.

Widener, Ralph W., Jr. "John S. 'Rip' Ford, Colonel, CSA." *Confederate Veteran* (May–June, 1993), 14–21.

———. "John S. 'Rip' Ford, Colonel, CSA." *United Daughters of the Confederacy Magazine*, XXXVII (May, 1984), 19–23.

Wight, Willard E. "Letters of Thomas B. Hanly, 1863–1864." *Arkansas Historical Quarterly*, XV (1956), 161–71.

Wills, W. Ridley II. "Tennessee's Greatest Stud—Belle Meade." *Filson Club Historical Quarterly*, LXV (1991), 58–79.

"A Woman of the South" *Confederate Veteran*, XXVIII (1920), 396.

"The Women of the South in War Times." *Confederate Veteran*, XXXI (1923), 78.

"The Wonder State of Arkansas." *Confederate Veteran*, XXXVI (1928), 166–68.

Woodruff, Mrs. Howard. "Bates County, Missouri: Abstracts of Administrations & Bonds, Book #1, 1854–1866." *Missouri Miscellany*, XII (September, 1981), 81–91.

———. "Boone County Marriages, 1841–1849." *Missouri Miscellany*, XV (March, 1983), 1–22.

———. "Doniphan's Expedition—War with Mexico, 1846, First Regiment of Missouri Mounted Volunteers." *Missouri Miscellany*, XI (March, 1981), 1–19.

Woodson, Mrs. A. A. "Great Generals That I Have Known." In *Recollections and Reminiscences, 1861–1865*, United Daughters of the Confederacy, South Carolina Division, 1903–1907; rpr. n.p., 1992.

Wooster, Ralph A. "The Arkansas Secession Convention." *Arkansas Historical Quarterly*, XIII (1954), 172–95.

———. "Wealthy Texans, 1870." *Southwestern Historical Quarterly*, LXXIV (1970–71), 24–35.

Wyatt, Lee T. III. "William S. Barry, Advocate of Secession, 1821–1868." *Journal of Mississippi History*, XXXIX (1977), 339–55.

Wyatt, Mrs. William A. "Confederate Veterans Buried in Hays County." *Hays County Historical and Genealogical Quarterly*, VI (September, 1972), 3–11.

X. X. "Who Was Last Soldier to Leave Burning City." *Southern Historical Society Papers*, XXXVII (1909), 317–18.

"Youngest General of the Confederate Army." *Southern Historical Society Papers*, XXXV (1907), 55–58.